LSAT
success

2004

Thomas O. White

THOMSON

PETERSON'S

Australia • Canada • Mexico • Singapore • Spain • United Kingdom • United States

COPYRIGHT © 2003 Thomas O. White

Previous editions, © 1996, 2000, 2002

Library of Congress Cataloging-in-Publication Data

White, Thomas O.

LSAT success/complete advice on preparing for the Law School Admission Test/ Thomas O. White
   p. cm.
  ISBN 0-7689-1219-9
   1. Law School Admission Test. 2. Law schools—United States—Entrance examinations. I. Title.
  KF285.Z9W477 1996
  340'.076—dc20   96-21949
                                         CIP

Printed in the United States of America

10 9 8 7 6 5 4 3 2 1   05 04 03

Contents

CONTENTS

ABOUT THE LAW SCHOOL ADMISSION TEST

Admission tests were first developed by law schools in the 1920s. Over the next three decades, a variety of tests were tried but attracted little interest or following in the field of legal education. But in 1947, the LSAT came along to change all of that. The first version of the LSAT did not build upon the previous experiments in law school admission testing. Rather, it was based upon the Pepsi-Cola Scholarship Test and a number of examinations that were developed for the U.S. Navy!

After two years, changes in the test's structure were introduced, and change has become the hallmark of the LSAT. Changes in content, structure, and timing were made fourteen times in the next forty-four years. Some of them were extensive, and others, like those of 1991, were more limited. These frequent changes alone would serve to make the LSAT unfamiliar to most test-takers, and the fact that it is completely different from the well-known verbal-mathematical standardized tests makes it that much more obscure.

As Dostoyevsky put it, "taking a new step, uttering a new word, is what people fear most." People will go to incredible lengths to convert a new or different experience into something they can recognize and "get a handle on." That is how most people choose to deal with the LSAT. Courses, books, and counselors expound all kinds of theories and strategies for converting the LSAT into something else, something comforting and familiar. Test-takers become disciples of these theories and strategies as they try to deal with their anxieties and concerns about the LSAT. Although many of the books, courses, and counselors are well-intentioned, virtually all of them fail to generate much more than the enthusiasm that they present as a substitute for the test-taker's lack of confidence and anxiety.

The vast majority of the failures of LSAT preparation share two root causes: One is conceptual, and the other is tactical. The conceptual flaw is the common perception on the part of teachers, writers, and advisers that the LSAT is complicated—enigmatic, tangled, and formidable. The tactical flaw is in depicting the test as an adversary of the test-taker. Making an enemy of the test *always* succeeds in appealing to people who are anxious, and this, combined with efforts at simplification, produces a large body of vulnerable test-takers who find the whole process extremely counterproductive.

With proper training, however, the LSAT can be seen differently, and the vulnerable test-taker becomes a thing of the past. By mastering the new insights, perspectives, and techniques provided here, you can be transformed from a potential victim to an exploiter of the LSAT. You can experience LSAT success.

Do not misunderstand. The path to LSAT mastery is no cakewalk, but it's far easier and more rewarding than battling a test adversary who has written the rules, the questions, and the answers and, for good measure, keeps the score. It's a contest that you cannot win. Far better to have the LSAT working *for* you, and this guide is designed to help you achieve that objective.

CRITICAL FACTORS IN TEST PERFORMANCE

Certain factors have a very high impact on LSAT performance. There is no practical value in fooling around with aspects of the test that have little impact. By learning techniques that put high-impact factors to work for you, you can improve your LSAT performance and succeed with the LSAT.

Anxiety

Anxiety results from the mystique of the LSAT and, for many, past experience with standardized tests. By confronting the factors that produce anxiety about the LSAT, you can have a substantial impact on your preparation and performance. By learning that your past experience with standardized tests is irrelevant to the LSAT and by learning new, more appropriate techniques to deal with it, you can remove another layer of anxiety. Anxiety-producing misinformation, contradiction, and exaggeration will be exposed and the apparent complexity of the LSAT shown to be an illusion.

✔ **AS YOU GAIN CONTROL OVER YOUR ANXIETY, YOU TAKE CHARGE OF THE TEST AND YOUR RELATIONSHIP TO IT.**

Academic Conditioning

Your past academic experience has taught you that a superior test performance results from attending lectures, taking and reviewing notes, reading, cramming, and memorizing everything you can. Naturally you conclude that the path to a superior LSAT score is the same—listening to lectures, taking and reviewing notes, reading, memorizing, and cramming into your head everything you can about the LSAT.

Wrong! *The LSAT is not an academic exercise and cannot be converted into one.* Working to convert the LSAT into something familiar is a waste of time. Getting ready for the LSAT is much more like athletics, business, or the military, in all of which a superior performance results from superior *training* and *planning*, not learning. The training techniques you will learn in this book will permit you to sidestep the negative consequences of your academic training.

✔ **FOR SUPERIOR PERFORMANCE ON THE LSAT, YOU MUST TRAIN.**

Reasoning

The LSAT tests your skill at being able to "think like a lawyer"—reasoning in the principal ways law schools and the legal system require. This way of thinking is generally unfamiliar to people who are considering a legal education, and the LSAT attempts to measure their aptitude for it. By providing you with techniques designed to respond to the reasoning requirements of the LSAT, this book will enable you to perform more successfully on every aspect of the test.

✔ **TRAINING IN THE FUNDAMENTALS IS CRUCIAL TO LSAT PERFORMANCE.**

HIGH-IMPACT TRAINING AND PLANNING

In the academic, or "sponge," method of test preparation, you soak up as much information as you can in the hope that you will be able to squeeze out important drops of knowledge when test time comes.

If you are proficient at the sponge method, you may feel that a few hours of your time in information gathering can result in effective preparation for the LSAT. Forget it. And forget the notion that you can achieve a superior performance by listening to lectures or practicing test questions and memorizing clever strategies without first getting a firm grip on the test basics.

✔ **A FOUNDATION OF LSAT-SPECIFIC TECHNIQUES PRODUCES THE HIGHEST IMPACT ON YOUR SCORE.**

When you acquire a new skill, the gains are often great. For example, after training in computer basics for a short time, you find you can get results you never could before. So it is with training in LSAT basics: If you use the techniques you will learn here to *train actively* for a short time, you will find you get big results. Then, and only then, will you be ready for practice with test questions and other theories of preparation.

LSAT STUDY PLANS

Each of the eighteen training sessions (fifteen Success Sessions and three Red Alerts) is relatively short and deals with a discrete subject, guiding you in the training techniques relevant to that subject. Remember, sessions are not designed as academic exercises.

✔**YOU CAN USE EACH SESSION INDEPENDENTLY.**

Using these sessions, you can tailor your training program to make the best possible use of the time available to you. Seven programs are mapped out in the following paragraphs. They are designed to be completed in as many as seven weeks or as little as 7 hours.

THE SEVEN-WEEK PROGRAM

The order of the eighteen training sessions is designed to take you through the training process in the course of thirty-five days. If you complete one session or pretest assignment each day and work five days each week, you will complete the full program in seven weeks. This is a healthy but not demanding pace. In this and the following lists, RA 1 refers to Red Alert 1; RA 2 refers to Red Alert 2; RA 3 refers to Red Alert 3, the 9-12-18 Test-Planning System; Diagnostic indicates the Diagnostic Test; and Positioning refers to Before You Begin: Establishing Your Success Position, which precedes the Diagnostic Test. S indicates a Success Session of training and planning; QS refers to a question set that you use for planning; and WS indicates a writing sample exercise.

Day	Assignment	Day	Assignment
1	RA 1	19	QS Relationships
2	Positioning	20	S 11
3	Diagnostic	21	QS Arguments
4	RA 2	22	QS Arguments
5	S 1	23	QS Arguments
6	S 2	24	QS Arguments
7	S 3	25	S 12
8	RA 3	26	QS Passages
9	S 4	27	QS Passages
10	S 5	28	QS Passages
11	S 6	29	QS Passages
12	S 7	30	S 13
13	S 8	31	S 14
14	S 9	32	WS 1
15	S 10	33	WS 2
16	QS Relationships	34	S 15
17	QS Relationships	35	Simulated LSAT
18	QS Relationships		

THE FIVE-WEEK PROGRAM

The five-week program is a variation of the seven-week program. It assumes that you complete one session or pretest assignment each day and work seven days each week. Again, you complete the training process over the course of thirty-five days. This program keeps you working each day at a reasonable pace.

THE FOUR-WEEK PROGRAM

The four-week program picks up the pace a bit. It assumes that you work six days each week, completing the program in twenty-four days. This further assumes that you will usually devote at least 1 hour of concentrated effort to the training each day—a little extra time in which to think through the exercise will help.

Day	Assignment	Day	Assignment
1	RA 1	13	QS—2 Relationships sets
2	Positioning	14	QS—2 Relationships sets
3	RA 2	15	S 11
4	S 1	16	QS—2 Arguments sets
5	S 2, S 3	17	QS—2 Arguments sets
6	RA 3, S 4	18	S 12
7	S 5	19	QS—2 Passages sets
8	S 6	20	QS—2 Passages sets
9	S 7	21	S 13
10	S 8	22	S 14, WS 1
11	S 9	23	S 15
12	S 10	24	Simulated LSAT

THE THREE-WEEK PROGRAM

The three-week program requires you to work at an accelerated pace. It includes all of the sessions and assumes that you will be able to put in 1½ to 2 hours of concentrated effort each day. It also assumes that you work six days each week, so you complete the program in eighteen days.

Day	Assignment	Day	Assignment
1	RA 1, Positioning	10	QS—4 Relationships sets
2	RA 2, S 1	11	S 11
3	S 2, S 3	12	QS—4 Arguments sets
4	RA 3, S 4	13	S 12
5	S 5, S 6	14	QS—4 Passages sets
6	S 7	15	S 13
7	S 8	16	S 14, WS 1
8	S 9	17	S 15
9	S 10	18	Simulated LSAT

THE TWO-WEEK PROGRAM

The two-week program sets a demanding pace. It compresses sessions and exercises. It assumes that you will be able to put in 2 or more hours of concentrated effort each day, for six days each week.

Day	Assignment	Day	Assignment
1	RA 1, Diagnostic	8	S 11, QS—4 Arguments sets
2	RA 2, S 1	9	S 12, QS—4 Passages sets
3	S 2, S 3	10	S 13, S 14
4	RA 3, S 4	11	WS 1, S 15
5	S 5, S 6	12	Simulated LSAT
6	S 7, S 8, S 9		
7	S 10, QS—4 Relationships sets		

THE ONE-WEEK PROGRAM

This program is cutting it very fine. It includes sessions that will produce the greatest impact in seven days of 2-plus hours of concentrated effort each day.

Day	Assignment	Day	Assignment
1	RA 1, Diagnostic	5	S 11, QS—4 Arguments sets
2	RA 2, S 1, S 2, S 3, RA 3, S 4	6	S 12, QS—4 Passages sets
3	S 5, S 6, S 7, S 8, S 9	7	S 13, S 14, S 15
4	S 10, QS—4 Relationships sets		

THE ONE-DAY PROGRAM

This program goes at warp speed. It assumes that you will spend seven hours with the sessions in the order set out. This can make a meaningful difference in your performance, but don't expect a miracle.

Assignment	Assignment
Success	S 6
RA 2	S 7
S 1	S 8
S 3	S 9
RA 3	S 13
S 4	S 14
S 5	S 15

GETTING STARTED

First, complete the Diagnostic LSAT to get a feel for the types of questions you will encounter and an assessment of your strengths and weaknesses. The next success sessions deal with two critical factors in test performance that do not appear directly on the LSAT: anxiety and academic conditioning. After this, the sessions concentrate on elements of the LSAT and the type of reasoning required by law schools and the legal system. The final sessions discuss techniques for handling the LSAT Writing Sample and the test environment.

There are two LSAT practice tests included in this book, as well as two more on the CD, each of which contains five complete sections of LSAT questions. You should train with practice questions. A limited number of practice questions are required to develop the techniques needed to prepare effectively for the LSAT. Once you develop the requisite skills, you can practice as much as you wish with questions that you can get from the Law School Admission Council.

Diagnostic LSAT

BEFORE YOU BEGIN: ESTABLISHING YOUR SUCCESS POSITION

The diagnostic test that follows can be used to develop basic performance information to position you relative to the demands of the LSAT. By completing the diagnostic test and recording your responses as described below, you will develop data about your reaction to a number of the critical aspects of the LSAT. The results of this positioning exercise provide a sense of your present state of test readiness as well as of those aspects of test performance that will benefit most from LSAT training.

WHAT ARE THESE POSITIONING EXERCISES?

The test-maker is interested in results only. Simply put, this means that you get credit for only the number of best answers the scoring machine finds on your answer sheet.

✔ **CREDIT IS GIVEN FOR THE NUMBER OF BEST ANSWERS ONLY.**

(We will refer to "best" rather than "right" answers throughout our work with the LSAT. The reason will become clear later.) The point to remember here is that the route you take to the answer is of no interest to the test-maker: Your score is the same whether you guess an answer or spend 20 minutes figuring it out. This is the first of many occasions where your interests greatly differ from those of the test-maker. How you select answers is crucial to your performance and its improvement, so the exercises in this session are structured to elicit basic information about the way you select answers, as well as the answers you select.

HOW DO YOU COMPLETE THE POSITIONING EXERCISES?

Before beginning, make certain that you will not be interrupted during the time required to complete the test or test sections. Turn off the phone, hang out your Do Not Disturb or Privacy Please sign, and secure the perimeter of your work area. No food, drink, smokes, or similar digressions are permitted. Pencils with erasers and a watch, clock, or other precise timing device are essential. No reference materials, scratch paper, or outside help may be used.

To reiterate, the LSAT score is determined only by the number of best answers marked on the answer sheet. Unlike similar standardized tests, there is no penalty for guessing when you don't know the answer. Omitted answers count as wrong answers. Selecting a wrong answer is no worse than omitting an answer, which means that you should never omit an answer, whether on the actual LSAT or in these introductory exercises.

✔ **ALWAYS GUESS WHEN YOU DON'T KNOW THE ANSWER.**

Follow the brief instructions that precede each set of questions. The time you take to read them is included in the time allotted for each exercise.

WHAT IS THE DIAGNOSTIC ANSWER SHEET?

A single section answer sheet for use with this diagnostic appears on page 11. Make copies of the page for each section of the test. While the answer sheet provides for a twenty-eight–question section, most LSAT test sections consist of twenty-four questions. Only the Passages section has twenty-eight questions. So for the twenty-four-question sections, be sure to use only the first twenty-four spaces on the answer sheet.

HOW DO YOU MARK THE DIAGNOSTIC ANSWER SHEET?

The format of the answer grid used with these exercises is different from that of typical standardized tests and of the actual LSAT. As is typical, there are five bubbles that correspond to the answer options for each question, but there are two additional bubbles in our diagnostic.

These bubbles contain the letters G and T (G for "guess" and T for "time").

1. Ⓐ Ⓑ Ⓒ Ⓓ Ⓔ Ⓖ Ⓣ

There are three possible situations that apply to every question you answer in the diagnostic. Be sure you understand them fully.

Situation 1

Situation 1 involves the certain answer selection that you make when you are sure of the best answer to a question. You blacken the space on the answer sheet that corresponds to your answer selection for that question.

Situation 2

Situation 2 involves guessing after consideration of the question and the answer options. When there are more than two answer options about which you are uncertain, make an additional mark on your answer sheet.

For example, suppose you consider question 1 and determine that answer option B is wrong, but you cannot narrow the other options. In fact, you cannot decide among the four remaining options—A, C, D, and E.

1. First, decide which of the four options is best, and blacken the space that corresponds to this selection.

2. Next, place an X over the space designated G (for "guess") on the answer sheet.

Situation 3

Situation 3 involves insufficient time. When you have had insufficient time to consider all questions on the exercise within the 35-minute period, you indicate this fact by making two marks on your answer sheet.

For example, suppose that you do not have time to consider question 1.

1. First, blacken the space that corresponds to your random selection or guess of an answer.

2. Next, place an X over the space designated T (for "time") on the answer sheet.

RECORDING YOUR ANSWERS

What is next? In order to determine your present position with respect to the various demands made of you by the LSAT, you must first com-plete the Answer and Analysis Sheet by following the instructions below. Once completed, you will analyze the data on the form and learn more about where you stand with respect to the LSAT.

On the Answer and Analysis Sheet, you will find a series of rows and columns. Record the data required down each column as you work your way across the rows. Place the answer choices you made in each exercise in the spaces provided.

Recording Best Answers

Recording the best-answer results is straightforward. If your blackened answer matches the Best Answer found in the answer section of this book, place a Y in the corresponding space in the Best Match column. If your blackened answer does not match the Best Answer, place an N in the corresponding space in the Best Match column.

Total the number of Ys and Ns, and enter those numbers in the Totals spaces in the Best Match column for that exercise.

Recording Guesses

Recording guessing results requires you to review both your original answers and the Best Match column. If you X'd a G on your answer sheet, place a Y in the corresponding space on the first of the two Guessing columns. Otherwise enter an N in that column. Only when you enter a Y in the first column do you refer to the Best Match column. If there is a matching Y for that question in the Best Match column, enter a Y in the second Guessing column.

Total the number of Ys and enter those numbers in the Totals spaces in the Guessing columns for that exercise.

Recording Times

Recording those answers where you had insufficient time requires you to review both your original answers and the Best Match column. If you X'd a T on your answer sheet, place a Y in the corresponding space on the first of the two Time columns. Otherwise, enter an N in that column. Only when you enter a Y in the first Time column do you refer to the Best Match column. If there is a matching Y for that question in the Best Match column, enter a Y in the second Time column.

Total the number of Ys and enter those numbers in the Totals spaces in the Time columns for that exercise.

What Is the Next Step?

Now you have the raw materials. Analyzing the exercise results comes next. As you will have gathered from your work on the answer key, we are looking at four different aspects of your performance—overall, question types, time, and guessing.

As you work through the analysis, remember that the exercises are designed to provide preliminary information about your performance, not to develop expectations for your performance. It is only in the course of your training that performance expectations will be established. And, by training, your performance will improve on all aspects of the LSAT.

OVERALL TEST POSITION

On the corresponding lines below, enter the total Ys for each exercise from the Best Match column on the answer key. After you enter this data, complete the three calculations indicated, and total the results.

Section 1   Total Ys____
Section 2   Total Ys____
Section 3   Total Ys____
Section 4   Total Ys____
Section 5   Total Ys____

Total Ys____ ÷ 124 × 100 ____%

The final calculation immediately above expresses your overall position as a percentage of questions for which you selected the best answer. Simply speaking, the LSAT is designed so that in order to get an average score, the test-taker (you) needs to select slightly more than 60 percent of the best answers. The nature of the LSAT scoring system is such that getting a small number of best answers above 60 percent results in a relatively large increase in the placement of that score on the LSAT scale. The higher the percentage of questions for which you selected the best answer, the stronger your position.

Guessing Position

Most people do some guessing on the LSAT. You were asked to indicate every question for which you were required to guess. To determine your guessing factor, enter on the corresponding lines below the total Ys for each exercise from the first Guessing column. Then complete the necessary calculations.

Section 1
(Relationships)   Total Ys____

Section 2
(Arguments)   Total Ys____

Section 3
(Relationships)   Total Ys____

Section 4
(Passages)   Total Ys____

Section 5
(Arguments)   Total Ys____

Section 1
(Relationships)   Total Ys____

Section 3
(Relationships)   Total Ys____

Total Ys____ ÷ 48 × 100____%

Section 2
(Arguments)   Total Ys____

Section 5
(Arguments)   Total Ys____

Total Ys____ ÷ 48 × 100____%

Section 4
(Passages)   Total Ys____

Total Ys____ ÷ 28 × 100____%

It is likely that the amount of guessing you have done varies from one question type to another. The higher the percentage, the more you were required to guess. By comparing percentages, you determine your relative need to guess.

The percentage of guessed answers that are Best Answers indicates your present position with respect to guessing. To determine this figure, enter on the corresponding lines the total Gs for each question type (Relationships, Arguments, and Passages) from the second Guessing column. Then enter the total Ys for each exercise from the first Guessing column. Complete the calculations.

Arguments $\dfrac{\text{Total Gs}}{\text{Total Ys}} \times 100 = $ ____%

Passages $\dfrac{\text{Total Gs}}{\text{Total Ys}} \times 100 = $ ____%

Relationships $\dfrac{\text{Total Gs}}{\text{Total Ys}} \times 100 = $ ____%

To the extent that any of these percentages exceeds 20 percent, your guessing is better than predicted by statistics. Your training will prepare you to guess best and to recognize when guessing will produce your highest possible score.

Time Position

On the answer blanks, you marked every question you did not have time to consider. To determine your position with respect to the use of available time, enter on the corresponding lines the total Ys from the Time column for each exercise. Then complete the calculations indicated.

Section 1
  (Relationships)   Total Ys____
Section 2
  (Arguments)   Total Ys____
Section 3
  (Relationships)   Total Ys____
Section 4
  (Passages)   Total Ys____
Section 5
  (Arguments)   Total Ys____

Section 1
  (Relationships)   Total Ys____
Section 3
  (Relationships)   Total Ys____

    Total Ys____ $\div$ 48 $\times$ 100____%

Section 2
  (Arguments)   Total Ys____
Section 5
  (Arguments)   Total Ys____

    Total Ys____ $\div$ 48 $\times$ 100____%

Section 4
  (Passages)   Total Ys____

    Total Ys____ $\div$ 28 $\times$ 100____%

It is likely that your position regarding the use of time varies from one question type to another. The higher the percentage, the more certain you can be that, for you, time is a major score factor with respect to that question type. A comparison of percentages will reveal your relative proficiencies. For most people, time appears to be the critical score factor on the LSAT. Further work will clearly identify for you what would be your optimal use of test time.

Question-Type Position

Finally, your performance is analyzed by the type of question. This analysis assumes that you have completed all five sections of the Diagnostic Test. Enter on the corresponding lines below the total Ys for each exercise from the Best Match column on the answer key. After you enter this data, complete the calculations indicated.

Section 1
  (Relationships)   Total Ys____
Section 2
  (Arguments)   Total Ys____
Section 3
  (Relationships)   Total Ys____
Section 4
  (Passages)   Total Ys____
Section 5
  (Arguments)   Total Ys____

Section 1
  (Relationships)   Total Ys____
Section 3
  (Relationships)   Total Ys____

    Total Ys____ $\div$ 48 $\times$ 100____%

Section 2
  (Arguments)   Total Ys____
Section 5
  (Arguments)   Total Ys____

    Total Ys____ $\div$ 48 $\times$ 100____%

Section 4
  (Passages)   Total Ys____

    Total Ys____ $\div$ 28 $\times$ 100____%

Most test-takers perform somewhat differently on the three question types. This reflects the fact that most test-takers perform differently when dealing with the three question types on the LSAT. Your position is set out in percentages that represent your question-type proficiency. When compared, these percentages indicate your relative strengths and weaknesses in working with the question types. The higher the percentage, the stronger your position.

This performance information is not reported to the law schools, but it is useful to you to determine the question types with which you are most and least proficient. Your training will have the greatest impact in those areas where you are weakest and the largest gains may be realized.

LSAT DIAGNOSTIC TEST ANSWER AND ANALYSIS SHEET

	Best Answer	B-Match (Y or N)	Guessing (Y or N)	G-Match (Y or N)	Time (Y or N)	T-Match (Y or N)
Section _____						
1. Ⓐ Ⓑ Ⓒ Ⓓ Ⓔ Ⓖ Ⓣ	____	____	____	____	____	____
2. Ⓐ Ⓑ Ⓒ Ⓓ Ⓔ Ⓖ Ⓣ	____	____	____	____	____	____
3. Ⓐ Ⓑ Ⓒ Ⓓ Ⓔ Ⓖ Ⓣ	____	____	____	____	____	____
4. Ⓐ Ⓑ Ⓒ Ⓓ Ⓔ Ⓖ Ⓣ	____	____	____	____	____	____
5. Ⓐ Ⓑ Ⓒ Ⓓ Ⓔ Ⓖ Ⓣ	____	____	____	____	____	____
6. Ⓐ Ⓑ Ⓒ Ⓓ Ⓔ Ⓖ Ⓣ	____	____	____	____	____	____
7. Ⓐ Ⓑ Ⓒ Ⓓ Ⓔ Ⓖ Ⓣ	____	____	____	____	____	____
8. Ⓐ Ⓑ Ⓒ Ⓓ Ⓔ Ⓖ Ⓣ	____	____	____	____	____	____
9. Ⓐ Ⓑ Ⓒ Ⓓ Ⓔ Ⓖ Ⓣ	____	____	____	____	____	____
10. Ⓐ Ⓑ Ⓒ Ⓓ Ⓔ Ⓖ Ⓣ	____	____	____	____	____	____
11. Ⓐ Ⓑ Ⓒ Ⓓ Ⓔ Ⓖ Ⓣ	____	____	____	____	____	____
12. Ⓐ Ⓑ Ⓒ Ⓓ Ⓔ Ⓖ Ⓣ	____	____	____	____	____	____
13. Ⓐ Ⓑ Ⓒ Ⓓ Ⓔ Ⓖ Ⓣ	____	____	____	____	____	____
14. Ⓐ Ⓑ Ⓒ Ⓓ Ⓔ Ⓖ Ⓣ	____	____	____	____	____	____
15. Ⓐ Ⓑ Ⓒ Ⓓ Ⓔ Ⓖ Ⓣ	____	____	____	____	____	____
16. Ⓐ Ⓑ Ⓒ Ⓓ Ⓔ Ⓖ Ⓣ	____	____	____	____	____	____
17. Ⓐ Ⓑ Ⓒ Ⓓ Ⓔ Ⓖ Ⓣ	____	____	____	____	____	____
18. Ⓐ Ⓑ Ⓒ Ⓓ Ⓔ Ⓖ Ⓣ	____	____	____	____	____	____
19. Ⓐ Ⓑ Ⓒ Ⓓ Ⓔ Ⓖ Ⓣ	____	____	____	____	____	____
20. Ⓐ Ⓑ Ⓒ Ⓓ Ⓔ Ⓖ Ⓣ	____	____	____	____	____	____
21. Ⓐ Ⓑ Ⓒ Ⓓ Ⓔ Ⓖ Ⓣ	____	____	____	____	____	____
22. Ⓐ Ⓑ Ⓒ Ⓓ Ⓔ Ⓖ Ⓣ	____	____	____	____	____	____
23. Ⓐ Ⓑ Ⓒ Ⓓ Ⓔ Ⓖ Ⓣ	____	____	____	____	____	____
24. Ⓐ Ⓑ Ⓒ Ⓓ Ⓔ Ⓖ Ⓣ	____	____	____	____	____	____
25. Ⓐ Ⓑ Ⓒ Ⓓ Ⓔ Ⓖ Ⓣ	____	____	____	____	____	____
26. Ⓐ Ⓑ Ⓒ Ⓓ Ⓔ Ⓖ Ⓣ	____	____	____	____	____	____
27. Ⓐ Ⓑ Ⓒ Ⓓ Ⓔ Ⓖ Ⓣ	____	____	____	____	____	____
28. Ⓐ Ⓑ Ⓒ Ⓓ Ⓔ Ⓖ Ⓣ	____	____	____	____	____	____
TOTALS	Ys____	Ys____	Ys____	Ys____	Ys____	Ys____
	Ns____	Ns____	Ns____	Ns____	Ns____	Ns____

Diagnostic Test

The questions in this section are based on a set of conditions. A diagram may be helpful in the answer selection process. Select the best answer to each question and mark the corresponding space on the answer sheet.

Questions 1–6

Eight businesses, A, B, C, D, E, F, G, and H, are moving into a new eight-story building. Two businesses will not locate on the same floor. Each business will occupy one entire floor. The floors of the new building are numbered one through eight from the ground floor to the top floor. Any plan for locating the businesses in the building must meet the following requirements:

B is to locate on the sixth floor.
D is to locate on the fourth floor.
E is to locate somewhere below D's floor.

1. If F locates on a floor directly below E, F can locate on floor

   (A) two
   (B) three
   (C) four
   (D) five
   (E) six

2. If A locates on a floor exactly three floors above E, A must be on floor

   (A) four
   (B) five
   (C) six
   (D) seven
   (E) eight

3. If A locates on the floor directly above C, which of the following is both a complete and an accurate list of the floors where C can locate?

   (A) two, seven
   (B) two, three
   (C) three, seven
   (D) one, two, seven
   (E) two, three, eight

4. If A locates on a floor somewhere above C, and if C locates on a floor somewhere above H, which of the following must be true?

   (A) C locates on a floor somewhere below D and above E.
   (B) C locates on a floor somewhere below E.
   (C) A locates on a floor somewhere above E and below D.
   (D) C locates on a floor somewhere above D.
   (E) A locates on a floor somewhere above D.

5. If F locates on a floor somewhere above G, and if G locates on a floor directly above H, which of the following could be true?

   (A) G locates on floor seven.
   (B) H locates on a floor somewhere above D.
   (C) H locates on a floor directly above B.
   (D) G locates on floor three.
   (E) F locates on a floor directly below E.

6. If A and E can locate only on even-numbered floors, which of the following CANNOT be true?

   (A) C locates on floor eight.
   (B) G locates on floor seven.
   (C) F locates on floor five.
   (D) E locates on floor two.
   (E) H locates on floor three.

Questions 7–12

The First National Bank has five branches, S, T, U, V, and W. The telephone system that connects the branches is not working properly. The branch managers have determined that they can place direct calls from their branches only to certain other branches. They have further determined that a branch can transfer calls to any branch to which it can place a direct call and can transfer calls only to such branches. Direct calls can be made only from:

S to V
T to S and U
U to T
V to T
W to S and U

7. Which of the following branches CANNOT receive calls from any other branch?

   (A) S
   (B) T
   (C) U
   (D) V
   (E) W

8. Which of the following offices can call S with exactly one transfer?

   (A) T only
   (B) U only
   (C) U and V only
   (D) T and W only
   (E) T and U only

9. How can T call V?

   (A) T can call V directly.
   (B) T can call S, which can transfer the call to V.
   (C) T can call U, which can transfer the call to V.
   (D) T can call W, which can transfer the call to V.
   (E) There is no way that T can call V.

10. If all lines are open, which of the following calls requires the greatest number of transfers?

    (A) T to V
    (B) S to T
    (C) V to S
    (D) U to V
    (E) W to T

11. If S's line is busy and all of the other lines are open, which of the following calls CANNOT be made directly, through a transfer, or through a series of transfers?

    (A) V to T
    (B) U to V
    (C) V to U
    (D) W to T
    (E) W to U

12. If T's line is busy and all of the other lines are open, which of the following calls can be made directly, through a transfer, or through a series of transfers?

    (A) U to V
    (B) U to S
    (C) V to U
    (D) V to S
    (E) W to V

Questions 13–18

Adam, Beth, Cal, Darla, Ed, and Fern are cousins.

No two cousins are the same age, but all have their birthdays on the same date.
The youngest is 17 years old and the oldest, Ed, is 22.
Fern is somewhere between Beth and Darla in age.
Adam is older than Beth.
Cal is older than Darla.

13. Which of the following must be true if exactly two of the cousins are between Cal and Fern in age?

    (A) Adam is between Fern and Darla in age.
    (B) Beth is younger than Darla.
    (C) Beth is 17 years old.
    (D) Fern is 18 years old.
    (E) Exactly one of the cousins is between Beth and Adam in age.

14. Which of the following must be true if Cal is 19 years old?

    (A) Adam is 19 years old and Darla is 21.
    (B) Beth is 19 years old and Adam is 20.
    (C) Beth is 20 years old and Adam is 21.
    (D) Darla is 17 years old and Beth is 21.
    (E) Fern is 19 years old and Adam is 20.

15. Which of the following could be the ages of Darla and Cal, respectively, if Beth is 17 years old?

(A) 18 and 19
(B) 18 and 20
(C) 18 and 21
(D) 19 and 21
(E) 19 and 22

16. Which of the following must be true if exactly two of the cousins are between Cal and Ed in age?

(A) Beth is younger than Cal.
(B) Fern is between Cal and Ed in age.
(C) Fern is older than Beth.
(D) Adam is 18 years old.
(E) Darla is 17 years old.

17. If Adam is one year older than Cal, the number of logically possible orderings of all six cousins by increasing age is

(A) 2
(B) 3
(C) 4
(D) 5
(E) 6

18. Which of the following is NOT possible?

(A) Darla is 19 years old.
(B) Fern is 19 years old.
(C) Darla is 20 years old.
(D) Fern is 18 years old.
(E) Fern is 20 years old.

Questions 19–24

Nell, Ray, Paul, Sarah, Ted, and Wendy are all of the members of a singing group. They meet once a week to rehearse.

Last week Ray arrived after Wendy but before Paul.
Ted arrived after Sarah but before Paul.
Nell arrived after Sarah but before Ray.

19. In which order could the group members have arrived at rehearsal?

(A) Nell, Wendy, Sarah, Ted, Ray, Paul
(B) Sarah, Ted, Nell, Ray, Paul, Wendy
(C) Sarah, Wendy, Ray, Nell, Ted, Paul
(D) Ted, Nell, Wendy, Ray, Paul, Sarah
(E) Wendy, Sarah, Nell, Ray, Ted, Paul

20. It could be true that Sarah arrived at rehearsal

(A) after Ray and before Paul
(B) after Wendy and before Ray
(C) with Nell
(D) with Ray
(E) with Ted

21. Which of the following CANNOT be true?

(A) Sarah and Wendy arrived together.
(B) Nell and Paul arrived together.
(C) Ray and Ted arrived together.
(D) Nell and Ted arrive together.
(E) Wendy and Nell arrive together.

22. What are the minimum and the maximum number of people, respectively, who could have arrived after Sarah and before Ray?

(A) 0..4
(B) 1..4
(C) 0..3
(D) 1..3
(E) 2..3

23. Which of the following is an accurate and complete list of the people who must have arrived at rehearsal before Ray?

(A) Nell, Sarah
(B) Sarah, Ted
(C) Sarah, Wendy
(D) Nell, Sarah, Wendy
(E) Nell, Sarah, Ted, Wendy

24. If exactly two people arrived at rehearsal after Nell and before Ray, they must be

(A) Ted and Wendy
(B) Sarah and Wendy
(C) Sarah and Ted
(D) Paul and Wendy
(E) Paul and Ted

SECTION 2   TIME—35 MINUTES   24 QUESTIONS

Evaluate the reasoning contained in the brief statements, and select the best answer. Do not make implausible, superfluous, or incompatible assumptions. Select the best answer to each question, and mark the corresponding space on the answer sheet.

1. Austin: Over time, solar energy will replace the depleting store of fossil fuels. So, development of solar energy should be a priority.

   Hanna: I disagree. Solar energy systems are crude and the supply of coal is sufficient for our needs.

   The misunderstanding between Austin and Hanna is based upon

   (A) different assumptions of the size of available fossil fuel
   (B) different beliefs about the environmental benefits of solar energy
   (C) different understandings of existing solar energy technology
   (D) different perspectives on time
   (E) different views of energy economics

2. Dictators well appreciate freedom, but for themselves. In their view, others do not deserve freedom. The contempt that a dictator feels for others is in direct proportion to the admiration that person has for absolute government.

   Given the above statement, people who respect universal political freedom would

   (A) admire the concept that absolute government be despots
   (B) understand political despots
   (C) appreciate their personal freedom
   (D) respect their fellow citizens
   (E) find few people who deserve freedom

3. Everyone who attended all of the seminars is bound to know enough to pass the examination.

   This assertion logically expresses which of the following?

   (A) It was nearly impossible to pass the exam if a person did not attend the seminar regularly.
   (B) Seminar attendance was low, and the examination failure rate was high.
   (C) Everybody who passed the test attended the seminar regularly.
   (D) Attendees did not have to do work outside the seminars in order to pass the examination.
   (E) The seminar presentations were consistently excellent.

4. Price and wage controls are the only way to control inflation. But wage controls limit worker spending, which, in turn, results in reduced corporate profits if price controls are in place.

   Assume the above statements are true. Which of the following statements also must be true if corporate profits are not decreasing?

   (A) If there is inflation, wage controls are not in place.
   (B) If there is inflation, it is not being controlled.
   (C) Workers have less money to spend.
   (D) Price controls are in effect.
   (E) Wage controls are in effect.

5. People who do not understand the laws of probability often explain random happenings as the work of supernatural forces. Those people would be much less likely to believe in the supernatural if they had knowledge of statistical probability.

The author of the above would agree most with which of the following?

(A) Supernatural forces must obey the laws of probability.
(B) There is a scientific explanation for every occurrence.
(C) Phenomenology is a valid form of understanding.
(D) Knowledge of the laws of probability reduces the likelihood of a person believing in the supernatural.
(E) Natural causes produce random happenings.

6. The distinctive yellow-green colors of Vincent van Gogh's paintings may have resulted from now known side effects of the drug digitalis. Digitalis was a commonly prescribed drug during the time van Gogh lived, and in portraits of the physician who treated van Gogh, he is holding a branch of foxglove, the plant from which digitalis is made.

The point of the passage is made primarily by

(A) presenting clear evidence of cause and effect
(B) presenting circumstantial evidence
(C) connecting digitalis to van Gogh's paintings
(D) citing specific documentary evidence
(E) referring to opinions of established authorities

7. The psychological stress of telling a lie produces certain physiological changes. By using appropriate instruments, the physiological symptoms of lying can be measured and result in reliable lie detection.

Which of the following, if true, most weakens the above argument?

(A) Lie detectors are sensitive machines that require constant maintenance.
(B) Lying is only moderately stress-inducing to some people.
(C) Lie detector operators must be highly trained and careful.
(D) Numerous kinds of psychological stress produce similar physiological symptoms.
(E) Measurement instruments such as lie detectors can be misused and abused.

8. Performing outstanding medical research requires more than a simple talent and more than a simple explanation. A drive to solve problems is clearly a part of it. Also critical is the ability to identify the right questions to ask. Thus, if we are to produce successful medical researchers, our universities must cultivate dedication and creativity rather than merely convey information.

If true, which of the following would be the strongest objection to the argument of the passage above?

(A) Researchers have a genuine curiosity about the world.
(B) Scientific talent is only a small facet of what makes an outstanding researcher.
(C) The proper function of our universities is not to produce outstanding researchers, but to create well-rounded graduates.
(D) Developing creativity in students is less important for the cultivation of research talent than is instilling a sense of dedication.
(E) Teachers often cause harm when they attempt to do more than convey information.

9. If they get customers to believe that earlier patrons have given large tips, cosmetologists can get larger tips from them. However, if cosmetologists give the impression that they are wealthy, their customers will not tip them at all.

Which of the following draws the most reliable conclusion from the passage?

(A) Wealthy people should not be cosmetologists.

(B) If a cosmetologist is wealthy, he or she will not usually receive big tips.

(C) If customers feel that a cosmetologist is not wealthy, they will tip generously.

(D) Customers often give tips according to their perceptions of the cosmetologist and of the actions of other customers.

(E) Patrons are not usually influenced by the quality of the service provided by the cosmetologist when they determine the amount of their tips.

10. Nursing-home residents have the right to refuse treatment. Forcing a resident to take sedatives, unless that person threatens the well-being of others, is a clear affront to human dignity, an illegal invasion of privacy, and an intolerable violation of the individual's right to think and make decisions about one's own welfare.

A major assumption in this argument is that

(A) residents in nursing homes are no threat to the well-being of others

(B) treatment in nursing homes is clearly harmful to residents

(C) sedating drugs should not be used as a treatment in nursing homes

(D) nursing-home residents are capable of making decisions about their own welfare

(E) the privacy rights of most residents of nursing homes are not protected

11. Unlike the more traditional energy sources of coal, gas, and nuclear energy, energy from the sun produces no major problems. It produces no pollution and requires no transportation from foreign lands. It threatens no one with radiation dangers and is not controlled by powerful corporations. Therefore, we should encourage people to use solar energy.

Which of the following statements, if true, most seriously weakens this argument?

(A) There have been very few studies of solar energy use by households.

(B) The cost of oil and gas could be regulated to make it less costly for home consumption.

(C) The cost of the equipment required to collect enough solar energy for a family of four equals the amount a family now pays for oil, gas, or nuclear produced energy in one year.

(D) Most critics of solar energy are connected to energy monopolies.

(E) An effective way for families to capture and store solar energy has not yet been developed.

12. Even though art need not have an intellectual appeal, neither is it something that immediately can be appreciated without previous experiences that have deepened one's capacity for appreciation. So it follows that to get full enjoyment from art, people must commit considerable time and effort to developing their ability to observe and understand art.

The point of the argument in the above paragraph is that

(A) the enjoyment of art has little to do with the intellect

(B) viewing art does not always result in an increase of a person's appreciation

(C) art has a universal appeal

(D) the ability to enjoy art often requires preparation

(E) art that is enjoyed usually deepens a person's capacity for appreciation

13. In France, as presidents have worked to expand their personal power, they have simultaneously achieved positive goals far beyond their own and far beyond those of their political parties. Well-executed struggles for presidential power contribute both to governmental effectiveness and qualitative improvements in public policy.

This author argues that

- **(A)** French presidents are responsible for governmental effectiveness
- **(B)** skillful exercises of presidential power are desirable, regardless of the reasons
- **(C)** presidential effectiveness in public policy is as important as political ideology
- **(D)** struggles to gain presidential power produce far-reaching beneficial results
- **(E)** a president's efforts to gain power counterbalance that individual's gains

14. The fact that one person is homely and another is beautiful is not viewed as morally wrong; yet, a drug dealer retiring on his millions while a retired clerk is forced to go on welfare is considered morally reprehensible. These differences in views result from the arbitrary, illogical, and inconsistent application of moral standards.

A critic of the stated position would most likely point out that

- **(A)** conditions created by nature can be differentiated from conditions created by society
- **(B)** beauty is often a burden, and society should not begrudge beautiful people their looks
- **(C)** people regularly maintain inconsistent views
- **(D)** looks are not as admirable as working
- **(E)** arbitrary distinctions and illogical judgments form the basis of moral standards

15. The different types of speech therapy based on experience produce virtually the same rates of success. While practitioner proponents of each type of therapy assert that their procedure is different from the others, studies of the results achieved by every one of these treatments show no significant differences in effectiveness.

It can be best inferred from the statement above that

- **(A)** there are few differences among the different types of speech therapies considered
- **(B)** the speech therapies discussed are less effective than other types of treatment
- **(C)** the differences among the various speech therapies considered are not causally relevant to their effectiveness
- **(D)** practitioner proponents differ substantially in their conceptions of therapeutic success
- **(E)** practitioner proponents ignore the connection between therapeutic experience and effectiveness

Questions 16–17

A sandhog claims that he has a list of thirty deceased workers who worked as a group on a tunnel that cut through a radon-intense area. He started his list after an oncologist reported that the incidences of cancer among sandhogs were five times greater than the incidence of cancer among other construction workers. The tunnel contractor states that its records show that no sandhogs working on the tunnel were exposed to more radiation than was safe.

16. If true, which of the following statements most damages the contractor's claim?

- **(A)** The medical records of the oncologist were accurate.
- **(B)** All thirty of the deceased sandhogs died of radiation-related cancer.
- **(C)** The contractor has denied requests to inspect its radiation records.
- **(D)** Sandhogs contract illness at higher-than-normal rates.
- **(E)** The remaining sandhogs that worked on the tunnel show no signs of illness.

17. Which of the following conclusions can be drawn most reliably from the passage?

    (A) Radiation did not cause cancer in the sandhogs.
    (B) The contractor is not being truthful about the radiation.
    (C) The records of the contractor are likely to be inaccurate or incomplete.
    (D) The sandhogs were exposed to radiation elsewhere rather than in the tunnel.
    (E) There is disagreement about the level of radiation that is safe.

18. The vast majority of people now depend on the media, both electronic and press, for information about criminal trials, instead of personal observation or spectator reports. Thus, the media serve as representatives of those private citizen observers and reporters of trials.

    Given that the public has the right to know about trials, the author's position above best justifies which of the following?

    (A) limiting nonmedia access to trials
    (B) censoring media reports on criminal court proceedings
    (C) sequestering juries in criminal trials that are covered by the media
    (D) expanding the right of the press to be present and cover trial proceedings
    (E) requiring prosecuting and defense lawyers to give press briefings in criminal trials

Questions 19–20

The excuse for not voting that is most commonly given by citizens is that the two major political parties do not offer competent candidates or meaningful policies and positions. The nonvoting citizen believes that by expressing dissatisfaction as a consumer in the political process by not casting his or her ballot, the parties will put forward better candidates and positions. But this misconceives the role of voter as that of consumer. In the marketplace, defection to another product or failure to purchase a product sends a powerful message that results in change, improvement, and innovation. But not voting in the political process will not produce a smorgasbord, but rather, will result in a menu with a single entree and two side dishes.

19. The author does NOT address which of the following?

    (A) the results from people not participating in the electoral process
    (B) consequences of a consumer's refusal to purchase a product
    (C) how citizens can effectively express dissatisfaction with the two major political parties
    (D) why many citizens refuse to vote
    (E) differences between the role of the voter and that of the consumer

20. The author attempts to make her point by

    (A) constructing a simile
    (B) discrediting an analogy
    (C) making a circular argument
    (D) offering a unique hypothesis
    (E) presenting new evidence

21. When your office is above the fourth floor, it has two exits.

    From which of the following can the above statement be logically deduced?

    (A) No offices on the fourth floor have two exits.
    (B) Unless it is above the fourth floor, an office does not have two exits.
    (C) All offices above the fourth floor have fire escapes.
    (D) Some offices on the fourth floor have two exits.
    (E) Two exit offices do not exist below the fourth floor.

22. The automation of industry throws people out of work; therefore, machines are harmful.

    The argument above is most like which of the following?

    (A) Hitler was a fascist; therefore, he was evil.
    (B) Fatty foods are harmful; therefore, eating butter is dangerous.
    (C) The senator steals public funds; therefore, he is dishonest.
    (D) Alcoholic beverages are high in calories; therefore, beer is fattening.
    (E) Pigeons spread diseases; therefore, birds are nuisances.

23. Five separate applications of the pesticide failed to rid the area of the mites. Only the most resistant of the mites survived each application. When the surviving mites reproduced, their offspring resisted the pesticide more effectively than did the parents.

Which of the following conclusions can best be drawn from the statement above?

(A) Normally, more pesticide-resistant mites tend to mate with less resistant mites.

(B) The mites that survived each exposure grew more pesticide resistant with each application.

(C) The pesticide applications did not coincide with the mating season of the mites.

(D) The pesticide was formulated to kill the mites in one application.

(E) Resistance to the pesticide is passed from parent to offspring.

24. Scientists have found through experimentation that baby female gorillas who were "nurtured" by inanimate mother substitutes that performed some parenting functions were unable to function as mothers when they had offspring. This teaches us that infants should not be placed in the care of babysitters and day-care centers but only should be raised by their natural mothers.

The conclusion reached by the author would be strengthened by which of the following?

(A) The scientists found that the baby gorillas in the experiments were very dependent on each other.

(B) The gorilla babies in the experiments would only accept food from the scientists, not from the "surrogate" mothers.

(C) Baby gorillas that had brief but regular exposure to their natural mothers were able to function as mothers later.

(D) Baby gorillas raised by females other than their own mothers were unable to function as mothers when they had offspring.

(E) Mature female gorillas that were "raised" by the mother substitutes could be taught many mothering functions when they had offspring.

SECTION **3**   TIME—35 MINUTES   24 QUESTIONS

The questions in this section are based on a set of conditions. A diagram may be helpful in the answer selection process. Select the best answer to each question and mark the corresponding space on the answer sheet.

Questions 1–6

A chef is preparing sauces using eight different ingredients—H, J, K, L, M, N, O, and P. According to the recipes, the following requirements apply to the use of the ingredients:

If J is used, both K and P must also be used.
M and N must always be used together.
If K is used, at least two of H, J, and O must also be used.
K and N cannot be used together.
M, O, and P cannot all be used in the same dish.
H, L, and P cannot all be used in the same dish.

1. Which of the following is an acceptable combination of ingredients for a sauce?

(A) H, J, K, O
(B) H, L, M, P
(C) L, M, N, P
(D) K, L, M, O
(E) M, N, O, P

2. Which of the following CANNOT be included in a sauce that contains M?

(A) J
(B) L
(C) N
(D) O
(E) P

3. In a sauce in which J is used, what is the smallest number of additional ingredients that would meet recipe requirements?

(A) 1
(B) 2
(C) 3
(D) 5
(E) 6

4. By the addition of exactly one more ingredient, which of the following could make an acceptable combination of ingredients?

(A) H, L, P
(B) J, N, M
(C) K, L, N
(D) K, M, P
(E) L, M, O

5. Which ingredient must be omitted from the combination H, J, K, L, P to meet the recipe requirements?

(A) H
(B) J
(C) K
(D) L
(E) P

6. Exactly how many ingredients can be used as the only ingredients of a sauce?

(A) 2
(B) 3
(C) 4
(D) 5
(E) 6

Questions 7–12

Point P is 20 miles along a straight line from point R.
Point Q is 10 miles along a straight line from point R.
Point S is 5 miles along a straight line from point Q.

7. Which of the following must be true?

(A) If S is 5 miles from R, then S is 25 miles from P.
(B) If R is 15 miles from S, then S is 35 miles from P.
(C) If Q is 15 miles from P, then S is 20 miles from P.
(D) If S is 5 miles from P, then Q is 10 miles from P.
(E) If Q is 10 miles from P, then S is 5 miles from P.

8. If R is 5 miles from S, which of the following must be true?

    (A) S is closer to P than to R.
    (B) S is closer to Q than to R.
    (C) S is closer to Q than to P.
    (D) S is closer to P than to Q.
    (E) S is closer to R than to P.

9. Which of the following CANNOT be true?

    (A) P is closer to Q than to R.
    (B) Q is closer to R than to P.
    (C) R is closer to P than to S.
    (D) R is closer to S than to Q.
    (E) S is closer to P than to R.

10. If Q is due west of R and R is due east of P, all of the following must be true EXCEPT:

    (A) Q is due east of P
    (B) Q is 10 miles from P
    (C) S is at most 15 miles from P
    (D) S is at most 15 miles from R
    (E) S is due east of P

11. If R is due west of P and S is 5 miles from P, which of the following must be true?

    (A) S is farther from P than from R.
    (B) R is farther from Q than from S.
    (C) S is farther from R than from Q.
    (D) S is farther from P than from Q.
    (E) Q is farther from S than from P.

12. If Q is due south of R and S is due north of Q, all of the following must be true EXCEPT:

    (A) S is farther from P than R is from P
    (B) R is farther from S than Q is from S
    (C) P is farther from Q than P is from R
    (D) Q is farther from R than S is from R
    (E) P is farther from R than Q is from R

Questions 13–18

Seven people—K, N, O, P, Q, R, and W—own condominiums in a four-story building.

> The floors are numbered one through four, consecutively, from bottom to top.
> Floor one has only one condo.
> Each of floors two, three, and four have two condos.
> K lives in a condo on one of the floors beneath R.
> P lives in a condo on one of the floors above the condos of Q and N.
> N and O live in condos on the same floor.
> Only one person owns each condo.

13. Which of the following must be true if K's condo is on the second floor?

    (A) Q's condo is on the first floor.
    (B) R's condo is on a floor below O.
    (C) N's condo is two floors above W.
    (D) R's condo is on the fourth floor.
    (E) W's condo is on the third floor.

14. Which of the following must be true if K's condo is on the third floor?

    (A) K's condo and Q's condo are on the same floor.
    (B) O's condo is two floors below R's condo.
    (C) W's condo is on the first floor.
    (D) Q's condo is on the fourth floor.
    (E) K's condo is on the first floor.

15. Which is a complete and accurate list of those owners whose condos could be on the fourth floor?

    (A) R, W
    (B) Q, R
    (C) P, W
    (D) P, Q, R
    (E) P, R, W

16. Which of the following is a complete and accurate list of the floors on which their condos could be located, if the condos of P and R are on the same floor?

    (A) two
    (B) three
    (C) four
    (D) two, three
    (E) three, four

17. Which of the following provides sufficient additional information to determine the floor location of every condo?

    (A) K's condo is on the first floor.
    (B) R's condo is on the second floor.
    (C) W's condo is on the first floor.
    (D) W's condo is on the second floor.
    (E) W's condo is on the fourth floor.

18. If P's condo is on the third floor, all of the following are true EXCEPT:

    (A) R's condo is one floor above K's condo
    (B) N's condo is one floor below R's condo
    (C) P's condo and K's condo are on the same floor
    (D) Q's condo is on the first floor
    (E) W's condo is on the fourth floor

Questions 19–24

B, C, D, E, F, and G are to be seated at a round table. Each of exactly six chair faces the center of the table and is directly opposite a chair across the table. The following requirements apply to the seating arrangements.

D must sit next to F.
B cannot sit next to F.
C cannot sit next to G.

19. If D is one of the two people who sit next to E, which of the following is a complete and accurate list of the other person who can sit next to E?

    (A) B
    (B) C
    (C) G
    (D) B, C
    (E) C, G

20. Who must sit in the chairs on either side of E if B sits next to D and if C sits next to F?

    (A) B and G
    (B) B and C
    (C) B and F
    (D) C and D
    (E) C and G

21. Who must sit directly across the table from F if C sits next to D and if E sits next to F?

    (A) C
    (B) B
    (C) D
    (D) E
    (E) G

22. If C sits immediately to the left of F and D sits immediately to the right of F, which is the total number of arrangements in which the others can be seated in relation to one another?

    (A) 1
    (B) 2
    (C) 3
    (D) 4
    (E) 5

23. Who must sit in the chairs on either side of G if C sits directly across the table from E?

    (A) C and D
    (B) D and E
    (C) E and F
    (D) B and E
    (E) B and F

24. If B sits directly across the table from F, each of the following could be true EXCEPT:

    (A) C sits directly across from E
    (B) C sits next to E
    (C) D sits next to E
    (D) G sits next to E
    (E) D sits directly across from G

| SECTION **4** | TIME—35 MINUTES | 28 QUESTIONS |

The questions in this section are based on what is stated or implied in the passage. Select the best answer to each question, and mark the corresponding space on the answer sheet.

Line It is not easy to describe the present position of legal opinion on advertising and free speech. Only a poet can capture the essence of chaos. Nor is it easy to foresee
5   how things will develop. Lacking any rationale for the First Amendment, with the courts depending on time-honored slogans to sustain conclusions, there is no obvious resting place, from the moment the slogans
10   cease to work their magic. At the present time, the courts are tending to bring a greater proportion of advertising within the protection of the First Amendment. And cases now proceeding through the courts,
15   such as the litigation concerning what egg producers can say about heart disease and cholesterol or what can be said about margarine in advertisements, will undoubtedly continue the process. Where will it
20   end?
         Some legal writers have sought to treat First Amendment rights as being, in some sense, absolute and have objected to what is termed the "balancing" by the
25   courts of these rights against others. But such "balancing" is inevitable if judges must direct their attention to the general welfare. Freedom to speak and write is bound to be restricted when exercise of these freedoms
30   prevents the carrying out of other activities that people value. Thus is it reasonable that First Amendment freedoms should be curtailed when they impair the enjoyment of life (privacy), inflict great damage on
35   others (slander and libel), are disturbing (loudness), destroy incentives to carry out useful work (copyright), create dangers for society (sedition and national security), or are offensive and corrupting (obscenity)?
40   The determination of the boundaries to which a doctrine can be applied is not likely to come about in a very conscious or

even consistent way. But it is through recognition of the fact that rights should be
45   assigned to those to whom they are most valuable that such boundaries come to be set. It is only in recent years that there has been any serious consideration of the relation of advertising to freedom of speech
50   and of writing. Now that the value of advertising in providing information has been accepted, it seems improbable that it will long be thought that this is true only for price advertising. And the action of the
55   Federal Trade Commission in treating prohibitions by professional associations of advertising by their members as anticompetitive will bring greater awareness of the informational role of advertising. Similarly,
60   the many studies of the failures of government regulatory agencies that have been made in recent years are bound to make the courts somewhat reluctant to expand and more willing to take advantage of
65   opportunities to contract the regulation of advertising. Where will it end? It seems likely that the law will be interpreted to allow the Federal Trade Commission to continue to regulate false and deceptive
70   advertising, but with greater freedom for what can be said in advertising than now exists, and with somewhat diminished powers for the various government agencies that regulate advertising.

1. Which of the following best describes the point of the passage?

    (A) The First Amendment is primarily a collection of slogans.
    (B) All advertising is protected by the right of free speech.
    (C) Courts must balance the right of free speech with others.
    (D) Advertising regulation has been a failure of the government.
    (E) More advertising will be protected by the First Amendment.

2. According to the passage, which of the following may NOT be limited by restrictions on the freedom of speech?

(A) advertising claims
(B) obscene films
(C) amplified music in a public park
(D) military secrets
(E) political rhetoric

3. According to the passage, which of the following is true?

(A) The Federal Trade Commission is losing its power to regulate false advertising.
(B) Price advertising is protected by the First Amendment.
(C) The First Amendment right of freedom to speak and write is absolute.
(D) Rationales for First Amendment rights are time-honored.
(E) Boundaries for First Amendment freedoms are consciously determined by the courts.

4. The author refers to "chaos" in line 4 to indicate which of the following?

(A) that the passage is written by a poet
(B) that the state of the law of free speech is disorganized
(C) that advertising and free speech are intermingled
(D) that it is difficult to describe the confusion in the law related to advertising and free speech
(E) that the essence of free speech applies to advertising

5. The passage suggests all of the following EXCEPT:

(A) government regulation of advertising is losing power
(B) advertising is pre-competitive
(C) government regulation of advertising will continue
(D) advertising is protected by the First Amendment
(E) government regulation of advertising is anticompetitive

6. According to the passage, limitations on free speech are permitted in order to protect

(A) the general welfare
(B) individual damages
(C) the national government
(D) sedition
(E) boundaries

7. According to the passage, all of the following are factors in the changing relationship of advertising to freedom of speech EXCEPT:

(A) failures of government agencies
(B) providing information to the public
(C) balancing of various rights
(D) assigning rights to those for whom they are most valuable
(E) the absolute nature of the freedom of speech

Line   The black experience in the United States, including slavery, the fight for full citizenship from the time of the Emancipation, and the enforced alienation that constantly
5   cuts into our natural identification with our country, has obviously been different from that of white people. And although, as passionate believers in democracy, black Americans identify themselves with broad
10   American ideals, their sense of reality springs, in part, from experiences with which some white people are reluctant to identify themselves even in their imaginations. Thus, when some white people in
15   the United States declare most twentieth-century American fiction to be the "American reality," black people respond by pointing out that this and this have been left out. And most of all, black people point
20   out that what white people would have the world accept as the image of black Americans isn't realistic.

    Each of the failings that has been identified by black people is found in both
25   second-rate works and in novels by some of America's most respected white authors. For example, I recall not more than five black Americans in the works of Hemingway and Steinbeck. They tend to ignore
30   black people, or, like the early Faulkner, who distorted black humanity to fit his personal versions of the Southern myth, they oversimplify black characters, seldom portraying them with the sensitively
35   balanced opposites—good and evil,

instinctual and intellectual, passionate and spiritual—that great literary art has projected as the image of human beings. Since the essence of literature is its ambivalence,
40 and since fiction is never so effective as when both potentials are operating simultaneously, it is unfortunate that these novels have been so one-sided.

Understandably, the attitude of black
45 people toward such fiction is one of great skepticism. This is borne out by a well-known black novelist's remark that some white Americans seem to disagree with black Americans over the nature of reality.
50 Historically, this disagreement is part of a larger conflict between, on the one hand, groups of Americans whose ancestors voluntarily immigrated to the United States many years ago and, on the other, minority
55 groups and more recently arrived immigrant groups, over the first's attempt to impose their image of "the American" upon the rest. This conflict, however, should not be misunderstood. For "the American" has not
60 yet (fortunately for the United States, its minorities, and perhaps for the world) been finally defined. Far from being socially undesirable, the tension surrounding what "the American" is to be is part of that
65 democratic process through which the nation works to achieve itself. Out of this tension the ideal American character—a type great enough to deserve the greatness of the land, a delicately poised unity of divergencies—is slowly being born.

8. Which of the following best describes the author's tone in characterizing the works by Hemingway, Steinbeck, and Faulkner in the passage?

   (A) aggravating
   (B) apologetic
   (C) indifferent
   (D) ironic
   (E) disapproving

9. Which of the following is the most essential property of literature according to the author?

   (A) obscurity
   (B) realism
   (C) sensitivity
   (D) ambivalence
   (E) imagination

10. Which of the following does the author of the passage explicitly criticize Hemingway for doing in his novels?

   (A) distorting the humanity of black characters
   (B) portraying black characters as unidimensional
   (C) including few black characters
   (D) exaggerating conflicts between black and white Americans
   (E) describing the black experience in an insensitive manner

11. It can be inferred from the passage that the author would most probably NOT agree with which of the following statements about the larger conflict described in the last paragraph?

   (A) It is good that this conflict has not yet been resolved.
   (B) It is through this conflict that the final image of "the American" is being developed.
   (C) This conflict is having a destructive impact on American society.
   (D) This type of conflict is to be expected in a democratic nation.
   (E) Disagreements between black Americans and some white Americans about twentieth-century American fiction can be viewed as part of this conflict.

12. The author of the passage apparently considers spirituality and passion to be

   (A) instinctual
   (B) antithetical
   (C) ambiguous
   (D) synonymous
   (E) suspect

13. Which of the following statements about great novels, if true, would most strengthen the author's assertions about literature and fiction in the second paragraph?

(A) Great novels usually depict the social environment accurately.

(B) Great novels usually contain characters who embody divergent qualities.

(C) Great novels usually portray characters in a sensitive manner.

(D) Great novels usually deal with themes of enduring importance.

(E) Great novels usually suggest a resolution for identified conflicts.

14. According to the passage, black Americans and some white Americans would NOT tend to disagree about which of the following?

(A) the nature of "the American"

(B) the vital importance of the democratic process in America

(C) the accuracy of Faulkner's depiction of black characters

(D) the representativeness of American reality as portrayed in most twentieth-century American fiction

(E) their respective experiences as Americans

Line There is a certain elemental appeal to the policy. People generally tend to think that if they pay money to have something made for them, they "own" it and should be able

5 to do with it as they please. Government people frequently express this kind of sentiment toward the spending of government money and seem not to understand why private firms might object to the

10 policy. They perceive the government policy to be fair, and any private firm that doesn't agree is, to put it bluntly, being greedy. The private firms, of course, tend to think that the government is trying to

15 get something for nothing. The truth is that when it comes to their rights as against those of their employees, private firms very well understand this principle of getting all the rights and benefits when one pays for

20 something. Within a firm, ownership of intellectual property and the profits resulting from the value of the intellectual property do not belong to the creative employee but to the shareholders of the

25 firm.

Yet government people do under-stand—even if they don't much like it—that private firms seem to lack incentives to develop and deliver their best products to

30 the government when the firms have no reasonable expectation of receiving a continuing stream of income from the product, so that, as a result, the government isn't getting a lot of the best technol-

35 ogy.

Some government people might think, "But, hey, a private firm has incentive to deliver the best technology to us (even though we have unlimited rights) because

40 it's OK with us if they take the thing to the commercial market." There are a couple of problems with this theory. One is that since the government claims an unlimited right to disclose the technology developed at public

45 expense to anyone for any purpose, the government has the power at any time to pull the rug out from under the commercial market (for in today's market, it is the valuable secrets embodied in the technol-

50 ogy that seem to determine its commercial value). Second, the government tends to want to "give away" valuable technology in which it has unlimited rights to other private firms whom the technology's

55 developer may see as its primary commer-cial market. Both of these can undermine the potential incentives that government people tend to think the private firm has retained.

60 It is worth pointing out that Congress has exacted a law to encourage small firms to develop and deliver to the government the highest quality, most innovative products, namely the Small Business

65 Innovation Development Act. This law gives participating small firms the right to retain ownership rights in patents developed at public expense, with a license back to the government to use the patent for govern-

70 mental purpose. In trying to decide whether to retain its broad unlimited rights policy, the government should think about whether it really needs "unlimited rights" in technology. It should ask itself why it needs

75 more than government purpose rights. It also should understand that one of the costs of the unlimited rights policy is that the government is likely to get delivery of less-than-high-quality products.

28

15. The primary purpose of the passage is to

(A) advocate an expansion of the Small Business Innovation Development Act

(B) explain the inability of the government to secure the best available technology

(C) propose a method to ensure business a continuing stream of income from technological products

(D) contrast the perspectives of government and industry people concerning technology

(E) encourage the government to surrender its unlimited rights policy as to technology

16. The passage uses the term "greedy" in line 13 to

(A) indicate the attitude of government workers toward private firms that sell technology to the government

(B) describe the attitude of private firms toward government procurement policy

(C) highlight the conflict between private and government views of technology purchased by the public

(D) contrast the sentiment of government people with that of private firms

(E) express the author's view of government policy toward technology acquisition

17. "Governmental purpose" in lines 69–70 describes which of the following?

(A) a restriction on the governmental use of technology

(B) an enlightened policy for private-firm technology development

(C) a license for the governmental use of technology

(D) the retention of ownership of technology by private firms

(E) a law to encourage the development of technology by private firms

18. Which of the following may be inferred from the passage?

(A) Private firms dislike dealing with the government.

(B) The government could get better technology than it does.

(C) The commercial value of technology is difficult to exploit.

(D) Intellectual property is owned by those who create it.

(E) People do not own property that they have paid for.

19. The author's attitude toward the "unlimited rights" policy of the federal government is best described as

(A) approving

(B) understanding

(C) questioning

(D) hostile

(E) neutral

20. Which of the following, if true, would most strengthen the author's argument?

(A) Technology is a small part of government acquisitions.

(B) The government acquires its most advanced technology on the open market.

(C) There is limited competition among technology companies.

(D) Less that 1 percent of government technology acquisitions are provided by small firms.

(E) Private firms seldom exploit the technology they develop for the government.

21. The government policy concerning the ownership of technology acquired from private firms is the same as

(A) that of private firms toward their creative employees

(B) that of shareholders toward the government

(C) that of employees toward their employers

(D) that of government employees toward private firms

(E) that of private firms toward government employees

Line Many scholars assert that the attempt to
regulate the behavior of business through
legislation is at best futile and at worst
deleterious. In making their argument,
5   advocates of nonregulation assume a
distinction between the morality of duty
and the morality of aspiration. They argue
that duties, which specify minimum
standards of human conduct, lend them-
10 selves to legal enforcement better than do
aspirations, which exhort one to realize
one's full potential. The advocates of
nonregulation also assume, quite justifiably,
that the problems associated with business
15 are primarily problems of aspiration; that is,
one may feel that a business is not doing all
it could to develop a new product. The
creation of a cumbersome network of
regulations to encourage aspiration, they
20 conclude, may make those subject to the
regulations abdicate independent, responsible judgment in those areas in which it is
most needed.
         However, the lawmaking problem
25 suggested by the distinction between duty
and aspiration, a distinction that is valid, is
not as insurmountable as the advocates of
nonregulation conclude. The law can and
often does make both individuals and
30 business aspire. When the law states that
citizens shall "not drive recklessly" or "not
ship in interstate commerce any vehicles
that do not meet minimum EPA standards,"
the law is making individuals aspire to drive
35 carefully and business aspire to produce
relatively pollution-free engines. Yet there is
some merit to the argument for nonregulation. Although the law can raise standards
as long as those standards are applied
40 generally, the standards are going to be the
result of compromises. Thus the business
that can far exceed the minimum standards
has no more legal obligation to do so than
does the business that can barely meet
45 those standards.
         But it is not inevitable that laws take
this form; in other words, there is nothing
inherent in the laws that encourage
aspiration that leaves those laws unenforce-
50 able. Laws could be predicated on what
can reasonably be expected of each
particular business, the more competent
businesses having to face higher standards
than the less competent. It is hard to

55 believe that juries do not already include
such considerations in their deliberations.
Admittedly, there would be difficulties in
enforcing such a system. Witnesses with
relevant expertise, records, evaluation of
60 the conditions prevailing within a particular
industry—all this and more—would be
needed so that a jury could determine what
is feasible and what is not.
         Unless we want to make excellence a
65 legal liability, it is unlikely that the law can
ever be a good mechanism for drawing out
of a business the best of which it is
capable. But we should recognize that it is
our own reluctance, and not any reason as
70 yet put forth by the advocates of nonregulation, that makes this so.

22. Which of the following is a major point
    made in the argument for nonregulation of
    business according to the passage?

    (A) The concept of aspiration is already
        the basis of the self-regulation of
        business because aspirations are vital
        to business growth.
    (B) The concept of aspiration has been shown
        to be a less useful basis for designing laws
        than has the concept of duty.
    (C) Laws that are intended to encourage
        aspiration actually discourage aspira-
        tion because such laws discourage the
        exercise of reflection, discretion, and
        initiative.
    (D) Because laws that encourage aspiration
        are unfair and ambiguous, they have
        been opposed by the majority of the
        public in the past and are likely to be
        opposed in the future.
    (E) Because there is at present little
        agreement as to which goals business
        should strive for, laws that encourage
        aspiration are difficult to enforce.

23. The primary purpose of the passage is best described as an effort to

(A) suggest some ways in which laws that encourage aspiration can be used effectively to regulate the behavior of business

(B) argue that the advocates of nonregulation have overemphasized the effect on business of laws that encourage aspiration while underestimating the effect of laws that specify duties

(C) discuss instances in which laws that encourage aspiration have had a desirable, although indirect, effect on both individuals and businesses

(D) rebut the argument that the distinction between the morality of duty and the morality of aspiration can and should be used in lawmaking

(E) contend that the distinction between the morality of duty and the morality of aspiration, however valid, should not be regarded as the basis of a valid argument against the regulation of business

24. According to the author, the advocates of nonregulation support their position by making which of the following arguments about duties and aspirations?

(A) Laws that designate duties are easier to enforce than are laws that encourage aspirations.

(B) Laws that designate duties should be of greater concern to society than should laws that encourage aspirations.

(C) Duties are easier to define than are aspirations.

(D) Businesses should be primarily concerned with duties and only secondarily concerned with aspirations.

(E) Businesses should be legally obligated to distinguish between duties and aspirations.

25. The author suggests that the most valid criticism of the enactment of laws that encourage aspiration that has been raised by the advocates of nonregulation is which of the following?

(A) In order to do business efficiently and profitably, a business must be able to change or modify its aspirations quickly.

(B) Many businesses are necessarily exempt from laws that encourage aspiration.

(C) Many of the laws that encourage aspiration apply to business in one country but not in another.

(D) The capabilities of different businesses vary, and such variation is not taken into account by laws that encourage aspiration.

(E) Laws that encourage aspiration are subject to the interpretation of only a few judges, whose opinions may not reflect the values of society as a whole.

26. According to the author, the assumption that the problems associated with business are primarily problems of aspiration is

(A) alarming
(B) verifiable
(C) unprecedented
(D) implausible
(E) sound

27. According to the author, the implementation of laws that encourage aspiration would be difficult because

   (A) evidence establishing a particular business's liability is not as likely to be available
   (B) information pertinent to each particular industry would have to be collected and analyzed
   (C) the liability of a business would have to be distinguished from the liability of its employees
   (D) businesses that are theoretical entities can be easily disbanded
   (E) the merits of conflicting, equally worthy aspirations would have to be considered

28. The author would most probably agree with which of the following statements about the relationship between business and laws that encourage aspiration?

   (A) Laws that encourage aspiration are noble but essentially unenforceable; therefore, laws that specify duties are more likely to regulate business behavior effectively.
   (B) Laws that encourage aspiration can be used to regulate only a few aspects of business behavior; therefore, only laws that specify duties should be applied to businesses.
   (C) Since many juries already consider aspiration to be an element of the law, it is unlikely that there would be very much difficulty in persuading juries to apply laws of aspiration to business behavior.
   (D) Since laws that specify duties and that are also effective imply aspirations, laws that explicitly encourage aspirations are a potentially useful legal mechanism for regulating business behavior.
   (E) Since many people are reluctant to make aspiration a legal responsibility, it is unlikely that the law can be used to regulate business behavior effectively.

Evaluate the reasoning contained in the brief statements, and select the best answer. Do not make implausible, superfluous, or incompatible assumptions. Select the best answer to each question, and mark the corresponding space on the answer sheet.

1. Recent research shows that millions of people in the United States still do not know that smoking cigarettes places people at very significant risk of health problems. This is the case, even though hundreds of millions of dollars have been spent to warn people of the hazards and risks of smoking. The inevitable conclusion is that the warnings placed on cigarette packs and in advertising have had no effect.

   If true, which of the following refutes the above argument?

   (A) Tobacco companies have had to be forced to warn smokers of the health dangers of smoking.
   (B) The majority of smokers are aware of the risks and hazards of their smoking.
   (C) Some smokers have legitimate reasons for smoking.
   (D) Some people who are aware of the hazards of smoking learned of them from mandatory warnings.
   (E) Smokers constitute the largest group of people who suffer from preventable illnesses in the United States.

2. Within available resources, the noble objective of greater safety in the office and factory has been actively pursued by the vast majority of businesses. By contrast, federal and state occupational health and safety regulations limit productivity and competitiveness—the country's most critical economic problems.

   If true, which of the following most weakens the above opinion?

   (A) Safety programs of businesses benefit from the intimate knowledge those enterprises have of the primary hazards in their activities.
   (B) Government health and safety regulations require inspection for and remediation of found hazards.
   (C) Governmental health and safety regulations have reduced costly accidents that previously reduced worker productivity.
   (D) Neither business nor government are aware of many occupational health and safety hazards.
   (E) Governmental health and safety regulations establish common standards, while individual business standards vary greatly.

3. Although it may seem to be counterintuitive, a country must reduce poverty and hunger concurrent with a reduction in the death rate if it hopes not to suffer a major growth in population. Poor and hungry people will feel the need to have many children until infant mortality decreases as the result of the benefits of economic growth.

   This argument would be weakened if it could be shown that

   (A) poverty and hunger do not necessarily account for a country's death rate
   (B) most large families consist of four different generations
   (C) infant mortality is not the primary reason for having many children
   (D) the rate of infant mortality need not increase when the death rate increases
   (E) in most wealthy countries, the benefits of economic growth are differentially distributed across the population

4. Singularity saves politicians from having to take infinite variations into account when they establish rules and regulations for diverse populations. A single set of rules and regulations fits all.

The main point of this commentary is that

(A) it is good when people are similar to one another
(B) the identification of variations among people is difficult
(C) rules and regulations cannot take diverse populations into account
(D) it is easier to treat a country's population as though it is homogeneous
(E) dealing with similar populations similarly is not just

5. Teachers provide information to students. But teachers should promote the use of that information by developing their students' abilities to create, think, and benefit from the use of their intellects. If schools are to educate, then teachers must demonstrate the development of ideas and the mind as well as pass along facts and opinions to students.

This comment implies which of the following?

(A) To develop the ability to think, a student must have a good teacher.
(B) Conveying facts and opinions is not good teaching.
(C) Education includes the cultivation of creative mental abilities.
(D) Teachers must be demonstrative if they expect to communicate effectively.
(E) Developing exercises that stretch the mind is the key to good teaching.

6. An owner of a large agribusiness explained to the foreign visitors that productivity improved significantly when crops were planted in long rows. Since virtually all planting, tilling, and harvesting is done by field machines, long rows reduce the number of turns that the equipment must make. Turns are difficult, take time, and prompt the field-machine operators to take a break. In short, long rows keep machines and their operators productive for more minutes each hour.

From the explanation, which of the following can be inferred about the way field-machine operators are paid?

(A) Operators are paid by the number of rows completed.
(B) Operators are paid by the amount of work done.
(C) Operators who produce more are paid more.
(D) Operators are paid by the hour.
(E) Operators are paid by the number of equipment turns made.

7. Contrary to the spin placed on her reelection, representative Anthony did not achieve a convincing victory. She points out that 60 percent of the voters cast ballots for her, but a mere 25 percent of eligible people voted for her. A substantial majority of registered voters did not vote. Clearly, she has the support of only a small minority of the people she represents.

This point of view is most weakened by ambiguous meaning of the word

(A) spin
(B) convincing
(C) majority
(D) support
(E) victory

8. Compared to a carnivore, an herbivore needs relatively few pounds of plants as food to be able to produce a pound of protein. Since carnivores feed on both herbivores and other carnivores, the accumulated consumption of thousands of pounds of plants is needed for a carnivore to produce a pound of protein.

This argument is best completed by which of the following?

(A) Herbivores produce protein faster than carnivores.

(B) A pound of carnivore protein has more food value than a pound of herbivore protein.

(C) The impact of people on plant resources would be much less if they substituted chicken for tuna in their diets.

(D) Carnivores' diets consist of more plants than meat.

(E) Chickens are a cheaper source of food than tuna.

Questions 9–10

It is argued that the problem of substantial unemployment of teenagers is due to the fact that the minimum wage makes it unprofitable to hire young people. But the fact that the percentage of people who are over 16 and employed is greater than ever before proves that the teenage unemployment problem is a myth.

9. The tactic used by the author to state her view against the minimum wage argument is to

(A) point out that the data used to describe the alleged problem is subjective

(B) show that the alleged cause of the problem is really an effect

(C) present data to support the conclusion that the minimum wage has increased employment

(D) describe that more people than ever before are employed

(E) demonstrate that the alleged problem is actually a pseudoproblem

10. If true, which of the following most weakens the author's point of view?

(A) A conclusion of a research study is that small-business owners are against a minimum wage.

(B) Most employers pay employees much more than the minimum wage.

(C) Of those who seek employment, virtually all of those over age 35 are employed while only 45 percent of those ages 20 and under are employed.

(D) Prior to the existence of a minimum wage law, there were times when teenage unemployment was as high as 75 percent.

(E) Loss of a job is rarely the result of the wage rate of the newly unemployed person.

11. Dr. Burns: If the medicine arrives today, the baby will be saved.

Dr. Mills: No, if the medicine arrives tomorrow, it will be just as good for the baby.

Dr. Mills' reaction to Dr. Burns' assertion indicates that she understood Dr. Burns to mean that

(A) nothing but medicine will save the baby

(B) if medicine arrives today, it will not arrive tomorrow

(C) today is the only day that medicine can arrive

(D) medicine arriving tomorrow will be of no use

(E) medicine will save the baby only if it comes today

12. At its annual meeting, the chairman of the board of Bransom, Inc., responded to a question about the lack of women senior executives by stating that 60 percent of the employees of the corporation are women. He then added that Bransom was committed to equal employment opportunities for women.

The basic flaw in the chairman's answer is that it

(A) confuses opportunity with action

(B) deflects the question by describing the number of women employees

(C) assumes that commitment meets the obligations of the corporation

(D) suggests that there are more women than men employees at Bransom

(E) interprets the question to focus on women executives

13. The Department of Agriculture will stop inspecting milk processing plants because no citations have been issued in the past two years.

If true, which of the following most strengthens the decision?

(A) Processors will cut corners if the threat of inspection is removed.
(B) Milk processing is very automated.
(C) The source of milk is known, so compensation can be had for any problem that occurs.
(D) The Department budget has been cut by 30 percent.
(E) The industry association has standards that exceed the legal requirements.

14. The ethereal state of the Lotophagai of Greek history was thought to result from eating the narcotic in the lotus fruit. But modern research with rats has shown that the smell of the fruit produces the sleepy, dreamy condition that identified the lotus-eaters.

This statement assumes that

(A) eating the narcotic in the lotus fruit has no effect on people
(B) the fragrance of the lotus enhances the narcotic effect of the fruit
(C) rats and humans are affected by the lotus fragrance in the same way
(D) the effect produced by eating the lotus fruit is greater than that produced by smelling the fruit
(E) it is the fragrance of the lotus fruit that is addictive rather than the narcotic

15. Mr. Wall teaches six high school classes each weekday. Professor Wall, his wife, teaches two courses each semester at the university. Professor Wall is in class 6 hours per week, and Mr. Wall is in class 5 hours each day. Professor Wall is paid 40 percent more than her husband. These differences are reasonable when the expectations for research of the two people are taken into account.

This description and explanation assumes that

(A) university teaching demands more research than high school teaching
(B) university teaching requires more education than does high school teaching
(C) equal pay for equal work does not apply in academic environments
(D) student contact hours for the Walls are similar
(E) university course preparation is more demanding than high school course preparation

16. Producing the fuel ethanol from corn is feasible but counterproductive and impractical because

(A) it could result in food shortages
(B) it provides a disincentive to oil and gas exploration
(C) it cannot meet the total world demand for fuel
(D) it requires more energy to produce ethanol than the ethanol provides
(E) it cannot substitute for certain fuels in the marketplace

17. Federal courts are the sole interpreters of the federal constitution. The federal constitution requires that funding of the federal courts is the responsibility of the federal legislature. The courts and the legislature are litigating a dispute over funding of judges' salaries. Judicial ethics precludes a judge from involvement in litigation that concerns that judge's finances.

Based upon this information, which of the following conclusions is most logical?

(A) The litigation will be determined by the legislature.
(B) The litigation will be determined by the federal courts.
(C) The federal legislature must defer to the federal courts in any salary dispute.
(D) The litigation will be determined by the courts and legislature compromising.
(E) No federal judge can participate in determining the outcome of the litigation.

18. Those people who have a hobby live longer than those who don't.

Those people who have pets live longer than those people who don't.

To live longer, you should get a pet, take up a hobby, or both.

If true, which of the following weakens the conclusion of this argument?

(A) Pet owners and hobbyists are more active than the general population.
(B) Pet owners and hobbyists, as a group, are less vulnerable to illness because they tolerate stress better than the general population.
(C) There is no difference between having a pet and having a hobby.
(D) People who have a cat and collect stamps have the same life expectancy as do those who have only one or the other.
(E) People who take up a hobby after contracting cancer live longer than those who do not take up a hobby.

19. Foolish behavior in teenagers correlates highly with conflict, stress, high-performance expectations, and other dynamic activities that seem senseless or confusing to them. Therefore, any evaluation of a teen's behavior must take into account the context in which the behavior occurs.

This analysis concludes that a teenager's behavior ought to be viewed as

(A) a series of unrelated events
(B) the result of personal confusion
(C) a part of her or his social environment
(D) a reflection of parental expectations
(E) the result of hormonal changes

20. Nearly continuous campaigning by both incumbents in and aspirants to national elected office is more democratic than the six-week period that many political scientists consider optimal. Little-known aspirants have time to meet the voters and gather resources for the campaign.

If true, which of the following most directly weakens the above position?

(A) Continuous campaigning confuses potential voters.
(B) Continuous campaigning causes incumbents to focus on the next election rather than on the people's business.
(C) Continuous campaigning produces voter disinterest.
(D) Continuous campaigning makes it more difficult to secure volunteers.
(E) Continuous campaigning eliminates many potential candidates who cannot afford to quit their jobs for months or years.

21. For the first time in this century, the most recent national census shows that towns with populations under 10,000 are growing more rapidly than cities of more than 1 million. This confirms that people prefer human scale environments to rich, high-density environments.

The above argument assumes that

(A) the populations of large cities is declining

(B) the environmental quality of cities is declining

(C) financial opportunities are the primary reason people live in large cities

(D) people find more financial opportunities in large cities than in small towns

(E) there are more rich people today than ever before

22. A recent restaurant review by a famous critic complained that the food needed more salt. This criticism is unwarranted at a time when research shows that salt can create health problems for many people. Restaurants should be encouraged to give their guests the opportunity to put as much salt as they prefer on their food.

If true, which of the following LEAST weakens the above argument?

(A) Salt takes a long time to permeate many foods.

(B) Most restaurants will accommodate requests for salt-free food preparation.

(C) Most people eat large amounts of fast and prepared foods that contain high levels of salt.

(D) Food flavors are enhanced only when salt is used during preparation.

(E) Salt is the leading cause of hypertension in people in the age cohort that most frequents restaurants.

23. A nationwide study of sibling rivalry shows that brothers and sisters continue to compete throughout their lives. The majority of those who volunteered to be interviewed for the study convinced the researchers that many of their daily actions were caused by sibling rivalry.

If true, which of the following most weakens the findings stated above?

(A) Short interviews tend to be less reliable than long interviews.

(B) Rivalry between sisters is more intense than between brothers.

(C) Causation is an elusive concept.

(D) The siblings who volunteered for the study are atypical.

(E) Competition is engaged in by many unrelated people.

24. It is a widely held belief that anemia in young women results from dietary iron deficiency. In truth, it results from the greater need that young women have for iron when compared to the total population.

This argument FAILS to

(A) define "deficiency" in terms of the need for iron in various populations

(B) state the number of young women who are anemic

(C) describe the reason that young women have a greater need for iron than do others

(D) make the relationship between iron and anemia clear

(E) identify the difference between dietary iron and other forms of iron

QUICK-SCORE ANSWERS

Section 1	Section 2	Section 3	Section 4	Section 5
1. A	1. D	1. C	1. E	1. D
2. B	2. D	2. A	2. E	2. C
3. D	3. D	3. C	3. B	3. C
4. E	4. B	4. E	4. D	4. D
5. D	5. D	5. D	5. E	5. C
6. A	6. B	6. C	6. A	6. D
7. E	7. D	7. D	7. E	7. D
8. C	8. C	8. C	8. E	8. C
9. B	9. D	9. C	9. D	9. E
10. D	10. D	10. E	10. C	10. C
11. B	11. E	11. C	11. C	11. E
12. E	12. D	12. B	12. B	12. B
13. D	13. D	13. D	13. B	13. E
14. C	14. A	14. B	14. B	14. C
15. D	15. C	15. E	15. E	15. A
16. E	16. B	16. C	16. A	16. D
17. A	17. E	17. B	17. C	17. E
18. E	18. D	18. B	18. B	18. B
19. E	19. C	19. E	19. C	19. C
20. B	20. B	20. E	20. B	20. E
21. B	21. C	21. B	21. A	21. D
22. D	22. E	22. D	22. C	22. C
23. D	23. E	23. D	23. E	23. D
24. A	24. D	24. C	24. A	24. A
			25. D	
			26. E	
			27. B	
			28. D	

EXPLANATORY ANSWERS

In the following answer guide, the credited responses appear in bold type, and the visualization that makes the credited response clear appears before the question set. Use the visualization to guide you in determining the credited answer.

SECTION 1

Questions 1–6

A, B, C, D, E, F, G, H

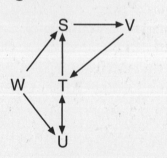

1. **The correct answer is (A).** two

2. **The correct answer is (B).** five

3. **The correct answer is (D).** one, two, seven

4. **The correct answer is (E).** A locates on a floor somewhere above D.

5. **The correct answer is (D).** G locates on floor three.

6. **The correct answer is (A).** C locates on floor eight.

Questions 7–12

S, T, U, V, W

7. **The correct answer is (E).** W

8. **The correct answer is (C).** U and V only

9. **The correct answer is (B).** T can call S, which can transfer the call to V.

10. **The correct answer is (D).** U to V

11. **The correct answer is (B).** U to V

12. **The correct answer is (E).** W to V

Questions 13–18

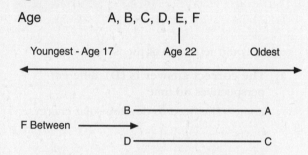

13. **The correct answer is (D).** Fern is 18 years old.

14. **The correct answer is (C).** Beth is 20 years old and Adam is 21.

15. **The correct answer is (D).** 19 and 21

16. **The correct answer is (E).** Darla is 17 years old.

17. **The correct answer is (A).** 2

18. **The correct answer is (E).** Fern is 20 years old.

Questions 19–24

Arrivals   N, P, R, S, T, W

Earlier   Later

W ——— R ——— P

S ——— T ——— P

S ——— N ——— R

19. **The correct answer is (E).** Wendy, Sarah, Nell, Ray, Ted, Paul

20. **The correct answer is (B).** after Wendy and before Ray

21. **The correct answer is (B).** Nell and Paul arrived together.

22. **The correct answer is (D).** 1..3

23. **The correct answer is (D)**. Nell, Sarah, Wendy

24. **The correct answer is (A)**. Ted and Wendy

SECTION 2

In the following answer guide, the credited responses appear in bold type and the guide that directs you toward the credited response appears within the answer choice context. The first reference is to the point of the argument and the second is to the nature of the issue involved.

1. **The correct answer is (D)**. different perspectives on time

   Point—The need to develop solar energy.

   Issue—Description question/characterizing points of view

2. **The correct answer is (D)**. respect their fellow citizens

   Point—Dictators disrespect those over whom they rule.

   Issue—Extension question/conclusion

3. **The correct answer is (D)**. Attendees did not have to do work outside the seminars in order to pass the examination.

   Point—Attendance results is sufficient knowledge to pass the exam.

   Issue—Extension question/conclusion

4. **The correct answer is (B)**. If there is inflation, it is not being controlled.

   Point—Wage and price controls limit inflation, spending, and profits.

   Issue—Extension question/conclusion

5. **The correct answer is (D)**. Knowledge of the laws of probability reduces the likelihood of a person believing in the supernatural.

   Point—Laws of probability explain many beliefs in supernatural forces.

   Issue—Extension question/conclusion

6. **The correct answer is (B)**. presenting circumstantial evidence

   Point—Digitalis accounts for the colors in van Gogh paintings.

   Issue—Description question/tactic

7. **The correct answer is (D)**. Numerous kinds of psychological stress produce similar physiological symptoms.

   Point—People undergo stress-induced physiological changes when they lie.

   Issue—Extension question/weakening evidence

8. **The correct answer is (C)**. The proper function of our universities is not to produce outstanding researchers, but to create well-rounded graduates.

   Point—Universities can produce successful researchers.

   Issue—Extension question/weakening evidence

9. **The correct answer is (D)**. Customers often give tips according to their perceptions of the cosmetologist and of the actions of other customers.

   Point—Patrons give large tips if they think that other patrons do and that their cosmetologists are not wealthy.

   Issue—Extension question/conclusion

10. **The correct answer is (D)**. nursing home residents are capable of making decisions about their own welfare

    Point—Nursing home residents have the right to determine their treatments.

    Issue—Extension question/assumption of capacity and competence

11. **The correct answer is (E)**. An effective way for families to capture and store solar energy has not yet been developed.

    Point—Encourage people to use solar energy because it is superior to other forms of energy.

    Issue—Extension question/weakening evidence

12. **The correct answer is (D)**. the ability to enjoy art often requires preparation

    Point—The ability to appreciate art must be acquired.

    Issue—Extension question/conclusion

13. **The correct answer is (D)**. struggles to gain presidential power produce far-reaching beneficial results

    Point—Working for power produces greater results than those sought.

    Issue—Extension question/conclusion

14. **The correct answer is (A)**. conditions created by nature can be differentiated from conditions created by society

    Point—Moral standards are inconsistently applied.

    Issue—Description question/different views have different causes

15. **The correct answer is (C)**. the differences among the various speech therapies considered are not causally relevant to their effectiveness

    Point—Different therapies produce different success rates.

    Issue—Extension question/conclusion

Questions 16–17

16. **The correct answer is (B)**. All thirty of the deceased sandhogs died of radiation-related cancer.

    Point—Thirty dead sandhogs were exposed to radiation that the contractor claims was safe.

    Issue—Extension question/weakening evidence

17. **The correct answer is (E)**. There is disagreement about the level of radiation that is safe.

    Point—Thirty dead sandhogs were exposed to radiation that the contractor claims was safe.

    Issue—Extension question/conclusion

18. **The correct answer is (D)**. expanding the right of the press to be present and cover trial proceedings

    Point—The media now serve as citizen representative observers at criminal trials.

    Issue—Extension question/conclusion

Questions 19–20

19. **The correct answer is (C)**. how citizens can effectively express dissatisfaction with the two major political parties

    Point—Not voting in the political process is not analogous to not purchasing in the marketplace.

    Issue—Description question/omission

20. **The correct answer is (B)**. discrediting an analogy

    Point—Not voting in the political process is not analogous to not purchasing in the marketplace.

    Issue—Description question/tactic

21. **The correct answer is (C)**. All offices above the fourth floor have fire escapes.

    Point—All offices above the fourth floor have two exits.

    Issue—Extension question/conclusion

22. **The correct answer is (E)**. Pigeons spread diseases; therefore, birds are nuisances.

    Point—Birds are nuisances because they are capable of spreading diseases.

    Issue—Extension question/conclusion

23. **The correct answer is (E)**. Resistance to the pesticide is passed from parent to offspring.

    Point—Pesticide resisting mites produce offspring that are more resistant.

    Issue—Extension question/conclusion

24. **The correct answer is (D)**. Baby gorillas raised by females other than their own mothers were unable to function as mothers when they had offspring.

    Point—Parenting skills are lost if babies are not raised by their mothers.

    Issue—Extension question/strengthening evidence

Section 3

In the following answer guide, the credited responses appear in bold type, and the visualization that makes the credited response clear appears before each question set. Use the visualization to guide you in determining the credited answer.

Questions 1–6

Ingredients

H, J, K, L, M, N, O, P

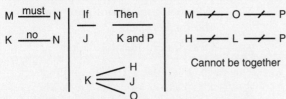

1. **The correct answer is (C)**. L, M, N, P

2. **The correct answer is (A)**. J

3. **The correct answer is (C)**. 3

4. **The correct answer is (E)**. L, M, O

5. **The correct answer is (D)**. L

6. **The correct answer is (C)**. 4

Questions 7–12

P, Q, R, S

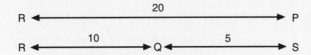

7. **The correct answer is (D)**. If S is 5 miles from P, then Q is 10 miles from P.

8. **The correct answer is (C)**. S is closer to Q than to P.

9. **The correct answer is (C)**. R is closer to P than to S.

10. **The correct answer is (E)**. S is due east of P.

11. **The correct answer is (C)**. S is farther from R than from Q.

12. **The correct answer is (B)**. R is farther from S than Q is from S

Questions 13–18

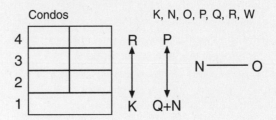

13. **The correct answer is (D)**. R's condo is on the fourth floor.

14. **The correct answer is (B)**. O's condo is two floors below R's condo.

15. **The correct answer is (E)**. P, R, W

16. **The correct answer is (C)**. four

17. **The correct answer is (B)**. R's condo is on the second floor.

18. **The correct answer is (B)**. N's condo is one floor below R's condo

Questions 19–24

Seating   B, C, D, E, F, G

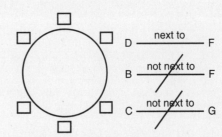

19. **The correct answer is (E)**. C, G

20. **The correct answer is (E)**. C and G

21. **The correct answer is (B)**. B

22. **The correct answer is (D)**. 4

23. **The correct answer is (D)**. B and E

24. **The correct answer is (C)**. D sits next to E

SECTION 4

In the following answer guide, the credited responses appear in bold type, and the guide that directs you to the place in the passage that accounts for the credited response appears within the answer choice context. The first reference is to the paragraph number in the passage that accounts for the credited response and the second number refers to the relevant sentence in the paragraph. The reference will appear as 2/4 for example. This means paragraph 2 and sentence 4 within paragraph 2.

1. **The correct answer is (E).** More advertising will be protected by the First Amendment.—Paragraph 1/Sentence 5

2. **The correct answer is (E).** political rhetoric—not listed in passage

3. **The correct answer is (B).** Price advertising is protected by the First Amendment.—Paragraph 2/Sentence 8

4. **The correct answer is (D).** that it is difficult to describe the confusion in the law related to advertising and free speech—Paragraph 1/Sentence 1

5. **The correct answer is (E).** government regulation of advertising is anticompetitive

6. **The correct answer is (A).** the general welfare—Paragraph 2/Sentence 2

7. **The correct answer is (E).** the absolute nature of the freedom of speech

8. **The correct answer is (E).** disapproving—Paragraph 2/Sentence 4

9. **The correct answer is (D).** ambivalence—Paragraph 2/Sentence 4

10. **The correct answer is (C).** including few black characters—Paragraph 2/Sentence 2

11. **The correct answer is (C).** This conflict is having a destructive impact on American society.—Paragraph 3/Sentence 4

12. **The correct answer is (B).** antithetical—Paragraph 2/Sentence 3

13. **The correct answer is (B).** Great novels usually contain characters who embody divergent qualities.—Paragraph 2/Sentence 3

14. **The correct answer is (B).** the vital importance of the democratic process in America—-Paragraph 3/Sentence 5

15. **The correct answer is (E).** encourage the government to surrender its unlimited rights policy as to technology—Paragraph 3/Sentences 3, 4, and 5

16. **The correct answer is (A).** indicate the attitude of government workers toward private firms that sell technology to the government—Paragraph 1/Sentence 3

17. **The correct answer is (C).** a license for the governmental use of technology—Paragraph 4/Sentence 2

18. **The correct answer is (B).** The government could get better technology than it does.—Paragraph 2/Sentence 1

19. **The correct answer is (C).** questioning—Paragraph 4/Sentence 4

20. **The correct answer is (B).** The government acquires its most advanced technology on the open market.—Paragraph 2/Sentence 1

21. **The correct answer is (A).** that of private firms toward their creative employees—Paragraph 1/Sentence 7

22. **The correct answer is (C).** Laws that are intended to encourage aspiration actually discourage aspiration because such laws discourage the exercise of reflection, discretion, and initiative.—Paragraph 1/Sentence 5

23. **The correct answer is (E).** contend that the distinction between the morality of duty and the morality of aspiration, however valid, should not be regarded as the basis of a valid argument against the regulation of business —Paragraph 1/Sentence 2, Paragraph 2/Sentence 1, Paragraph 4/Sentence 2

24. **The correct answer is (A).** Laws that designate duties are easier to enforce than are laws that encourage aspirations.—Paragraph 1/Sentence 3

25. **The correct answer is (D).** The capabilities of different business vary and such variation is not taken into account by laws that encourage aspiration.—Paragraph 2/Sentence 6

26. **The correct answer is (E).** sound—Paragraph 1/Sentence 4

27. **The correct answer is (B)**. information pertinent to each particular industry would have to be collected and analyzed—Paragraph 3/Sentence 4

28. **The correct answer is (D)**. Since laws that specify duties and that are also effective imply aspirations, laws that explicitly encourage aspirations are a potentially useful legal mechanism for regulating business behavior.

Section 5

In the following answer guide, the credited responses appear in bold type, and the guide that directs you toward the credited response appears within the answer choice context. The first reference is to the point of the argument and the second is to the nature of the issue involved.

1. **The correct answer is (D)**. Some people who are aware of the hazards of smoking learned of them from mandatory warnings.

   Point—Warnings have no effect.

   Issue—Extension question/conclusion

2. **The correct answer is (C)**. Governmental health and safety regulations have reduced costly accidents that previously reduced worker productivity.

   Point—Safety regulations limit productivity and competitiveness.

   Issue—Extension question/weakening evidence

3. **The correct answer is (C)**. infant mortality is not the primary reason for having many children

   Point—Infant mortality drives having children.

   Issue—Extension question/weakening evidence

4. **The correct answer is (D)**. it is easier to treat a country's population as though it is homogeneous

   Point—Single rules simplify matters for politicians.

   Issue—Extension question/conclusion

5. **The correct answer is (C)**. Education includes the cultivation of creative mental abilities.

   Point—Education should include instruction in the use of information taught.

   Issue—Extension question/conclusion

6. **The correct answer is (D)**. Operators are paid by the hour.

   Point—Productivity depends on the amount of time spent working each hour.

   Issue—Extension question/conclusion

7. **The correct answer is (D)**. support

   Point—Anthony has little support of her constituents.

   Issue—Extension question/weakening evidence

8. **The correct answer is (C)**. The impact of people on plant resources would be much less if they substituted chicken for tuna in their diets.

   Point—Herbivores produce protein much more efficiently than carnivores.

   Issue—Extension question/conclusion

Questions 9–10

9. **The correct answer is (E)**. demonstrate that the alleged problem is actually a pseudoproblem

   Point—Employment of people who are 16+ is at a record high despite a minimum wage.

   Issue—Description question/tactic

10. **The correct answer is (C)**. Of those who seek employment, virtually all of those over age 35 are employed while only 45 percent of those aged 20 and below are employed.

    Point—Employment of people who are 16+ is at a record high despite a minimum wage.

    Issue—Extension question/weakening evidence

11. **The correct answer is (E)**. Medicine will save the baby only if it comes today.

    Point—Medicine will save the baby.

    Issue—Extension question/NOT conclusion

12. **The correct answer is (B).** deflects the question by describing the number of women employees

Point—Number of women senior executives, not the percentage of women employees.

Issue—Description question/tactic

13. **The correct answer is (E).** The industry association has standards that exceed the legal requirements.

Point—Inspections identify no violations.

Issue—Extension question/conclusion

14. **The correct answer is (C).** rats and humans are affected by the lotus fragrance in the same way

Point—Smelling, not eating, causes a sleepy, dreamy condition.

Issue—Extension question/assumption

15. **The correct answer is (A).** university teaching demands more research than high school teaching

Point—An inverse relationship between pay and time-in-class is justifiable.

Issue—Extension question/assumption—research expectations

16. **The correct answer is (D).** it requires more energy to produce ethanol than the ethanol provides

Point—Producing ethanol from corn is counterproductive.

Issue—Extension question/conclusion

17. **The correct answer is (E).** No federal judge can participate in determining the outcome of the litigation.

Point—Ethics require judges not decide matters of financial self-interest.

Issue—Extension question/conclusion

18. **The correct answer is (B).** Pet owners and hobbyists, as a group, are less vulnerable to illness because they tolerate stress better than the general population.

Point—People who have a pet or hobby live longer.

Issue—Extension question/weakening evidence

19. **The correct answer is (C).** a part of her or his social environment

Point—Teen behavior correlates with the types of activities and context they experience.

Issue—Extension question/conclusion

20. **The correct answer is (E).** Continuous campaigning eliminates many potential candidates who cannot afford to quit their jobs for months or years.

Point—Continuous campaigns for national office are more democratic than time-restricted campaigns.

Issue—Extension question/weakening evidence

21. **The correct answer is (D).** people find more financial opportunities in large cities than in small towns

Point—More rapid population growth in small towns rather than big cities confirms an environmental preference of people.

Issue—Extension question/assumption

22. **The correct answer is (C).** Most people eat large amounts of fast and prepared foods that contain high levels of salt.

Point—Salt levels in restaurant food should be at patron discretion.

Issue—Extension question/NOT weakening evidence

23. **The correct answer is (D).** The siblings who volunteered for the study are atypical.

Point—Sibling rivalry continues through life and causes daily actions of siblings.

Issue—Extension question/weakening evidence

24. **The correct answer is (A).** define "deficiency" in terms of the need for iron in various populations

Point—Anemia in young women is not caused by a dietary deficiency but a greater need for iron.

Issue—Description question/ambiguous terminology

PREPARATION ANXIETY BRINGS US TOGETHER

I ask, "Are you ready for the LSAT?"

You respond, "Sure!"

Now that we have established the obligatory positions, we deal with the concerns that bring us together. You are very interested in doing well on the LSAT. You want me to tell you how to do well and to be quick about it. In short, you will do as well as you are able, when we successfully tear down the test-related barriers that threaten your performance.

The first barrier is test anxiety. Test anxiety is familiar to you—by this time in your academic career, you have undoubtedly experienced symptoms of anxiety during a test. There is a question about an unfamiliar subject; you cannot remember a fact, etc. Test anxiety is unlikely to be a barrier to your best performance. Research has shown that anxiety during a test rarely impairs performance, though occasionally a person will become so upset that performance suffers significantly. But, unless you have already experienced such extreme test anxiety, it is unlikely the LSAT will provoke a similar reaction.

PREPARATION BARRIER?

The second barrier is preparation anxiety. It is an obstacle to best performance for many, if not most, test-takers. It does impair LSAT performance and we must remove it.

Most people sense that the LSAT is different from other tests. They feel the test preparation strategies that have worked for them in the past may be insufficient when it comes to the LSAT. However, because they don't know what else to do, they do nothing, sign up for a test-prep course, or go through their time-tested preparation rituals. In spite of their efforts, many people remain uncertain about their readiness. The preparation barrier remains standing. Something tells them that their efforts are no preparation at all, and anxiety grows as their date with the test draws near.

DO YOU HAVE SYMPTOMS OF PREPARATION ANXIETY?

High achievers and perfectionists are the most susceptible to preparation anxiety. Although your past achievements testify to the contrary, you often feel unsure of your ability to perform well and, as a consequence, become very anxious when facing a critical test. You know that perfection is almost impossible to achieve, and your efforts are doomed from the start. Mild symptoms of preparation anxiety include tension, restlessness, boredom, disorganization, and a sense of being overwhelmed. Those more seriously affected experience depression, physical complaints, insomnia, appetite change, and shifts in their interpersonal behaviors.

In nearly all instances, preparation anxiety manifests itself in procrastination: the avoidance of meaningful preparation. If you have a severe case of preparation anxiety, you will be committed to the notion of preparation—starting tomorrow or maybe next week. If the anxiety is less severe, you are likely to resort to familiar preparation rituals. You will read books about the test. You may enroll in a prep course, where you take notes for future study. Although no effective preparation actually takes place, you will try to persuade yourself otherwise, while your anxiety grows. If any of this sounds familiar, be assured that you are not alone. The majority of those facing the LSAT suffer the same symptoms.

IS THE PREPARATION-ANXIETY BARRIER REAL OR IMAGINED?

Some LSAT anxiety is appropriate. After all, the test is difficult, and the score is all-important. But a colossal case of LSAT anxiety makes no sense at all—it is like being home alone on a dark night when the floor creaks, a door squeaks, shadows seem to dance, and the wind whistles at the window. The hair stands up on the back of your neck, and your heart begins to race. You have haunted-house syndrome. Imagination takes over and projects horrors of every description onto the LSAT, and you convince yourself the score will be a measure of your worth as a person and reveal your inadequacies to the world.

You are in needless pain. Do not project your fears onto the LSAT and give the syndrome a chance to undermine your removal of the barriers between you and your best performance. Sure, the LSAT is the most important factor in law school admission, but it does not measure your worth or predict your success in life. It simply does not merit projecting any such meaning onto it.

WHAT CAUSES PREPARATION ANXIETY?

Whatever form your anxiety takes, fear of the unknown is the barrier that is the root cause of preparation anxiety. How do you control the unknown? Most top-notch students prepare for every possible eventuality. They "study every-thing." Since there is no obvious "everything" where the LSAT is concerned, you experience a loss of control. This feeling of no control over LSAT performance has four principal factors: anticipation, mystification, misinformation, and overcomplication.

✔**MOST PEOPLE ANTICIPATE THAT THE LSAT WILL BE IMPOSSIBLE.**

Most people who take the LSAT believe that they will not be able to consistently perform the difficult tasks it requires. They **anticipate** a poor performance on the test and are convinced there is little or nothing they can do about it. They sense that they have no control over the LSAT, and a classic case of preparation anxiety follows.

Most people feel **mystified** about what the LSAT measures, how the score is determined, what use is made of the score, and a passel of similar puzzlements. This lack of certainty feeds their sense of being unable to control their test preparation or performance.

Misinformation about the LSAT abounds, usually taking the form of contradictions, exaggerations, and everything from gossip to gospel. It travels by the printed word and by word of mouth. Nearly everyone who has come into contact with the test becomes a source, and even the official word seems contradictory. For example, some time ago, in its information book, the test-maker stated, "The LSAT measures skills and knowledge that typically develop over a long period of time, so that you cannot prepare for the test by making a last-minute effort to master specific subject areas." Although the types of questions included on the LSAT have not changed, the test-maker currently sells a kit ". . . with hints and explanations that help you improve your skills."

The seeming **complexity** of the LSAT also contributes to a feeling of anxiety and loss of control. Five sections, three types of questions, a writing sample, raw scores, scaled scores, cut scores, percentiles, index numbers, and all the rest create a barrier that can prevent your best performance.

Where does this leave you?

Most people find themselves behind the preparation-anxiety barrier. To begin the barrier-removal process, you recognize its existence. Do not deny it or try to rationalize it. Accept your feelings.

Acceptance is essential to your removing your anxiety barrier. You need to use your anxiety to power your understanding of the LSAT. Understanding the LSAT will give you the control you need to perform your personal best. And the best way to begin your understanding is to gain control over your anxiety through training.

What is the key to anxiety reduction?

When you feel that you are in control of a situation, you have little or no anxiety. Therefore, the key to reducing preparation anxiety is control, and the key to control is developing choice, familiarity, and positivity.

When you are told that you must do something, you feel that you have no control over the situation, and your anxiety increases. However, if you choose to do the same thing, you put yourself in control. Thus, the first key to control over preparation anxiety is to **choose** the LSAT rather than have it imposed upon you.

While it is true that you must take the LSAT if you intend to go to law school in the United States or Canada, the choice to attend law school is yours. Deciding to take the LSAT puts you in control and consequently reduces preparation anxiety. You are doing what you want to do, not what you must.

Familiarity with the test further enhances your sense of control and further reduces preparation anxiety. Effective training for the LSAT will show you exactly what to expect of the test and how to respond to it. This knowledge will give you more of the control you need to overcome preparation anxiety.

Positive thoughts, feelings, images, and attitudes also contribute to a sense of control. If, during training, you keep on thinking about an exam you failed five years ago, and you imagine that everyone registered for the LSAT will outperform you, or you picture questions full of long Latin phrases, and you are sure you will blacken the wrong spaces on the answer sheet, chances are good that you will experience significant loss of control and suffer a near-terminal case of preparation anxiety.

But if you think that the LSAT is totally predictable (it is), you are confident that you can take advantage of its weaknesses (you can), you can visualize the question types that are always asked on the LSAT (they always are), and you are convinced that one of the 12,000 scores in the top 10 percent is waiting for you (yes, it is), then you will be in control, the preparation barrier will be rubble, and your test training will be both powerful and effective.

When you encounter a negative experience during training, convert it into a positive experience. For example, if you miss a question, recall that no one gets all the so-called right answers and that it is possible to miss as many as eighteen questions and still score in the top 10 percent on the LSAT.

By deciding that it is you who wants to take the LSAT, by becoming fully informed about the test and the appropriate responses to it, and by developing a positive attitude toward the test and your training for it, you will take control and overcome your preparation anxiety.

Practice worrying!

Worry practice is useful and effective. Throughout your life, people have encouraged you to overcome barriers with the words "don't worry." As you face the LSAT, your parents, friends, spouse, and others assure you that "Everything will be OK. Don't worry, you always do well." Accept such encouragement, but do not mistake it for positive thinking or a good training practice.

Worry about the LSAT.

Irrespective of how often you are told not to, you will worry about the LSAT. And, perhaps ironically, it's a good idea. Constructive worrying

about the LSAT should motivate you to explore effective test-taking techniques and to implement a personal training plan, and it is through these things that you gain control over the test.

However, **how you worry** is very important if the worry experience is to be positive and not produce a barrier to performance or undermine your training program. The essentials of effective worrying are: identifying the threat, exploring the options available for dealing with it, and installing a safety net.

How does worry practice work?

When you practice worrying, you gain control of what threatens you, and you remove it as a barrier. You determine the worst that can happen and implement a plan that takes that outcome into account.

Suppose that studying for a multiple-choice test has never resulted in good scores for you. Naturally, you worry about having the same experience with the LSAT. Factor in the cost of a prep course and the potential loss of pride of your family and friends, and you can gauge the embarrassment that a low score will cause you. This is a threat.

What options are available to you? One option is not to prepare for the LSAT at all—just take the test without telling anyone, since you don't believe preparation will help your performance anyway. Then when you don't do well, no one will be the wiser. This may help you deal with your preparation anxiety, but it won't help you achieve your goal of your best test score. A wiser course is to train hard for the LSAT, even if this training should turn out to have little effect. Explain to your family and friends that the test is very tough and the outcome very uncertain, but you will work as hard as you can to do well. Then if you don't do well, they will be prepared.

Next you develop and install your safety net. Even if you do not do well, the worst that can happen is that you have wasted a large amount of time and money getting ready and taking the test and applying to law schools. If, after all this, you perform no better than you would have done without preparation, you are no further behind than you were, and your family and friends will know that you worked hard. While this would not be a happy circumstance, it can get no worse than this, and this is not all that bad. The status quo is your safety net.

Do relaxation and concentration help reduce anxiety and keep that preparation barrier down?

There is much evidence that people perform best when they are relaxed and able to concentrate. Training that facilitates relaxation and concentration will enhance your performance and counter preparation anxiety.

There is a straightforward training process that encourages relaxation and concentration. If it seems hokey, let me assure you it is not. You can practice its three steps frequently during your training period. The first step involves **breath control**—when you begin to feel anxious or tense, pause in what you are doing and take three deep breaths. Inhale slowly and fully, then slowly and fully exhale. As you breathe deeply, execute step two, which is to **dismiss all thoughts of the past and future**. Put recollections of past performance and speculation about future performance out of your mind. Such thoughts are distracting and have no relevance to the task at hand. Finally, **focus exclusively on the immediate task**—nothing more and nothing less. Try it. You will be relaxed and your powers of concentration restored. You will be in control.

As you have learned in this session, control is the key to managing preparation anxiety, and training, including constructive worrying, is the key to control. By following the training regimen in this book, you will gain control over your preparation anxiety, tear down the barrier it poses to your best performance, and improve your LSAT results.

Success Session 1

Your academic training and conditioning can impede LSAT performance. Yes, it's true. The learning and testing techniques that have helped you in school can be barriers that actually lower your LSAT score. Even worse, the greater your academic learning and testing proficiency, the greater the risk to your test score. The objective of this success session is to train you to remove the barriers that arise from your academic conditioning.

Can you rely upon academic prowess?

Academic success is probably a major contributor to your interest in law school and the legal profession that have, in turn, led you to the challenge of the LSAT. You probably have some confidence in your academic ability. You have learned that a superior academic performance depends upon superior conditioning and study and test-taking techniques. Therefore, you reason that the conditioning and techniques that have produced good academic results for you in the past should also produce a superior LSAT score. For your reasoning to be correct, the LSAT should be a form of academic performance—but this is not the case.

✔**THE LSAT IS NOT AN ACADEMIC EXERCISE.**

For this reason, relying upon academic conditioning and techniques may actually place barriers that impair rather than enhance your LSAT performance. By training to circumvent these barriers, you can dramatically improve your score potential.

✔**AVOIDING EFFECTIVE ACADEMIC TECHNIQUES CAN ACTUALLY IMPROVE YOUR LSAT SCORE.**

Skeptical?

Sure you are. Skepticism is one of those successful academic techniques. You have been conditioned to question, and you insist on being convinced. And unless I can convince you that your academic conditioning must be put aside, your test training and LSAT performance will suffer, so here we go.

Isn't the LSAT a test like any other test?

No, it is not—at least not the kind of test with which you are familiar.

Your academic conditioning has provided you with a clear picture of a test. For example, you are supposed to have acquired certain information in Professor Smoot's course. To measure the extent to which you have succeeded in this, Smoot requires you to answer a series of questions she has prepared. You know the information, answer the questions, and do well. That's a test.

Because it is called Law School Admission Test, your academic conditioning leads you to expect it to have the characteristics of the familiar test. Even the format of the LSAT confirms this expectation—questions and answers, paper and pencils, time limits. But appearances are deceiving. Exactly what information is measured by the LSAT? What are you expected to know? The meaning of *carmagnole*? The formula for determining the surface area of a basketball? Everything? Nothing?

Aha! Now you know why the LSAT is not a test like the academic tests with which you are so familiar. Your knowledge of vocabulary, grammar, mathematical formulae, computation, facts, opinions, and other such information is not measured by the LSAT. In short, precious little substantive knowledge is required by the LSAT.

To further add to the possible deception, the LSAT is not designed to measure what it appears to ask. Rather, it is designed to measure your ability to select the best answer from the options provided by the test-maker. Selecting the best answer from provided choices is very different in form and content from answering a question about a subject that you are expected to know. Avoiding the barrier that associates the

Law School Admission Test with a familiar classroom or licensing test is essential to you scoring as well as you might on the LSAT. At the risk of oversimplification, do not think of the LSAT as a test. The LSAT is not a test!

WHAT LEARNING TECHNIQUES ARE BARRIERS TO YOUR BEST LSAT PERFORMANCE?

Barrier—Convert the Unfamiliar into the Familiar

When faced with the unfamiliar, we tend to respond by doing something familiar and comfortable. Thus, the majority of those facing the LSAT enroll in a "course" that they believe will teach them the substantive information required for the test—but, as we have just seen, the LSAT requires no substantive information.

As a substitute for effective preparation, weeks are wasted in the familiar classroom context searching for a way to convert the LSAT into the familiar (and comfortable?) academic test. The search is futile. It is a barrier that does little more than generate more preparation anxiety. Those who recognize the futility of traditional classroom preparation often attempt to sharpen their academic test-taking techniques by slogging through hundreds of LSAT questions. But this type of practice reinforces techniques that, when applied, likely constrain LSAT performance.

✔DON'T TRY TO CONVERT THE LSAT INTO THE FAMILIAR STUDY, STUDY, STUDY BARRIER.

In an academic course, generally, success is achieved by studying. Your academic conditioning dictates that study is the best way to learn the information needed to perform well on a test. Consequently, you have been conditioned to "study." In the LSAT context, study means answering and reviewing answers to questions that will not appear on the test. Such study wastes time and amplifies preparation anxiety because, if you're honest with yourself, you know that nothing of consequence is happening. The "study" barrier prevents you from productive training for success on the LSAT.

✔DON'T SUBSTITUTE THE COMFORT OF APPARENT STUDY FOR EFFECTIVE LSAT TRAINING.

Barrier—Effort Does Not Equal Excellence

Academic lore has it that excellent performance is a function of effort—no pain, no gain. You believe that if you work hard, you will do well on academic tests. "Hard work" generally means committing information to memory, but since the "information" required by the LSAT has virtually nothing to do with your test performance, the hard work with which you are familiar has no value in the context of this test. Studying hundreds of LSAT questions misses the point. LSAT excellence depends on consistent execution of a basic reasoning task, not repetitious grunt work.

✔DON'T SUBSTITUTE "HARD WORK" FOR EFFECTIVE LSAT TRAINING.

The Generalization Barrier

Academic rewards come regularly to those who discover the general concept that explains many specific observations. Those who are academically proficient anticipate the presence of consistency in a test and look for answers that are consistent with ones that have gone before. The LSAT anticipates this anticipation. Don't anticipate consistency in LSAT questions and answers—the opposite is often the case. The only reward for such anticipation and generalization is a barrier that produces a consistently low test score.

✔EACH LSAT QUESTION IS INDEPENDENT OF EVERY OTHER LSAT QUESTION.

Barrier—Complex Drives Out Simple

Your academic conditioning discourages choosing the simple or superficial answer to a test question and encourages you to search for the complex and thorough. When this conditioning is projected onto the LSAT, the test-taker frequently selects a less-than-appropriate answer because the best answer seems "too simple." Don't bypass the simple LSAT answer choice just because it would not be a strong response on an academic test.

✔ **THE SIMPLE ANSWER IS OFTEN THE BEST ANSWER TO AN LSAT QUESTION.**

Barrier—Reading for Information

In an academic context, reading is the primary way to acquire information. When the LSAT presents a reading passage, the conditioned reaction is to read it for the information it contains. But the passages you will find in the LSAT are not there to present information that you must commit to memory for future use. Such memorization would only detract from the purpose of LSAT reading passages, which is to provide a familiar vehicle through which your reasoning skill might be measured.

✔ **DO NOT READ THE LSAT FOR THE INFORMATION IT PRESENTS.**

Information acquisition is not among the purposes of the LSAT. Effective manipulation of information is an objective of the LSAT. Avoid erecting a reading-for-information barrier to your best performance on the test.

Barrier—Persuaded by Logic

Perhaps the most hazardous item of academic conditioning is the belief that a logical presentation is destined to be the most persuasive one. Confidence in what you know and understand of reality can lead to many an incorrect answer on the LSAT. The logic employed in the LSAT involves structure rather than reality.

✔ **THE BEST ANSWER TO AN LSAT QUESTION OFTEN DEFIES REALITY AS YOU KNOW IT.**

WHAT TEST-TAKING TECHNIQUES ERECT BARRIERS TO YOUR BEST LSAT PERFORMANCE?

The Well-Worn Path Barrier

People who are successful at academic test taking generally follow a clear path to good grades. They find a routine or pattern that leads them to a consistently strong test performance. For example, they apply the first-to-last strategy, answering the first question first and proceeding through the questions in the order presented. Many standardized tests anticipate this strategy—the SAT, for example, presents questions in the order of least to most difficult. The LSAT is not

such a test. LSAT questions are designated by a number that corresponds to a number on the answer sheet. There is no other purpose for the order of questions. Generally, there is no benefit that results from answering LSAT questions in the order presented.

✔ **CONSIDER QUESTIONS IN THE ORDER THAT WILL PRODUCE THE HIGHEST SCORE FOR YOU.**

The Completion-Delusion Barrier

Academic conditioning promotes the delusion that you can enhance your test performance by considering every question and answering every question to the extent that time allows. For virtually everyone who takes the LSAT, the opposite is true. **No points are gained by simply completing the entire LSAT.** Your score results exclusively from the number of correct answers you select. In fact, it is by not completing the test that most people will reach their top test score.

✔ **RARELY WILL COMPLETING THE LSAT PRODUCE YOUR BEST PERFORMANCE.**

The Perfectly Impossible Barrier

Academic conditioning encourages the held belief of students that a flawless performance is the test-taker's objective. For the LSAT, this objective is virtually impossible to achieve. Instead of striving for impossible perfection, the well-trained LSAT test-taker will expect to get certain types of questions wrong and will concentrate on those questions that are most likely to produce the highest possible score for the examinee.

✔ **PLAN FOR A GREAT SCORE, NOT AN IMPOSSIBLE PERFECT PERFORMANCE.**

The Question-Is-the-Question Barrier

Academic conditioning suggests that what appears to be an LSAT question is the "real" question; that is, the question is the sentence that ends with a question mark. This expectation of most LSAT test-takers is confusing because, on the LSAT, it is the answer choices that define the questions, not the questions themselves. Most LSAT questions are vague. Only by careful consideration of the answer choices can you clarify the questions and select the best answer.

✔ON THE LSAT, THE ANSWER IS THE QUESTION.

Barrier—Hard Questions Count More

Academic tests often reward correct answers to difficult questions with more points than are awarded for less difficult ones. This common practice does not apply to the LSAT. While LSAT questions vary considerably in difficulty, the scoring rule is clear and simple—one question, one point. Answering the ten least difficult questions yields exactly the same number of score points as would answering the ten most difficult questions.

✔ANSWER THE LEAST DIFFICULT LSAT QUESTIONS BEFORE ANSWERING THE MOST DIFFICULT ONES.

The BYO Barrier

Academic conditioning prompts a "bring-your-own" strategy in most test-takers. In other words, successful academic test-takers have preconceived notions about what the questions and answers will be, and they tend to find what they're looking for. This is often referred to as psyching out the test. This test-taking strategy is of no value with the LSAT. This is because the LSAT provides all questions and all acceptable answers. Having your own questions or answers in mind or generating your own answers can only lead to confusion that produces a barrier to your best performance.

✔AVOID THE TEMPTATION TO BRING YOUR OWN QUESTIONS OR ANSWERS TO THE LSAT.

The Assumption Barrier

A superior performance often results from making the invited assumptions on an academic test. Students know the subject matter, the professor, the text, and the context in which the test is being given. It is natural and justifiable to make assumptions about test questions when they are presented in these circumstances. The LSAT exploits this conditioning by inviting many assumptions. But the LSAT is different—there is no course, no subject matter, no professor, no text, and, thus, there is no context. Without a meaningful context, invited assumptions about test questions or answers become barriers to the best possible performance on the LSAT. Making an invited assumption is not only inappropriate but puts your best test score at risk. The LSAT is context-free and should be dealt with accordingly.

✔MAKE NO ASSUMPTIONS WHEN TRYING TO SELECT THE BEST ANSWER TO AN LSAT QUESTION.

The Bingo Barrier

Avoiding the bingo barrier is one of the most difficult challenges the LSAT test-taker faces. The combination of the multiple-choice format of the LSAT and the BYO strategy of test-takers generates the "bingo barrier." Its mechanics are as follows. The test-taker reads the LSAT question and proceeds to develop an answer to the question asked, without regard to the proffered answer options. This mental answer is then compared to each of the answer choice options on the test. A match is sought. If the match is found, bingo!

But what if there is no match? The test-taker becomes anxious and frustrated. Was the question misunderstood? Is there a mistake on the test? What is wrong with the answer the test-taker developed? Whatever the explanation, the process is wasteful, unnecessary, and a major barrier to a top performance on the LSAT.

The bingo barrier develops from the misconception that the best technique for selecting an LSAT answer is to match the answers provided on the test with one the test-taker develops. For reasons that are accounted for by the types of answer choices provided on the LSAT, you should use only the choices provided by the test itself when selecting the "best" LSAT answer. Once again it is important to remember that the LSAT is not a test of knowledge or substance. Your charge does not involve the development of the best answer you are capable of producing. Your charge is to **select** the best answer from the limited choices provided. Avoid the bingo barrier and your performance on the LSAT will improve.

✔DO NOT USE THE BINGO TECHNIQUE TO SELECT LSAT ANSWERS.

The Cream-of-the-Crop Barrier

Academic conditioning directs the test-taker to seek the best possible answer, the cream-of-the-crop answer, to every question on the traditional test. But the LSAT is not a traditional test. The LSAT is not burdened with a need to provide the best possible answer. Since the answer choices are provided, all of the choices can be seconds or cream-of-the-crop answers. Indeed, you should expect that the best answers to questions presented on the LSAT do not appear as an answer choice.

If the best possible cream-of-the-crop answers were to appear among the five LSAT answer choices, they would usually be obvious and readily selected by the vast majority of test-takers. This would defeat the purpose of the LSAT. The purpose of the test is to differentiate among test-takers according to certain abilities. This purpose would not be well served by a test on which most test-takers produced very similar results. In order to guarantee that its purpose is achieved, the LSAT tactic is to provide one answer choice that is not at all the best possible answer but one that is somewhat better than the others. This cream-of-the-crop tactic makes the task of selecting the best answer much more difficult for the test-taker and advances the objective of the test—to differentiate among very able test-takers. The cream-of-the-crop answer is the best one of the five answer options; it is usually not the best possible answer. Remember, "best," in LSAT parlance, means best among the five choices. Avoid the best barrier as you avoid the test barrier. For the LSAT, you can avoid humbling barriers if you constantly remind yourself that test is not test and best is not best.

✔ **THE BEST ANSWER TO AN LSAT QUESTION IS THE CREAM OF THE CROP.**

The Substantivitis Barrier

Superior performance on most academic tests results from effectively dealing with a case of "substantivitis." The test-taker effectively demonstrates on the academic test that substantive information has been acquired and is available for application to various problems, circumstances, situations, and the like. Superior performance on the LSAT, on the other hand, results from effectively demonstrating that the test-taker can consistently apply the reasoning process required by law schools to various problems, circumstances, and situations presented on the test. This process is largely free of substance. In fact, substance frequently becomes a barrier to the best possible performance on the LSAT.

Imagine that there is question material on the LSAT that deals with substantive matters about which you know a great deal. It is a great temptation to believe that your substantive knowledge is being tested. In fact, it is difficult to believe otherwise. You are likely well condi-

tioned to react to the substantive material rather than to the process that the LSAT is attempting to assess. If you react to the substantive material of the question, you face a barrier to your best performance. Avoid the barrier by avoiding substantivitis. Deal only with the process required by the LSAT and you will avoid the substantivitis barrier.

✔ **IN SELECTING LSAT ANSWERS, CONCENTRATE ON FORM, AND AVOID BECOMING INVOLVED WITH SUBSTANCE.**

Barrier—Fair Means Unpredictable

Finally, your previous academic conditioning promotes the notion that a fair test is one that is unpredictable. If you know and understand the substantive information presented in the academic course, you can do well in responding to any question that may appear on a test. If the questions are any more predictable than this, the test is not perceived as fair in the sense that a person can do well by knowing only the information to which the test is limited. If the test deals only with the material in one lecture of a thirty-lecture course, it is very predictable and not likely to be perceived as fair by most students. So it should follow that for the LSAT to be fair, as it must be in order to be effective in deciding the admissions of students to law school, it should also be unpredictable.

The idea of its unpredictability is reinforced by the point made earlier in this session: The LSAT does not measure the subjects customary to academic or other standardized tests, such as facts, vocabulary, grammar, mathematical formulae, and the like. But, as you have seen elsewhere in this session, the LSAT reality is often the opposite of what you might expect, and the matter of its predictability is no exception. The LSAT is totally predictable. Each of the subsequent success sessions provides techniques that can be used to take advantage of this predictability.

As noted earlier, the LSAT is designed to differentiate among test-takers. This differentiation cannot be left to chance by the test-maker. The differentiation must be totally predictable. Without this predictability, the test would not serve its purpose. So, the test is designed to consistently produce the same, predictable results. If you think or believe otherwise, you will confront a barrier to your best performance. To avoid this barrier, treat the LSAT as a ruler. It remains constant so that the measurement results are consistent and predictable. Each edition of the test is the same. Each question set measures the same things in the same way—over and over.

✔THE LSAT IS TOTALLY PREDICTABLE.

You cannot quickly change your academic conditioning and the attendant learning and test-taking techniques it has taken you many years to develop just for the very limited purpose of achieving your best LSAT performance. Do not expect such a change of yourself. You will likely be disappointed. In any event, it is not necessary.

Rather than changing anything, concentrate on learning something new. Accept and learn the techniques found in this and subsequent success sessions. By learning new techniques, you can avoid the barriers that you will face if you treat the LSAT as an academic exercise. If you learn new techniques, your LSAT preparation experience will be interesting and useful, and your test score will benefit.

Success Session 2

FAMILIARITY BREEDS SUCCESS!

As you become familiar with the LSAT, you become able to avoid those aspects of the "test" that are barriers to your best performance. As you learned in the first session, the greatest barriers to your best performance are those academic test-taking tactics that you have developed over your years of formal education. As you will learn in this session, familiarity with the LSAT provides you with the ability to treat the test as what it is rather than what it appears to be.

WHAT IS SUCCESS FOR THE LSAT?

For you, LSAT success means a high score. By contrast, the LSAT succeeds when it effectively differentiates among those who aspire to law school. Through differentiation, the LSAT provides law schools with a simple way of ranking applicants for admission.

As noted in the previous session, you have been conditioned to believe that a test is designed to measure the extent to which you have acquired and can use information acquired in your academic studies. Your conditioning tempts you to project such a purpose onto the LSAT, and this temptation is reinforced by much of the rhetoric and rumor that surrounds the test. Your conditioning clouds your view of the LSAT.

A clear view of the results expected of the LSAT will allow you to bypass your academic conditioning and related temptations. The LSAT is nothing more or less than a device for distributing people along the 61 points of its score scale. That's right, the LSAT succeeds when it places you with one of 61 predetermined groups of test-takers and assigns one of 61 scores to you and the others in your group.

✔ **THE PURPOSE OF THE LSAT IS TO DISTRIBUTE TEST-TAKERS.**

No matter how great a test-taker's abilities and knowledge, the LSAT will assign all who take it one of the 61 points of its score scale. For example, only 20 percent of all test-takers can score in the top 20 percent. Not all test-takers can achieve a high score; if they could, the LSAT would fail in its purpose. Consequently, the test is designed to ensure that scores are distributed as expected, not concentrated. The LSAT is designed to succeed. As you will soon learn, success is built in.

WHAT IS THE JUSTIFICATION FOR THE LSAT?

There are two basic justifications offered for the use of the LSAT. The first involves the claimed correlation between LSAT scores and law school performance; that is, students who earn the highest LSAT scores also will get the highest first-year examination grades in law school. The relationship of the average first-year law school grades of the school's students to their LSAT scores establishes the association of the test to grades for the law school as a whole. This relationship is referred to as the school's correlation coefficient. The coefficient is expressed as a number between 0 and 1, with 0 indicating no relationship and 1 a perfect relationship. Law schools justify their use of the LSAT on the basis of correlation coefficients as low as .20 or as high as .65.

The second justification concerns the correlation of LSAT questions with basic law school activities. Specifically, the form of Passages questions reflects the form of the casebooks that law students must read and analyze. The forms of Arguments and Relationships questions reflect those found in the Socratic discussions and the examinations of law school. (See the comparisons given on the following pages.)

Whether you are persuaded by these justifications is of little consequence, since the law schools are persuaded and they have accepted the LSAT as the predominant factor in the admission decision. Accept this reality and the LSAT's use as a ranking device, and you will be in the best position to take advantage of its attributes as you train for your LSAT success.

How does the LSAT work?

To succeed, the LSAT must be reliable—in the jargon, it must "measure" consistently. In fact, to do its job properly, it should perform consistently in all of its outcomes. If it does not perform consistently, the scores from one administration—say, October of one year—could not be compared meaningfully with those from another—say, December of the next year. How can the necessary consistency, and thus LSAT success, be ensured? There is a straightforward and effective way to assure consistency: Be sure that every edition of the LSAT requires that the same exercises are done in the same way. When the same activities are measured in the same way, the outcomes will be consistent. This requirement for consistency—an LSAT design requirement—assures that the test is predictable.

✔**BECAUSE THE LSAT MUST PERFORM CONSISTENTLY, IT MUST BE PREDICTABLE.**

LSAT predictability is the principal advantage you have as you train for success and take the LSAT. Because the LSAT is predictable, it is possible to know exactly what to train for and exactly what you will face when you take the test.

Obviously, there is no need for you to experience anxiety about the unknown characteristics of the LSAT. This is because there are NO unknown characteristics of the LSAT. By design and definition, the characteristics of the LSAT must be known. It is academic conditioning that tells you the test content cannot be predicted in specific terms. LSAT content is totally predictable.

What are the basic elements of the LSAT?

In keeping with its predictability, every LSAT consists of the same basic elements. There are six of these basic elements to every LSAT—sections, directions, statements, questions, answers, and time.

Sections

While they are commonly referred to as test sections, these elements are, in fact, separate tests. It is important to understand that each LSAT consists of five of these tests, as well as a Writing Sample. Although there is only one LSAT score, there are five different tests on every LSAT.

A section is defined by time and by the type of questions it contains. Each test section is 35 minutes long. One section consists of questions about reading passages (sometimes referred to as reading comprehension questions). This is the **Passages** section. It is scored. One section consists of questions about relationships (sometimes referred to as analytical or logic-games questions). This is the **Relationships** section. It also is scored. Two sections consist of questions about arguments (sometimes referred to as logical reasoning questions). These are the **Arguments** sections. They, too, are scored.

There is one so-called **Experimental** section. This section is not scored. It is used to test questions for use on future editions of the LSAT. It consists of the same types of questions as are included in one of the scored sections.

Last and least, there is a **Writing Sample**. The Writing Sample is provided to law schools along with your test score, but it is not scored.

Directions

Each section comes with directions. The directions tell you what you are expected to do on that section. Directions are important.

Statements

A statement precedes most question and answer-choice sets. The statement provides certain information, some of which is relevant to the questions and answer choices that follow the statement. It is easy to confuse statements and questions.

Questions

There are approximately 100 scored questions on the LSAT. These questions generally are distributed across the separate test sections as follows, though any section may vary by one or two questions.

- Passages—28 questions
- Relationships—24 questions
- Arguments—24 questions in each of two Arguments sections

Answers

Each LSAT question is followed by five answer choices or options. This means that there are some 500 answer choices on every LSAT.

The Correlation of LSAT Passages Questions with Law School Tasks

Law school casebooks require the student to read and interpret edited appellate court opinions that use difficult grammar and complex reasoning.

Excerpt from a Professional Responsibility Casebook

It is plain that reversal of convictions that are infected by improper and prejudicial newspaper publicity, though necessary to protect the right of a defendant to a fair trial, no matter how heinous his crime would seem to be, is an expedient and not a cure. Such reversals cast a heavy burden, financial and otherwise, on the public and the defendant. For example, in this case, even though the improper publicity has not resulted in a new trial, it imposed a substantial and otherwise unnecessary expense on the taxpayers of the County of Passaic. As has been indicated above, there was to be no sequestration of the jury until the full complement of 14 had been chosen. But, when the prejudicial matter appeared in the two local papers on successive days, the trial court felt obliged to abandon the plan and to order immediate sequestration as jurors were accepted. Empaneling of the jury took three weeks. Sequestration began on the second day of trial and after only one juror had been sworn. The cost to the public of maintaining the jurors during that long period before a single bit of evidence could be offered in support of the indictment was wholly unnecessary but for the newspaper articles. Many curative measures have been proposed to curb improper crime reporting and trial of defendants by newspaper. Among them are greater use of the contempt power, legislation making it a criminal offense to divulge or publish prejudicial material pending a criminal trial, and the recognition of such pretrial publicity as a violation of the federal civil rights statute, on the ground that it deprives the defendant of a fair trial.

In the excerpt from Justice Frankfurter's opinion quoted earlier, he suggested that frequently the improper pretrial stories are published with the prosecutor's collaboration. In our case such collaboration was not shown. But the news accounts suggest that the inflammatory factual material (which was never proved at the trial) was furnished by the police. If true, such conduct is censurable and worthy of discipline. Control of the matter is largely in the hands of the prosecutor and local police authorities.

Excerpt from an LSAT Passages Section

The conception of order in the news varies with each type of disorder. In news about natural disasters, order is defined as the preservation of life and property; despite the concern for nature, flood stories do not often worry
(5) about how the flood may harm the river. Among technological disasters, plane crashes are usually more newsworthy than the winter breakdowns of tenement furnaces, even if they result in the same number of deaths. Yet, here as elsewhere, disorder news is affected
(10) by whose order is being upset.
Social disorder is generally defined as disorder in the public areas of the society. A protest march in which three people die would be headline national news, whereas a family murder that claimed three victims
(15) would be a local story. Disorders in affluent areas or elite institutions are more likely to be reported than their occurrence elsewhere. In the 1960s, the looting of a handful of stores on New York's Fifth Avenue received as much attention as a much larger looting spree taking
(20) place in a ghetto area that same day. Peaceful demonstrations on college campuses, especially elite ones, are usually more newsworthy than those in factories or prisons. But the major public area is the seat of government; thus, a trouble-free demonstration in front of
(25) a city hall or a police station is news, whereas that in front of a store is not. Ultimately, social disorder is equated with political disorder; similarly, social order is viewed as the absence of violent or potentially violent threats to the authority of public officials, particularly the president.
(30) Beneath the concern for political order lies another, perhaps even deeper, concern for social cohesion, which reflects fears that not only the official rules of the political order but also the informal rules of the social order are in danger of being disobeyed. This is apparent in the
(35) nonpolitical stories that either become or do not become news. Hippies and college dropouts of the 1960s were newsworthy in part because they rejected the so-called Protestant work ethic; even now, drug use by the young, and its consequences, is in the news more than alcohol
(40) use because it signifies a rejection of traditional methods of seeking oblivion or mind expansion. The romanticization of the past as an era in which formal and informal rules were obeyed betrays the same fear of contemporary disintegration, and the frequent celebration
(45) of past ways in the news may reflect an implicit ideal of the future. As Eric Sevareid put it during the live television coverage of the marriage of Princess Anne of England: "A people needs the past to hold them together."

The Correlation of LSAT Arguments Questions with Law School Tasks

Law school examinations and in-class Socratic discussions require the student to consider and evaluate arguments in hypothetical situations.

This brief exchange is an excerpt from a first-year class in contracts.

Professor: Ms. Jones, suppose you represent the dealer who sold a motorcycle to a 16-year-old who refuses to pay for it, saying she is a minor, and therefore her contract with the dealer is unenforceable by law. You find out that the 16-year-old lives 50 miles outside the city and works downtown. She commutes every day. She also lives in an apartment by herself. Do these facts give you any ideas?

Student: Uh. . . .

Professor: What argument could you make to stick this 16-year-old hoodlum, this reneging infant, with the contract she willingly entered?

This Arguments question appeared on a recent LSAT.

2. No law should restrict the use of alcohol to any particular age group. Americans think that alcohol causes problems like drunk driving. In fact, repressive attitudes toward alcohol cause drunk driving, because children who are prohibited from drinking develop the unhealthy notion that drinking is a symbol of maturity and adult freedom. In the United States, where alcohol use is discouraged and attitudes are repressive, there are twice as many alcohol-related traffic fatalities per capita as there are in France, where drinking is a normal, routine part of family life.

The author's argument would be most greatly weakened if it were true that

The Correlation of LSAT Relationships Questions with Law School Tasks

The formats of law school examinations and class discussions require the determination of various relationships.

Torts—Section 3.
(Time: One hour and 30 minutes)

A, an inexperienced but licensed airplane pilot, rents from X a small dual-control plane manufactured by Y and invites B, a friend, and C, an experienced pilot, to fly with him. At 2,000 feet, owing to a defect, the control mechanism operated by A fails, and A asks C to take over. C refuses until too late to avert a crash on M's land. A, D, the plane, N, a trespasser on M's land, and P, an employee of M, are hurt. What are the liabilities?

This question from a first-year Torts examination poses a hypothetical fact scenario requiring the ordering of various persons, objects, events, and so on.

This LSAT problem requires the ordering of various persons, objects, and events.

Every morning, commuters P, Q, R, S, and T board a train at the city terminal. The train makes six subsequent stops, numbered 1 through 6, consecutively. Each of the commuters leaves the train at a different stop, and at one of the stops no one leaves.

P always leaves the train at an odd-numbered stop.
Q is always the third of the five commuters to leave the train.
S always leaves the train after R, and none of the other four commuters leaves the train at a stop that comes after R's stop but before S's stop.

Time

You are allotted 35 minutes to complete each LSAT section. Of the many factors that determine the LSAT score, time is the most important one. While the test-maker states that time is not a factor in the design of the LSAT, the truth is that time accounts for test-takers' selection of greater numbers of wrong answers than any other factor involved in the test.

✔ **FOR MOST PEOPLE, TIME IS THE PRINCIPAL FACTOR IN THEIR LSAT SCORE.**

Most people find that the allotted 35 minutes is insufficient to consider each question in a test section carefully. Most respond to this time pressure by reducing the time they take to consider individual questions. As we will see in Red Alert 3, The 9-12-18 Test-Planning System, reducing the time you take to consider individual questions may reduce your score. Thus, time becomes a significant performance factor.

Also important is the fact that each LSAT section is separately timed, and you cannot transfer time from one test section to another. For example, if you complete the Passages section in 30 minutes, you cannot use the 5 remaining minutes to start another test section, nor can you return to an earlier section you were unable to complete in the 35 minutes allotted. This means that you must treat every LSAT section as a separately timed test.

✔ **THE LSAT IS ESSENTIALLY FIVE SEPARATE TESTS AND A WRITING SAMPLE.**

How does the LSAT perform?

The LSAT has difficulty as it strives to successfully meet its stated objective of ranking applicants to law schools so that the very skilled and superskilled are meaningfully differentiated for admission selection. In terms of actual performance, the LSAT does not meet its ranking objectives very well. For example, rather than distributing test-takers across the score scale, the LSAT tends to bunch test-takers at various places on the scale. The test maker explains this phenomenon variously.

Whatever the explanation, you will design your LSAT performance strategy to take advantage of this tendency in the test. It is a strategy that can produce the best test result for you.

What does the way the LSAT performs mean to you?

Because the LSAT's sole purpose is to rank you in relation to others, it should come as no surprise to you that the test is only concerned with your performance in relation to that of others. And, in contrast to the academic conditioning that focuses on the number of questions you answer correctly, the LSAT's performance is based upon the number of wrong answers you and all other test-takers select. Where your number of wrong answers places you among all test-takers is the only information of interest to the test-maker and the law schools.

If all of you fail to select the necessary number of wrong answers, the test-maker concludes that the test is too easy. Since the LSAT is not an academic test, this cannot be solved by asking harder questions, using more obscure information in statements, or requiring more complex calculations to turn stated information into useful information. What the test-maker must do is construct better wrong answers, and this is very difficult to do. What is difficult for the test-maker gives an advantage to the savvy test-taker, as you will find in future sessions.

✔ **WRONG ANSWERS PROVIDE THE KEY TO YOUR BEST LSAT SCORE.**

By training yourself to control the number of wrong answers you select, you reduce performance anxiety and avoid academic conditioning that could limit your test score. You will train to take advantage of what might be called the "wrong-answer weakness" of the LSAT.

A review of past tests yields the following table. (Numbers will vary slightly, depending on the test form.) You would need to choose the specified number of wrong answers in order to be grouped with the percentage of test-takers indicated.

Number of Wrong Answers	% of Test-Takers with More Wrong Answers	% of Test-Takers with Fewer Wrong Answers
7	99.9	0.1
18	95	5
21	90	10
25	80	20
29	70	30
32	60	40
37	50	50

✔**YOU MUST SELECT AT LEAST TWENTY WRONG ANSWERS TO SCORE IN THE BOTTOM 90 PERCENT OF TEST-TAKERS.**

To follow up on the significance of wrong answers, remember that you are not penalized for guessing on the LSAT. Whether you select a wrong answer or no answer, the impact on your score is the same, so there is no advantage to leaving any blanks on your answer sheet. Also, you can gain no advantage from knowing that some LSAT questions are more difficult than others. LSAT answers are not weighted, so each answer contributes equally to your score.

Your success strategy is to answer every question on the LSAT; guessing, if you must. Your success strategy is to seek out and answer every easy question before spending time on difficult questions.

WHAT DOES THE WAY THE LSAT PERFORMS MEAN TO LAW SCHOOLS?

The least significant aspect of the LSAT's performance is its apparent similarity to the work law students do. However, the fact that its various characteristics resemble those of law-school texts and classroom and examination activities appears to make some people in the law schools more comfortable with its use than would be the case if no similarity existed.

The LSAT is a common comparative factor among law schools. With minor exceptions, every law school in the United States and Canada requires every applicant to present an LSAT score as part of the application process. This facilitates the comparison of applicants. Each applicant's test score can be compared with every other applicant's test score. Rankings are easily determined and lines are easily drawn.

Scores over 3 years old are not routinely reported to law schools, so the LSAT score is current. Thus, when comparing applicants, law schools can minimize their dependence on evaluations or academic records reflecting work performed at different times. The LSAT provides them with a comparison of applicants based upon a common recent experience.

The LSAT score is easily defensible. If you get a low score, the score is fully and exclusively attributable to you—not to the law schools, admission officers, professors, counselors, or under-graduate schools. The score is a single "objective" number and not very susceptible to interpretation.

As pointed out previously, the correlation between LSAT performance and first-year law school grades is offered as a justification for the use of the LSAT. Law schools routinely interpret this correlation as a prediction of first-year grades and of overall performance in the school, operating on the assumption that the higher the LSAT score, the higher the law school grades and the better the law school performance.

✔**THE ASPECT OF THE LSAT THAT IS MOST SIGNIFICANT TO LAW SCHOOLS IS THE FACT THAT IT MAKES THEIR REJECTION DECISIONS EASY.**

Not only does the LSAT rank every applicant, but, because its score results are preset, law schools are able to predict the number and nature of test scores at any given point, knowing nothing more than the number of test-takers.

HOW DOES THE LSAT INFLUENCE THE LAW SCHOOL "REJECTION DECISION"?

The vast majority of applications for admission to law school are rejected. There are places in a law school class for some 60 percent of those who apply. For this and other reasons, the average law school aspirant applies to some five law schools. The result is that nearly 90 percent of all applications are wasted. Put another way, if the selection system worked perfectly, only about 10 percent of applications would be accepted. Since the system is far from perfect, many more than 10 percent are accepted.

Virtually all of the law school rejection decisions made by directors of rejection (who you should know prefer to be addressed as directors of admission) can be accounted for by the LSAT score and undergraduate grade point average (GPA). This does not mean that other factors are not taken into account in the admission decision, but that, after all is said and done, the LSAT and GPA usually can explain the decision to accept or reject, other factors notwithstanding.

To facilitate decision making, the vast majority of law schools combine the LSAT and GPA into an admission index. Each school determines the weight to be given to applicants' LSAT and GPA and calculates each applicant's admission index.

✔**FOR EACH LAW SCHOOL TO WHICH YOU APPLY, YOUR ADMISSION INDEX IS A FUNCTION OF YOUR LSAT SCORE AND YOUR GPA.**

All applicants can then be ranked by admission index and admitted or rejected according to the policies and practices of that law school. The next page contains an illustration of this process.

The relative weight law schools assign to the LSAT score and GPA is all-important to the admission index. Assuming that all applicants have a GPA of at least 2 on a 4-point scale, a survey of the admission indices of 150 law schools shows that the effective weight of the LSAT is more than that of the GPA. For 45 percent of the schools, the LSAT score accounted for some 70 percent of the index. If you have a relatively strong GPA, you will want to apply to those schools that weigh the GPA most. If you have a relatively strong LSAT score, you will want to apply to those that weigh the LSAT most.

✔**KNOW HOW MUCH WEIGHT THE LSAT SCORE WILL BE GIVEN BY THE LAW SCHOOLS TO WHICH YOU APPLY.**

WHAT DOES THE LSAT MEASURE?

The test-maker says the LSAT measures the ability to "read and comprehend complex texts, manage and organize information, and process information to reach conclusions." All of this begs the question.

✔**IN ADDITION TO THE REQUIRED REASONING ABILITIES, THE LSAT MEASURES YOUR SPEED, ACCURACY, AND SKILL AT PLANNING, DISCIPLINE, AND MECHANICS.**

Your prior academic conditioning emphasizes speed over accuracy rather than the optimal balance between the two. The LSAT, however, indirectly measures your ability to break through your academic conditioning to find and consistently apply an optimal balance between speed and accuracy as you work your way through the test questions and answer choices.

Your academic conditioning suggests that you should study for a test, and the test will measure your success at such study. But the total predictability of the LSAT suggests that you plan for the test, and the test will measure your success at such planning. Also, indirectly, the LSAT measures your self-discipline in following a plan and avoiding the limitations that academic conditioning could place as a barrier to your best LSAT score.

Its final measurement is of your skill at the mechanics of test taking. For example, transcription is a critical skill. LSAT test-takers often make errors in transcribing their answers from the test book to the answer sheet. By avoiding transcription errors and other mechanical mistakes, you can avoid a barrier to receiving your best possible LSAT score.

In constructing your test plan, we will consider both the selection of wrong answers and the factors that are measured indirectly by the LSAT.

UCS University
Computer Services

Memorandum

To: Director of Rejection
University Law School

From: Computer Services

Re: Applicants Ranked by Index

Please find enclosed the list of
applicants to University Law School,
ranked according to the calculated
index. If targeted entering class size
is 75 (assuming 75% of those we accept
will attend), you must reject all but
about 100 applicants. The top 100
candidates on the enclosed list have
index scores of 83.2 or above.

PAGE 5

Rank	Index	Name
83	84.4	EDWARDS, J. O.
84	84.3	ELLSWORTH, M. S.
85	84.2	CARDIN, L. P.
86	84.1	THOMAS, O. G.
87	84.1	BAKER, B. E.
88	84.1	SAUNDERS, H. J. M.
89	84.0	WILLETT, S. A.
90	84.0	BECKER, A. R.
91	83.9	DENNY, S. C.
92	83.7	SELIGMAN, S. A.
93	83.5	SCHLOSS, J. R.
94	83.5	MCELVEEN, E. E.
95	83.5	DEMEO, H. L.
96	83.4	GUTH, R.
97	83.4	GUZZO, M. A.
98	83.3	KOCHIS, N. M.
99	83.2	BROWN, A. T.
100	83.2	VANLOVEREN, S. A.
101	83.1	CORDERO, J. M.
102	83.0	BRIGLIN, R. V.
103	83.0	KETELTAS, T. C.
104	82.9	MCELROY, G. S.
105	82.8	BEVERSDORF, E. C.
106	82.8	HEDLUND, M. Q.
107	82.7	ENDERS, J. R.
108	82.6	EAMES, T. P.
109	82.5	COTT, M. A.
110	82.5	PECK, P. J.
111	82.3	HILL, F. X.

Success Session 3

YOUR TEST-TRAINING PLAN BEGINS WITH A STRATEGY.

Given that the LSAT is predictable, your LSAT success is best assured by a good training plan and a good performance plan. A good plan requires a solid strategic base. In this instance, a solid strategic base for you must take into account that strategy upon which the LSAT is based. Thus, we begin this session with a brief analysis of the strategy upon which the LSAT is based.

WHAT IS THE LSAT's PREPARATION STRATEGY?

The LSAT is based upon a carefully prepared strategy that ensures that the expectations—yea, requirements—for the LSAT are met each time the test is administered. First and foremost, if the LSAT does not perform consistently as expected, the value of the test is lost. So the test-maker spares nothing to make certain that every time an LSAT is administered, the test results are those specified. The LSAT is not prepared, administered, scored, and results reported. *Au contraire.*

✔ **THE TEST-MAKER'S STRATEGY IS TO KNOW HOW THE TEST WILL PERFORM BEFORE IT IS ADMINISTERED.**

The adage of the trial lawyer applies equally to the LSAT: "Never ask a witness a question if you don't know what the answer will be." The LSAT is not improvised. It is fully scripted, planned in every detail. Long before the test is administered, test scores and their structure for the specific edition of the LSAT involved have been determined. By the time an LSAT is administered, all that remains for the test-maker to do is connect individual test-takers to the predetermined scores. This is done by administering the test to you and others. To belabor the point, "predetermined" means that the LSAT is predictable. You will use that predictability.

At the core of the LSAT strategy is a plan. The LSAT plan establishes detailed objectives for the test, identifies the variables involved, determines the optimal mix of the variables needed to meet the objectives, and mixes the variables consistently. The test-maker has developed this planning process over a long period and at great expense. Contrary to the advice or propaganda some people may offer to you, you have neither the time nor the resources to develop a competing process—nor should you try—nor should they try.

WHAT IS YOUR PREPARATION STRATEGY?

As you know, most people's LSAT preparation strategy is to practice past or simulated LSAT questions and to review analyses of the questions and the answer choices. This usually means practicing test-taking habits, mechanics, and skills that are not appropriate to the LSAT, which results in the expenditure of a great deal of effort and little score improvement for most people. For some, this practice strategy actually impairs rather than improves test performance.

Your strategy, on the other hand, is to take advantage of the LSAT's strategy. All the hard work has been done for you. Your job is to take advantage of the hard work and use the model provided for you.

✔ **AT THE CORE OF YOUR TEST-TRAINING STRATEGY IS YOUR PLAN.**

To best succeed, you will follow the model of the test performance plan designed for the LSAT. You will begin, as does the LSAT model, by establishing your objectives for the test. Next you will identify the factors or activities that will be meaningful in achieving your objectives. Then you will determine the optimal mix of variables needed to meet the objectives. And finally, you will execute your plan consistently to ensure that your objectives are realized through your performance.

WHAT ARE YOUR OBJECTIVES?

At this point, you have only one objective. You want a superior LSAT score. A score in the ninety-ninth percentile would do very nicely. In the context of your test plan and the purpose of the LSAT, this objective has little meaning. Put simply, it is too general. For practical purposes, the LSAT consists of five separate tests and a writing sample. Only four of the tests contribute to your score.

The more specific your objectives, the better your plan will be. At the minimum, a good test plan will have an objective for each of the separate tests that make up the LSAT. It will include the number of wrong answers planned for each test. It will also include a procedure to follow for achieving this wrong-answer objective. This procedure will take into account each of your test-performance factors and the predictable attributes of the LSAT.

WHAT IS MEANT BY TEST-PERFORMANCE FACTORS?

Your level of anxiety, academic test-taking habits and mechanics, reasoning skill, time use, and self-discipline are the major factors that influence performance on the LSAT. Facts, perspectives, and other such information are of very little consequence. The training in this book is designed to minimize the impact that the factors of anxiety and entrenched academic test-taking habits and mechanics have on your performance. By learning and applying procedures that take advantage of the LSAT's nature, you will be able to avoid any negative impact these performance factors might have on your test score.

The reasoning skill required by law schools is a critical performance factor on the LSAT. For most people it is the most important factor by far. Your training regimen should include regular monitoring of this skill as you refine it, and your test plan should be modified to take improvement in your reasoning into account.

Self-discipline is the most difficult of all performance factors to build into your plan. Only you know if you are strict or lax in following the test-taking procedures you train to use. Avoid being overly optimistic in this regard—there is a great tendency to believe that each of us enjoys a generous measure of self-discipline, but the evidence consistently proves the contrary. If self-discipline, sometimes referred to as concentration, persistence, focus, or effective time-management does not come naturally to you, do not plan on it to contribute positively to your training and test performance. To the contrary, plan on it being a barrier to your best performance, and make your greatest effort to avoid those practices that depend on a large infusion of self-discipline.

WHAT IS AN OPTIMAL MIX?

The LSAT establishes an optimal mix of performance factors to ensure that the test results are precisely those desired; for example, that the proportion of test-takers that will produce a score of 150 satisfies the number that is the objective for the test. Among other things, this effort leads to the structuring of the LSAT as separate tests, the inclusion of a specific number of questions in each of the tests, the selection of certain types of questions, the allocation of time for each test, and the following of a particular presentation pattern. To achieve an optimal mix, many experiments with the LSAT variables are conducted, increasing this, decreasing that, changing something else. Once the variables produce exactly the results intended, the test is ready to be administered.

As with the LSAT strategy, your optimal mix of performance factors is the one that best ensures that your objectives are achieved. Just enough worry to make sure that you are in control of the training and testing process is best. Balancing your speed of working on the questions against the accuracy of your answers so that you select the expected number of wrong answers is crucial. Mechanics are important—the sequence in which you consider questions, the order in which you examine answer choices, the recording of your answers in the test book, the transcription of answer choices onto the answer sheet, and others.

HOW ABOUT CONSISTENT PROSECUTION?

As you will understand better when you learn more about the structure of each of the question types on the LSAT, it is difficult for the test itself to perform consistently. It is also difficult for you to perform consistently over the course of the 205-minute LSAT. Yet, your best performance will depend on consistency.

✔ **CONSISTENT EXECUTION OF YOUR TEST PLAN AND CONSISTENT PROSECUTION OF THE TASKS REQUIRED WILL CONTRIBUTE POSITIVELY TO YOUR PERFORMANCE AND TEST SCORE.**

WHERE DO YOU START YOUR TEST PLAN?

You will recall that the LSAT consists of five separately timed tests and a Writing Sample. Each of the five tests consists of four sets of questions and answer choices. Thus, the LSAT is made up of twenty of these question/answer sets. A good way to visualize this is to think of the LSAT as consisting of twenty minitests of six or seven questions each.

✔ **THE QUESTION/ANSWER SET IS THE FOCUS OF YOUR TEST PLAN.**

WHAT MAKES UP THE LSAT MINITESTS?

A Passages question set consists of one reading passage and the questions and answer choices related to it. There is a passage and seven questions that have five answer choices each. A Relationships question set consists of the facts and rules common to the problem and the six questions and the five answer choices related to each question. An Arguments question set consists of six questions and the five answer choices related to each of the questions. A short paragraph provides the material upon which one or two Arguments question sets depend.

Your ability to handle the Passages question sets may differ from the way you handle the Relationships or Arguments sets; so your test plan will reflect these differences. Also, your test plan will be dynamic. It will change as you gain proficiency in the following:

- Leveraging the one basic reasoning task required by the LSAT
- Taking advantage of the LSAT's total predictability
- Exploiting your wrong-answer advantage
- Combating obfuscation, the test-maker's only tool
- Conquering the multiple-option trick
- Employing special mechanical and transcription techniques
- Mastering critical question-visualization techniques
- Preparing your Writing Sample in advance
- Avoiding the test habits that lower your score
- Using the 9-12-18 planning system

As you train, the optimal mix of your performance factors will change, and, as the optimal mix changes, so will your plan.

RED ALERT

THE 9-12-18 TEST-PLANNING SYSTEM

YOUR TEST-PLANNING PROCESS STARTS HERE.

Your test plan is developed by using a system that takes into account your test performance strengths and weaknesses. It is important that you carefully follow the process that is described here. Your best performance is in the balance.

WHAT IS THE 9-12-18 SYSTEM?

The 9-12-18 test-planning system is based on the same process used in establishing the optimal mix of factors needed for the LSAT to meet its objectives. The process is well described by the proverb "The proof of the pudding is in the eating"—that is, the way to test whether something works as intended is to try it. Through the inclusion of a set of experimental questions on every test, the LSAT learns exactly how these questions perform and exactly how test-takers perform with respect to these questions. This pretest process produces the information upon which the LSAT bases the performance plan for the development of each form of the test.

The pretest process is effective for the LSAT because it avoids conjecture. This process can be equally effective for you, because it avoids the academic conditioning that leads you to aim your performance expectations away from what is reality toward what you wish reality to be. There is no ambiguity about your performance—what you see is what you get, and what you get is a function of the process upon which you choose to base your test plan.

When you are presented with a set of LSAT questions and the related answer choices, performance factors influence your approach, including the method you use to select your answer choices. The only record of your consideration of test questions is your answer selection. How you go about choosing an answer is of no consequence to your score. Thus, you will base your test plan on the results of your

answer selection activity, giving no consideration to your selection process. Through the implementation of the 9-12-18 process, you will establish the optimal mix of factors required for you to establish and meet your LSAT performance objectives.

Each of the principal test-performance factors—reasoning skill, speed, accuracy, planning, discipline, and mechanics—manifests itself in your selection of answers. Thus, your plan, like that of the LSAT, takes advantage of this performance result.

The 9-12-18 test-planning system is based on your selection of answers to a set of LSAT questions. You will choose a set of questions from the LSAT diagnostic and practice tests in this guide and consider the questions and related answer choices, then you select answers for 9 minutes. The results of your performance will be recorded for later analysis. You will then give the same set of questions and related answer choices further consideration for an additional 3 minutes and record the results of your performance in those 3 minutes. Finally, you will give the set of questions and related answer choices an additional 6 minutes' consideration and record the results of this performance as well. Following this 9-12-18 process, you will analyze your performance results.

CONSIDER THE FOLLOWING EXAMPLE CAREFULLY.

Suppose that you are working at selecting the credited or best answers to a set of six Relationships questions. Each Relationships section-test consists of four sets of six questions and their related answer choices, to be completed in 35 minutes. You calculate that there are about 9 minutes in which to complete all six questions in the set (four question sets into 35 minutes), so you decide to allocate 1½ minutes to each question. At the end of 9 minutes, you have completed the selection of six answers. The purpose of the next part of the exercise is for you to reconsider the questions and related answer choices and change the choices you first made if you determine a better choice is available. Since you next have an additional 3 minutes to work, you follow the same strategy you used for the 9 minutes; you divide the time equally and spend an additional half minute on each question. After reconsidering each question, you change two answers. With the last 6 minutes you have available, you decide to concentrate on four questions about which you are unsure. As a result, you change three answers.

You next compare your answer choices to the key. Of the six answers you selected during the first 9 minutes, you find that only two were credited or best answers. Of the answer choices you selected after the 3 additional minutes (for a total of 12 minutes), three were credited or best. Of the answer choices you selected after the additional 6-minute period (for a total of 18 minutes), all six were credited or best.

Summarized, your performance on this question set was as follows:

9 minutes	$2 \times 4 + 0 = 8$
12 minutes	$3 \times 3 + 1 = 10$
18 minutes	$6 \times 2 + 2 = 14$

WHAT DOES THIS PROCESS SHOW?

The first number in each formula represents the number of credited or best answers selected in that period of time. When you considered the question set for 9 minutes, you selected only two credited or best answers. When you spent 12 minutes, you selected three credited or best answers, and when you spent 18 minutes, you selected six credited or best answers.

The second number in the calculation represents the projection of your one-set performance onto the entire 35-minute, four-set Relationships section-test, were you to perform with the same accuracy as you did on the one set. Thus, in the first formula, the number of best answers (2) is multiplied by 4 (the full four question sets in the section-test).

The second formula shows what happens if you decide to work on just three question sets during the time allocated for the separate section-test. This means that there is an average of about 12 minutes ($12 \times 3 = 36$) available for each set. The number of best answers (3) is multiplied by 3 (the three sets you intend to complete) to project your one-set performance

onto the entire section-test, were you to perform on three question sets with the same accuracy as you did on the one.

The third formula shows what happens if you decide to work on only two question sets during the time allocated for the section-test. This means that there is an average of about 18 minutes ($18 \times 2 = 36$) available for each set. The number of best answers (6) is multiplied by 2 to project your one-set performance onto the entire section-test, were you to perform on two question sets with the same accuracy as you did on the one set.

The third number in the formula represents the credited or best answers that will result from guessing on question sets that you do not otherwise consider. Recall that you should always guess on an LSAT question, even when you have not considered it. Since there are five answer choices to every question, a guess has a one-in-five chance of being the best answer. There are six questions per set on the Relationships section-test; consequently, over a six-question set, chance alone will result in your selecting one best answer, even though you give that question no other consideration.

Obviously, if you consider all four question sets in the section-test, you get no guessing bonus. If you consider three of the four question sets, you get a guessing bonus of one. If you consider two of the four question sets, you get a guessing bonus of two. This results from the fact that, even though you have not considered a particular six-question set, you have arbitrarily selected (guessed) an answer for each of those questions.

The total of best answers, the fourth number in the formula, shows how you would perform on the whole section-test, were you to consider and complete four, three, or two question sets. In the example, you can see that you will select the fewest wrong answers on the section-test if you consider only two question sets and guess your answers for the other two.

This pretest process produces your optimal balance between speed and accuracy on the Relationships section-test of the LSAT. The example shows that by considering all four question sets (a total of twenty-four answers), you can plan on selecting sixteen (twenty-four total answers minus eight best answers) wrong answers. By considering just three question sets, you can plan on selecting fourteen wrong answers—not a large difference. However, by considering only two question sets, you can plan on selecting ten wrong answers, an improvement of 75 percent over your performance if you completed all four sets.

The 9-12-18 system uses your performance to establish the optimal balance between speed and accuracy for you. In the example, this performance produces your basic test plan for the Relationships section-test. On the Relationships section-test, you will select the fewest wrong answers if you stress accuracy over speed. The faster you are forced to go the more inaccurate your selection process becomes.

This Relationships' performance may not apply to the other two types of sections-tests on the LSAT. Following is an example that expands this 9-12-18 strategy to a full four section-test LSAT. Hypothetical results on each of the four section-tests are summarized in the same way as in the preceding example.

Relationships Section-Test

9 minutes	$2 \times 4 + 0 = 8$
12 minutes	$3 \times 3 + 1 = 10$
18 minutes	$6 \times 2 + 2 = 14$

Arguments Section-Tests
(remember, there are two Arguments section-tests)

9 minutes	$3 \times 4 + 0 = 12 \times 2 = 24$
12 minutes	$6 \times 3 + 1 = 19 \times 2 = 38$
18 minutes	$6 \times 2 + 2 = 14 \times 2 = 28$

Passages Section-Test

9 minutes	$3 \times 4 + 0 = 12$
12 minutes	$5 \times 3 + 1 = 16$
18 minutes	$5 \times 2 + 2 = 12$

These calculations result in the following sample test plan:

Relationships section-test	2 sets at 18 minutes each
Arguments section-test	3 sets at 12 minutes each
Arguments section-test	3 sets at 12 minutes each
Passages section-test	3 sets at 12 minutes each

The total score of 68 that results from this plan contrasts with the total of 44 that would result if every question-answer set were given consideration. By focusing on the optimal balance between speed and accuracy, an increase of more than 50 percent in LSAT performance results.

How do you develop your own LSAT success plan?

The 9-12-18 system of test-plan development starts with three pretests, or minitests, each of which measures and evaluates your test performance factors through a single set of six questions. The first minitest involves a Relationships question-set, the second an Arguments question-set, and the last a Passages question-set (all of which you can pull from the full-length LSATs included in this guide). The results of these minitests are used to establish the optimal mix of the principal test performance factors for you as they apply to the different question types found on the LSAT.

Use a watch, clock, alarm, or timer on each pretest. The three minitests can be completed at different times or in a single 1-hour period. Try to take the minitests in a quiet place, under reasonably relaxed circumstances, and at a time when you will not be interrupted.

You will have 18 minutes to complete each minitest. Your objective is to select as many best answers as you can in the first 9 minutes, then to select as many best answers as you can in an additional 3 minutes, and finally to select as many best answers as you can in an additional 6 minutes.

The pretest process will be unfamiliar and may, at first, appear to be somewhat complicated. Review the directions carefully, and you will have no problems.

How do you take the pretests?

There are five steps to completing each of the minitests.

STEP 1

Set your timer for 9 minutes. Read the directions at the top of the set of questions. Then answer as many questions in the set as you can in 9 minutes. Circle your answers. Do not be concerned if you do not complete all of the questions. At the end of 9 minutes, stop. These answers become your 9-minute set.

STEP 2

Next, give yourself an additional 3 minutes. Go back to the set, and answer any questions you did not get to in the first 9 minutes, or review the questions you answered in the first 9 minutes, and change your answers if you wish.

This brings the total minutes expired to 12. Place a box beside each of the answers you selected during this 3-minute period. If you did not change an answer, place a box beside the circled answer. If you changed the answer, place a box beside the new selection. The boxed answers represent your 12-minute set. Do not erase or change the circles you placed beside questions during the first 9 minutes.

STEP 3

Finally, give yourself an additional 6 minutes. Go back to the set, and answer any questions you did not get to in the first 12 minutes, or review the questions, and change answers if you wish. This brings the total minutes used to 18. Place an asterisk beside each of the answers you selected during this 6-minute period. If you did not change an answer, place an asterisk beside the boxed answer. If you changed the answer, place an asterisk beside the new selection. The answers identified with asterisks are your 12-minute set. Do not erase or change the circles or boxes you placed beside questions during the first 12 minutes.

STEP 4

Turn to the appropriate Quick-Score Answers section for the question-sets used in the minitests (page 39 for the Diagnostic LSAT, page 191 for Practice Test 1, and page 229 for Practice Test 2). For each set, determine the number of best answers you selected in the 9-minute set (circled), 12-minute set (boxed), and 18-minute set (asterisked). Enter those numbers on the Pretest Performance Tracking Worksheet on page 75. Alternatively, you can use the following calculation form.

STEP 5

Complete the calculations indicated.

Relationships Set

Circles _____ × 4 + 0 = _____
Boxes _____ × 3 + 1 = _____
Asterisks _____ × 2 + 2 = _____

Largest total _____

Arguments Set

Circles _____ × 4 + 0 = _____
Boxes _____ × 3 + 1 = _____
Asterisks _____ × 2 + 2 = _____

Largest total _____

Passages Set

Circles _____ × 4 + 0 = _____
Boxes _____ × 3 + 1 = _____
Asterisks _____ × 2 + 2 = _____

Largest total _____

WHAT'S NEXT?

To develop your first test plan, enter in the blanks below the number of sets that corresponds to the largest total for each of the four section-tests.

Relationships section-test _____ sets
Arguments section-tests (2) _____ sets
Passages section-test _____ sets

As your training progresses, you should monitor your performance on question sets by updating your Pretest Performance Tracking Worksheet (page 75) as you complete additional section-tests. As your training results in more consistent and improved use of time, your optimal balance between speed and accuracy will change. The changes will be reflected in your test plan.

There are two major components to your test plan. One is your question-set performance, and the other is your section-test strategy. Your performance on each question set determines whether your section-test strategy is to complete four, three, or two question sets in each section-test. You want to produce the optimal balance between speed and accuracy for each of the three different types of section-tests (five tests in all).

Your combined strategies for the five section-tests will constitute your test plan.

Pretest Performance Tracking Worksheet

Relationships

Minitest	1	2	3	4	5	6	7	8
Circles (9 minutes) x 4 + 0 =								
Boxes (12 minutes) x 3 + 1 =								
Asterisks (18 minutes) x 2 + 2 =								
Largest Total								
From 4, 3, or 2 sets?								

Arguments

Minitest	1	2	3	4	5	6	7	8
Circles (9 minutes) x 4 + 0 =								
Boxes (12 minutes) x 3 + 1 =								
Asterisks (18 minutes) x 2 + 2 =								
Largest Total								
From 4, 3, or 2 sets?								

Passages

Minitest	1	2	3	4	5	6	7	8
Circles (9 minutes) x 4 + 0 =								
Boxes (12 minutes) x 3 + 1 =								
Asterisks (18 minutes) x 2 + 2 =								
Largest Total								
From 4, 3, or 2 sets?								

Success Session 4

WHAT IS THE BASIC LSAT COMPONENT?

As you determined in the previous session, the question set is a critical component of the test plan: It facilitates your management of time, maximizes your sense of control, and avoids much of your academic conditioning. And the basic component of the set is the LSAT question. While generally referred to as a single question, in fact, this question component presents a multielement profile.

WHAT IS THE LSAT QUESTION PROFILE?

The LSAT question profile is simple, and every question fits it. The profile has four elements. First are the directions, which make three important points. They tell you that every section-test is separately timed, that you are to select the best answer to each question, and that notes must be made in the test book, not on scratch paper, the work surface, or a shirt sleeve.

The second element is a statement. The statement provides the context for the questions. The statement varies in both length and structure. For a Relationships question, the statement presents a small number of facts and rules. The statement for an Arguments question is also short and consists of a small number of facts and/or conclusions. In contrast, Passages statements are lengthy extracts from journals and similar sources.

Following the statement is the question. LSAT questions are short. Remember, questions are not questions in the customary academic sense. Each question can be viewed as a variation on one of three basic types—that which must, could, or cannot be true given the information presented in the statement and question.

The fourth element of the profile is the answer choice, the most important element of the profile for the test-taker. Answer choices give meaning to the question and effectively become the question. For example, the question "Which of the following must be true?" can only derive meaning when it is considered in the context of the five answer choices.

HOW CAN THE ANSWER CHOICES BE DESCRIBED?

In the recent past, LSAT answer choices have appeared in two formats: the single-option format and the multiple-option format. Only the single-option format has been used on the most recent tests. It is very unlikely that a multiple-option answer choice will appear on an LSAT that you take. However, a brief description of the multiple-option answer choice is included here. If the time available to you permits, read through the description. In any event, do not spend any substantial time with the multiple-option answer-choice description.

The Single-Option Answer Choice

The single-option format presents five answer choices following a brief question. Your objective is to select the best answer choice from among the five options presented.

The question is identified by its number, which, as is conventional, corresponds to one on the LSAT answer sheet. The answer choices are identified by letters.

1. If Ms. Stark sits next to Mr. Taylor, which of the following must be true?

    (A) One of the Reeds sits next to one of the Starks.
    (B) The Vines sit opposite the Reeds.
    (C) The Taylors sit together.
    (D) The Vines sit together.
    (E) One of the Taylors sits next to one of the Reeds.

The Multiple-Option Answer Choice

The multiple-option answer choice has a number of characteristics that make it more difficult than the single-option answer choice. Most significant among them is that more than one of the answer choices can be best and that five answer options are effectively expanded into seven. (This is illustrated in the diagram below. Note that only five of the possible seven are actually used.) Because there can be more than one best answer, the test-maker doesn't have to work so hard to produce wrong answer choices. The complexity of the answer structure makes the selection of the best answer more difficult for the test-taker. So, with less effort than is required by the single-option format, the test-maker can produce a more difficult question. Following is an example.

2. If Mr. Vine sits next to Mr. Taylor, which of the following must be true?

   I.   All fathers sit next to each other.
   II. Three daughters sit next to each other.
   III. Each father sits next to his daughter.

  (A) I only
  (B) II only
  (C) I and II only
  (D) II and III only
  (E) I, II, and III

As you can see, the multiple-option format initially presents only three choices, any or all of which may meet the conditions set by the question. The answer-choice structure then presents five lettered single or multiple options from which to select one best answer.

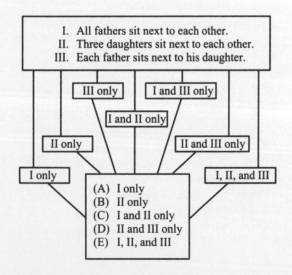

The multiple-option trick?

When first encountering the complexities of the multiple-option format, many test-takers believe they are the victims of an insidious plot. They find the format problematic and confusing. However, this response is not called for; in fact, in most circumstances the format provides you with an advantage I call the multiple-option trick. Perhaps this accounts for the demise of this answer type?

Looking at the preceding example, review the five letter-designated answer choices. You will notice that II appears in answer choices B, C, D, and E. If you could determine the status of choice II, you would be able to eliminate four answers and identify the best answer. Suppose that you study the facts and determine that choice II cannot be true. If choice II cannot be true, neither can answers B, C, D, and E. The only answer not discarded is A, which thus must be the best selection.

Presto, you have selected the best answer by having to consider only choice II! The example shows the multiple-option trick at peak power. Usually the test-maker makes application of the trick helpful but not determinative, as here. Since using the trick has no downside risk for you, you can apply it every time you encounter the multiple-option format.

Where is the "none of the above" answer choice?

"None of the above" is another answer choice that test-makers frequently use to make their work easier by not having to produce a best answer. All answers can be bad. There is no "none of the above" answer choice on the LSAT.

WHAT IS THE BASIC REASONING TASK REQUIRED BY THE LSAT?

In addition to the four-element profile, all LSAT questions also have a reasoning task in common. The primary reason that the LSAT is useful to law schools is that it measures applicants' skills at reasoning in the principal way the schools and the legal system require.

However, the best information a single question can contribute to the measurement is very limited. Only after accumulating information from many test questions does the LSAT provide sufficiently precise results to be useful to the law schools. To get a reasonably accurate result, many individual measurements have to be taken, so the LSAT involves some 100 questions. If these questions measured a variety of skills, the test would be unable to give reasonably reliable information about each one, but because it measures a singe skill, the results are reasonably consistent.

The single skill measured by the LSAT is difficult to describe in precise or familiar terms, though it can be relatively easily understood in terms of the task it requires. A good analogy is to aspirin, whose workings scientists have been unable to explain precisely despite vast amounts of research, although they can observe the results of its operation and understand its nature in terms of those results. By observing the basic task in operation, the LSAT can understand it in terms of the results produced.

✔**FOR OUR PURPOSES, THE BASIC REASONING TASK THE LSAT DEMANDS CAN BE CALLED "CONDITIONAL REASONING," THOUGH THIS IS NOT TO SUGGEST A FORMAL LOGICAL CONCEPT OR ANYTHING FORBIDDING.**

CAN THE BASIC TASK BE ILLUSTRATED?

Following is a problem placed in the LSAT format, with the four elements of the question profile identified.

DIRECTIONS
Answer the following question as quickly as you can. Circle the best answer choice.

STATEMENT
The oak is a deciduous, hardwood tree known for the fact that it always produces a nut commonly called an acorn.

QUESTION
1. If it has been determined that a specific tree produces acorns, which of the following descriptions of the tree must be true?

ANSWER CHOICES
(A) It is a deciduous tree.
(B) It is an acorn tree.
(C) It is a hardwood tree.
(D) It is an oak tree.
(E) It is an unknown species of tree.

The statement tells you that a tree called an oak has certain attributes or conditions. Among them are that it is deciduous, is a hardwood tree, and always produces acorns. The question, which involves a tree that produces acorns, is designed to exploit the statement that precedes it.

The statement uses the words "always produces . . . an acorn" to suggest more than it actually tells you, encouraging the assumption that a tree that produces acorns must be an oak. However, the statement only tells you that in order for a tree to be an oak, it must produce acorns—it does not tell you that a tree that produces acorns must always be an oak.

In the spirit of the LSAT, the question also exploits what the statement does not tell you. The question asks you to identify a tree by providing you with only one of the three conditions (attributes) that the statement says are necessary for a tree to be an oak. No matter what that condition (acorn), its existence does not identify the object (oak) to a certainty. For the acorn to be sufficient to establish the tree as an oak, the statement would have had to clearly state that a tree that produces an acorn is always an oak, and the statement said no such thing.

However, you remember from your basic botany course that acorns are only produced by an oak tree. No other tree produces acorns. Besides, your own experience tells you this is so. What does this mean? This means nothing! Nothing!

No matter how certain you are about acorns and oaks, the information from your botany course and experience is outside of the test; it is not in the statement, and it has no relevance in the context of the LSAT question. Outside information can often and clearly be detrimental under certain test circumstances. Avoid it. Use only the information the LSAT provides to you when selecting answers.

✔**NO EXTERNAL INFORMATION IS REQUIRED FOR YOU TO BE ABLE TO SELECT THE BEST ANSWER TO AN LSAT QUESTION.**

While the LSAT does not go out of its way to set traps of the acorn question type, it often sets such traps. Using only the information you are given is the most effective way to avoid the BYO information and calculations—academic conditioning that has been so helpful to you in previous test situations.

✔ AVOID EXTERNAL INFORMATION WHEN SELECTING AN LSAT ANSWER CHOICE.

Now you know why answer choice E is the best choice. It is the only one of the five that must be true. The other choices could be true, but, based on the information provided, they also could be untrue. You just don't know, and since the question asks you what you know to a certainty—what *must* be true—answer choice E is your only option. You are certain that you don't know.

✔ THE BASIC REASONING TASK IS FOUND IN EVERY LSAT QUESTION.

Unfortunately, the basic reasoning task is seldom presented as obviously as it is in the oak-acorn example. If it were, the LSAT would be even more predictable than it is. It would be too easy and would not be able to differentiate among people very well. The law schools would have little use for it, and the LSAT would have to find some other application for the many questions in its inventory. To make certain that this scenario is not realized, the LSAT goes to great pains to mask the basic reasoning task. This could be called camouflage, concealment, disguise, or—my personal favorite—"obfuscation."

WHAT IS OBFUSCATION?

Obfuscation is the LSAT's primary tool. Obfuscation makes it difficult for the test-taker to see the basic reasoning tasks in most LSAT questions. The greater the degree of obfuscation, the more difficult the selection of an LSAT answer choice becomes for the test-taker. Nevertheless, the basic reasoning task is there—it is the essence of every LSAT question. In fact, the basic reasoning task must be there if the test is to measure your skill in dealing with it. With some training, you can become effective at locating the basic task, avoiding the academic conditioning the problem sets out to exploit, and selecting the best answers consistently.

In this next example of the basic reasoning task, you are asked to answer a question about cards. Give it a try, and see if you can notice how the LSAT could obfuscate your route to the best answer. Once again, the basic elements of the problem have been identified—just remember, they won't always be spelled out in this way.

DIRECTIONS

Answer the following question as quickly as you can. Circle the best answer choice.

STATEMENT

The card-master holds four cards in a stack. Each card has a single letter on the front side and a single number on the back side. The master states that if a card has a vowel on one side it will have an even number on the other side. The master places the four cards on a table with the visible sides showing A, B, 1, and 2, respectively.

QUESTION

2. Of the following, which names only the cards that must be turned over to determine whether what the master said is true?

ANSWER CHOICES

(A) The cards showing A and B.
(B) The cards showing A and 1.
(C) The cards showing A and 2.
(D) The cards showing A, B, and 1.
(E) All four of the cards.

A method for dealing with the four cards on the table can be depicted as follows:

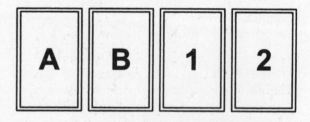

First, remember that each card has a number on one side and a letter on the other. The card-master has said that if a card has a vowel on one side, it has an even number on the other. Circle only those cards that you have to turn over to determine if the card-master's statement is true.

The object is a card with a vowel on one side (front); the condition is an even number on the other side (back). There are four cards. As with the oak-acorn example, this question is designed to exploit your conditioning.

Remember, no outside information. You are not being asked about all possible cards, alphabetic or numeric. It may appear to you that the question seeks to establish some universal proof, but the question only deals with four cards. Review the question carefully—it asks you to do what you can to establish the truth of the card-master's statement. In this context, what technique is available to you to establish that which is true? There is only one—to locate evidence that disproves the statement.

In your quest for such evidence, you consider each card. The first one has an A on the side you can see. A is a vowel. (Note that you do need this outside information.) This card is the object of the statement. By turning it over, you will determine if the condition is met. If the card has an even number on the reserve side, you will have learned no more than what the statement told you. But, if an odd number appears on the reverse side, you will establish that the card-master's statement is untrue. Thus, you must turn the A-card over.

The second card has a B on the side you can see. B is not a vowel but a consonant. It is not the object of the statement. In fact, it is irrelevant to your problem, whatever is on the back. Neither the statement nor the question says anything about consonants. This card is no help to you, and you need not turn it over.

The third card shows a 1, an odd number. If you turn it over and a consonant appears, you will gain no evidence concerning the question. But if you turn it and a vowel appears, you will establish that the card-master's statement is untrue. Thus, you must turn this card over.

The fourth card has a 2, an even number. If you turn this card over and find a consonant on the other side, you will gain no evidence concerning the question. Remember that there is nothing in the statement or question that would preclude there being an even number on a card with a consonant on its reverse side. Should you turn this card and find a vowel, you have no more evidence about the truth of the card-master's statement than you had before. Thus, there is no reason to turn the 2-card.

After consideration, you deduce that the best answer choice is (B). Only answer-choice (B) involves the object of the question and the relevant condition. The basic reasoning task leads to the selection of the best-answer choice.

Obfuscation tactics make this example of the cards more difficult than the oak tree question. By inviting you to assume that even numbers cannot appear on cards with a consonant, the LSAT could obfuscate the basic reasoning task. Then, by inviting you to read the question as if your task were the opposite of what you are actually asked to do (that is, to confirm the card-master's statement rather than disaffirm it), the LSAT could further obfuscate the basic reasoning task. Such obfuscation tactics maintain the effectiveness of LSAT questions, and some obfuscation tactics work better than others.

WHAT ARE THE TYPES OF OBFUSCATION TACTICS?

Three of the five general types of obfuscation tactics used on the LSAT involve varying the presentation of the basic task. First, the context in which the basic task is presented is varied. For example, three seemingly different section-tests are used—Arguments, Passages, and Relationships. Within each of these section-tests, the appearance of the questions is varied to add to the impression that many different tasks are required. The question structure is emphasized in the mind of the test-taker, who tends to concentrate on differences in form and overlook the essential similarity of LSAT questions. Varying the presentation of the basic task causes the LSAT's focus to seem different from what it really is.

Related to the obfuscation-by-variation tactic is the use of excess or excessive information. Although it is employed elsewhere on the test, this tactic is seen best in the Passages statement, which gives the test-taker much more information than is needed to respond to the question-answer choice sets. The test-taker concentrates on the information presented, trying to understand and retain the data by using processes that have proven effective in past test experiences. Thus, the test-taker becomes absorbed in processes that detract from work on the real LSAT task.

The third obfuscation tactic involves the omission of information in the statement and question. The test-taker gets the impression that there is insufficient information to respond to the question, and this "missing" data grabs and keeps the test-taker's attention away from the basic reasoning task involved. While it often may appear otherwise, the information needed to respond to the question is always given—what is not stated is often as informative as what is stated.

These three tactics generally create difficulties with question location for the test-taker. The test-taker uses limited test time seeking rather than responding to the question. You can minimize the impact of these tactics by remembering that the basic task of reasoning with objects (including nonmaterial ones) and conditions is always the same and by avoiding activities that do not involve this basic task.

The last two obfuscation tactics are less obvious than the first three and pose greater difficulties for most test-takers. They are the invited assumption and the invited question.

You experienced the invited assumption tactic in both the oak-tree and card-master examples. In the oak-tree example, you were invited to assume that every tree that produces acorns is an oak. In the card-master example, you were invited to assume that cards with even numbers on one side had to have vowels on the other. You were also invited to assume that cards with consonants on one side had odd numbers on the other. Each of these assumptions was invited by a familiar or probable pattern (vowel = even, consonant = odd) or by external knowledge (acorns occur only on oak trees). The invited assumption usually involves these or other familiar patterns or external knowledge. Avoid the assumption tactic by identifying and using only the patterns and information presented in the problem.

The invited question is also very difficult for the well-conditioned test-taker to resist. The invited question obfuscation tactic often shows up on television quiz shows—the host reads only a few words of the question and a contestant blurts out an answer. A more subtle form of the same thing was involved in the card-master example. Although the question invited you to identify cards that might confirm the truth of the card-master's statement, the operative question required you to identify only those cards that could disprove the truth of the statement. The question asked was not the operative question. You will find that nearly all LSAT questions are generic and unclear. Consequently, they invite interpretation. Effective interpretation of the questions best results from a review of the answer choices. Seldom can interpretive data be found other than in the answer choices.

✔**BY CONSIDERING ONLY THE FIVE ANSWER CHOICES, YOU CAN RESIST THE INVITATION TO ANSWER A QUESTION THAT IS NOT ASKED.**

Success Session 5

WHAT ARE RELATIONSHIPS QUESTIONS ABOUT?

Of the three LSAT question formats, Relationships questions present the basic task most obviously. This clarity can assist you in developing the skills and procedures you need for handling the basic task in the other two LSAT problem formats. Note also that of the three question formats, Relationships is also the most difficult for most people to master. Thus, we begin specific problem-type training with Relationships. Working on Relationships first gives you additional time to get the basic task in this context under control and thus, helps to maximize your test performance.

WHY ARE RELATIONSHIPS QUESTIONS SO DIFFICULT?

In short, the reason Relationships questions are difficult is that they are unfamiliar and require the consistently exact application of the basic reasoning task. Most test-takers are familiar with and relatively proficient at test questions that require recall or are based upon contexts with which they have experience. Questions about definitions, formulas, and facts require the test-taker to recall memorized information and to, perhaps, apply it. Questions about the concepts, procedures, and theories presented in lectures, texts, and class discussions depend on the test-taker's assimilation of teachers' and writers' perspectives. These experiences and acquired perspectives permit the test-taker to consider points of view, arguments, and the like when responding to a question. Relationships questions require a much different application of the skill that I refer to as the basic task of conditional reasoning.

✔ RELATIONSHIPS QUESTIONS REQUIRE VERY LITTLE RECALL, NOR DO THEY INVOLVE LEARNED PERSPECTIVES, POINTS OF VIEW, OR ARGUMENTS. CONSEQUENTLY, THEY ARE UNFAMILIAR, DISCOMFORTING, AND DIFFICULT.

HOW MANY QUESTIONS ARE THERE IN A RELATIONSHIPS SECTION-TEST?

There are four sets of Relationships questions in each 35-minute section-test. Generally, there are six questions in each of the four sets, though, occasionally, you will find as few as five or as many as seven questions in a set when the LSAT has had to deviate from the norm to get the test performance required. Thus, there are almost always twenty-four questions in a Relationships section-test.

✔ THE FOUR SETS OF QUESTIONS IN THE SECTION-TEST ARE CRITICAL TO YOUR TEST PLAN.

WHAT ARE THE COMPONENTS OF A RELATIONSHIPS QUESTION?

As you will recall, the LSAT problem profile has four components—directions, statements, questions, and answer choices.

The directions for Relationships questions are brief. What they do say, however, is pertinent: "Each group of questions is based on a number of conditions. You are to choose the best answer to each question." Interpreted, this means that the best answer is the only one of the five options that satisfies all the relevant conditions involved in the question.

Thus, you gain an advantage. For example, if you are finding it difficult to select between two answer options to a Relationships question, you *know* that only one meets all of the conditions. You should be able to resolve your dilemma quickly by finding the condition that differentiates between the two answer options. In this way, you avoid a trap that captures many test-takers, who repeatedly review the same answers in the same way in the futile hope that the best answer will eventually reveal itself.

How do Relationships questions work?

The Directions

The directions for Relationships questions are brief and not very enlightening. The LSAT tells you that questions are based on a set of conditions and that you are to select the response that most accurately and completely answers the question. And that's it! The important thing you are not told is that the conditions that appear in the statement apply to all questions, and the conditions that appear in a question apply *to that question only*. As you will soon learn, the response that most accurately and completely answers a question will be the only answer option that satisfies all of the conditions applicable to that question. There is no ambiguity to resolve when dealing with Relationships problems.

The Statement

Relationships statements usually consist of two parts, designated here as facts and rules. Although the facts and rules are short and seemingly simple, there is a possible complication unique to Relationships questions. While each question in a set shares the common statement, some problems include an additional statement embedded in the question itself. In general, about two thirds of Relationships questions include one of these supplemental statements. Supplemental statements can also overrule or disable a fact or rule that appears in the common statement. Be alert!

The facts and rules in the common statement apply to all questions in the set. The facts and rules in a supplemental statement apply only to the questions in which they appear.

✔**WHEN THE LSAT PLACES A SUPPLEMENTAL STATEMENT WITHIN A QUESTION, THE ADDED STATEMENT APPLIES ONLY TO THAT QUESTION.**

Note again that not only does the supplemental statement apply solely to the question in which it is found, but it may contradict another such statement placed in a different question in the set.

In the facts portion of the statement, the LSAT presents the variables involved in the question set. By including many variables in the statement, the LSAT is able to obfuscate the fact that only a few are actually relevant to the set of questions. Test-takers become confused by the presence of many variables, with their potential for vast numbers of combinations. They then spend much time trying to sort through the variables and their combinations, or they move to another question set in the hope that it will be less forbidding. You can avoid these detrimental reactions by looking to the rules and questions to render the facts manageable.

✔**CONCENTRATING ON THE RULES AND QUESTIONS REDUCES THE NUMBER OF POSSIBLE VARIABLES AND COMBINATIONS TO THE RELEVANT FEW.**

When applied to the facts, the rules portion of the statement generally yields a number of conditions. And it is these conditions that are referred to by the questions. The rules limit the number of conditions you have to consider in selecting the best answer to a Relationships question. Taken together, the facts and rules define the conditions applicable to the questions and usually eliminate many possible conditions.

The Question

The question circumscribes or brackets the answer selection to be made. As described previously, it also may add facts and rules to those that are common to the entire question set, further narrowing the relevant conditions with which you must deal. However, the question seldom reduces the relevant conditions to one.

Relationships questions are very straightforward. There are only three basic questions.

- Which of the following *must* satisfy the conditions/be true?
- Which of the following *could* satisfy the conditions/be true?
- Which of the following *cannot* satisfy the conditions/be true?

In most Relationships section-tests, you will find more *must* and *could* questions and fewer *cannot* questions. The LSAT is able to vary the presentation of these basic questions. The questions and their variations are illustrated in the diagram below.

The first variation shows the supplemental statement format. The second is the converse of the basic question, requiring the selection of the answer option that is an exception to the

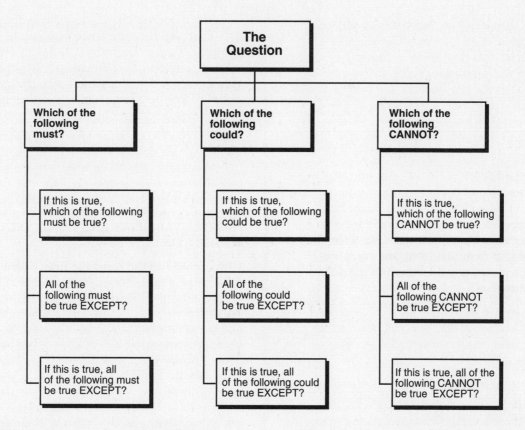

conditions required by the question. The last variation combines the supplemental statement format with the converse of the basic question.

The LSAT also varies the appearance of questions by slipping synonyms in here and there. For instance, "might" may be substituted for "could" and "has to" or "is" may substitute for "must."

And that about tells it all for Relationships questions. You have reviewed all of them. Learn the elements and the variations and there will be no surprises on the Relationships section-test on the LSAT. *You now can predict every Relationships question that will appear on the LSAT.*

The Answers

The LSAT's selection of answer options gives you the wrong-answer advantage. Not only are there just five answers from which to select, but four of them do not satisfy one or more of the conditions required by the problem. As you learned previously, it is difficult for the LSAT to produce attractive wrong answers, since every wrong answer fails to satisfy one or more of the conditions required by the combined statement and question. The LSAT attempts to disguise this weakness, but, for most answer options, it is relatively easy to detect. In fact, for most

questions using the single-option format, the failure is easy to detect in at least three of the five answer options.

✔**THE LSAT USUALLY OFFERS JUST ONE ATTRACTIVE WRONG ANSWER OPTION.**

Wrong answers follow patterns that can assist in your detection of them. Recall that the best answer option is the only one that satisfies *all* of the relevant conditions. If the question is "Which of the answer options **must** be true?" options that *could* be true or *cannot* be true are wrong—they fail to satisfy all of the conditions.

If the question is "Which of the answer options **could** be true?" options that *cannot* be true are wrong. They, too, fail to satisfy all of the conditions. (Note that the LSAT accepts that an answer choice that **must** be true satisfies a question asking for the choices that *could* be true.)

If the question is "Which of the answer options **cannot** be true?" options that *must* be true and *could* be true are wrong, failing as they do to satisfy all of the conditions.

With Relationships questions, the LSAT usually uses the **too-little-too-much** technique (and a variation we will deal with a little later) to create wrong answer options. This simply means that the answer option overstates or understates conditions that would satisfy the question.

Notice that the following example of a Relationships problem employs a supplemental statement in the question. For the purposes of illustration, all of the answer options offered here are wrong. This would not be the case with an actual LSAT question. Remember also that the identifiers used here do not appear on the LSAT.

STATEMENT

Facts

The twelve-member board of directors of Acme International, Inc., is divided into four committees: the Audit Committee, the Finance Committee, the Planning Committee, and the Shareholder Relations Committee.

Rules

At least one of the directors is a member of the Audit, Finance, and Planning committees.

At least one of the directors is a member of the Audit, Finance, and Shareholder Relations committees.

QUESTION

1. If each committee has three members, and no two committees share more than two members, which of the following must be true?

ANSWER CHOICES

(A) All members of the Audit Committee are members of the Planning Committee.

(B) No member of the Audit Committee is a member of the Planning Committee.

(C) The Audit and Finance committees have at least two members in common.

(D) The Planning and Shareholder Relations committees have only one member in common.

(E) The Audit Committee has exactly twice as many members in common with the Finance Committee as does the Shareholder Relations Committee.

Since the question asks for that which **must** be true, wrong answers will be those that *could* or *cannot* be true.

Answer option (A) overstates what must be true. The supplemental statement requires that no more than two of the three members of a committee be shared with another committee. Thus, all three committee members *cannot* be shared by two committees.

Answer option (B) understates what must be true. The common statement requires that one director be a member of both the Audit and Planning committees. Thus, it *cannot* be that no committee members are shared by the two committees.

Answer option (C) overstates what must be true. The common statement requires that *one* member of the Audit and Finance committees be shared, not two. The supplemental statement requires that no more than two members of a committee be shared with another committee—it does not require that two members be shared. Thus, it *could* be that two committee members are shared by two committees, but it is not necessarily so.

Answer option (D) both understates and overstates what must be true. The common statement does not require that the member of the Audit, Finance, and Planning committees be the same person who is shared by the Audit, Finance, and Shareholder Relations committees. It is possible but not required. The supplemental statement requires that no more than two members of a committee be shared with another committee. It does not require that any members be shared. Thus, it *could* be that the Planning and Shareholder Relations committees have only one member in common, but it need not be so.

Answer option (E) illustrates a variation of the **too-little-too-much** technique sometimes used by the test-maker. It is wrong because it is far too precise to meet the stated conditions. This technique can be disconcerting and distracting to a test-taker who fails to recognize it and tries to develop some conclusive proof.

By identifying a condition implicit in the answer option that fails to satisfy the question, you can determine that an answer is wrong and dump it. The wrong-answer patterns and obfuscatory tactics are summarized below.

For **must** questions, wrong answer options are those that *could* or *cannot* satisfy required conditions, even though they use

- the **too-little-too-much** tactic
- the **overprecision** tactic

For **could** questions, wrong answer options are those that *cannot* satisfy required conditions, even though they use

- the **too-little-too-much** tactic
- the **overprecision** tactic

For **cannot** questions, wrong answer options are those that *must* or *could* satisfy required conditions, even though they use

- the **too-little-too-much** tactic
- the **overprecision** tactic

HOW DOES THE LSAT CREATE MORE DIFFICULT QUESTIONS?

As you have seen, making more difficult questions is not simply a matter of asking tougher questions. Rather, in order to create more difficult questions, the LSAT must develop better answers. The LSAT wants the substantial majority of questions on any section-test to be of medium difficulty, with some 40–60 percent of test-takers selecting the best answer. It wants a smaller proportion of questions to be relatively easy, with more than 60 percent of test-takers selecting the best answer. And it is important that an even smaller proportion is to be relatively tough, with fewer than 40 percent of test-takers selecting the best answer.

To adjust the difficulty level of a question or question set, the LSAT use two basic techniques. First, the complexity of the relationships can be varied. This is demonstrated in the preceding example by the inclusion of the supplemental statement, which defines the size of the committees and limits the nature of their composition.

✔**IN GENERAL, THE GREATER THE COMPLEXITY OF THE STATED RELATIONSHIPS, THE MORE DIFFICULT THE QUESTION.**

The second technique used by the LSAT to create more difficult questions involves the answer options. Again, this is demonstrated in the preceding example. Answer options (A) and (B) are determined to be wrong by direct reference to a condition in the statement or the question. If all the wrong answer options could be similarly eliminated, the question would be relatively easy; it is made slightly more difficult by the inclusion of answer options (C), (D), and (E), which require a more complicated review of conditions to determine that they are wrong.

With respect to your test plan, it makes sense to complete questions in the order of increasing difficulty. This strategy applies even more to question sets than to questions within sets. However, except for using the techniques described above, the LSAT provides no clear clues about the difficulty of questions.

✔**UNLIKE MANY OTHER STANDARDIZED TESTS, THERE IS NO ORDER OF DIFFICULTY AMONG LSAT QUESTIONS OR QUESTION SETS.**

Later question sets are no more difficult than earlier ones, nor are later questions harder than earlier ones. Fatigue may sometimes make later question sets appear to be more difficult, but this is illusory.

HOW DO YOU BEST HANDLE THE COMPLEXITY OF RELATIONSHIPS QUESTIONS?

Visualization is a critical efficiency device for working with the format of Relationships questions. How do you visualize? If you are told to put yourself in Mary's position and that John is standing to Mary's left and Betty to her right, what do you project onto the screen in your mind? If you "see" three people in a line, two women together and a man on one end or the other, your visualization technique is working well. If you "see" a woman, another woman, and a man standing in a line from left to right, your visualization is slightly more efficient, because you have defined the exact placement of the three on the basis of Mary's position. If you "see" something else or nothing at all, you will find the **node-and-line** visualization technique particularly helpful.

By using a single visualization as the basis for selecting answers to many questions, you maximize your use of test time and minimize the potential for confusion. The technique uses nodes to depict variables (usually things) and lines to depict connections (usually relationships) between them. Below is a visualization of the John-Mary-Betty statement in the previous paragraph.

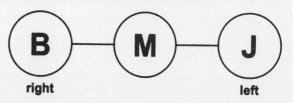

right   left

HOW DO YOU APPLY THE VISUALIZATION TECHNIQUE?

First, you read the facts and rules. It is rare that these alone will provide sufficient information for you to develop an effective visualization, so you must next scan the questions. At this point, the core of information you will be working with becomes clear, and you can begin your visualization.

You usually will find some space to record your visualization on the pages of the question set, but occasionally you will encounter a full page with no white space. Scratch paper and shirt cuffs are forbidden. What to do? Just fold the preceding or succeeding page in half, and use the space thus exposed.

In the LSAT, relationships are defined in relative rather than specific terms. You will find such statements as "Mary is older than John and John is younger than Betty." You will not read that "Mary is 10, John is 8, and Betty is 12." The most efficient visualization must anticipate this lack of specificity and allow for the shifts that inevitably will be required by the questions.

You must remember that the lines in your visualization do not depict exact relationships—they are more akin to rubber bands, capable of extending or contracting as circumstances require. In fact, a squiggly line can be used to remind you of this important point. (The varieties of visualization will be thoroughly illustrated in the next success session.)

After you complete your visualization, consider the questions. As you work through them, you may have to adjust your visualization slightly to accommodate a supplemental statement or some other attribute of the question. Consider each answer option, remembering that your objective is to identify the condition that will make it wrong by failing to satisfy the requirements of the question and statement. Use comparison, identifying the conditions in the answer option and comparing them to those in your visualization. When you find the condition that fails to satisfy the requirements, dump that answer choice. One unsatisfactory condition is sufficient to eliminate an answer choice—compare no more.

Repeating the process, you select the best answer option and circle it in the test book. Once you have completed all six questions in the set, transfer all of your answers to the answer sheet *at the same time*. This provides a natural break for you before you move on to the next Relationships problem.

Success Session 6

WHAT ARE ARGUMENTS AND PASSAGES QUESTIONS ABOUT?

This session will consider both Arguments and Passages, the other two question formats found on the LSAT. These formats appear to be more familiar than Relationships questions to most people, but appearances can be deceiving. While the formats may seem familiar to you, the material is not. In fact, the LSAT selects material that is extremely unlikely to be familiar in order to make sure that your reasoning skill is being measured, not your knowledge of the material. You should not treat Arguments and Passages as if they were academic material simply because there is a superficial resemblance in the formats.

While Arguments and Passages appear to be very different from each other, they share many common characteristics that are more important to your test performance than their perceived differences. In this session we will examine the similarities of the two formats, and in later sessions we will consider in detail their distinctive qualities.

WHAT ARE THE COMPONENTS OF ARGUMENTS AND PASSAGES PROBLEMS?

Like Relationships problems, both Arguments and Passages problems present the four-component LSAT problem profile: directions, statements, questions, and answer options. The directions and statements of Arguments and Passages problems differ in notable respects, while the questions and answers are very similar. (Directions will be discussed in detail in Sessions 8 and 9.)

WHAT ARE THE CHARACTERISTICS OF THE STATEMENTS?

The most apparent difference between Arguments and Passages statements is their format. Passages statements are long and heavy on detail. They contrast with Arguments statements, which are short and offer little detail. These differences conceal their underlying similarity: Each statement presents an argument.

Applied to the LSAT, the term "argument" means that the statement involves premises, propositions, and reasons that lead to, support, or imply a conclusion. The combination of different elements in the argument produces the conditions upon which Arguments and Passages questions and answer options are based.

The fact that Arguments and Passages statements both involve arguments should be comforting to most test-takers. The argument provides a context and a starting position for the consideration of questions and answer options that seem to be similar to those encountered in an academic environment. This perceived similarity seems to be sufficient to make the average test-taker more comfortable with these question types than with Relationships. Whether for this reason or others, Arguments are the least difficult for most test-takers. Passages are more difficult for most test-takers, and, finally, Relationships, as noted previously, the most difficult.

WHAT ARE THE QUESTIONS LIKE?

Arguments and Passages questions are very much alike. They are of two basic types: the **description question type** and the **extension question type**.

Description questions ask you to select the answer option that best embodies or describes the conditions set out in the statement. They look familiar because they refer to the statement or the conditions presented. Description questions often relate directly to key words or concepts found in the statement. Consider this example of a description question type.

1. According to the passage, the Technocrats were

    (A) twentieth-century politicians
    (B) frustrated modern inventors
    (C) overpaid factory workers
    (D) precursors of today's scientists
    (E) nineteenth-century economists

The extension question asks you to select the answer option that best represents an extension of the conditions set out in or required by the statement. An example of the extension question type follows.

1. The passage suggests that which of the following might occur if governments increased control over the means of public communication?

   (A) Newspapers would become more conservative.
   (B) Free speech would be threatened.
   (C) Individual rights to privacy would be better respected.
   (D) Citizens would be more considerate of diversity.
   (E) The content of radio programs would be more informative.

The reasoning task involved in Arguments and Passages problems is the same as in all LSAT questions. Because the task is the same, the questions have the same basic format. As you learned in previous sessions, there are three basic question types that require you to determine which of the answer options must, could, or cannot satisfy the conditions. As you remember, these questions are put quite directly in the Relationships section-test, but the LSAT is less direct in the Arguments and Passages section-tests. Seldom is a basic question asked directly, so each question type needs to be identified before you can proceed to the answer options.

✔ **IN ARGUMENTS AND PASSAGES PROBLEMS, YOU NEED TO IDENTIFY THE QUESTION THAT IS BEING ASKED.**

While this identification can be challenging, the wrong-answer advantage that results is worth the effort. The work of identification is assisted by the LSAT's dominant use of **could** questions in both the Arguments and Passages section-tests. (*Must* and *cannot* options do appear regularly, but they are far less frequent than **could** answer options.) As you recall, every wrong answer to a **could** question is an answer option that *cannot* satisfy the conditions. Most test-takers identify *cannot* wrong answer options more readily than either *must* or *could* options. For these reasons, and perhaps some others, Arguments questions are, on average, the least difficult for test-takers.

Arguments and Passages questions share another common trait: Neither one adds to or alters information contained in the statement.

✔ **IN AN ARGUMENTS OR PASSAGES QUESTION, THERE IS NEVER A SUPPLEMENTAL STATEMENT TO CONFUSE OR OBFUSCATE.**

HOW IS THE INTERACTION BETWEEN QUESTIONS AND ANSWERS STRUCTURED?

The questions and answer options for Arguments and Passages are presented in three formats. The first is the **question-and-answer** format with which you are likely to be very familiar. As the name implies, a question is posed to which the answer options are responses. The second format is the **question-question** format, in which the question asks you to select the question that is answered by the information given or implied by the statement. The last format is **sentence completion**. The question is the first part of the sentence that the answer options complete in various ways. There is no question mark involved in this question format.

The variety of formats serves to obfuscate the question. The formats are summarized in the illustration on page 91. Although they are included in order to leave nothing to chance, the multiple-option format is very unlikely to appear on the LSAT and you should spend only a minimal amount of time considering it.

WHAT ARE THE ANSWER CHOICES LIKE?

Answer options to Arguments and Passages questions are similar in structure.

Description questions are drawn directly from the statement, and the LSAT has little leeway in interpreting the information when constructing questions and answer options for this type of problem presentation.

✔ **ANSWERS TO DESCRIPTION QUESTIONS CONNECT DIRECTLY TO THE STATEMENT.**

The direct connection between statement and question means that the focus of the question is immediately apparent. This often seems too easy to test-takers, so many of them seize the opportunity to convert a relatively straightforward question into one that is much more difficult by entertaining assumptions or interpretations that are unwarranted and not called for.

Question Formats

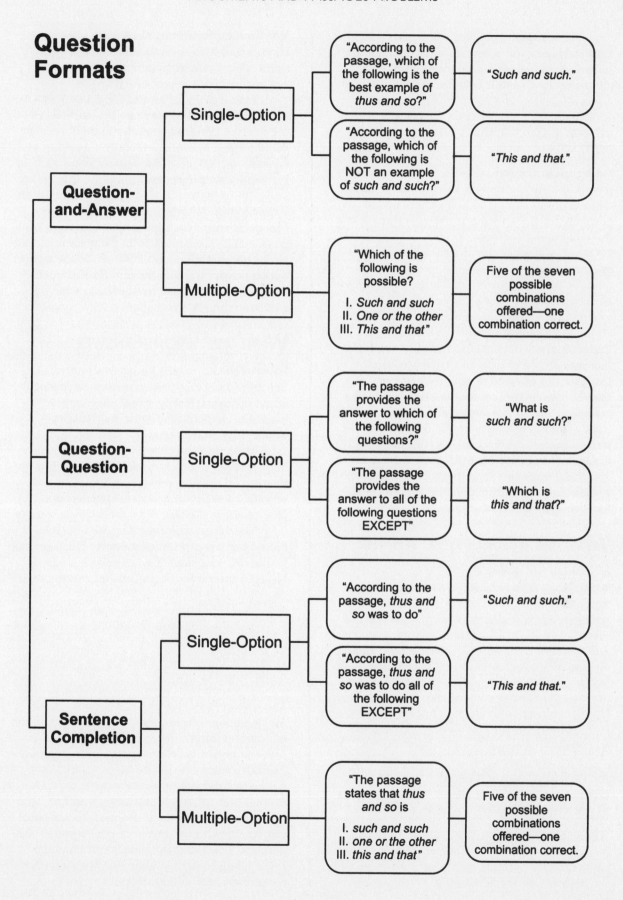

When constructing extension questions, the LSAT interprets the information contained in the statement and, thus, is much more likely to obfuscate the question or its focus.

✔ ANSWERS TO EXTENSION QUESTIONS CONNECT TO INTERPRETATIONS OF THE STATEMENT.

More than in any other LSAT format, you need to rely on the answer options to cut through any existing obfuscation. The best-answer option generally provides a focus for the question that the other answer options do not.

You will recall that the LSAT eliminates questions that do not work as predicted. A question-and-best-answer combination that does not attract a consensus of those it was designed to snag is discarded. This gives you a big advantage where Arguments and Passages questions are concerned, because the questions that pass all of the trials and are placed on the LSAT are not going to be followed by best-answer options that are too obscure to be identified. The best-answer choice is right in front of you. Selecting it can be difficult, but the wrong-answer advantage assists your efforts with Arguments and Passages even more than it does with Relationships. Recall that the wrong-answer advantage is one of the most powerful tools you have for dealing with the LSAT.

WHAT DISTINGUISHES THE WRONG-ANSWER OPTIONS?

Every wrong answer on the LSAT fails to satisfy the conditions required by the combination of statement and question. It is worth repeating that even though the LSAT attempts to disguise it, it is relatively easy to detect this failure in most answer options. You won't be surprised to hear that there are certain disguises that obfuscate more effectively than others, nor will you be shocked to find out that these are the very disguises the LSAT uses for the wrong-answer options in the Arguments and Passages section-tests.

✔ BY TRAINING YOURSELF TO IDENTIFY WRONG-ANSWER DISGUISES, YOU ENHANCE YOUR WRONG-ANSWER ADVANTAGE.

When you combine the fact that the LSAT usually includes just one attractive wrong-answer option among the four offered with your knowledge of the disguises and understanding of the wrong-answer patterns for the three basic question types, you will be positioned to take full advantage of the wrong-answer options to every Arguments and Passages question.

Take a moment to recall that the best-answer option is the only one that satisfies all of the relevant conditions set out in the statement and question. When you identify a question as a variation of "Which of the answer options could be true?" the options that cannot be true fail to satisfy all of the conditions and are wrong. With a variation of "Which of the answer options cannot be true?" the options that must and could be true fail to satisfy all of the conditions and are wrong. With a variation of "Which of the answer options must be true?" the options that could and cannot be true fail to satisfy all of the conditions and are wrong.

WHAT ARE WRONG-ANSWER DISGUISES?

The LSAT uses four basic disguises for wrong-answer options. Briefly stated, they are the **same-language** disguise, the **too-little-too-much** disguise, the **true but** disguise, and the **false-assertion** disguise.

It is not beneath the LSAT to use disguises. That is, a particular wrong-answer option may simultaneously wear a same-language and a false-assertion disguise.

The **same-language** disguise is simple. It consists of a repetition of the same language that was in the statement. This disguise attracts test-takers because it connects directly to the statement, and the language is usually so obscure as to create an impression of subtle significance.

The **too-little-too-much** disguise is used to overstate or understate something in the answer option so that it fails to satisfy the conditions required by the question.

The **true but** disguise means what it says. The answer option is true, but it does not satisfy the conditions required by the statement and the question. It attracts the test-taker because it is true and makes good sense. Its veracity obscures its irrelevance.

The **false-assertion** disguise is used to misstate information in the answer option. That is, the answer option misinterprets or wrongly characterizes a proposition or conclusion in the problem. It is often combined with the same-language disguise. It is attractive because it is obscure and authoritatively put.

How do Arguments and Passages problems work?

Your knowledge of wrong-answer patterns and disguises will assist you in the identification of wrong-answer options. By dumping wrong-answer options, you can expeditiously locate the cream-of-the-crop answer option—the best answer option—the one that satisfies the conditions required by the statement and question. The way wrong-answer patterns and disguises are combined is illustrated in the following discussion.

STATEMENT

It is worth repeating that studies show that teenagers' exposure to the news is one measure of the extent of youthful political involvement in this society. In addition, the patterns of exposure to the news that develop during the teens continue throughout life. Even though we have confidence in these observations, the conclusions drawn from them by many media experts are simply not valid because so little is understood about the variables that are involved.

QUESTION

1. Which of the following best states the conclusion to which the author's statements lead?

ANSWER CHOICES

(A) It is worth studying teenagers' exposure to the news.

(B) Confidence in the observations of the variables that are involved in patterns of exposure to the news supports the conclusions drawn by many media experts.

(C) Understanding teenagers' exposure to the news is critical to understanding human behavior.

(D) The conclusions of many media experts about exposure to the news involve little-understood variables.

(E) Adult patterns of exposure to the news will ultimately reflect the fact that teenagers are more politically active.

This question calls for selection of the answer option that **could** satisfy the conditions set out in the statement and question. Wrong-answer options are those that **cannot** satisfy the conditions.

Answer option (A) is the best selection, though it is unlikely that you would select it as best after a quick reading. A careful reading will disclose that there is nothing in the answer option that conflicts with the conditions in the statement and question. It is an attractive cream-of-the-crop answer.

Answer option (B) is a **cannot** wrong-answer option in a **same-language** disguise. Every word of this answer is taken from the statement, which connects it to the statement and makes it seem attractive. However, it cannot satisfy the statement conditions because, among other reasons, confidence cannot support the conclusions of media experts.

Option (C) is a **cannot** wrong-answer option in **too-much** and **same-language** disguises. The answer option overstates by using much of the language of the statement to declare that what was "one measure" is actually "critical" and that it encompasses not just "youthful political involvement" but all "human behavior." By using what could be misperceived as paraphrase rather than overstatement, the answer might attract a few test-takers.

Option (D) is a **cannot** wrong-answer option in a **true but** disguise. The answer option is a "true" statement, but it is irrelevant to the question posed. The author's conclusion, not the media experts', is what is sought.

Option (E) is a **cannot** wrong-answer option in **false-assertion** and **same-language** disguises. It misstates the information given. Among many other things, there is no mention in the statement of the degree of teenage political activity involved, nor is it suggested that such activity is related causally to exposure to the news.

What are the variations on the wrong-answer disguises?

The ways the LSAT varies the four basic disguises are often fuzzy, although they are predictable. Their outlines are always identifiable, and they frequently can assist your identification of the basic disguise and wrong-answer pattern. However, for this knowledge to work to your advantage, you have to have or develop a certain tolerance of imprecision.

✓IT IS IMPORTANT THAT YOU NOT GET CAUGHT UP IN TRYING TO IDENTIFY WRONG-ANSWER DISGUISES PRECISELY. YOUR SENSE THAT THEY ARE WRONG IS SUFFICIENT.

In the examples that follow, note that the number of answer options fluctuates atypically between four and five, depending on the number of variations being illustrated. For each LSAT question there will always be four wrong-answer choices and one best choice.

Same-Language Variations

There are four variations on the **same-language** wrong-answer disguise that the LSAT usually uses.

- The first reaches an incorrect conclusion, using the language of the statement.
- The second contradicts the statement, using the language of the statement.
- The third refers to a topic or point not in the statement, using the language of the statement.
- The fourth misinterprets points made in the statement, using the language of the statement.

STATEMENT

It is worth repeating that studies show that teenagers' exposure to the news is one measure of the extent of youthful political involvement in this society. In addition, the patterns of exposure to the news that develop during the teens continue throughout life. Even though we have confidence in these observations, the conclusions drawn from them by many media experts are simply not valid because so little is understood about the variables that are involved.

QUESTION

1. Which of the following can be inferred from the statement?

ANSWER CHOICES

(A) Youthful political involvement in this society is extensive.

(B) The variables that are involved in patterns of exposure to the news support the conclusions drawn by many media experts.

(C) Patterns of exposure to the news are measured by observation.

(D) The conclusions of many media experts about youthful political involvement are based on little-understood variables.

This question requires an answer option that **could** satisfy the conditions set out in the statement. Wrong-answer options will be those that *cannot* satisfy the conditions.

Option (A) is a **cannot** wrong-answer option in which the **same language** is used with a dash of **too much** to express an incorrect conclusion. There is nothing in the statement to suggest that youthful political involvement is extensive.

Option (B) is a **cannot** wrong-answer option using the **same language** to contradict the statement. The statement says that the variables are the reason media experts' conclusions are invalid. This is the opposite of supporting the conclusions.

Option (C) is a **cannot** wrong-answer option using the **same language** as the statement to refer to a different topic or point. There is nothing in the statement to suggest the method used to measure patterns of exposure to the news.

Option (D) is a **cannot** wrong-answer option that misinterprets a point in the statement while using the **same language** as the statement. The statement does not indicate what the experts' conclusions are based on, although it is possible to interpret it as suggesting that observations were involved. To infer that the variables provide the base of their conclusions is a clear misinterpretation of the statement.

Too-Little-Too-Much Variations

There are four primary variations on the **too-little-too-much** wrong-answer disguise used by the LSAT.

- One contradicts the statement, taking a part of the statement for the whole.
- Another agrees with the statement, taking a part of the statement for the whole.
- Another is too narrow, answering part of the question but not all of it.
- The last is too broad, answering all of the question and much more.

STATEMENT

It is worth repeating that studies show that teenagers' exposure to the news is one measure of the extent of youthful political involvement in this society. In addition, the patterns of exposure to the news that develop during the teens continue throughout life. Even though we have confidence in these observations, the conclusions drawn from them by many media experts are simply not valid because so little is understood about the variables that are involved.

QUESTION

1. Which of the following best describes the observations of exposure to the news made in the above statement?

ANSWER CHOICES

(A) It can be comprehensively measured by youthful political involvement.

(B) It can measure youthful political involvement in all societies.

(C) It can measure youthful political involvement.

(D) It measures political involvement in most societies, and its patterns explain both teenage and adult behavior.

This question calls for the selection of the answer option that **could** satisfy the conditions set out in the statement and question. The wrong-answer options are those that cannot satisfy the conditions.

Option (A) is a **cannot** wrong-answer option that contradicts the statement by declaring that exposure to the news is comprehensively (**too much**) measured by youthful political involvement. The statement indicates just the opposite—that youthful political involvement is measured by exposure to the news. It also ignores the second observation in the statement—patterns of exposure to the news that develop during the teens continue throughout life—thus taking a part of the statement for the whole.

Option (B) is a **cannot** wrong-answer option that agrees generally with the statement but overstates it (referring to "all societies" instead of "this society"). It also ignores the observation that patterns of exposure to the news that develop during the teens continue throughout life, thus taking a single observation for the whole.

Option (C) is a **cannot** wrong-answer option that takes the first observation in the statement into account but understates it (**too little**) in that it ignores the second observation entirely.

Option (D) is a **cannot** wrong-answer option that goes too far in that it answers the question and much more. It declares that exposure to the news measures all political involvement (not just among teenagers) in most societies (not just this society) and that its patterns explain all behavior (no behavior is involved in the statement).

True-But Variations

There are five primary variations on the **true but** wrong-answer disguise used by the LSAT. The wrong-answer option is true, but

- it refers to a part of the statement not involved in the question.
- it does not match the information in the statement, although it is a logical response.
- it is not responsive to the question, although it is a logical response.
- it answers a different question.
- it implies a point or judgment not made in the statement.

STATEMENT

It is worth repeating that studies show that teenagers' exposure to the news is one measure of the extent of youthful political involvement in this society. In addition, the patterns of exposure to the news that develop during the teens continue throughout life. Even though we have confidence in these observations, the conclusions drawn from them by many media experts are simply not valid because so little is understood about the variables that are involved.

QUESTION

1. Which of the following best summarizes the observations about exposure to the news made in the above statement?

ANSWER CHOICES

(A) Accurate studies do not always reach accurate conclusions.

(B) Exposure to the news changes over a lifetime in response to changes in the way news is reported.

(C) Those reporting news should take teenagers' interests into account.

(D) Exposure to the news is a lifelong experience.

(E) Patterns of exposure to the news are important to media experts.

Again, the best answer option is one that **could** satisfy the conditions set out in the statement and the question. Wrong-answer options are those that cannot satisfy the conditions.

Answer option (A) is a **cannot** wrong-answer option that may be true, but it makes reference to parts of the statement (the studies and the invalidity of the experts' conclusions) that are not involved in the question.

Option (B) is a **cannot** wrong-answer option that may be true, but it does not match the statement, which declares that the patterns of exposure to the news continue rather than change over a lifetime.

Answer option (C) is a **cannot** wrong-answer option that may be true, but it is not responsive to the question, which focuses on observations drawn from studies about exposure to the news.

Option (D) is a **cannot** wrong-answer option that may be true, but it is answering a different question, not the one asked.

Option (E) is a **cannot** wrong-answer option that may be true, but it implies a point or judgment that is not made in the statement—that patterns of exposure to the news are important to media experts.

False-Assertion Variations

There are four variations on the **false-assertion** wrong-answer disguise:

- The first misinterprets or negates a statement premise.
- The second uses a false assertion to contradict the statement.

- The third uses a false assertion to agree with the statement.
- The fourth is a logical response but does not match the premises of the statement.

STATEMENT

It is worth repeating that studies show that teenagers' exposure to the news is one measure of the extent of youthful political involvement in this society. In addition, the patterns of exposure to the news that develop during the teens continue throughout life. Even though we have confidence in these observations, the conclusions drawn from them by many media experts are simply not valid because so little is understood about the variables that are involved.

QUESTION

1. Which of the following best describes the conclusions reached by the media experts referred to in the above statement?

ANSWER CHOICES

(A) Youthful political involvement is a measure of teenagers' exposure to the news.

(B) Youthful political activity is the result of increased exposure to the news.

(C) Youthful political involvement is measured by media experts.

(D) The conclusions are not valid because the observations upon which they are based are not complete.

This question again requires that you select the answer option that **could** satisfy the conditions set out in the statement. Wrong-answer options are those that cannot satisfy the conditions.

Answer option (A) is a **cannot** wrong-answer option that misinterprets or negates a premise of the statement (that exposure to the news measures political involvement) by making the false assertion that political involvement measures exposure to the news.

Option (B) is a **cannot** wrong-answer option that uses a false assertion that contradicts the statement. It declares that there is a causal relationship between political activity and exposure to the news.

Option (C) is a **cannot** wrong-answer option involving a false assertion that agrees with the statement to the extent that it notes that political involvement is being measured. It is false because it asserts that media experts do the measuring, a fact neither included nor implied in the statement.

Answer option (D) is a **cannot** wrong-answer option that is a logical response to the question but makes the false assertion that observations are not complete. This assertion does not match the premise in the statement that experts' conclusions are not valid because little is understood about the variables involved.

HOW DIFFICULT ARE ARGUMENTS AND PASSAGES QUESTIONS?

As noted earlier, the LSAT wants the substantial majority of questions on each section-test to be of medium difficulty, with some 40 to 60 percent of test-takers selecting the best answer. A smaller proportion of the questions are to be relatively easy, with more than 60 percent of the test-takers selecting the best answer. And a smaller proportion are to be relatively tough, with fewer than 40 percent of test-takers selecting the best answer.

In Arguments and Passages section-tests, there is no order of difficulty among sets. Question sets appearing later in a section-test are not necessarily more difficult, nor are questions appearing later in a question set harder, than those that come first. Later questions sometimes appear to be more difficult, but this is usually due to the cumulative effect of having reviewed many questions and answer options. Fatigue may make later question sets appear more difficult, but, while the fatigue may be real, the apparent difference in difficulty is not.

Success Session 7

RELATIONSHIPS PROBLEMS—
CRITICAL DETAILS

There is one Relationships section-test on each LSAT, which translates into some 25 percent of the questions. Relationships question sets appear in four forms: the line-up, cluster, map, and schedule contexts.

Since there are four sets of Relationships questions on each 35-minute section-test, this might suggest that each of these contexts will be represented on each section-test. In fact, a section-test may include only two or three of them. The line-up, cluster, and schedule contexts appear with much greater frequency than does the map context. In fact, the map context has been almost completely phased out by the LSAT, and it is unlikely that you will encounter it. However, it will be covered just in case.

IN WHAT ORDER SHOULD YOU CONSIDER RELATIONSHIPS PROBLEMS?

While individual experiences differ, certain contexts are generally more difficult for test-takers than others. The line-up context is generally the least difficult, the cluster and map contexts somewhat more difficult, and the schedule context usually the most difficult. Therefore, you should work on them in that order, from least to most difficult. Recall that there is no benefit from getting the best-answer choice for a more difficult question when compared to the least difficult question-answer choice combination.

✔ **WORK ON RELATIONSHIPS PROBLEMS IN THE ORDER OF DIFFICULTY OF THEIR CONTEXTS—FROM THE LINE-UP TO THE CLUSTER, MAP, AND SCHEDULE CONTEXTS.**

In most instances, the question sets do not appear on the section-test in the order in which it is best to consider them. So your first assignment when beginning a Relationships section-test is to identify the context of each of the four question sets and number the sets in the order you will work them.

After completing this task you turn to the specific contexts.

WHAT IS THE LINE-UP CONTEXT?

Most question sets include at least one question using the **line-up** context. You are already familiar with this context in its basic form. It involves simply putting items in a required order. A teacher arranges the students in a row, from shortest to tallest, from fastest to slowest, or from youngest to oldest—this is what is meant by the line-up context.

HOW DO YOU WORK WITH THE LINE-UP CONTEXT?

You begin by reading the statement, noting the facts and rules.

> ARF dog food comes in six sizes—Small, Medium, Large, Jumbo, Giant, and Colossal.
>
> Colossal weighs more than Large.
> Large weighs more than Small.
> Medium weighs less than Jumbo.
> Large weighs more than Giant.
> Giant weighs more than Jumbo.

The facts and rules announce the line-up context and suggest that the question set will focus on weight. A brief review of the questions confirms this suggestion. Now that the focus for the questions is clear, you can visualize the problem.

The facts tell you that ARF comes in six sizes. These are the variables that will become nodes in your visualization. Abbreviate them as S, M, L, J, G, and C. (The LSAT generally uses names beginning with different letters to facilitate their abbreviation.)

✔**CHECK YOUR WORK TO BE CERTAIN THAT EACH VARIABLE IS INCLUDED.**

The differences in weight are expressed in the relative terms "lighter" and "heavier." The lines in the visualization will depict these transitive relationships.

✔**AGAIN, RUN A CHECK TO BE CERTAIN THAT EACH RELATIONSHIP IS REPRESENTED.**

Then combine these representations into a single visualization. After you complete the visualization, consider the questions. Do not return to the statement for any reason. This is a time-waster and is to be avoided.

✔**AS YOU WORK THROUGH THE QUESTIONS, REFER TO THE VISUALIZATION ONLY.**

1. Which of the following must be true?

   (A) Large is heavier than Jumbo.
   (B) Large is lighter than Jumbo.
   (C) Small is lighter than Medium.
   (D) Large is lighter than Giant.
   (E) Giant is heavier than Small.

This is a **must** question. Refer to the visualization, and start work with answer option (A). You determine that Jumbo weighs less than Giant, which weighs less than Large. This means that Large is heavier than Jumbo, and option (A) is the best answer. Since you know there can be only one answer that satisfies all conditions, and you have determined that option (A) does this, there is no reason to go any further in considering options. Testing every answer option can be a big time-waster, avoid it.

2. Which of the following CANNOT be true?

   (A) Jumbo is heavier than Large.
   (B) Jumbo is lighter than Large.
   (C) Small is lighter than Medium.
   (D) Large is heavier than Giant.
   (E) Giant is heavier than Small.

This is a **cannot** question. Again, refer to the visualization, and start work with answer option (A). As you noted in the previous question, Jumbo weighs less than Giant, which weighs less than Large. This means that Jumbo cannot be heavier than Large. Option (A) is the best answer—it satisfies all conditions. There is no reason to go beyond (A) in considering options.

Notice that the best answers for questions 1 and 2 are opposites. The LSAT frequently uses such an approach. By being alert to take advantage of this circumstance, you can reduce the time required to respond to questions and become more efficient.

3. How many sizes must be lighter than Giant?

   (A) 0
   (B) 1
   (C) 2
   (D) 3
   (E) 4

This is a **must** question. The wrong answers are those that *could* or *cannot* be lighter than Giant. By referring to the visualization, you determine that Jumbo weighs less than Giant, and Medium weighs less than both. You also determine that, because both Large and Colossal weigh more than Giant, they *cannot* be lighter. Finally you determine that Small *could* be lighter than Giant. Thus, three sizes either *could* or *cannot* be lighter than Giant, leaving two that **must** be lighter. Therefore, option (C) is the best answer.

4. How many sizes must be heavier than Jumbo?

   (A) 1
   (B) 2
   (C) 3
   (D) 4
   (E) 5

This is a **must** question. The wrong answers are those that *could* or *cannot* be heavier than Jumbo. By referring to the visualization, you determine that Jumbo weighs more than Medium, which *cannot* then be heavier. You also determine that Jumbo could be lighter than Small, which means that Small *could* be heavier. Thus, two sizes either *could* or *cannot* be lighter than Giant, leaving three that must be heavier. Option (C) is the best answer.

5. If a new Kennel size is added to the ARF line of dog food, and it is lighter than three of the six original sizes, which of the following must be true?

   (A) Giant is heavier than Kennel.
   (B) Large is heavier than Kennel.
   (C) Jumbo is heavier than Kennel.
   (D) Small is lighter than Kennel.
   (E) Small is heavier than Kennel.

FIRST STEP IN VISUALIZING
THE VARIABLES

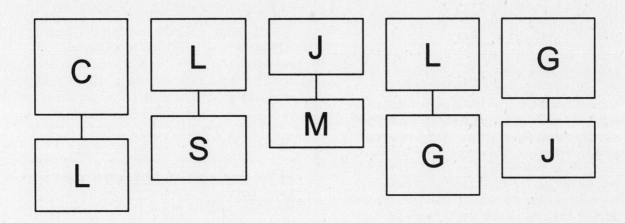

SECOND STEP IN VISUALIZING
THE VARIABLES

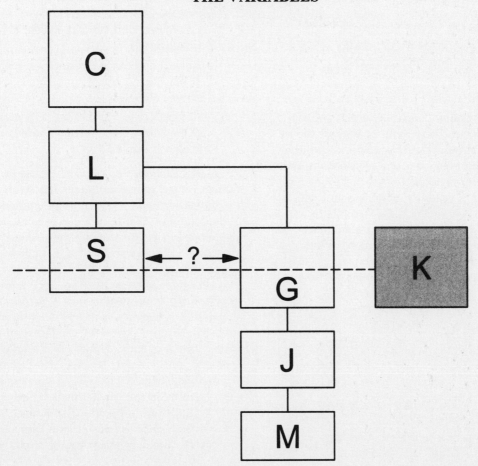

This is a **must** question that involves a **supplemental statement**. The wrong answers are those that *could* or *cannot* be true. First you must add the supplemental information to the visualization (K on page 101). By referring to the augmented visualization, you determine that Colossal and Large are the two heaviest sizes; what is uncertain is the third size that is heavier than Kennel. A review of the conditions discloses that you have no information through which certainty can be reached. Thus, it is likely that the best answer will not involve the uncertainty. Answer option (A) directly involves the uncertainty: Since Giant *could* be heavier than Kennel, option (A) is wrong. Because Large weighs more than all sizes other than Colossal, it **must** be heavier than Kennel, making option (B) the best answer. Since you know that only one answer option satisfies all conditions, and you have determined that (B) satisfies all conditions, there is no reason to consider further options.

6. If a new Kennel size is added to the ARF line of dog food, and it is heavier than three of the six original sizes, which of the following CANNOT be true?

(A) Kennel is heavier than Small.
(B) Kennel is heavier than Jumbo.
(C) Kennel is heavier than Giant.
(D) Kennel is lighter than Large.
(E) Kennel is lighter than Jumbo.

This is a **cannot** question that involves a **supplemental statement**. The wrong answers are those that *must* or *could* be true. First you must add the supplemental information to the visualization. The supplemental information, though conflicting with that in question 5, yields the same visualization. What is uncertain is the third size that is lighter than Kennel. Again, a review of the conditions discloses that you have no information through which certainty can be reached.

Thus, once more it is likely that the best answer will not involve the uncertainty. Answer options (A) and (C) directly involve the uncertainty: since Kennel could be heavier than Small and Giant, (A) and (C) are wrong. Because Jumbo weighs less than all sizes other than Medium, it must be lighter than Kennel, and option (B) must be true, making it wrong when what is asked for is a **cannot** answer. And because Large weighs more than all sizes other than Colossal, it must be heavier than Kennel, and option (D) must be true, making it similarly wrong. Thus, the best answer is (E).

WHAT IS THE CLUSTER CONTEXT?

You probably have some familiarity with the **cluster** context. On the LSAT, the cluster context usually appears in problems involving groups and individuals within those groups. It introduces the complications that arise when individuals have dual status or are affected by more than one set of conditions. Some conditions may apply to groups only, some to individuals within groups, some to individuals alone, and some to combinations of these. This complication tends to make the cluster context somewhat more difficult than the line-up context.

HOW DO YOU WORK WITH THE CLUSTER CONTEXT?

As usual, you begin by reading the statement, with its facts and rules, to determine the context. You will recognize the following statement from the previous session.

> The twelve-member board of directors of Acme International, Inc., is divided into four committees: the Audit Committee, the Finance Committee, the Planning Committee, and the Shareholder Relations Committee.
>
> At least one of the directors is a member of the Audit, Finance, and Planning committees.
>
> At least one of the directors is a member of the Audit, Finance, and Shareholder Relations committees.

The facts present a board of twelve directors and four committees. These are the potential variables. By scanning the questions, you determine that their focus is committee membership, so the committees become the nodes in your visualization: A, F, P, and S. The relationships are depicted by the lines in your visualization. Always check to be certain that each variable and relationship is visualized.

In this instance, you will need to produce two visualizations, because the facts and rules leave an uncertainty. The director who is a member of the Audit, Finance, and Planning committees may or may not be the director who is a member of the Audit, Finance, and Shareholder Relations committees. The first visualization depicts the facts and rules if there are two directors (X and Y) satisfying the conditions; the second one depicts the facts and rules if there is just one director (Z) satisfying the conditions.

After completing the visualization, consider the questions, recalling that you will be referring only to the visualization as you work through the questions.

1. Which of the following must be true?

   (A) At least one member of the Finance Committee is a member of the Planning Committee.

   (B) No member of the Planning Committee is a member of the Shareholder Relations Committee.

   (C) The members of the Finance and Planning committees are the same people.

   (D) The members of the Planning Committee are different from those of the Finance and Shareholder Relations committees.

   (E) The members of the Shareholder Relations Committee are the same as those on the Finance Committee.

This is a **must** question. Note from the visualizations that at least one member of the Finance Committee is a member of the Planning Committee. Since this option satisfies the conditions of the question, circle answer choice (A). Since you know that only one answer option satisfies all conditions, and you have determined that (A)

satisfies all conditions, there is no reason to consider further options.

2. Which of the following could be true?

   (A) No member of the Audit and Planning committees is the same person.

   (B) No member of the Audit Committee is a member of the Finance Committee.

   (C) Some members of the Audit Committee are members of the Finance Committee.

   (D) No member of the Finance Committee is a member of the Planning Committee.

   (E) No member of the Shareholder Relations Committee is a member of the Audit Committee.

This is a **could** question. You note from the visualizations that at least one member of the Audit Committee is a member of the Planning Committee. Therefore, answer choice (A) cannot be true, and it fails to meet the question conditions and is a wrong-answer option. Next you consider answer choice (B). From the visualizations you determine that at least one member of the Audit Committee is a member of the Finance Committee. Therefore, answer choice (B) cannot be true, and it fails to meet the question conditions and is a wrong-answer option. Then you consider answer choice (C). The visualization shows you that at least one

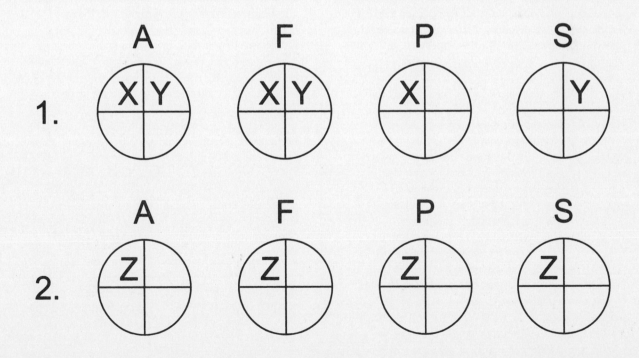

member of the Audit Committee is a member of the Finance Committee. Since answer choice (C) is true, it could be true and it meets the conditions specified. It is the best-answer choice, it satisfies all conditions, and there is no reason to consider further options.

3. If the fewest number of members possible meet the Board organization conditions and Carter is the only common member of two committees, which of the following could be FALSE?

   (A) Carter is a member of the Planning Committee.
   (B) Carter is a member of the Shareholder Relations Committee.
   (C) Carter is a member of the Planning and Shareholder Relations Committees.
   (D) Carter is not a member of the Planning Committee.
   (E) Carter is a member of both the Finance and Shareholder Relations Committees.

This is a **could** question with a **supplemental statement** that establishes the second visualization as the accurate representation of the question's conditions. Note that "could be false" also implies "could be true." It also is true that "could be false" subsumes that which must be false. From the visualizations, you determine that Carter is a member of all four committees. Since all answer choices but (D) provide that Carter is a member of one or more of the committees, it is the only answer choice that could be false. Answer choice (D) is the best option.

4. If Gates is the only director that the Audit and Finance committees have in common, which of the following must be true?

   (A) Gates is a not a member of the Planning Committee.
   (B) Gates is a not member of the Shareholder Relations Committee.
   (C) The Planning and Shareholder Relations committees do not have at least one member in common.
   (D) The Finance and Planning committees do not have at least one member in common.
   (E) Gates is a member of all four Board committees.

This is a **must** question with a supplemental statement that establishes the second visualization as the accurate representation of the question's conditions. Note on the visualization that Gates (Z) is a member of the Audit and Finance committees and a member of the Planning and Shareholder Relations committees. Since option (E) is the only one that satisfies the conditions of the question, it is the best answer choice. Also notice that this question is a variation of the previous question 3. The LSAT often uses this technique with Relationships questions. Be on the alert for it!

5. If Martin is the only director that the Planning and Shareholder Relations committees have in common, which of the following could be true?

   (A) Martin has to belong to both the Finance and Shareholder Relations committees.
   (B) Martin does not belong to both the Audit and Finance committees.
   (C) The Finance and Planning committees have to have only Martin in common.
   (D) Martin has to belong to at least three different Board committees.
   (E) Martin has to belong to all four Board committees.

This is a **could** question with a **supplemental statement** that suggests that visualization two applies to the question. However, nothing in the supplemental statement provides that some Board member other than Martin could not satisfy the first condition in the statement and that some other Board member, also not Martin, could not satisfy the second condition in the statement. Put another way, nothing in the conditions requires that Martin is the Board member that is common to all committees. This being true, all answer choices that require that Martin be on committees are not true and each is not the best answer choice. On the other hand, nothing requires that Martin be a member of either the Audit or Finance committees, thus answer choice (B) meets the conditions specified, it could be true and is the best answer choice.

6. If Titus and Varga are the only members of the Finance Committee, and neither is a member of all four committees, which of the following must be true?

- **(A)** Titus is a member of the Audit and Planning committees.
- **(B)** Titus and Varga are not both members of the Audit Committee.
- **(C)** Titus is a member of the Audit and Shareholder Relations committees.
- **(D)** Titus and Varga are not both members of the Planning Committee.
- **(E)** Varga is a member of the Planning and Shareholder Relations committees.

This is a **must** question with a **supplemental statement** that establishes the first visualization as the accurate one. By reference to that visualization, you can determine that Titus and Varga are X and Y, but you have no information to help you establish which is which. You consider the answer options in order. As to (A), Titus *could* be a member of the Audit and Planning committees. Since *could* is a wrong answer to a **must** question, option (A) is dumped. As to (B), the visualization establishes that Titus and Varga are both members of the Audit Committee, so it *cannot* be that they are not. This makes option (B) wrong, and you dump it. As to (C), Titus *could* be a member of the Audit and Shareholder Relations committees. As with (A), *could* is a wrong answer to a **must** question, so (C) is dumped. As to (D), Titus and Varga *cannot* both be members of the Planning Committee. Option (D) satisfies the conditions and is the best choice. There is no need to consider option (E).

WHAT IS THE MAP CONTEXT?

You are not likely to be familiar with the **map** context, which is a type of spatial or relative-location exercise. It has many of the attributes of the line-up, although line-ups are deployed in two-dimensional space instead of in a single line.

A few terms the LSAT consistently uses are worthy of review. To indicate a precise direction, the LSAT uses such terms as "due," "directly," or "exactly." Therefore, "due north" means precisely north—0° and 360° on the compass. "North" means northerly; that is, anything in the northern direction bounded by the east/north/west hemisphere. "Northeast" means northeasterly; that is, anything in the direction of the quadrant bounded by north and east. These conventions apply to each of the compass directions—north, east, south, and west.

HOW DO YOU WORK WITH THE MAP CONTEXT?

As with the other contexts, you begin by reading the statement, with its facts and rules.

There are nine gasoline stations in the town of Mountain View: Amoco, Boron, Chevron, Exxon, Gulf, Hess, Mobil, Shell, and Texaco. The stations are located as follows:

> Amoco, Boron, Chevron, and Exxon are all west of Gulf, and all of the others are east of Gulf.
>
> Boron and Chevron are both due west of Gulf, and Amoco is due north of Boron.
>
> Exxon is due south of Chevron, and Mobil is due northeast of Gulf.
>
> Hess is due north of Mobil, and Shell and Texaco are both due south of Mobil.

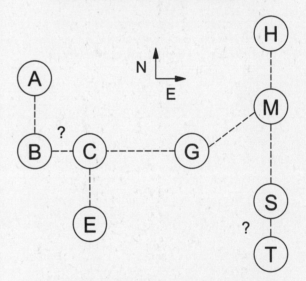

The statement establishes the map context and suggests that direction and distance will be the focus of the question set. A brief look at the questions confirms this suggestion. Now you record your visualization.

The facts tell you that there are nine stations: A, B, C, E, G, H, M, S, and T. These variables will be the nodes in the visualization. The differences in direction are expressed in relative terms, and the lines in the visualization will depict these transitive relationships. As always, check to be certain that each relationship is visualized, and be especially careful not to confuse direction with relative distance.

Complete your visualization, and consider the questions. Note that, because directions are relative, you should take care to consider the answer options from the position declared in the question. Remember to refer to the visualization only.

1. Hess lies in which direction from Chevron?

   (A) due east
   (B) southeast
   (C) due north
   (D) northeast
   (E) southwest

Even though it does not use the term, this is a **must** question. Locate C and H by referring to the visualization. H is east of C but also north. Thus, answer options (A), (B), and (C) cannot be true. They do not meet the conditions and are dumped. Option (D), however, does meet the north and east conditions of the question and is the best-answer option. There is no need to consider option (E).

2. If a person were to travel directly west from Mobil, what is the maximum number of stations the person could encounter?

   (A) 0
   (B) 1
   (C) 2
   (D) 3
   (E) 4

This is a **could** question. From M's position on the visualization, you determine that B, C, E, G, S, and T are all south and cannot be due west of M. *Cannot* is the wrong answer to a **could** question. H is north of M and *cannot* be due west of it. Again, *cannot* is the wrong answer to a **could** question. Since A is due north of B, which is southwest of M, A **could** be directly west of M, depending on how far north A is from B. All nine variables are thus accounted for, and only A **could** be directly west of M. Answer options (A), (C), (D), and (E) *cannot* be true; they do not satisfy the question conditions and are dumped. Option (B) satisfies the conditions and is the best answer.

3. Which of the following could be true?

   (A) The Hess, Shell, and Texaco stations are south of the Gulf station.
   (B) The Boron, Chevron, and Exxon stations are north of the Gulf station.
   (C) The Amoco, Shell, and Texaco stations are north of the Gulf station.
   (D) The Hess and Amoco stations are south of the Gulf station.
   (E) The Chevron and Boron stations are southwest of the Gulf station.

This is **could** question. From G's position on the visualization, you determine that H is north of M, and, because M is northeast of G, H must also be northeast of G, not south. Since *cannot* is the only wrong answer to a **could** question, you have determined that (A) *cannot* be true; it is a wrong-answer choice. Answer choice (B) provides that both Boron and Chevron are north of the Gulf station. The second condition in the problem statement declares that B and C are "due" west of G. Therefore, by virtue of this rule, they *cannot* be north of G and answer choice (B) does not meet the required conditions of the problem; (B) is a wrong-answer choice. You next determine that A is north of B, and, because B is due west of G, A must also be north of G. You know that S and T are due south of M, but they could be north or south of G. Option (C) satisfies the conditions of the question and is the best answer. There is no reason to consider the remaining answer choices because only one choice satisfies all required conditions.

4. How many stations must be south of the Boron station?

   (A) 1
   (B) 2
   (C) 3
   (D) 4
   (E) 5

This is a **must** question. Referring to the location of B on the visualization, you determine that A is north of B, and both B and C are due west of G. This means A, C, and G *cannot* be south of B. Because E is south of C, and both B and C are due west of G, E must also be south of B. Since *could* and *cannot* are the only wrong answers to a **must** question, A, C, and G do not satisfy the conditions of the question, and E does. Since B is due west of G, M is northeast of G, and H is north of M, H and M *cannot* be south of B and do not satisfy the conditions of the question. There is no information about how far south S and T are from M, so they could be as far south as to be south of B, but they might not be. S and T do not satisfy the conditions. Answer options (B), (C), (D), and (E) *cannot* be true; none of them meets the question conditions. Answer option (A) does satisfy the conditions of the question, and it is the best-answer option.

5. Which of the following could be true?

(A) The Amoco station is due west of the Gulf station.

(B) The Exxon station is west of the Boron station.

(C) The Boron station is east of the Exxon station.

(D) The Hess station is due east of the Chevron station.

(E) The Mobil station is south of the Exxon station.

This is a **could** question. By referring to your visualization, you see that A's east-west position is determined by the position of B. Since B and C are due west of G, and A is due north of B, A *cannot* be west of G. Thus answer choice (A) *cannot* be true; it is a wrong answer to a **could** question. The visualization shows you that E's east-west position is determined by the position of C. Since C **could** be west of B or vice versa, E **could** be west of B. Option (C) satisfies the question conditions and is the best-answer choice. There is no reason to consider the remaining answer choices because only one choice satisfies all required conditions.

6. What is the maximum number of stations that could be southeast of the Amoco station?

(A) 4
(B) 5
(C) 6
(D) 7
(E) 8

This is a **could** question. Studying the visualization, you determine that A is due north of B and, consequently, that B *cannot* be southeast of A. Since *cannot* is the only wrong answer to a **could** question, B does not satisfy the conditions of the question. There is no information in the statement or question from which you can determine that B and A are not westernmost among the stations, nor can you determine how far north of B station A is located. So if A is located sufficiently far north, all stations other than B **could** be southeast of A. This means that seven stations **could** be southeast

of A, and answer options (A), (B), (C), and (E) *cannot* be true. They do not meet the conditions and are dumped. Option (D) does satisfy the conditions and is the best-answer option.

WHAT IS THE SCHEDULE CONTEXT?

You may have some familiarity with the schedule (or "assignment") context. As used on the LSAT, it expands upon the complication of the cluster context, with some conditions applying to individuals, some to locations, some to times, and some to combinations of the three. This complication generally makes the schedule context the most difficult of the five Relationships contexts, which is why you should plan to work on schedule problems last when working on the Relationships section-test of the LSAT.

HOW DO YOU WORK WITH THE SCHEDULE CONTEXT?

You begin, as with all Relationships questions, by reading the statement to establish the facts and rules. The sample problem that follows is probably more difficult than any you will find on the LSAT. It is included to make the point that appearances can be deceiving. Despite its difficulty, the question set can be managed by following the Relationships protocol that is quickly becoming familiar to you.

A circus presents a twelve-act show in three rings. Ring 1 is adjacent to ring 2, which is adjacent to ring 3. During a show, which is divided into four equal segments, each act is presented exactly once. Three acts are presented simultaneously in each segment. The acts are: acrobats, bears, clowns, dogs, elephants, horses, jugglers, lions, seals, trapeze artists, unicyclists, and wire-walkers.

> Only ring 2 has wire-walking, unicycling, and trapeze rigging.
>
> The lions and bears must perform in ring 3, the only ring with a cage.
>
> Because of the cage, the clowns, elephants, and horses cannot perform in ring 3.
>
> Two adjacent rings may not present an animal act at the same time.
>
> The acrobats, dogs, and lions perform at the same time.
>
> The trapeze artists and wire-walkers cannot follow immediately after each other, and the clowns must perform between the two to provide relief from the tension.

The many facts and rules tell you that this is the schedule context and suggest that order and location are the ideas on which the question set will focus. A brief survey of the questions confirms this suggestion. Now you are ready to visualize a schedule.

The facts tell you that there are twelve acts (individuals), four time slots, and three rings (locations). The individuals are A, B, C, D, E, H, J, L, S, T, U, and W. The intersection of time and location determines the nodes of your visualization, which results in a 3 x 4 matrix. Check to be certain that each variable is included, and apply the rules to the individuals, noting the results in the matrix as follows.

The first rule tells you that T, U, and W perform only in ring 2. The second rule tells you that L and B perform only in ring 3. Since rule three provides that animal acts cannot be presented in adjacent rings at the same time, rule four provides that dogs and lions (and acrobats) perform at the same time, and rule two provides that lions perform in ring 3, it follows that dogs must perform in ring 1 (not adjacent to another animal act) and acrobats in ring 2. *You have now determined all of the acts for ring 2: A, T, U, and W.*

Rule two provides that C, E, and H cannot perform in ring 3, and ring 2 is full, so C, E, and H must perform in ring 1 with D. *This determines all of the acts for ring 1: C, D, E, and H.*

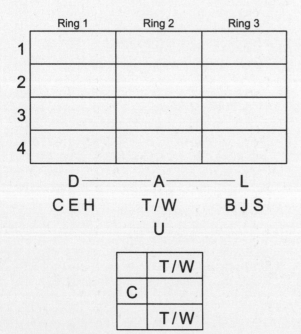

The remaining acts must perform in ring 2. *Thus you have determined all of the acts for ring 3: B, J, L, and S.*

Take note that the clowns must perform between the trapeze artists and the wire-walkers.

1. Which of the following must be true?

    (A) There are no animal acts in ring 1.
    (B) There are no animal acts in ring 2.
    (C) All acts presented in ring 3 are animal acts.
    (D) All acts presented in ring 2 are animal acts.
    (E) Animal acts perform in all three rings.

This is a **must** question. Beginning with answer option (A), you refer to your visualization and determine that dogs perform in ring 1. Option (A) *cannot* be true, as it does not satisfy the conditions of the question, and is dumped. Moving on to option (B), you refer to the visualization and determine that A, T, U, and W perform there. None is an animal act, so option (B) is true, does satisfy the conditions of the question, and is the best answer. There is no reason to consider options (C), (D), and (E).

2. Which three acts CANNOT start the show in rings 1, 2, and 3, respectively?

    (A) elephants, trapeze artists, bears
    (B) horses, unicyclists, seals
    (C) dogs, acrobats, lions
    (D) clowns, wire-walkers, jugglers
    (E) elephants, unicyclists, jugglers

This is a **cannot** question. Beginning with answer option (A), you refer to the visualization and determine that E performs in ring 1, T in ring 2, and B in ring 3. There is no other information to suggest that it **cannot** be true, so option A *could* be true, does not satisfy the conditions of the question, and is dumped. Working with option (B), you refer to the visualization and determine that H performs in ring 1, U in ring 2, and S in ring 3. As with option (A), option (B) *could* be true and is therefore dumped. Answer option (C) goes the same way, since (D) performs in ring 1, together with A in ring 2 and L in ring 3, and option (C) could be true. When you arrive at option (D), you refer to the visualization and determine that C performs in ring 1, W in ring 2, and J in ring 3. However, C *must* perform between W and T; therefore, C and W **cannot** perform at the same time, and option (D) **cannot** be true, satisfies the conditions of the question, and is the best answer. There is no reason to consider option (E).

3. If the lions are presented in the first segment, which of the following must be true?

(A) The clowns are the third act presented.
(B) The elephants are the second act presented.
(C) The wire-walkers are the fourth act presented.
(D) The horses are the first act presented.
(E) The bears are the third act presented.

This is a **must** question with a **supplemental statement**. The supplemental statement dictates that D (ring 1), A (ring 2), and L (ring 3) are the first acts presented. This means that either T or W **must** perform second in ring 2, since C **must** perform between them. This means that C **must** be among the third acts presented. Answer option (A) **must** be true, satisfies the conditions of the question, and is the best answer. There is no reason to consider options (B), (C), (D), and (E).

4. If the trapeze act is presented second, which of the following could be true?

(A) The elephant act is presented second.
(B) The lion act is presented third.
(C) The clown act is presented fourth.
(D) The wire-walkers' act is presented third.
(E) The acrobats' act is presented last.

This is a **could** question with a **supplemental statement**. From the supplemental statement that T is presented second and the requirement that an act be presented between it and W, it follows that W must be presented fourth. Since C must be presented between T and W, it must be third. We know that D, A, and L must be presented together, and the only time left for them to perform is first.

Answer choice (A) tells you that E performs second. Referring to the visualization, you determine that there is no reason this *cannot* be true. Since this option satisfies the question conditions, you circle answer choice (A) as the best-answer choice. Because there is only one answer choice that meets all of the conditions of the problem, there is no reason to consider options (B), (C), (D), and (E).

5. If the acrobats are presented in the first segment, which of the following CANNOT be true?

(A) The unicyclists are presented second.
(B) The horses are presented second.
(C) The seals are presented second.
(D) The jugglers are presented second.
(E) The elephants are presented second.

This is a **cannot** question with a **supplemental statement**. The supplemental statement dictates that D, A, and L are the first acts presented. Either W or T must perform second in ring 2, since C must perform between them. This means that U must be among the third acts presented. Answer option (A) *cannot* be true, satisfies the conditions of the question, and is the best answer. There is no reason to consider options (B), (C), (D), and (E).

6. If the clowns and dogs are presented in the second and fourth segments, respectively, which of the following could be true?

(A) The unicyclists are presented first.
(B) The horses are presented third.
(C) The wire-walkers are presented second.
(D) The acrobats are presented first.
(E) The elephants are presented fourth.

This is a **could** question with a **supplemental statement**. The supplemental statement dictates that D, A, and L are the fourth acts presented. Either W or T must perform first in ring 2, since C must perform second between them. This means that U *cannot* be among the first acts presented. Answer option (A) *cannot* be true, does not satisfy the conditions of the question, and is dumped. As to answer option (B), supplemental statement says that C performs second and D fourth in ring 1. This means that E or H **could** perform third, since there is no information that dictates they cannot. Answer option (B) **could** be true, satisfies the conditions of the question, and is the best answer. There is no reason to consider answer options (C), (D), and (E).

A practice exercise

To get a sense of each of the types of Relationships questions, turn to one of the complete tests in the book. Scan through each of the Relationships sets and identify the type of context that each question set presents.

Success Session 8

In this session you will work with Arguments problems separately from Passages. There are two Arguments section-tests in every LSAT. This means that Arguments comprise about half of all of the questions on the test. Quantitatively, Arguments are twice as important as other question types. This means that you should concentrate on Arguments until you are performing consistently with them.

WHAT IS THE FUNDAMENTAL APPROACH TO ARGUMENTS PROBLEMS?

An Arguments section-test contains between 3,000 and 4,500 words, with 4,000 the average. If you use all of the time allotted to reach the section-test material, you must read at the rate of about 115 words per minute. While not too fast for careful reading, this is not a slow pace. Taking into account the time you need to make decisions about answer options, you may find that such a reading pace is demanding and difficult to maintain.

Your pace when reading carefully will influence your optimal balance between speed and accuracy. You should also be mindful of the fact that answer options, not statements, provide much of the reading burden in an Arguments section-test. In order to keep your test-taking mechanics consistent throughout, there is a small task you should complete before you begin an Arguments section-test. Only one or two Arguments questions are based on a common statement, so the questions are not presented in sets. It is up to you to establish the question-answer sets for each Arguments section-test.

✔ **YOU, RATHER THAN THE LSAT, PACKAGE THE QUESTIONS INTO SETS.**

You will package the questions into sets of six. Sets are easily built by combining questions 1 through 6, 7 through 12, etc., as summarized below. In this way, you create four sets of Arguments questions in each 35-minute section-test.

- Question set 1: questions 1–6
- Question set 2: questions 7–12
- Question set 3: questions 13–18
- Question set 4: questions 19–24+

IN WHAT ORDER SHOULD ARGUMENTS QUESTION SETS BE CONSIDERED?

Previously it was stated that you should work on the least difficult question set first and the most difficult last. However, when this principle is applied to Arguments questions, a problem arises. Because Arguments question-answer sets do not share a common statement, it is very time-consuming to place them in a clear order of difficulty. In general, the effort it takes to identify the questions in terms of their difficulty outweighs any advantage you might realize from the effort. So, simply work through Arguments questions in the order in which they appear.

Instead of reordering question sets according to their difficulty, you will approach the questions according to your test plan. If your plan is to complete all four question sets in the section-test, you will work through the questions in sets of six.

If your plan is to complete three question sets, you have a choice of two strategies. The more straightforward one is to work through the first three sets of questions and guess the answers to the fourth set. A more sophisticated strategy is to omit six questions as you work through the four question sets. Pass over six long question-answer combinations or question-answer sets that you find confusing, since you have the poorest prospects of selecting the best-answer options to these questions. (Of course, you will select answers to the omitted questions by guessing.) Either question-selection strategy will meet the objectives of your test plan and maximize your wrong-answer advantage.

If your plan is to complete two question sets in a section-test, you apply the strategy described above, in this instance either working through the first two sets of questions and guessing your answers on the last two sets or omitting twelve questions as you work through the four question sets, passing over twelve long question-and-answer combinations or confusing questions.

HOW ARE ARGUMENTS PROBLEMS CONSTRUCTED?

Arguments are generally drawn from informal sources. Letters to the editor are good sources, because they are often implausible and unpersuasive while appearing to be logical. Advertisements are also used for source material, because they often encourage unjustified assumptions. Books, periodicals, editorials, speeches, and reported conversations provide Arguments statements, too. Whatever the source, the statement has usually been heavily edited to ensure that it is compatible with the LSAT format.

Each argument is selected because it has three major characteristics. **Evidence**, or a premise, is always involved. And a point or purpose—the **conclusion**—is also involved. A **structured process** connects the evidence and conclusion. This process is sometimes called reasoning, and it accounts for the Arguments sections being called tests of "logical reasoning" by many people. This designation is misleading, however, since no formal logic is required, even when the form and content of the argument are unfamiliar.

✔**NO KNOWLEDGE OF FORMAL LOGIC IS REQUIRED FOR YOU TO HANDLE ARGUMENTS PROBLEMS EFFECTIVELY.**

To summarize, every argument is selected because it involves evidence that is used to support or reach a conclusion through a structured process. But the customary order of a series of pieces of evidence leading to a conclusion is not always followed by the LSAT. The order of presentation varies. Sometimes the conclusion is placed in the statement. It may come first, last, or between pieces of evidence. It also may be placed in the answer options. And evidence may be placed in the statement or in the answer options.

Possible arrangements of Arguments problems look like this:

Evidence → Conclusion
Conclusion ← Evidence
Evidence → Conclusion ← Evidence

HOW DO ARGUMENTS QUESTIONS WORK?

As you know, the profile of an Arguments problem is the same as for other LSAT problems. There are directions, a statement, questions, and answer options.

The Directions

In the directions the LSAT tells you to evaluate the reasoning contained in brief statements and that the best answer is a "conceivable solution to the particular problem posed" by the question. The LSAT also says that the best answer is the one that does not require you to make what are by common-sense standards implausible, superfluous, or incompatible assumptions.

For many test-takers, these directions obfuscate rather than clarify what is expected of them. It is difficult to extract the practical meaning of the directions from the language used by the LSAT. However, the directions can be translated into more familiar terms, especially when it comes to wrong-answer options. And you know how important it is to your performance to be able to identify wrong-answer options to LSAT questions. Identifying and dumping wrong-answer options is the most efficient way of selecting the best-answer options—the cream of the crop.

To reiterate, a wrong-answer option is one that does not satisfy the conditions of the statement and question. Thus, if the question seeks an answer that **must** satisfy the conditions, answer options that *could* or *cannot* satisfy the conditions are wrong choices. If the question seeks an answer that **could** satisfy the conditions, options that *cannot* satisfy the conditions are wrong. And last, if the question seeks an answer that **cannot** satisfy the conditions, answers that *must* or *could* satisfy the conditions are wrong.

There are two basic reasons why an answer option can fail to satisfy the required conditions of the question: One is that it conflicts directly with the statement, and the other is that it makes unjustified assumptions. Directly conflicting options are usually not difficult to identify.

In the matter of the unjustified assumption, the wrong answer looks like it satisfies the required conditions only because you make a related but unjustified assumption. So all you have to do is avoid making unjustified assumptions when working through Arguments questions—this seems to pose no great challenge.

And it is not much of a challenge if you heed the directions we looked at earlier. Translated, the LSAT's directions tell you that unjustified assumptions are those that exceed the terms of the statement, are inconsistent with the terms of the statement, or are unfounded given the terms of the statement. Avoid these things, and you will identify wrong-answer options readily and efficiently select best answers, right? Not exactly!

Unfortunately, experience shows that this is easier said than done. Assumptions are the stock-in-trade of the able student, for whom the ability to justify assumptions and positions persuasively is a necessary skill rewarded in examination papers, essays, debates, and other such exercises. The temptation to apply this ability in the context of the LSAT can be almost irresistible to the able student. When a test-taker gives in to this temptation, the result is the erroneous selection of a wrong-answer option as the best answer to an Arguments question, so fight the unjustified-assumption trap with everything you've got. Your Arguments section-test performance will benefit.

✔ **AVOID EVERY ASSUMPTION THAT IS NOT CLEARLY SUPPORTED BY THE ARGUMENTS STATEMENT.**

The Statement

Arguments statements are generally short. Their brevity can make them seem deceptively simple. The brevity is often the result of the LSAT's strategy of obfuscation by omission. Many Arguments questions seek omitted evidence or a conclusion—in other words, the information required to complete the argument.

Arguments statements always involve a position or point of view. Although the position or point of view may not be clearly articulated, the statement is never neutral. Identify the point of view presented. It makes dealing with the problem much more straightforward.

A statement consists of 75 to 125 words. It defines the context for either one or two question-and-answer sets. Usually a statement supporting two questions has a relatively smaller reading burden than a statement supporting only one.

The Question

Arguments questions are straightforward. They directly present the decision that must be made. They do not contain supplemental statements, which means that questions never modify or add to the argument. In most section-tests, there are more instances of the statement supporting one question than two. When two questions are supported by a single statement, each question is independent of the other.

As was discussed in the preceding session, there are two basic Arguments question types: **description** questions and **extension** questions. There are two variations on the description question:

- One requires you to recognize the point, purpose, premise, or reasoning of a statement.
- The other requires you to recognize a stated presumption.

There are four variations on the extension question:

- The first requires you to identify a pattern.
- The second requires you to identify inferences and conclusions.
- The third requires you to identify assumptions.
- The fourth requires you to assess evidence.

These six variations in description and extension questions cover all of the questions that will appear in the Arguments section-test.

✔ **YOU NOW CAN PREDICT EVERY ARGUMENTS QUESTION THAT WILL APPEAR ON THE LSAT.**

The Answers

The answer options complete the Arguments question; without them the question has little practical meaning. Take a typical Arguments question: "Which of the following is the underlying point of the above?" You are being asked, "What's the point?" As you know, this is not an invitation to extemporize or demonstrate your ability to synthesize. Your activity should be confined to the selection of the answer options that best satisfy the conditions of the question and statement. You achieve this by viewing each answer option in relation to the question. Only then can you select answers in the way the LSAT requires.

✔**THE ANSWER OPTIONS PRESENT YOU WITH A FIELD OF CHOICES FROM WHICH YOU MUST DECIDE. YOU SELECT ONLY FROM THE FIVE OPTIONS PRESENTED.**

Your objective with Arguments questions is to identify wrong-answer options quickly so that you can locate the best answer to the question posed.

In addition to obfuscating by omission, the LSAT will attempt to disguise both the question and the wrong-answer options. Often, the LSAT does not present the question explicitly. This means that you must first determine whether you are being asked to select the answer option that must, could, or cannot satisfy the conditions of the question and statement. And, until you work through the answer options, it is very difficult to tell which statement conditions are relevant and which are not. In order to make the best use of the time available, you need to minimize the number of times you deal with an answer option. The decision technique you will use to work through answer options involves **comparison** and **contrast**.

Comparing an answer option against the statement only one time meets the objective of efficiency. Repeating the same process is a time-wasting score drain. The answer options are compared against the conditions required by the statement and question. When the comparison makes it clear that an answer option fails to satisfy the conditions, you know that it is a wrong-answer option and chuck it.

If comparison fails to produce all four wrong answers, contrast the remaining options (usually two). Using this technique often makes it possible to identify differences that highlight the failure of one of the answer choices to satisfy the conditions required by the statement and question.

✔**COMPARISON AND CONTRAST FACILITATE YOUR IDENTIFICATION OF WRONG ANSWERS AND YOUR DECISION MAKING ABOUT ANSWER OPTIONS.**

To review the patterns of wrong-answer options, think of them in terms of an *if-then* format. *If* you determine that the question seeks an answer option that **could** satisfy required conditions, *then* options that *cannot* satisfy all of the conditions are wrong. These **could** questions are the most frequently asked in the Arguments section-test. *If* you determine that the question seeks an answer option that **must** satisfy

required conditions, *then* options that *could* or *cannot* satisfy all of the conditions are wrong. And *if* you determine that a question seeks an answer option that **cannot** satisfy required conditions, *then* options that *must* or *could* satisfy all of the conditions are wrong.

To make wrong-answer options attractive, the LSAT disguises them by using the **same-language**, **too-little-too-much**, **true but**, and **false-assertion** disguises we have met before. The patterns and disguises are combined in the following summary of wrong-answer options.

For **could** questions, wrong-answer options are those that *cannot* satisfy required conditions, even though they use

- the **same-language** disguise
- the **too-little-too-much** disguise
- the **true but** disguise
- the **false-assertion** disguise

For **must** questions, wrong-answer options are those that *could* or *cannot* satisfy required conditions, even though they use

- the **same-language** disguise
- the **too-little-too-much** disguise
- the **true but** disguise
- the **false-assertion** disguise

For **cannot** questions, wrong-answer options are those that *must* or *could* satisfy required conditions, even though they use

- the **same-language** disguise
- the **too-little-too-much** disguise
- the **true but** disguise
- the **false-assertion** disguise

Knowing wrong-answer patterns and disguises is advantageous to you, as is knowing that the LSAT usually includes just one very attractive wrong-answer option among the four offered. When you combine this knowledge with the ability to predict the six basic questions that appear and reappear on the Arguments section-test, you will be ready for anything.

WHAT IS THE BEST RESPONSE TECHNIQUE FOR ARGUMENTS QUESTIONS?

Even though the question appears after the statement, the first thing you do is *read the question*. You need to determine whether it is a **could**, **must**, or **cannot** question. Note your decisions next to the question. You want to be able to tell as quickly as possible which information in the statement is relevant to the question and which is superfluous. Reading the question first gives you clues about what will be relevant.

Now *read the statement*. As you do so, highlight or underline key words, assertions, and the conclusion, if there is one. If there is no conclusion in the statement, it is likely that the question will ask for a conclusion in some form.

Next, *work through each answer option*. As you work through the answer options, you will use comparison and contrast to identify the options that fit a wrong-answer pattern, keeping alert for disguises. When you find a condition in an answer option that fails to satisfy the requirements of the question or statement, you chuck it. Repeating this process as necessary, you *select the best answer option and circle it in the test book*.

Once you have completed all of the questions in the set of six, you *transfer all your answers to the answer sheet* at the same time. This gives you a natural, albeit brief, break before you move on to the next Arguments question-answer set.

HOW DO YOU WORK WITH THE SIX BASIC ARGUMENTS QUESTIONS?

The LSAT uses six basic question types in the Arguments section-test. The techniques used to work through them are detailed in the following paragraphs. These techniques are applicable to any version or variation of the six questions. It might also help you familiarize yourself with the thinking required if, after this discussion, you review each question and answer option, specifically identifying the disguises used by the LSAT. (For example, option (C) in question 4 uses the **same language** as the statement to disguise the wrong answer. Option (B) in question 3 takes advantage of the **true but** disguise, and option (B) in question 1 applies the **false-assertion** disguise to a wrong-answer choice.)

Description Questions

Description questions make direct reference to the argument. There is no need to go beyond the argument to identify the answer option that satisfies the conditions of the question and statement. Description questions take two forms. The first asks you to identify a point, purpose, premise, or form of reasoning used in the argument. The second asks you to identify a stated presumption.

A *what's-the-point?* question uses a direct format that takes the form "Which of the following best describes (or is) the point, purpose, premise, or form of reasoning used in the argument?" An example follows. Remember to read the question first.

1. Too little staging rather than too much is the failure of producers of wild animal movies. The indifference recently displayed by an "Animals in the Wild" film crew is hard to excuse as it zealously filmed a newly born killer whale agonizingly drowning in an overwhelming flood tide.

Which of the following is the underlying point of the above?

(A) Producers should not stage animal action shots.

(B) Producers should document the inhumanity of whalers, because their cruelty can be stopped only by exposure.

(C) Producers should not continue as observers when doing so is incompatible with humane behavior.

(D) Producing real-life films is a brutal business, because it requires people to sacrifice their feelings in order to record events.

(E) Producers should commit themselves to reducing suffering and promoting humane behavior.

The question in this example asks you to select the answer option that **could** express the point of the statement. The first sentence of the statement clearly accepts staging, whereas answer choice (A) rejects it. Thus, (A) cannot satisfy statement conditions and is wrong. Answer option (B) cannot satisfy required conditions because it refers to matters not involved in the statement, such as the inhumanity of whalers and the prevention of cruelty. Options (D) and (E) are wrong for the same reason as (B). They refer to matters not involved in the statement, such as people's feelings and their obligations. Thus, answer option (C) is the best selection, since it does not require anything inconsistent with the statement.

The second form of description question asks you to identify a *stated presumption*. The format for this question type is usually direct, although the LSAT varies the question structure.

The following example uses a conversation structure. Read the question first.

2. *Mark*: Everyone who was a fighter pilot during the Korean War suffered battle fatigue.

Harry: That is untrue. Many veterans of the Korean War who were in the infantry had an acute psychological reaction to their wartime experience.

Harry's response indicates that he interpreted Mark's remark to mean that

(A) fighter pilots are more likely to have suffered battle fatigue than any others

(B) only those who were fighter pilots suffered from battle fatigue

(C) battle fatigue is a mental rather than physical reaction to stress

(D) flying fighter planes was more stressful than being a foot soldier

(E) some who were not fighter pilots suffered battle fatigue

The question in this example requires careful reading. It asks you what Harry presumes Mark meant. Answer options (A) and (D) *cannot* satisfy the required conditions because they compare such items as the likelihood of battle fatigue and differences in job stress. Nothing in the statement suggests such comparisons. Option (C) *cannot* satisfy the required conditions because there is nothing in the statement to suggest a disagreement about the nature of battle fatigue. Option (E) *cannot* satisfy the required conditions because it is Harry's position, not Harry's interpretation of Mark's position. Option (B) is the best selection because it does not conflict with the conditions of the statement in any way.

Extension Questions

Extension questions require you to go beyond the argument to identify the answer option that satisfies the question and statement conditions. You will have to draw inferences or define assumptions or reach conclusions. The answer options do not connect to the statement directly.

Extension questions take four forms, in which you are asked to identify a matching pattern, determine inferences and conclusions, recognize assumptions required for a conclusion, or assess evidence.

Pattern questions ask you directly to select the answer option that has a structure or

principle in common with or analogous to that of the statement. Rarely, you might be asked to identify a logical flaw in a statement. It takes the form "The above is most like which of the following?"

3. The automation of industry throws people out of work; therefore, machines are harmful.

The argument above is most like which of the following?

(A) Hitler was a fascist; therefore, he was evil.

(B) Fatty foods are harmful; therefore, eating butter is dangerous.

(C) The senator steals public funds; therefore, he is dishonest.

(D) Alcoholic beverages are high in calories; therefore, beer is fattening.

(E) Pigeons spread disease; therefore, birds are nuisances.

This pattern-recognition question asks you to select the answer option that *could* satisfy the requirements of the statement and question. Many people approach such a question by trying to find a rational explanation for a similarity in subject matter between the statement and the answer option. This technique is not productive. Rather, you should compare the statement and answer option to determine a difference between them. Option (A) is wrong for a number of reasons. It *cannot* satisfy the question conditions because of the verb in the first phrase of the statement: "Throws" is active, while "was" in the answer is not. Also, the subject of the first and second phrases in the answer option is the same ("Hitler" and "he"), while in the statement it is different ("automation" and "machines"). Option (B) also exhibits the first-phrase verb difference ("throws" versus "are"). For the same reason, answer option (D) is wrong. There are other differences, if you want to seek them out, but you should avoid such unnecessary hunts when taking the test. Option (C) is also a wrong answer. The verb pattern in the statement and answer is the same, but the subject pattern is not: In the statement the subjects of the two phrases are different ("automation" and "machines"), but they are the same in the answer option ("senator" and "he"). So the best answer option is (E), which shares both the verb and subject patterns of the statement.

While the pattern is not always based on sentence structure, very often an analysis at the sentence level will quickly produce the best answer.

Inference and conclusion questions ask you to select the answer option that expresses an inference or conclusion drawn from the statement. The format is very direct, asking, "Which of the following conclusions can be logically inferred?"

4. Children perceive the world spontaneously and unself-consciously. But as they grow into adulthood, learning more facts about reality, they lose their capacity for direct perception and immediate response.

If the statements above are true, which of the following conclusions can be logically inferred?

(A) Children's perceptions are better than those of adults.

(B) Facts are unimportant in the process of perceiving.

(C) Children and adults do not perceive the world in the same way.

(D) It is impossible for adults to recapture spontaneous perception.

(E) Children do not distinguish clearly between fact and fantasy.

This conclusion question asks you to select the answer option that *could* satisfy the requirements of the statement and question. Answer option (A) does not satisfy the conditions because it introduces a value term, "better," as a conclusion. There is nothing in the statement or question to suggest values. Option (B) is wrong for the same reason—the value term here is "unimportant." Option (D) is wrong because it declares that something cannot be recaptured, when the statement gives no indication that what is lost—spontaneous perception—cannot be regained. Option (E) introduces two concepts, fantasy and distinguishing, that are not suggested in any way by the statement. This leaves option (C) as the best answer, since it offers nothing contrary to the conditions of the statement and question.

Assumption questions ask you to select the answer option that provides the evidence necessary to permit the conclusion in the statement to be reached. The question format is usually direct. It asks, "The above requires (or is based on) which of the following assumptions?"

5. Since Byron's fingers are so short and stubby, he will never be an outstanding pianist.

The statement above is based on which of the following assumptions?

(A) The size and shape of fingers are important attributes for a professional musical career.

(B) Piano playing requires long, thin fingers.

(C) Physical characteristics can affect how well one plays the piano.

(D) Byron is not a particularly able pianist.

(E) No amount of practice will make a difference in Byron's playing ability.

The question asks you to select the answer option or options that express the assumptions that *could* be made in order to satisfy the requirements of the statement and question. Recall that you must always try to identify the conclusion when you read an Arguments statement. In this statement, the conclusion is "he will never be an outstanding pianist." Answer option (A) is a wrong answer to a *could* question. The conclusion in the statement involves only the type of pianist ("outstanding"), not whether the pianist is an amateur or professional or has a musical career or not. The references made in (A) *cannot* account for the conclusion, and it is a wrong answer. Because the statement clearly implies that Byron plays the piano, even though he does not have long, thin fingers, answer choice (B) contradicts the statement and cannot satisfy its conditions.

"Short" and "stubby" are physical characteristics. If physical characteristics can affect the way a person plays the piano, as answer choice (C) states, the length and shape of Byron's fingers could account for the conclusion that he will never be an outstanding pianist. Thus answer choice (C) is the best answer. There is no need to consider answer options (D) and (E) since (C) satisfies all of the conditions in the question, and there is only one answer option that satisfies all conditions.

Evidence-assessment questions appear in a number of forms in the Arguments section-test. They ask you to select the answer option that strengthens or weakens an argument, criticizes an argument, or distinguishes between fact and opinion in an argument. The format for the evidence-assessment question varies, but it is usually direct.

6. The British economy is stagnant, which can only be the result of its overgenerous governmental programs of social aid.

Which of the following, if true, most seriously weakens the view expressed above?

- **(A)** Britain spends a lower percentage of its national income on medical care than does prosperous Germany.
- **(B)** Several countries in the world have found that certain governmental social-aid programs have absorbed an unexpectedly high percentage of government revenues.
- **(C)** The governmental social-aid programs of Britain meet many of the needs of its citizens and residents and yet cost less than similar programs elsewhere.
- **(D)** The Scandinavian nations, with more comprehensive governmental social-aid programs than Britain's, have similar economies that are thriving.
- **(E)** Italy, which has few governmental social-aid programs, has for many years been in economic difficulty to a degree that equals or exceeds that of Britain.

This evidence-assessment question asks you to select the answer option that **could** weaken the statement. The fact that the word "most" is used to modify "weaken" is of no importance; this degree of refinement is virtually never involved on the LSAT. You will need to identify the conclusion in the statement—"The British economy is stagnant."

Answer option (A) does not satisfy the requirements of the question and statement. It is wrong because nothing in the option suggests the proportion of income the Germans spend on social-aid programs. Also, it involves only medical care, which is just one social-aid program; therefore, it *cannot* be related to the statement. Options (B) and (C) *cannot* satisfy the statement conditions and are wrong because, among other things, they fail to indicate the condition ("stagnant"?) of the economies to which Britain's economy is being compared. Option (E) is wrong because it fails to indicate whether the amount Italy spends on its few social-aid programs is more, less, or the same as that spent by Britain. It *cannot* be related to the statement. This leaves (D) as the answer option that weakens the

argument, because nothing in it conflicts in any way with the statement, and it affirms that countries with more comprehensive social-aid programs and economies similar to Britain's are not stagnant ("thriving").

ARE THERE CUE CLUES IN ARGUMENTS PROBLEMS?

Arguments statements and answer options are replete with cue words. These words indicate the nature of the information that follows them. For example, the appearance of the word "therefore" cues you that the conclusion is coming up. There are a bundle of similar cue words. They are not worth committing to memory, but a read-through may prove beneficial to your test performance. Some conclusion cues follow.

- so
- indicates
- therefore
- suggests
- hence
- proves
- thus
- means
- accordingly
- shows
- can be inferred
- nevertheless
- results
- however
- follows

There are also a number of cue words whose presence generally indicates that the information that follows is evidence. The evidence that it cues may or may not be relevant. Representative words are listed below.

- given
- inasmuch as
- since
- as
- because
- but
- assume
- except
- suppose
- despite
- if
- notwithstanding
- insofar as
- although

Success Session 9

WHAT ARE THE FUNDAMENTALS OF PASSAGES PROBLEMS?

There is one Passages section-test on each LSAT, with four Passages problems in the section-test. Each Passages problem fits the LSAT profile: directions, a statement, a question, and answer options. Each statement supports a set of questions and answer options. There are seven questions per set, making the total number of questions in a section-test twenty-eight.

HOW ARE PASSAGES PROBLEMS CONSTRUCTED?

For the most part, Passages are taken from law reviews and similar journals. This is not to suggest that some knowledge of law is required or even beneficial in working through Passages problems. In fact, the statements are chosen and edited to avoid jargon and legalese. They involve diverse topics—from technical subjects to topics drawn from the social sciences, the humanities, and other fields.

✔ **PASSAGES STATEMENTS ARE CHOSEN FOR THEIR COMMON CHARACTERISTICS, NOT FOR THEIR SUBJECT MATTER.**

From the LSAT's perspective, the topic of the statement is irrelevant. What is critical to the LSAT is that the Passages statements have six major characteristics:

- point of purpose
- key words or concepts
- authorities
- enumerations
- unusual words or phrases
- competing perspectives

The fact that Passages problems have common characteristics that are the critical attributes necessitates an adjustment in the way you read. You have most likely been conditioned to read material of the type presented in material like Passages statements for information and understanding. However, successful performance on the LSAT Passages section-test depends upon you avoiding this conditioning.

✔ **WITH PASSAGES STATEMENTS, YOU READ FOR THE CHARACTERISTICS OF THE STATEMENT, NOT FOR INFORMATION OR UNDERSTANDING OF THE TOPIC.**

HOW DO YOU HANDLE ALL OF THE PASSAGES READING?

As you have seen from your previous work, Passages problems impose a substantial reading burden on test-takers—nearly twice that of the other LSAT section-tests. The Passages reading burden is a major factor in your performance on the Passages section-test, much more so than with Relationships and Arguments problems. There are between 4,000 and 7,500 words in a section-test. This means that to complete all of the reading in a long section-test, a pace above 200 words per minute must be maintained. The required pace can go even higher when the time needed to select the best-answer options is taken into account, since, for Passages problems, the questions and answer options require as much reading as the statements. It is difficult, if not impossible, to read carefully at this pace.

✔ **YOUR READING PACE CLEARLY INFLUENCES YOUR BALANCE BETWEEN SPEED AND ACCURACY.**

By testing your pace, you can estimate the time you will need to complete the reading in the Passages section-test. Read the following example carefully. Keep a record of the time it takes you to complete the reading. Then divide the number of words in the statement (some 550) by the number of minutes you took to read the statement. This tells you your speed at reading a Passages statement. Suppose you took 5 minutes to read the statement carefully: This means that you read the statement at a pace of 110 words per minute.

Line   Blackmail may be defined as the sale of information to an individual who would be incriminated by its publication, and at first glance it appears to be an efficient method

5   of private enforcement of the law (the moral as well as the positive law). The value of the information to the blackmailed individual is equal to the cost of the punishment that the individual will incur if 10 the information is communicated to the authorities and he is punished as a result, and so he will be willing to pay up to that amount to the blackmailer for the information. The individual is thereby punished, 15 and the punishment is the same as if he had been apprehended and convicted for the crime that the blackmailer has discovered, but the fine is paid to the blackmailer rather than to the state.

20   Why, then, is blackmail a crime? One scholar's answer is that it results in underdeterrence of crimes punished by nonpecuniary sanctions because the criminals lack the resources to pay an 25 optimal fine. The blackmailer will sell his information to the criminal for a price lower than the cost of punishment if the criminal cannot pay a higher price. A more persuasive explanation of why blackmail 30 follows directly from the decision to rely on a public monopoly of law enforcement in some areas of enforcement, notably criminal law. Were blackmail, a form of private enforcement, lawful, the public 35 monopoly of enforcement would be undermined. Overenforcement of the law would result if the blackmailer were able to extract the full fine from the offender. Alternatively, the blackmailer might sell his 40 incriminating information to the offender for a price lower than the statutory cost of punishment to the criminal, which would reduce the effective cost of punishment to the criminal below the level set by the 45 legislature. This problem, however, could be solved by a system of public bounties equal to the cost of punishment (or lower, to induce the enforcement industry to contract to optimal size). Then the black- 50 mailer could always claim a bounty from the state if the criminal was unable to pay a price equal to the optimal fine.

Consistent with this analysis, Axel's studies show that practices indistinguish- 55 able from blackmail, though not called by that name, are permitted in areas where the law is enforced privately rather than publicly because the overenforcement

problem is not serious. No one seems to 60 object to a person's collecting information about his or her spouse's adulterous activities and threatening to disclose that information in a divorce proceeding or other forum in order to extract maximum 65 compensation for the offending spouse's breach of the marital obligations.

Blackmail and bribery appear to be virtually identical practices from the standpoint of the analysis of private 70 enforcement. The blackmailer and the bribed official both receive payment in exchange for not enforcing the law. We therefore predict that in areas where there is a public monopoly of enforcement, 75 bribery, like blackmail, will be prohibited, while in areas where there is no public monopoly, it will be permitted. And so we observe. The settlement out of court of negligence claims is a form of perfectly 80 lawful bribery, although the term is not used in these situations because of its pejorative connotation.

If you read at the pace of 110 words per minute and assume a Passages section-test of about 5,000 words, you will be able to read 75 percent of the full burden of the Passages section-test or put another way, three of the four Passages problems. The reading burden puts a premium on the techniques you use to work through each Passages problem. You especially want to avoid rereading or other repetitive activities.

IN WHAT ORDER DO YOU CONSIDER PASSAGES PROBLEMS?

You should work on the least difficult Passages problem first and the most difficult last. There are two major factors determining Passages difficulty. The first and dominant one is the reading burden of the problem. (As elsewhere, "problem" refers to the combined statement, questions, and answer options.)

✔THE GREATER THE READING BURDEN, THE MORE DIFFICULT THE PROBLEM.

The other factor is the subject matter of the statement. While we have said that the statement subject matter is less significant than it appears to be, many test-takers are significantly less proficient at reading a statement about a subject they dislike or find difficult.

✔**REORDER PASSAGES PROBLEMS ACCORDING TO THEIR DIFFICULTY.**

You will proceed by working on the problems according to their degree of difficulty, from least to most difficult. This means that you must first rank the problems by length. (The greatest variation in length occurs within the combination of seven questions and answer options that follow each statement.) You then consider the subject matter of the statements—if a statement involves subject matter that is problematic for you, rank that statement last. Otherwise, work through Passages problems in the order of their length, with the shortest first and the longest last.

Of course, the number of problems you will work through depends on your test plan. If your plan is to complete all four Passages problems in the section-test, you will work through all the questions in sets of seven. If your plan is to complete three problems, you will work through your selected three sets of questions and guess your answer selections on the fourth set. If your plan is to complete two problems, you will work through the first two question sets and guess your answer selections on the last two sets.

How do Passages questions work?

The Directions

In the directions to Passages questions, the LSAT tells you to select the best answer to the question based upon what is stated and implied in the statement. Beyond acknowledging the presence of the two basic question types—the description and extension types—these directions do not give you any information.

The Statement

Passages statements obfuscate by their basic structure. They are relatively long, generally between 500 and 550 words, and much of the material in them is not relevant to the questions. But the length of the statement presents most readers with fewer difficulties than do its other attributes. The absence of familiar structure can be disconcerting, and there are no titles to go by. Each statement has been heavily edited beforehand, with the result that the purpose of the statement is unclear, especially since it appears outside of its original context. The statement is compressed into three to five paragraphs, and the paragraphs often do not reflect different topics or points. The grammar is generally awkward, and the writing is in a technical, rather than journalistic, style.

The line numbers placed beside each statement are used to mark five-line increments, which facilitates the making of references to statement material in the questions. When a question refers to a specific word in the statement, the line number is used to indicate the location of that word.

Opinion is involved in virtually every Passages statement, although the point of view, purpose, or position is often veiled. The form and substance these opinions take are likely to be unfamiliar to you, and they can be confusing if you let yourself become involved with them.

✔**OVERLOOKING FORM AND CONTENT PERMITS YOU TO AVOID CONFUSION AND FOCUS ON THE ELEMENTS OF THE STATEMENT THAT ARE REALLY INVOLVED IN THE QUESTIONS.**

You will recall that the pertinent elements of the statement are its point or purpose, key words or concepts, authorities, enumerations, unusual words or phrases, and competing perspectives. Most statements present competing perspectives, although the presentation may at first appear to be balanced by viewing the topic "on the one hand" and "on the other hand." Even if it is camouflaged, one of the views is preferred by the author. Key words and concepts usually can be identified by their being repeated or elaborated upon. References to authorities include such statements as "The Task Force study shows . . ." Enumerations are usually found in the statement and take the form "Examples of these are dogs, cats, canaries, tropical fish, and horses." Unusual words or phrases also appear regularly. Some examples are "syntactics," "on-all-fours," "credence goods," "post-Pigovian," "prose models," and "gentry controversy."

In other words, the statement presents elements upon which the set of questions and answer options is based. It supports all of the questions in the set.

The Question

Passages questions are limited in their coverage and structure. They directly state the decision to be made by test-takers. They do not contain supplemental statements. Passages questions do not modify or add to the statement, and each question is independent of every other one.

When a question refers to a line number, that reference ought to be taken in context. This means that you should consider the material before and after the specific reference at the same time that you look at the referenced material.

As you recall, there are two basic Passages questions types: description questions and extension questions. The variations on these questions are similar to those used in Arguments questions, but they are not exactly the same.

The three variations on the description question require you to select an answer option that presents:

- the summary, principal point, or purpose of the statement
- some specific detail
- some meaning in context

The summary, point, or purpose question almost always appears in Passages question sets. The four variations of the extension question require you to:

- identify a perspective
- identify a context
- identify a pattern
- assess evidence

These seven points cover all the types of questions that appear on a Passages section-test.

✔YOU NOW CAN PREDICT EVERY PASSAGES QUESTION THAT WILL APPEAR ON THE LSAT.

The Answers

The answer options complete the question, which, by itself, means very little. The typical Passages question asks, "Which of the following best summarizes the point?" It does no more than tell you that the selection of an answer option will be necessary. Only when it is connected to the answer options does the question become sufficiently specific to permit answer selection.

✔THE ANSWER OPTIONS PRESENT THE REAL DECISION TO YOU.

As with Arguments, you will use **comparison** and **contrast** to work through the answer options. These techniques assist you in detecting wrong-answer disguises and identifying differences between options.

With most Passages problems, it is not clear whether the question requires the selection of an answer option that must, could, or cannot satisfy the question and statement conditions. This means that, before you work through the answer options, you must first determine the nature and, to the degree possible, the focus of the question. Is it must, could, or cannot? Does it focus on an enumeration, authority, unusual word, or some other statement characteristic? By doing this, you can take best advantage of the time available, minimizing the number of times you deal with the statement and answer options.

✔REPEATED REVIEWS OF THE SAME MATERIAL ARE EFFICIENCY-BUSTERS OF THE WORST KIND.

Your efficiency objective is to compare an answer option against the statement conditions just once. When the comparison shows that an answer option fails to satisfy the conditions, you chuck it. In the contrast technique, one answer option is contrasted with another. This is useful when the comparison of an answer option against the required conditions has yielded more than one possible best answer. Contrasting answer options often identifies differences in them that make it clear that one or both fail to satisfy the required conditions.

✔COMPARE AND CONTRAST FOR EFFICIENT WRONG-ANSWER IDENTIFICATION.

Take a moment to recall the other aids we have employed to identify wrong-answer options efficiently: the wrong-answer patterns and disguises. For a question seeking an answer that **could** satisfy required conditions, the pattern predicts that options that *cannot* are wrong. These **could** questions are the ones most often asked on the Passages section-test. Questions asking for an answer that **must** satisfy required conditions are not completed by options that *could* or *cannot* satisfy all of the conditions. And questions asking for an answer that **cannot** satisfy required conditions are not completed by options that *must* or *could* satisfy the conditions.

As to disguises, the LSAT uses the **same-language, too-little-too-much, true but,** and **false-assertion** strategies to create answer options that are attractive but do not satisfy the conditions of the question and statement.

These patterns are combined in the following summary of wrong-answer options.

For **could** questions, wrong-answer options are those that *cannot* satisfy required conditions, even though they use:

- the **same-language** disguise
- the **too-little-too-much** disguise
- the **true but** disguise
- the **false-assertion** disguise

For **must** questions, wrong answer options are those that *could* or *cannot* satisfy required conditions, even though they use:

- the **same-language** disguise
- the **too-little-too-much** disguise
- the **true but** disguise
- the **false-assertion** disguise

For **cannot** questions, wrong-answer options are those that *must* or *could* satisfy required conditions, even though they use:

- the **same-language** disguise
- the **too-little-too-much** disguise
- the **true but** disguise
- the **false-assertion** disguise

Another strategy used by the LSAT to disguise the best answer option is **paraphrasing**. This disguise obfuscates the best answer and adds to the attractiveness of answer options that use the same language as the statement. Recognizing that an answer option paraphrases the statement can keep you from discarding it too quickly. Carefully check answer options that are clear paraphrases—they often satisfy all the required conditions.

WHAT IS THE BEST RESPONSE TECHNIQUE FOR PASSAGES QUESTIONS?

Efficient use of time is important to your performance on all LSAT section-tests. Passages provide you with many opportunities for efficiency. Your challenge is to take advantage of the opportunities.

The first order of business is to determine and mark the order in which you will work through the four Passages statements and question sets. Using the techniques described earlier in this session, you rank the Passages problems according to their difficulty, numbering them in the order in which you will work through them.

Next, you begin to work on the statement you designated as first. Orient yourself to it briefly by taking 10 to 20 seconds to read the first sentence of each paragraph. This gives you a sense of the statement's orientation before you scan the questions. Both this and the question scan are important preparation for the one careful reading of the statement that follows.

Scan the questions. As you know, they are short and serve primarily as cues, but they often provide a good idea of the characteristic in the statement that is their focus. A clear example is the question that refers you to a specific line in the statement. Mark that line during your scan so that you can concentrate when it comes to the careful read-through.

During the scan, designate the questions as **description** (D) or **extension** (E) types. This is so you can work through description questions first. Working through the questions that make direct reference to the statement first will improve your familiarity with the statement before you reach the extension questions that require you to go beyond the statement.

Next, read through the statement carefully, focusing on the six characteristics and discarding the residual. There are two alternative techniques that facilitate this objective. The first is unfamiliar—as you read, use a marking pen to cross out extraneous material, leaving only the common characteristics for later reference. Not only does this make reference to the characteristics easy, but it eliminates the potential distraction of superfluous portions of the statement. But this procedure creates insecurity in many test-takers, because the blackened text is gone, and there is no turning back. However, the marked out text is unnecessary and a distraction.

> Blackmail ~~may be defined as the sale of information to an individual who would be incriminated by its publication, and at first glance it~~ appears to be an efficient method of private enforcement of the law ~~(the moral as well as the positive law). The value of the information to the blackmailed individual is equal to the~~ cost of the punishment ~~that the individual will incur if the information is communicated to the authorities and he is punished as a result, and so he will be willing to pay up to that amount to the blackmailer for the information. The individual is thereby punished, and the punishment~~ is the same as if he had been apprehended and convicted for the crime ~~that the blackmailer has discovered, but the fine is paid to the blackmailer rather than to the state.~~

The second technique is more familiar to most test-takers. It involves underlining or highlighting the common characteristics for later reference. (For an example, see page 124.)

In using either of these techniques, you are connecting the statement to the predetermined

Blackmail may be defined as the sale of information to an individual who would be incriminated by its publication, and at first glance it appears to be an efficient method of private enforcement of the law (the

5 moral as well as the positive law). The value of the information to the blackmailed individual is equal to the cost of the punishment that the individual will incur if the information is communicated to the authorities and he is punished as a result, and so he will be willing to pay up

10 to that amount to the blackmailer for the information. The individual is thereby punished, and the punishment is the same as if he had been apprehended and convicted for the crime that the blackmailer has discovered, but the fine is paid to the blackmailer rather

15 than to the state.
Why then is blackmail a crime? One scholar's answer is that it results in underdeterrence of crimes punished by nonpecuniary sanctions because the criminals lack the resources to pay an optimal fine. The

20 blackmailer will sell his information to the criminal for a price lower than the cost of punishment if the criminal cannot pay a higher price. A more persuasive explanation of why blackmail follows directly from the decision to rely on a public monopoly of law enforcement in

25 some areas of enforcement, notably criminal law. Were blackmail, a form of private enforcement, lawful, the public monopoly of enforcement would be undermined. Overenforcement of the law would result if the blackmailer were able to extract the full fine from the

30 offender. Alternatively, the blackmailer might sell his incriminating information to the offender for a price lower than the statutory cost of punishment to the criminal, which would reduce the effective cost of punishment to the criminal below the level set by the

35 legislature. This problem, however, could be solved by a system of public bounties equal to the cost of punishment (or lower, to induce the enforcement industry to contract to optimal size). Then the blackmailer could always claim a bounty from the state if the criminal was

40 unable to pay a price equal to the optimal fine.
Consistent with this analysis, Axel's studies show that practices indistinguishable from blackmail, though not called by that name, are permitted in areas where the law is enforced privately rather than publicly

because the overenforcement problem is not serious. No

45 one seems to object to a person's collecting information about his or her spouse's adulterous activities, and threatening to disclose that information in a divorce proceeding or other forum, in order to extract maximum compensation for the offending spouse's breach of the

50 marital obligations.
Blackmail and bribery appear to be virtually identical practices from the standpoint of the analysis of private enforcement. The blackmailer and the bribed official both receive payment in exchange for not

55 enforcing the law. We therefore predict that in areas where there is a public monopoly of enforcement, bribery, like blackmail, will be prohibited, while in areas where there is no public monopoly, it will be permitted. And so we observe. The settlement out of

60 court of negligence claims is a form of perfectly lawful bribery, although the term is not used in these situations because of its pejorative connotation.

Point and Purpose

Blackmail . . . appears to be an efficient method of private enforcement of the law. . . .

Were blackmail, a form of private enforcement, lawful, the public monopoly of enforcement would be undermined.

blackmail . . . permitted in areas where the law is enforced privately. . . .

where there is no public monopoly, it will be permitted.

Key Words and Concepts

Blackmail

cost of the punishment . . . is the same as if he had been apprehended and convicted for the crime.

cost of punishment . . . set by the legislature.

Blackmail and bribery appear to be virtually identical practices . . . payment in exchange for not enforcing the law.

Authorities

One scholar's answer. . . .

Axel's studies show. . . .

Enumerations

collecting information about his or her spouse's adulterous activities, and threatening to disclose that information . . . to extract maximum compensation for the offending spouse's breach of the marital obligations.

The settlement out of court of negligence claims is a form of perfectly lawful bribery. . . .

Unusual Words and Phrases

public monopoly of law enforcement

optimal fine

a system of public bounties equal to the cost of punishment

Competing Perspectives

Why then is blackmail a crime? . . . it results in underdeterrence of crimes. . . .

A more persuasive explanation . . . is that the decision to discourage blackmail follows directly from the decision to rely on a public monopoly of law enforcement in some areas. . . .

analysis of the statement. You know that the **point** or **purpose, key words** or **concepts, authorities, enumerations, unusual words** or **phrases,** and **competing perspectives** in the statement will be the focus of the questions. No other material will be involved in the questions.

✔**DO NOT WASTE TIME WITH EXTRANEOUS MATERIAL.**

Return to the statement earlier in this session. Using whichever technique you prefer, read the statement carefully and note the point or purpose, key words or concepts, authorities, enumerations, unusual words or phrases, and competing perspectives. After you have completed your reading, review the samples here and compare your results. Beside the underlined sample on page 124 are extracts of the noted material organized under headings reflecting the six characteristics used by the LSAT to select Passages statements.

Now you are ready to work through the description questions and then the extension questions. Determine whether the question seeks a must, could, or cannot answer option. Examine the answer options in order, using the techniques of comparison and contrast to identify the options that match a wrong-answer pattern. Be alert for the LSAT's disguises. When you find an answer option that fails to satisfy the requirements of the question and statement, you chuck it. *Repeat the process until you have selected the best-answer option. Circle it in the test book.*

Once you have completed all of the questions in a set, *transfer all of your answers to the answer sheet* at the same time. This provides you with a natural break before moving on to the next Passages statement and question set.

Passages answers may be presented in both the single- and multiple-option formats. Recall that the multiple-option format permits one, two, or all three of the Roman numeral choices to satisfy the conditions required by the statement and question. In most Passages section-tests, the multiple-option format is used very sparingly.

HOW DO YOU WORK WITH THE SEVEN BASIC QUESTIONS?

Description Questions

Description questions always refer directly to the passage statement. Refer to the statement if

necessary to make a decision about the conditions, but make only one such reference back.

Description questions take three forms. They ask you to recognize the principal point or purpose of the statement, identify a specific detail in the statement, or determine the meaning of a term or concept in context. (All of the examples of questions and answer options that follow are based on the previous passage about blackmail and bribery.)

Principal point or purpose questions employ a direct approach of the form "Which of the following best describes (or is) the principal point or purpose of the passage?"

1. Which of the following best summarizes the main point of the passage?

   (A) Blackmail and bribery are valuable forms of law enforcement.
   (B) Private law enforcement is more efficient than public law enforcement.
   (C) Punishment under private and public law enforcement is the same.
   (D) The law enforcement industry should contract to optimal size.
   (E) When public law enforcement is not threatened, blackmail and bribery are permitted.

Although not directly, the question asks for the answer option that **could** satisfy the required conditions. Answer option (A) makes a value judgment not made in the statement. The statement indicates that blackmail is an *efficient* method of private law enforcement but nowhere says that it is a *valuable* form of law enforcement or even a *valuable* form of *private* law enforcement. Option (A) does not satisfy the conditions of the statement and is wrong. (Be particularly alert to answer options that make value statements, which often employ the **too-little-too-much** disguise.) Answer option (B) *cannot* satisfy the required conditions because it compares the efficiency of public and private law enforcement. No such comparison is made in the statement. Option (C) is wrong because it involves a peripheral point, not the *main* point of the statement. It is an example of the **true but** wrong-answer option, as is option (D). Option (D) reflects the point made on line 49 of the statement but has nothing to do with the question, which seeks the *main* point of the statement. Option (E) is the best answer.

Specific detail questions also have a direct format. They focus on enumerations, a key word or concept, or an unusual word or phrase. Specific detail questions usually require a **must** or **cannot** answer option.

2. According to the passage, which of the following sets the cost of punishment?

(A) the blackmailer
(B) the offenders
(C) the legislature
(D) the criminal
(E) the bribed officials

This is a **must** question. The blackmailer may set the *tribute* to be paid, but the tribute is not the cost of punishment. Answer option (A) does not satisfy the statement conditions and is wrong. Nothing in the statement suggests that the offenders, criminals, or bribed officials set the cost of punishment. Besides, they are practically the same in the context of this question. For both reasons, answers (B), (D), and (E) are wrong. Option (C) is best, and the statement makes the point clearly in lines 33–35.

Meaning-in-context questions use a straightforward format. They require direct reference to the statement, but the reference is to the context and not to the specific words involved. The meaning is drawn from the context, not from the dictionary.

3. In line 36, "public bounties" refers to

(A) a claim made to establish optimal fines for blackmailers
(B) a way to ensure that blackmailers receive the statutory cost of punishment
(C) a way to ensure the optimal size of the law enforcement industry
(D) a claim paid by the state to blackmailers to induce enforcement
(E) a way to ensure that optimal punishment is enforced by blackmailers

This is a **could** question. Answer option (A) fails to satisfy the conditions and is wrong. It declares that optimal fines are established by claims, a concept suggested nowhere in the statement. The statement does declare that blackmailers could make claims (lines 39–40) but also suggests that such claims would be made to collect an amount equal to the optimal fine, not to establish the fine. Option (C) is drawn from a

parenthetical aside (lines 37–39) on the meaning of public bounties and is thus a wrong-answer option. Option (D) states the purpose of public bounties to be the inducement of enforcement, a concept that is outside the scope of the statement and therefore wrong. Answer option (E) fails similarly. Nowhere does the statement deal with the concept of optimal punishment. This leaves (B) as the best-answer selection.

Extension Questions

Extension questions always require that you go beyond the statement to arrive at the answer. You are required to make inferences and assumptions and draw conclusions from material you find in the statement. Reference to the statement may be helpful.

Extension questions take four forms. You are asked to determine a perspective, select the context from which the statement came, identify a pattern, or assess evidence.

Perspective questions ask you directly to select the answer option that reflects the view, attitude, or purpose of the statement's author or some other person involved with the statement. They may seek either general or specific perspectives. While they may go beyond the statement, they also may connect directly to material in the statement, often bridging the area between description and extension questions.

4. Which of the following best describes the author's attitude toward bribery?

(A) It will be permitted in divorce proceedings.
(B) It will be encouraged when overenforcement is not a serious problem.
(C) It will be used in order to extract maximum compensation.
(D) It will be permitted where there is no public law enforcement monopoly.
(E) It will be permitted where private law enforcement is not a serious problem.

This is a **could** question. Answer options (A) and (C) fail to satisfy the statement conditions, since all the references to divorce proceedings in the statement involve something akin to blackmail, not bribery, which is the focus of the question. There is nothing in the statement to suggest that the overenforcement mentioned in option (B) is encouraged or should be. (B) is a wrong-answer option. Option (E) also fails to satisfy the statement conditions, since there is no reference in the statement to private law enforcement being a serious problem, let alone its connection to bribery being permitted. Answer (D) is the best option and connects to the point made in lines 58–59.

Context questions are easily understood but not so easily dealt with. They ask you to determine the source of the statement or the text that either precedes or succeeds the statement. It is very difficult to determine context from a few paragraphs, but comparing and contrasting are often helpful techniques.

5. Which of the following law review articles is the most likely source of this passage?

   (A) "The Private Enforcement of Law"
   (B) "Public Monopoly of Law Enforcement"
   (C) "Comparing Bribery and Blackmail"
   (D) "A Critique of Out-of-Court Settlements"
   (E) "Bounties as a Means of Law Enforcement"

This is another **could** question. Answer options (C), (D), and (E) are not likely candidates when contrasted with (A) and (B). They deal narrowly with specific matters considered in the statement. The statement provides the context for these answer options, not vice versa as the question requires. By comparing answer options (A) and (B) to the statement, it becomes clear that the focus of the statement is on private law enforcement, of which blackmail and bribery are examples and to which the public law enforcement monopoly is antagonistic. Because the passage concentrates on private enforcement, option (B) does not satisfy the statement conditions and is a wrong answer. Answer (A) is the best option.

Pattern questions ask you to identify answer options that are structurally or logically analogous to a point or concept expressed in the statement. These questions are sometimes obscure. Use the answer options to bring clarity to the question.

6. Which of the following most closely parallels the author's example of perfectly lawful bribery in the passage (lines 59–62)?

   (A) A plea bargain made by a public prosecutor with an indicted defendant
   (B) A pardon given by a governor to a convicted felon
   (C) A fine paid by a traffic violator to a magistrate
   (D) A holiday turkey given by a vendor to a city purchasing agent
   (E) A donation given by a landowner to a senator running for reelection

This a **could** question. The perfectly lawful bribery referred to in lines 59–62 is a variation of the process described in lines 54–55: "payment in exchange for not enforcing the law." The payment described in answer option (C) is made as a result of the enforcement of the law, the opposite of bribery. Thus, this answer is wrong. The payments described in options (B), (D), and (E) are not made in exchange for nonenforcement of the law. They too are wrong. Answer option (A) is the best answer. By accepting a plea bargain ("payment in exchange") for not pursuing the indictment ("not enforcing the law"), the public prosecutor's action parallels that of accepting a settlement for not pursuing a negligence claim in court.

Evidence-assessment questions take various forms in the Passages section-test. All ask you to select the answer option that strengthens, weakens, criticizes, or distinguishes between fact and opinion in the statement. The format for evidence-assessment questions varies slightly, but it is direct.

7. Which of the following, if true, most strengthens the author's position on the legality of blackmail?

(A) Blackmail is not a crime in all countries where law enforcement is a public monopoly.

(B) Bribery flourishes in countries where public law enforcement is weak or nonexistent.

(C) Blackmail of such private dispute—resolution professionals as labor arbitrators is very rare.

(D) Bribery of such public dispute—resolution professionals as judges is very rare.

(E) Blackmail is a crime in all countries where people can choose between private and public law enforcement.

Once again, this is a **could** question. If answer choice (A) were true, it would weaken the author's position, not strengthen it. It *cannot* satisfy the question and statement conditions and is wrong. Answer options (C), (D), and (E) do not satisfy the required conditions, since they refer to matters not included in the statement. Use of the contrast technique makes it clear that there is no practical difference between answer options (C) and (D), and, consequently, each is wrong. This leaves answer option (B) as the best answer.

The techniques used to work through the seven examples of Passages questions are applicable to all versions of those questions. If you found yourself attracted to a wrong-answer option as you worked through the questions, you might benefit from returning to that option and identifying the disguise that made it attractive. By becoming familiar with the disguises that attract you, you can avoid being misled by them in the future.

Success Session 10

HOW DOES THE 9-12-18 SYSTEM APPLY TO YOUR RELATIONSHIPS TRAINING?

In Red Alert 3 (pp. 71–75), you learned and applied the techniques of the 9-12-18 test-planning system to a Relationships question set. You will recall that the 9-12-18 system is based on two concepts. First, your performance is maximized by identifying and planning on achieving your optimal balance between speed and accuracy.

This will probably mean that you achieve your goal of selecting fewer wrong-answer options by planning to work on fewer question sets than the number available in the section-test. (Remember, always guess on the question-answer sets that you do not work on.) Second, you use a process similar to the LSAT's to find your optimal speed and balance on each section-test.

✔ **UTILIZING THE 9-12-18 PLANNING SYSTEM, YOU WILL DETERMINE WHETHER IT MAXIMIZES YOUR SECTION-TEST SCORE TO COMPLETE FOUR, THREE, OR TWO QUESTION SETS IN THE 35 MINUTES ALLOWED.**

As you apply the techniques presented in the previous Relationships success sessions, they will become familiar and easy to use. As they do, you will probably experience a change in your optimal balance between speed and accuracy, and the familiarity you gain will give you a greater sense of control over the LSAT, and you will experience reduced anxiety. Familiarity will also improve your proficiency with the question sets. The combination of greater control and improved proficiency will result in more accurate answer selection. You will identify wrong answers and, consequently, best answers more efficiently. And with this increase in efficiency, you may have to adjust your test plan.

HOW DO YOU DEVELOP YOUR RELATIONSHIPS SECTION-TEST PLAN?

Suppose that your initial Relationships question-answer set (in Red Alert 3) indicated that you would achieve optimal performance by completing three of the four question sets in a section-test (and only guessing on the fourth). Working with the Relationships training techniques described in the previous sessions, you will apply the 9-12-18 process to the Relationships question-answer sets presented in the LSATs in this book and update your performance record (page 75) with the results.

After working through these techniques a number of times, you may notice that your test results suggest that you make a change in your plan for balancing speed and accuracy. It now may be clear that completing all four sets of questions on the Relationships section-test would yield a better score than completing only three and guessing on one.

✔ **CHANGE YOUR TEST PLAN ONLY WHEN THE RESULTS OF THE 9-12-18 PROCESS INDICATE IT.**

Having arrived at this point does not mean that you should put your Relationships training aside and concentrate on other aspects of the test. You must maintain your level of familiarity and proficiency by working through the Relationships sessions regularly and monitoring your performance with 9-12-18 system as you work through the various Relationships question-answer sets in the simulated LSATs in this book.

HOW DO YOU USE RELATIONSHIPS SECTION-TESTS?

This session closes by describing how you can use the twenty-four Relationships question-answer sets that appear on the three complete LSATs in this book. They are to be used one at a time. Each time you review Sessions 5 and 7, take one of the Relationships question-answer sets on an LSAT and update your performance record. You should work through the Relationships training techniques at least six times and complete at least six question-answer sets. Working on more question-answer sets could result in continued improvement. If it does, keep going. If you become consistent in your performance, stop.

Upon completion of at least six training and update sessions, your performance record is likely to have stabilized, and your plan for the Relationships section-test will be "set." Your plan will indicate the number of question-answer sets you should complete and the number you should guess on the Relationships section-test at any sitting of the LSAT.

HOW DO YOU TAKE RELATIONSHIPS QUESTION-ANSWER SETS?

To reiterate the process, first you read the statement and scan the questions until you are satisfied that you understand the general focus of the questions. Then you complete your visualization. For your visualization to be effective, it must represent all of the conditions set out in the facts and rules of the statement. It should be the sole reference you need for the efficient and accurate identification of the wrong and best answers to every question. Thus, time spent on your visualization is time well spent. Depending upon your reading speed, you can comfortably allocate 3 to 5 of the first 9 minutes you spend on a question set reading the statement, scanning the questions, and preparing your visualization.

After completing the visualization, select answers to the number of questions you can comfortably handle in the remainder of the first 9 minutes allocated to the pretest set. It is important that you not push your pace beyond your comfort level.

At the end of the 9-minute period, you will have selected an answer for each of the six questions in the set through your own combination of considering and guessing. Place a *circle* around these answer choices, which constitute your 9-minute set.

Next, take an additional 3 minutes (for a total of 12) to reconsider questions and answer selections. You can be flexible, either focusing on questions you did not have time to consider in the first 9 minutes or reviewing questions about which you were uncertain. Without erasing or changing the circles you made during the first 9 minutes, place a *box* beside each of

the answers you selected during this 3-minute period. If you did not change an answer, simply place a box beside the circled answer. If you did, place the box beside the new selection. The boxed answers are your 12-minute set.

In the final 6 minutes, go back and answer any questions you did not get to during the first 12 minutes, or review and change answers if you wish. Be flexible. Concentrate on questions about which you are uncertain, and take care not to rethink previously selected answers about which you are confident. Place an *asterisk* beside each of the answers you selected during this 6-minute period, without erasing or changing the circles and boxes you made during the first 12 minutes. If you did not change an answer, place an asterisk beside the boxed answer. If you did, place an asterisk beside the new selection. The answers identified with asterisks are your 12-minute set.

After you have completed the pretest, turn to the Answer Keys for the question-answer set you completed at the back of the book. For each set, determine the number of best answers you selected during the 9-minute set (circled), 12-minute set (boxed), and 18-minute set (asterisked). Apply the numbers to the following formula, and complete the calculations indicated.

The largest total indicates the optimal number of question sets (two, three, or four) that you transfer to the Pretest Performance Tracking Worksheet (page 75). As you develop this record, it will clearly indicate the number of Relationships question sets you should plan to complete when taking the LSAT. Completing this number will yield the highest test score for you.

Relationships Set

Circles _____ × 5 + 0 = _____

Boxes _____ × 4 + 1 = _____

Asterisks _____ × 3 + 2 = _____

Largest total _____

To repeat, every time you work quickly through Sessions 5 and 7, reviewing the main points, you complete one of the question-answer sets. This process will take about 30 minutes. Don't be tempted to complete a set without working through the techniques; it is familiarity with and proficiency in the use of the techniques that will have the greatest impact on your performance. Conversely, working through a series of question-answer sets without first working through the techniques is the least effective way of making an impact on your performance. You want high impact, not low impact or no impact.

✔ **TRAINING WITH THE TECHNIQUES—THEN UPDATING YOUR PERFORMANCE RECORD WITH THE RESULTS OF A QUESTION-ANSWER SET—IS THE KEY TO THE DEVELOPMENT OF YOUR TEST PLAN.**

As your performance improves, your test plan reflects the changes. Upon the completion of at least six or seven sets provided in this book, you will have a performance record that is stable. You will know whether your optimal performance will result from completing two, three, or four question sets. You will have a test plan for the Relationships section-test of the LSAT.

Only after your performance and test plan have stabilized will practicing question-answer sets serve to maintain your achievements. Now your challenge becomes having the discipline to stick to your plan during the actual LSAT.

✔ **ONLY BY FOLLOWING YOUR PLAN CAN YOU MAXIMIZE YOUR TEST PERFORMANCE AND SCORE.**

SHOULD YOU DO MORE QUESTION-ANSWER SETS?

Once you have completed six training workthroughs, you probably will have realized the high-impact gain that you were looking for before taking the LSAT. For most, further workthroughs and sets will have much less impact, if any. But it is important to maintain familiarity and proficiency, and some people find they can also maintain control through regular practice. In any event, you may want to work with additional Relationships question-answer sets.

There are three good sources of additional sets. The first is this guide—the simulated LSATs can be used as a source of question sets. Also, Law School Admission Services sells disclosed tests. And finally, there are a number of preparation books that contain little more than simulated tests. (If you use these, take care that the questions use only the same specifications as the LSAT itself. It is not helpful to work with questions that employ different structures.)

You can use test materials that are not presented as question-answer sets by converting them into sets. This is exactly what you do when taking the LSAT. You isolate a question-answer set and think of it as "the test" until you have completed it. Then you move on to the next set. By breaking the test down into its components, you gain maximum control over it and are in the best position to execute your test plan.

WHAT ARE THE DIRECTIONS FOR COMPLETING THE QUESTION-ANSWER SETS?

Complete a question-answer set only after you have worked through the Relationships training techniques in Sessions 5 and 7. The directions are the same for each of the Relationships question sets you choose from the Diagnostic Test or Practice Tests 1 and 2. Each set of questions is based on a number of conditions. A diagram is helpful in the answer selection process. Choose the best answer to each question from the five options presented, and mark your answers as described in the text.

Success Session 11

How do you apply the 9-12-18 system to Arguments problems?

You completed an Arguments question-answer set in Red Alert 3 (pp. 71–75), where you learned the techniques of the 9-12-18 test-planning system. The system uses question-answer sets to help you identify your optimal balance between speed and accuracy on each section-test. With this information you can plan your total test performance.

The LSAT rewards working smart rather than working hard. You maximize your performance by selecting best answers, not by rushing through questions and answers. In the Arguments section-test, most people select fewer wrong answers as best when they plan on working with less than all the available question sets.

✔ **YOU DECIDE TO MAXIMIZE YOUR SECTION-TEST SCORE BY COMPLETING FOUR, THREE, OR TWO QUESTION SETS IN THE 35 MINUTES ALLOTTED.**

The techniques presented in the previous Arguments sessions will become familiar and easy to apply to Arguments problems as you work with them. As you apply them, you may find that your optimal balance between speed and accuracy changes. The familiarity you have developed will give you a greater sense of control and reduce your anxiety. Familiarity will also improve your proficiency with the question-answer sets. The combination of greater control and improved proficiency will result in more accurate answer selection. You will identify wrong answers more efficiently and, consequently, select more of the best answers. This increase in efficiency may lead to a change in your test plan.

How do you develop your Arguments section-test plan?

You are probably becoming very familiar with the process of using ongoing practice information to revise your test plan. It has been ex-plained previously, so feel free to skim the next few paragraphs if you are already comfortable with the process.

Suppose your initial Arguments question-answer set (in Red Alert 3) indicated that you would achieve your optimal performance by completing three of the four question sets in a section-test (and guessing on the fourth set). Working with the training techniques explained in the previous two sessions, you will use the 9-12-18 process to update your performance record with the results. After you have worked through a number of question-answer sets, your performance record may dictate making a change in your plan of optimal performance. For instance, the results may now make it clear that you will achieve a better score by completing all four sets of questions on the Arguments section-test than you would by completing only three question sets and guessing on one.

✔ **YOU WILL CHANGE YOUR TEST PLAN ONLY WHEN THE RESULTS OF THE 9-12-18 PROCESS INDICATE IT.**

Even after you have arrived at a stable balance between speed and accuracy, working through Arguments question-answer sets will maintain and enhance your level of familiarity and proficiency. Always work through the technique sessions first, and then monitor your performance with 9-12-18 question-answer sets that appear in the simulation LSATs that appear in this book.

How do you use Arguments question-answer sets?

This session ends suggesting that you complete at least six Arguments question-answer sets. Identify them on the simulation LSATs and complete them one at a time. Each time you work through all of the techniques in Sessions 6 and 8, complete one of the question-answer sets. Use the results to update your performance record. This means you should review the Arguments training techniques at least six times and complete at least six question-answer sets.

✔**UPON COMPLETION OF THE SIX TRAINING AND UPDATE SEQUENCES, YOU SET YOUR PLAN FOR THE ARGUMENTS SECTION-TESTS.**

After six times through the sequence, your performance record is likely to have stabilized, and your plan can be set. It will indicate the number of question-answer sets you should complete and the number you should guess on the Arguments section-test of the LSAT.

HOW DO YOU TAKE ARGUMENTS QUESTION-ANSWER SETS?

On question-answer sets you should follow the procedure of reading the question first and then the statement, looking for and noting key words, concepts, and the conclusion, if any. Next, select your answer options. Repeat this procedure for the number of questions you can comfortably cover in the first 9 minutes allocated to the pretest set. It is important that your pace not exceed your comfort level. At the end of the 9-minute period, you will have selected an answer for each of the six questions in the Arguments set. Depending upon your pace, some of your answers may have been selected by guessing. *Circle* your answer choices. These constitute your 9-minute set.

Next, use an additional 3 minutes to reconsider the questions and the answers you selected in the 9-minute period. Your use of the additional time will vary depending on the work you completed during the first 9 minutes: You can work through questions you did not have time to consider in the first 9 minutes or review questions about which you are uncertain. Place a *box* beside each of the answers you select during this 3-minute period. If you did not change an answer, place a box beside the circled answer. If you changed an answer, place a box beside the new selection. The boxed answers are your 12-minute set. Do not erase or change the circles you placed on the question sheet during the first 9 minutes of the pretest.

The next step is to use an additional 6 minutes. Go back to the set and answer questions you did not get to during the first 12 minutes, or review and change answers as necessary. Be flexible in using this period. Concentrate on questions about which you are uncertain, but avoid reworking previously selected answers about which you are confident. Place an *asterisk* beside each of the answers you select during this 6-minute period. If you did not

change an answer, place an asterisk beside the boxed answer; if you did, place the asterisk beside your new selection. The answers identified with asterisks are your 18-minute set. Again, be sure not to erase or change the circles or boxes you placed on the question sheet during the first 12 minutes of working on the question-answer set.

After the question-answer set is completed, refer to the Quick-Score Answers at the back of the book. Determine the number of best answers you selected during the 9-minute (circled), 12-minute (boxed), and 18-minute (asterisked) question-answer sets. Complete the calculations called for below. The results of these calculations are transferred to your Pretest Performance Tracking Worksheet (page 75). Enter the number of question sets that represent your optimal balance between speed and accuracy. As you work through the question-answer sets and develop your performance record, the pattern of your greatest efficiency will emerge.

This pattern will indicate the number of Arguments question sets you should plan to complete on the actual LSAT—the number that will yield the highest test score for you.

Circles _____ × 5 + 0 = _____
Boxes _____ × 4 + 1 = _____
Asterisks_____ × 3 + 2 = _____

Largest total _____

This "largest total" figure indicates the optimal number (2, 3, or 4) of question sets you will enter on your Performance Tracking Worksheet.

For the 9-12-18 process to work most effectively, you should complete a question-answer set only after you have reviewed the Arguments test-training techniques in Sessions 6 and 8. Do this before each pretest. It will take about 30 minutes. The familiarity and proficiency you gain with the techniques through this procedure will have the greatest impact on your performance and your test score. Going through a series of question-answer sets without first working through the training techniques is the least effective way of having an impact on your performance. And your objective is high impact, not low or no impact.

✔**ONCE YOUR PERFORMANCE ON ARGUMENTS QUESTION-ANSWER SETS IS STABILIZED, SO IS YOUR TEST PLAN.**

After six or more question-answer sets have been completed, your performance record should be sufficiently comprehensive to provide you with stable information. You will develop your test plan for the Arguments section-tests on the basis of this performance record. You will plan to complete two, three, or four question sets, depending on the optimal balance you have discovered between your speed and accuracy. Then your challenge is having the self-discipline to stick to your plan during the actual LSAT.

✔**FOLLOW YOUR PLAN TO MAXIMIZE YOUR TEST PERFORMANCE AND SCORE.**

SHOULD YOU DO MORE QUESTION-ANSWER SETS?

Once the high-impact gain you wanted before taking the LSAT is realized, further workthroughs and question-answer sets will have much less, if any, impact on your score. But it is important to maintain familiarity and proficiency with Arguments, and practice with question-answer sets provides a positive maintenance regimen for many prospective test-takers. For others, regular workthroughs of the techniques in Sessions 6 and 8 will maintain readiness.

If you want to practice with additional Arguments problems, there are three good sources of additional sets. Besides the simulated tests in this book, Law School Admission Services sells disclosed tests. And there are a number of preparation books containing little more than simulated tests. (If you use such books, make certain that the problems are constructed to the same specifications as the real LSAT questions.)

When practicing with test materials, first convert them into question sets. This is exactly the same process you will use when taking the LSAT. You identify a question set, view that set as the test until you have completed it, then move on to the next set or test. By segmenting the section-test into its four component sets, you gain maximum control over the test, which puts you in the best position to execute your test plan.

WHAT ARE THE DIRECTIONS FOR COMPLETING THE QUESTION-ANSWER SETS?

In each of the Arguments question-answer sets you choose from the three tests in this book, evaluate the reasoning contained in the brief statements, and select the best answer. The best answer is a "conceivable solution to the particular problem posed" by the question and does not require you to make what are, by commonsense standards, implausible, superfluous, or incompatible assumptions.

Complete each question-answer set only after you have worked through the Arguments training techniques in Sessions 6 and 8.

Success Session 12

HOW DO YOU APPLY THE 9-12-18 SYSTEM TO YOUR PASSAGES TRAINING?

In Red Alert 3 (pp. 71–75) you learned the 9-12-18 test-planning system, including its application to a Passages problem. The system uses question-answer sets to help you identify your optimal balance between speed and accuracy. This information is then used to develop your plan for the Passages section-test. Remember that working through fewer question sets than are available on a Passages section-test usually produces more best answers than rushing through all of the questions.

✔ QUESTION-ANSWER SETS HELP YOU DETER-MINE WHETHER YOU WILL MAXIMIZE YOUR SECTION-TEST SCORE BY COMPLETING FOUR, THREE, OR TWO QUESTION SETS IN THE 35 MINUTES ALLOTTED.

Passages test-taking techniques will become familiar and easy to apply as you work with them. Familiarity will give you a sense of control over and reduce your anxiety about the questions. It will also improve your proficiency with the question-answer sets. The combination of greater control and improved proficiency will result in more accurate answer selection. You will be able to identify wrong answers more efficiently and, consequently, select more of the best answers. As this happens your balance between speed and accuracy may change, and your test plan will change accordingly.

HOW DO YOU DEVELOP YOUR PASSAGES SECTION-TEST PLAN?

Once again, we will go through the process of using question-answer set information to revise the test plan. It is the same process that has been explained previously, so, if you are comfortable with the question-answer set process, skim the next paragraphs.

Suppose your initial Passages question-answer set (in Red Alert 3) indicated that your optimal performance would result from complet-ing three of the four question sets on a section-test (and guessing on the fourth set). Working with the Passages training techniques you have learned, you will use the 9-12-18 process to update your performance record with the results. After you have worked through a number of question-answer sets, your performance record may suggest making a change in your plan for optimal performance. For instance, your efficiency may have improved so that your perfor-mance record shows you will achieve a better score by completing all four sets of questions on the Passages section-test rather than by complet-ing only three question-answer sets and guessing on one. This calls for a change in your test plan for the section-test.

✔ CHANGE YOUR TEST PLAN ONLY WHEN INFORMATION FROM THE 9-12-18 QUESTION-ANSWER SET PROCESS INDICATES THAT A CHANGE IS DUE.

Avoid the temptation to stop working through the Passages techniques and question-answer sets at the point where your Passages performance record indicates that completing all four question sets will yield your best score. The workthroughs maintain and enhance your familiarity and proficiency.

HOW DO YOU USE PASSAGES QUESTION-ANSWER SETS?

There are twelve Passages question-answer sets in the three simulation LSATs in this book. After you have completed working through all of the Passages techniques in Sessions 6 and 9, com-plete one of the question-answer sets. Then use the results to update your performance record. Work through the Passages test-training tech-niques at least six times and complete at least six question-answer sets.

After you have been through the sequence six times, your performance record is likely to have stabilized. Your performance record can then be translated into a plan for the number of ques-tion sets you will complete and the number you will guess on the Passages section-test of the LSAT.

How do you take Passages question-answer sets?

On Passages question-answer sets you should begin by reading the first sentence of each paragraph in the statement. Then scan the questions, noting the types of questions, key words and concepts, and any references to line numbers in the statement. Next, read the statement carefully, looking for elements of the six-part pattern. Underline or highlight the point or purpose, key words or concepts, unusual words or phrases, authorities, enumerations, and competing perspectives. All other information in the statement is extraneous.

Now you are ready to work through the questions and answer options. Complete the number of questions you can comfortably address in the first 9 minutes allocated to the question-answer set. Maintain your pace at the comfort level. At the end of the 9-minute period, you will have selected an answer for each of the six questions in the Passages set. Depending upon your pace, some of your answers may have been selected by guessing. *Circle* your 9-minute answer choices—this is your 9-minute set.

Next, take an additional 3 minutes to reconsider the questions and the answers you selected in the 9-minute period. Vary your use of the additional time according to the work you completed during the first 9 minutes. First work through questions you did not have time to consider in the first 9 minutes. Then review questions about which you were uncertain. Place a *box* beside each of the answers you selected during this 3-minute period. If you did not change an answer, place a box beside the circled answer. If you did, place the box beside the new selection. The boxed answers are your 12-minute set. Do not erase or change the circles you placed on the question sheet during the first 9 minutes of the question-answer set.

The next step is to use an additional 6 minutes. Return to the set and answer questions you did not get to during the first 12 minutes, or review questions and answers, making changes as necessary. Concentrate on questions about which you are still uncertain, but avoid reworking previously selected answers about which you are confident.

Place an *asterisk* beside each of the answers you selected during this 6-minute period. If you did not change an answer, place an asterisk beside the boxed answer. If you did, place the asterisk beside your new selection. The answers identified with asterisks are your 18-minute set. Again, do not erase or change the circles or boxes you placed on the question sheet during the first 12 minutes of the question-answer set.

After the question-answer set is completed, refer to the Quick-Score Answers at the back of the book. Determine the number of best answers you selected during the 9-minute (circled), 12-minute (boxed), and 18-minute (asterisked) question sets. Complete the calculations called for, and then transfer the results of these calculations onto your question-answer set Pretest Performance Tracking Worksheet (page 75). Enter the number of question sets that represents your optimal balance between speed and accuracy. As you work through the question-answer sets and develop your performance record, the pattern of your greatest efficiency will emerge. This pattern will indicate the number of Passages question sets you plan to complete—the number that will yield the highest score for you.

Circles _____ × 5 + 0 = _____
Boxes _____ × 4 + 1 = _____
Asterisks _____ × 3 + 2 = _____

Largest total _____

This "largest total" figure indicates the optimal number (2, 3, or 4) of question sets you will enter on your Performance Tracking Worksheet.

For the question-answer set process to work effectively, you should complete a question-answer set only after you have reviewed the Passages test-training techniques in Sessions 6 and 9. Do this before each question-answer set. This should take you about 30 minutes. The familiarity and proficiency you will gain through this process will produce the greatest impact on your performance and your test score. Going through a series of question-answer sets or question sets without first working through the training techniques will have little, if any, impact on your performance. And your objective, as you know, is high impact.

After the six plus question-answer sets have been completed (one in Red Alert 3), your performance record should be sufficiently comprehensive to provide you with stable information. You will develop your test plan for the Passages section-test on the basis of this performance record. You will plan to complete two, three, or four question sets, depending on the optimal balance between your speed and accuracy. Then your challenge is having the self-discipline to stick to your plan during the actual LSAT.

✔**FOLLOW YOUR PLAN TO MAXIMIZE YOUR TEST PERFORMANCE AND SCORE.**

How many question-answer sets should you complete?

Once the high-impact gain you wanted before taking the LSAT is realized, further workthroughs and question-answer sets will have much less, if any, impact on your score. But it is important to maintain familiarity and proficiency with Passages, and practice with question-answer sets meets this objective for many prospective test-takers. Others maintain their efficiency by regular workthroughs of Sessions 6 and 9.

If you want to work with additional Passages question sets, there are three good sources. The first is this guide—if you choose, you can use the simulated tests included here as a source of additional question sets. Law School Admission Services sells disclosed tests, and there are a number of preparation books containing little more than simulated tests. (If you use these, be sure the problems are constructed to the same specifications as the real LSAT questions.)

When practicing with test materials, break down the section-tests into question-answer sets. This is exactly the same process you will use when taking the LSAT. You identify a question-answer set, viewing it as **the test** until you have completed it, and then move on to the next set or test. By dividing the section-test into its four component sets, you gain maximum control over your practice and test-taking, which puts you in the best position to execute your test plan.

What are the directions for completing the question-answer sets?

For each of the Passages question-sets you choose to practice with, select the best answer option to the question on the basis of what is stated or implied in the statement.

Success Session 13

There is one Writing Sample on the LSAT. It is important to understand the various objectives and uses of the Writing Sample, as well as the mechanics of completing it successfully.

What are the LSAT's objectives for the Writing Sample?

The LSAT declares four objectives for the Writing Sample. The first is to elicit a clear expression of your position on the assigned topic. The second is to determine the care with which you support your position. The third is to secure information about your skills in organization, vocabulary, and grammar. The last is to determine how well you write.

This is a heavy burden for a 30-minute Writing Sample to carry, especially since test-takers have no information about the topic in advance. As a practical matter, a 30-minute Writing Sample cannot achieve the formidable objectives set for it. But this does not mean that these objectives can be ignored. A realistic plan for the Writing Sample must take the objectives into account.

How do law schools use your Writing Sample?

A copy of your Writing Sample accompanies each report of your LSAT score. Law schools use this in various ways. The vast majority of them file the Writing Sample and make no other use of it. Some use a deficient Writing Sample to disqualify applicants. A few use it to identify students who might benefit from writing instruction in the law school context. Infrequently the Writing Sample is used to differentiate between applicants who present otherwise indistinguishable admission credentials.

✔ **THERE IS NO EVIDENCE THAT LAW SCHOOLS USE THE WRITING SAMPLE TO IDENTIFY APPLICANTS WITH GREAT POTENTIAL AS LAW STUDENTS OR LEGAL WRITERS.**

What are the objectives for the Writing Sample?

Both the nature and use of the Writing Sample dictate your single objective: to ensure that it cannot be used in any way to disqualify you for admission.

Given its limitations, the Writing Sample certainly gives you no opportunity to impress anyone with your writing skill. What it does give you is the opportunity to demonstrate one or more serious failings, such as illegible handwriting, not addressing the assigned topic, not following directions, not producing a cogent sample, and using inappropriate vocabulary or grammar.

✔ **A GOOD PLAN IS CRUCIAL TO PRODUCING A WRITING SAMPLE THAT WILL NOT DISQUALIFY YOUR LAW SCHOOL APPLICATION.**

You will develop a plan for reaching your objective that takes into account organization, vocabulary, and the mechanical aspects of writing. It will include the preparation of an outline on scratch paper provided at the test center exclusively for use on the Writing Sample.

What is your task on the Writing Sample?

As with other aspects of the LSAT, the Writing Sample is not what it seems. As we have seen, it cannot meet fully the objectives set for it, nor does it meet the expectations raised by your academic conditioning. The Writing Sample is no term paper or exam essay. It does not require journalistic or creative writing. The type of writing required resembles the completion of forms more than anything else.

✔**THE REAL TASK IS TO GIVE A ONE-SENTENCE RESPONSE TO EACH OF THE DEMANDS OF THE WRITING SAMPLE.**

It is most important that you avoid the temptation to extemporize or be inventive. This can best be ensured by sticking to the directions.

WHAT ARE THE ELEMENTS OF THE WRITING SAMPLE?

The Directions

The Writing Sample directions tell you that how well you write is more important than how much you write. Law schools are mainly interested in how clearly you express the position you take on the topic; how carefully you support that position; and your organization, vocabulary, and writing mechanics.

You are told to write on the assigned topic only. Under no circumstances should you write on a topic of your choosing. Why prepare a writing sample in advance on your own topic when you can use the LSAT's topic and satisfy the expectations exactly? No special knowledge about the topic is expected or required, but you are expected to write on the topic assigned.

You are also advised that there is no right or wrong answer to the topic. The LSAT does not evaluate the position you take, nor are the law schools provided with model answers or model Writing Samples. As with all LSAT questions, the LSAT uses the Writing Sample topic to elicit a response. There is no interest in your knowledge of the topic.

Time is short. You are told that you have 30 minutes to plan, organize, and write your sample. This places a premium on your plan for completing the Writing Sample. Remember coloring books and being told to color inside the lines? The Writing Sample is like that: Only the writing on the lined area in the booklet is reproduced and sent to the law schools. The space provided is more than enough to accommodate your sample, provided you follow your plan. Just be sure that you limit your writing to a reasonable size that fits easily between the lines. Use the black pen provided by the LSAT so that your Writing Sample will reproduce clearly.

Legible handwriting is imperative. If your writing is not entirely legible, print. If your printing is not entirely legible, draw. Make certain that your writing sample can be read easily.

✔**AVOID PRODUCING A WRITING SAMPLE THAT IS HARD TO READ.**

If you need to be convinced, imagine a law professor on the admission committee who is faced with a choice between reading your illegible exam papers for three or four years or your competitor's perfectly legible ones.

The directors provide you with an advantage. You are told exactly how to produce your Writing Sample. Follow the directions, and you will satisfy the LSAT's expectations and complete a Writing Sample that cannot be used to disqualify your law school application.

The Topic

All Writing Sample topics have a similar, predictable layout. They are made up of three components—positions, conditions, and evidence. In the following example, the components are spelled out. These headings do not appear on the LSAT, but the components are obvious and cannot be confused.

There are two positions and two conditions in each topic. The positions are stated first, the conditions follow, and then comes the evidence.

Positions

As a trustee of Whistler College, you will soon vote on how a recent donation of $1 million will be used. Write an argument in support of applying the donation to the development of either the Art Department or the Economics Department. Two considerations guide your decision:

Conditions

- Enrollments at Whistler have been decreasing in the last few years.
- Disharmony between faculty and students has been increasing in the last few years.

Evidence

For years, the Art Department has had an inadequate staff and limited course offerings, and what has been offered has not been of good quality. This gift would enable the college to hire four excellent people, including an artist-in-residence. One or two could round out the course offerings in art history, and others could do something about the lack of courses in studio art. That should change the department's image. It should also attract some new art majors or at least keep students from leaving. Quite a few potential art majors have been lost in recent years because of the poor quality of the department. The best that could be expected from the improvement is a decent Art Department.

In contrast, the money could make the already strong Economics Department more than excellent. Its expansion would result in its being the best in Whistler's part of the country. But such an expansion presents some risk. The Economics Department is already causing problems. The economists think one way politically; the majority of the student body thinks another way. Healthy disagreement in an academic setting is acceptable, but out-and-out rebellion is very problematic. Whistler is a small, tightly knit community, and it is important that harmony be maintained.

✔**PREPARATION OF THE WRITING SAMPLE OUTLINE IS COMPLETED IN 5 TO 7 MINUTES.**

HOW DO YOU DEVELOP YOUR WRITING SAMPLE OUTLINE?

Even before you read the topic, you should take the first step in your Writing Sample plan. Write down the following outline on the scratch paper provided.

    I. Positions
    II. Condition 1
        A. Evidence item 1
        B. Evidence item 2
    III. Condition 2
        A. Evidence item 3
        B. Evidence item 4
    IV. Summary

As you read the Writing Sample topic, extract the information called for by the outline and place it in the appropriate place in the outline format. All of the information you need is provided in the topic. The outline uses the information and organization of the topic to establish the structure of the Writing Sample. An example based on the preceding topic follows.

I. Positions
   Trustee
   Vote to use million for Art Dept.

Under the positions heading, two points are noted. The first is the position or perspective from which you will write. In this instance, the topic is to be viewed from the perspective of a college trustee. The LSAT will always indicate this perspective. It is there for you to use.

The second point is the position that you will advocate. It makes no difference which position you choose, as long as you choose one. Any ambivalence, however, will make a difference—it wastes time and introduces confusion. To avoid ambivalence, select the position you will advocate before you go to the test center to take the LSAT. In fact, decide right now! Determine whether you will always advocate position one or position two for any Writing Sample topic. Then, be disciplined enough to consistently advocate the position you selected.

II. Condition 1
    Decreasing enrollment over years
    A. Evidence item 1
       Poor quality of Art Dept. overcome by:
          studio art program addition
          art history curriculum expansion

    B. Evidence item 2
       Strong Economics Dept. will get all students it normally would without getting donation

Decreasing enrollment is the first condition to be addressed. The first item of evidence is drawn directly from the topic as presented; the second is not drawn directly from the topic but is consistent with it.

III. Condition 2
     Disharmony between faculty and students over years
     A. Evidence item 3
        Add four art faculty members with views compatible with students' views
     B. Evidence item 4
        Using donation to expand economics faculty will exacerbate existing disharmony, because faculty members will choose more like themselves

Faculty-student disharmony is the second condition to be addressed. Evidence item 3 is drawn directly from the topic, while item 4 is an extension of material given in the topic.

> IV. Summary
> Using donations for Art Dept.
> will increase enrollment and
> improve faculty-student
> harmony

The summary statement reiterates how the conditions will be answered by the position selected.

HOW DO YOU PRODUCE YOUR WRITING SAMPLE?

You will organize your Writing Sample in much the same way that a lawyer makes a jury presentation. Advocate the position you selected, writing positively and confidently in support of it. Avoid weighing the pros and cons of the competing positions, and steer clear of improvisations, inspirations, and uncertainties.

✔ **SPEND ABOUT 15 MINUTES COMPLETING YOUR WRITING SAMPLE.**

The necessary steps can be summarized as follows:

1. State your position and what you will prove.

2. Select and support your position with available proof.

3. Summarize what you have proved.

Based upon the outline, your Writing Sample should be structured into four paragraphs. In paragraph one, you use one sentence to state your position and a second sentence to state what you will establish.

> As a trustee, I will vote to use the
> million-dollar donation for the
> development of the Art Department
> at Whistler College. Using the donation
> to expand the art faculty and hire an
> artist-in-residence will result in an
> increase in enrollment at the college
> and a reduction in the disharmony
> between faculty and students.

In paragraph two, use one or two sentences to present an item of evidence that meets the first condition, using the topic material. Then use a second sentence or two to support the position you chose or oppose the position you did not choose. If you opt for the latter, be sure to explain the position you oppose.

Responding to the first condition by supporting your position with two items of evidence is sufficient for the second paragraph. Some test-takers feel compelled to write more in paragraph two. If you must, use another sentence or two to support the position you chose or oppose the position you did not choose.

> Recently, many students left
> Whistler or chose not to enroll at the
> college because of the poor quality
> of the Art Department. By using the
> donation to develop a studio art
> program and to support the expansion
> of the art history curriculum, the
> Art Department will become
> attractive to students who previously
> left or did not consider Whistler, and
> enrollment at the college will increase.
> Conversely, using the donation to
> improve the Economics Department
> will not lead to an increase in
> enrollment at Whistler, because
> the strength of the economics
> faculty already attracts all of
> the economics students who consider
> going to college here.

Paragraph three has the same structure as paragraph two. Use one or two sentences to present an item of evidence that meets the second condition, using the topic material. Then write a sentence or two to support the position you chose or oppose the position you did not choose. Again, support of your position on the second condition with two items of evidence is sufficient to complete the third paragraph, though, if you must write more, it is all right to use another sentence or two to support the position you chose or oppose the position you did not choose.

The disharmony between faculty and students will be reduced by using the donation to add four faculty members to the Art Department. Selecting new faculty members whose political views are more compatible with those of the students will result in an improved balance between the political views of faculty and students. Were the donation used to expand the economics faculty, the present faculty members would choose new members whose political views were the same as their own, and the existing disharmony between faculty and students would be increased.

In paragraph four, summarize how the position you selected will satisfy the topic conditions. This paragraph should be brief—no more than two sentences.

In conclusion, by using the million-dollar donation to improve the Art Department at Whistler College, the trustees will have acted to ensure that student enrollment increases and that harmony between faculty and students is enhanced.

Upon completion of the Writing Sample, proofread your work and correct the vocabulary, grammar, punctuation, and spelling.

✔ **MAKE SURE YOU LEAVE 5 MINUTES TO PROOFREAD YOUR WRITING SAMPLE.**

Do not vary this structure. It applies to every Writing Sample.

Suppose that you selected the second position. As noted earlier, the position you choose makes no difference with respect to the Writing Sample. You would follow the same plan and produce a similar Writing Sample.

As a trustee, I will vote to use the million-dollar donation for the development of the Economics Department at Whistler College. Using the donation to improve the economics faculty will result in an increase in enrollment at the college and a reduction in the disharmony between faculty and students.

Recently, enrollment at Whistler has declined. By using the donation to turn the already strong Economics Department into the best in the region, we will attract students who presently choose to go elsewhere. The student body will grow on a foundation of excellence. Conversely, using the donation to improve the Art Department will result, at best, in a decent program that will not be good enough to attract any more students than now attend Whistler.

The disharmony between faculty and students will be reduced by using the donation to add faculty members to the Economics Department. New faculty members will be chosen whose political views are more compatible with those of the students, and this will result in a balance of views within the Economics Department. Thus, there will be greater harmony between the students and the economics faculty because there will be less difference between their views. Were the donation used to expand the art faculty, the disharmony between the economics faculty and the students would not be reduced and would continue to cause problems for Whistler.

In conclusion, by using the million-dollar donation to improve the Economics Department at Whistler College, the trustees will have acted to ensure that student enrollment increases and that harmony between faculty and students is improved and maintained.

✔ **BY STRICT ADHERENCE TO YOUR PLAN, YOU WILL BE ABLE TO PRODUCE WITH EFFICIENCY A WRITING SAMPLE THAT SATISFIES THE LSAT'S OBJECTIVES AND YOURS.**

WHAT PRINCIPLES OF VOCABULARY, GRAMMAR, PUNCTUATION, AND MECHANICS ARE IMPORTANT TO YOUR WRITING SAMPLE PERFORMANCE?

For the same reason that the LSAT uses the same-language disguise on the LSAT, you should use the same language as is used in the topic. Not only does this sound convincing, but it helps you avoid misusing words. Misuse will not be a problem if you use only words that are familiar and have clear meaning for you.

Avoid clichés or idiomatic expressions: They invariably offend someone. Never use a pronoun other than "I." "It," "they," and the like often have unclear referents. Avoid legalese in any form.

You should already be familiar with the rules of grammar required to produce a Writing Sample. The following alerts are reminders of a few matters of particular importance: Sentences must be complete; adjectives modify nouns and adverbs modify verbs or adjectives; parallel construction is required; and double negatives should be avoided.

Use only two forms of punctuation on your Writing Sample—the period and the comma. Avoid the need to use any other form of punctuation. Keep it simple, correct, and safe from mistake.

There are three mechanical items that are of concern. Paragraphs should be indented. The passive voice should be avoided; it is difficult to use properly, especially under pressure. And last, avoid contractions. They make a less powerful presentation.

Success Session 14

WRITING PRACTICE SESSIONS

The Writing Sample practice sessions differ from those involving Relationships, Arguments, and Passages. The 9-12-18 planning system is not applicable to the Writing Sample, in which there is no need to balance speed and accuracy. The objective is to complete the Writing Sample with a cogent argument that responds clearly to the assigned topic by taking one of the given positions and satisfying the stated conditions.

WHAT IS YOUR WRITING SAMPLE PLAN?

The techniques you worked through in Session 13 provide the basis for your plan, which is designed to take advantage of the predictability of the Writing Sample. Except for the specific words, you should have the structure and all the structural details of your Writing Sample fixed in advance of the test.

As with all sections of the LSAT, time is a critical factor. The plan permits you to take maximum advantage of the 30 minutes available for the Writing Sample. Your objective is to use the 30 minutes to connect your predetermined structure to the test topic and complete the required writing. First you fill in the outline, which is used to structure the components of your Writing Sample, and then you write the actual sample.

HOW DO YOU USE THE WRITING SAMPLES IN THIS SESSION?

There are three Writing Sample pretests at the end of this session. They are to be used to familiarize yourself with the process you will follow in completing the actual LSAT Writing Sample. After you have completed working through all of the techniques in Session 13, complete one of the practice samples. Take no more than 30 minutes.

Upon completion of the sample, go through and criticize your performance, sentence by sentence. Be certain that you have executed all aspects of your plan. If you have, you will have produced a legible and cogent writing sample. If you can identify a weakness or omission, review all of the techniques in Session 13. Only after this review, complete another sample, and repeat your critique.

HOW MANY SAMPLES SHOULD YOU COMPLETE?

Complete one to five writing samples. Once you complete a Writing Sample that satisfies your plan, there is no improvement to be realized by completing additional samples. You can use any remaining sample topics to maintain your familiarity with the Writing Sample techniques.

While there is little reason to seek out further Writing Samples, the disclosed tests offered by Law School Admission Services include a Writing Sample topic. Some LSAT preparation books also provide topics, but if you use such preparation books, you must make certain that the topics are constructed to the same specifications as those of the LSAT.

WHAT ARE THE DIRECTIONS FOR THE WRITING SAMPLE?

The general directions for the Writing Sample, which were discussed in Session 13, apply to the practice exercises as well. Your are to complete a short writing exercise on the assigned topic. You have only 30 minutes to plan, organize, and write the sample. You must write only on the topic specified.

There is no right or wrong answer to the topic. No special knowledge is expected or required. Law schools are interested in how clearly you express the position you take on the topic and how carefully you support that position. They are interested in organization, vocabulary, and writing mechanics. How well you write is more important than the amount you write. The schools understand that you will be writing under pressure and are limited to a short time in which to produce the finished sample.

Your writing should be confined to the lined area in the booklet, since only this area will be reproduced for the law schools. You will have enough space in the booklet if you plan carefully, write on every line, avoid margins, and limit your writing to a reasonable size. Be certain that you write legibly.

WRITING SAMPLE TOPIC 1

The First Church of Newhope, having outgrown its 150-year-old building, has moved into a new facility and is trying to decide what to do with the old building. As a member of the committee charged with making the decision, you must write an article in support of selling the old building to Newhope University or renting it to the Lutheran Church. Two considerations guide your decision:

- There is a high risk of vandalism in the area where the old church building is located.
- First Church income has been steadily declining over the past three years.

The real estate market is depressed at the present time, and the University's offer to buy the church for $200,000 is 40 percent greater than any other offer received. The University will use the building as a student rathskeller, selling beer and snacks as well as holding dances and parties. The University needs an immediate answer, because it is committed to opening a rathskeller within six months to overcome student and community concerns about the problems caused by the lack of such a facility. Many church members object to the use planned by the University, and some residents of the neighborhood in which the church is located are very upset about the noise and traffic that would result from the University's purchase.

The Lutherans are remodeling their Sunday school and want to rent the old church for about a year. They can only pay rent of $400 per month, and minimal upkeep on the building is $5,000 a year. The use by a church satisfies those who object to the use planned by the University, but others are concerned because the building will only be occupied on Sunday. Some church members feel that the real estate market will be stronger in a year and there will be more options then, while others feel that property in the area is depreciating in value and the church will have to find another tenant, which will be very difficult.

WRITING SAMPLE TOPIC 2

As the director of the Atreeta State Park, you must write in support of one of two staff recommendations to the state Parks Department on how to alleviate the crowded conditions in and damage to the natural character of Atreeta that has resulted from a recent increase in wilderness hiking and camping. One recommendation is to reduce the number of trails and designated camping areas and install a booking system to limit the number of visitors using the park at any one time. The other recommendation is to increase the number of trails and designated camping areas and charge a fee for the use of the park. Two Parks Department policies guide your decision:

- Encouraging more people to enjoy wilderness backpacking and camping.
- Preserving the natural wilderness environment for public enjoyment.

By decreasing the number of trails and campsites, damage would be confined to specific small areas of the park, and the enforcement of rules designed to prevent damage would be made easier. The reservation system would eliminate overcrowding and, by designating trails and campsites, ensure that hikers and campers enjoy the solitude of the wilderness. But, by confining park users and requiring reservations, the park objectives of spontaneity and freedom to enjoy the natural environment would be destroyed.

By increasing the number of trails and campsites in the park, more people would be able to hike and camp comfortably, while damage would be less concentrated and easier to repair. The fee would provide funds to make any needed repairs. But the fee would tend to reduce the number of people using the park, and more trails and campsites would make it more difficult to enforce park rules.

152

WRITING SAMPLE TOPIC 3

As the conductor of the Ventara Symphony Orchestra, you must give your decision on whether to try to offset a serious operating deficit for the coming year by increasing ticket prices or by lengthening the concert schedule and including a greater number of more popular programs in the schedule. Two considerations guide your decision:

- Most of the orchestra's grant support depends upon its maintaining its very strong artistic reputation.
- For the past three years, orchestra ticket sales have averaged only 70 percent of capacity.

Increasing ticket prices by 35 percent would produce sufficient revenue to meet the projected operating deficit, provided that ticket sales increased to 85 percent of capacity. Some advisers have indicated that higher ticket prices would result in reduced attendance, and that there is some risk that a price increase would alienate some of those who now provide grants to the orchestra.

The orchestra's income should increase with the presentation of more concerts, but the musicians' contract does not permit more concerts, and, despite the financial problems, the musicians are likely to demand increased salaries for additional work. Also, while scheduling more popular concerts should increase attendance, such concerts do not enhance the orchestra's reputation and, in the eyes of many, detract from it.

Success Session 15

In this final session, you will put the finishing touches on your LSAT training techniques. The first part of the session briefly reviews the critical test performance factors you have been concentrating on. If you are uncertain about any of the test-taking techniques as you work through the review, stop and go back to the session that deals with the subject. Work through the techniques until your uncertainty is put to rest.

The second part of the session alerts you to a variety of minor factors that also influence your test performance and discusses quick-and-easy techniques for controlling them.

WHAT ARE THE CRITICAL TEST PERFORMANCE FACTORS?

Anxiety

Preparation anxiety and test anxiety influence your performance. Control is the key to managing them. You gain control by choosing to take the test, familiarizing yourself with it, thinking positively, and worrying constructively. You choose to accept the LSAT challenge and all of the baggage that travels with it. You make yourself familiar with the test and its use in every practical detail. You develop techniques that allow you to have a positive response to every aspect of the LSAT. You recognize worry as the sign of a loss of control, which triggers a response that will work to regain that control.

Conditioning

Conditioning is even more important to your test performance than anxiety. Nearly all of your former academic and test-taking conditioning is potentially detrimental to your LSAT performance. You have neither the time nor reason to alter it. Your strategy is to avoid your conditioning and, as a consequence, minimize its influence on your performance. Learning specific techniques for handling every aspect of the test renders your conditioning irrelevant to the LSAT.

The Basic Reasoning Task

The basic reasoning task, which is required by every LSAT question, can be characterized as conditional reasoning. Each of the three types of LSAT questions presents the conditional reasoning task in a different format, but every one asks you to determine which evidence or conclusion satisfies the conditions presented in the statement and question. More specifically, you are asked to determine the evidence or conclusion that **must**, **could**, or **cannot** satisfy the given conditions.

The Techniques

Good techniques yield optimal LSAT performance. The right techniques ensure that you perform the basic reasoning task effectively and consistently. They neutralize the test-maker's strategy of obfuscation. The test-maker uses unfamiliar contexts, varied structures, ambiguities, illusions, distractions, complexities, and multiple formats to obfuscate the basic reasoning task. Various disguises— **same language, too-little-too-much, true but,** and **false assertion**—are also used. Your techniques consistently and expeditiously guide you through the jungle of obfuscation directly to the familiar reasoning task.

Discipline

Discipline is required for you to develop your section-test plan. Maintaining the discipline of working through the LSAT by question sets is the keystone of your performance. The discipline of completing the pretest question sets provides you with the information upon which you base your plan for optimum performance (highest score). Having the discipline to consistently execute the techniques within the context of your plan maximizes your performance.

WHAT SHOULD YOU DO WHEN THE TEST IS IMMINENT?

The Date

You choose the date on which you will take the LSAT. The most important factor to consider when making the choice is readiness. Use the fact that the LSAT is administered four times a year to your advantage. Unlike performance on many other standardized tests, LSAT performance does not improve clearly with educational level. Aside from specific test preparation, there seems to be no significant improvement in test performance after the completion of two years of college. So you have many test dates from which to choose. After you are ready, choose the test date that makes you most comfortable. For example, June may be most comfortable for students, teachers, or people in the ski-resort business.

The Site

Register to take the test at a site that gives you an advantage. For many, the "home-court advantage" is a major performance plus. Others trade familiarity for small size. A huge test site with central check-in, room assignments, and other complexities can trash a large reserve of control in short order, whereas a small center sometimes provides the advantages of informality and low tension. Find out about the location and size of test centers from Law School Admission Services if you think that either might give you an advantage.

Wherever you choose to take the LSAT, familiarize yourself with the site in advance. Know exactly how you will travel there and what you will do with your car when you arrive. Many a person has lost test-taker control to campus parking, rearranged for a homecoming football game. If you cannot visit the site before the test date, get there early and check it out. Then leave the test area and return just before test time.

Locate the rest room at the test site and the most direct route to it from the test room. This is important since, if you have to use the rest room during the test, it is on your time. There is usually a 15-minute break between the second and third section-tests.

Light is also a matter of concern. Trying to concentrate on the LSAT when you are sitting in a dark corner of an auditorium or staring into the sun is not advantageous. If the light at your assigned seat is inadequate, seek out the proctor and insist, politely but firmly, that you be moved.

Avoid distractions. If you are easily distracted, you should not sit at the back of a room of 200 people, each of whom will provide you with at least one distraction in the course of the test. For you, it's "down in front."

What Should You Do When the Test Is Tomorrow?

The Tools

You will need some obvious and not-so-obvious tools to take the LSAT. Get them together early on the day before the test. The No. 2 pencil is tool number one, as answer sheets must be completed in pencil. Prepare and take four pencils to the test—they should have full erasers and not be needle sharp. (Needle-sharp pencils lacerate answer sheets, and their points splinter. Slightly blunted points are best.) The Writing Sample must be completed in pen, and pens are provided at the test. Though it is not explicitly sanctioned, many test-takers prefer to use their own pens. They should have black ink and be erasable, which eliminates the need for crossing out. The resulting neat look is a plus in ensuring that your Writing Sample does not disqualify you. If you wish to use a highlighter for marking Passages or Arguments problems, bring at least two in the colors of your choice.

A reliable watch or equivalent time-minder is essential to your performance. Before you begin to work through a section-test, calculate and write at the starting point of each question set within it the exact time you have planned to be at that point. This makes your time checks easy to perform as you track your pace through each question set.

The test-maker discourages the ingestion of food at the test center, but the test is long, and administrative procedures at some centers make the testing time even longer. How does a conscientious test-taker reconcile a desire not to transgress by eating with the equally strong desire not to have a growling stomach disturb the test center? Those who have resolved this dilemma successfully strongly advise against the crunchy, the smelly, and the gooey. Pretzels, potato chips, or celery sticks crunch noisily when eaten. Worse still are beef jerky, pepperoni, and cheese. Their capacity for olfactory offense is nearly limitless. Avoid fudge, toffee, nougat, and the like, since they are sticky and endanger neat paperwork. Otherwise, it is the test-taker's choice—cookies and candy work well. During cool weather, jacket pockets are good for holding food. The marsupial sweatshirt with the pouch in the front carries a lot, is comfortable, and gives convenient access to your food. Make sure you snack between, not during, question sets.

If you take medication, be sure that you have a supply with you. Aspirin or some alternative form of medicine may prevent a distracting headache. Smoking is not permitted at LSAT test centers. If it will help, get your nicotine gum prescription filled before the test. The test is not a good time to go cold turkey.

The Run-Up

Two basic strategies are advocated for the time just before the test. Advocates of the Jell-O strategy believe that it is best to sit back and let your plan and techniques gel during this period. Ben-Gay advocates claim that a little warm-up working one last set of questions is the best way to spend it. Studies have shown that neither strategy has a greater impact than the other on performance.

What is significant is that you avoid either "zoom" or "doom and gloom." Extremes of emotion and activity can have a negative impact on your performance. Maintaining emotional equilibrium and your typical level of activity will ensure that you are in the best position to concentrate during the test. Follow a regimen that encourages a sense of relaxation. If a good party the night before is a shortcut to relaxation for you, try to avoid relaxing too far. There is no evidence that a roaring hangover leads to poor test performance, but the LSAT is hard enough without helping it along.

Adjust your personal schedule to the hour of the test. If you are not a morning person and are scheduled to take the LSAT in the morning, set your alarm to give you sufficient time to come out of your morning fog before the test starts.

WHAT SHOULD YOU DO WHEN THE TEST IS NOW?

The Routines

On the day of the test, proceed as normally as possible, especially with respect to your schedule, level of activity, and intake of food and liquid. Staying as close as possible to your regular schedule supports you in carrying out your planned response to the predictability of the LSAT. Changing all of your routines in honor of test day is counterproductive, since it disrupts your plan. Eating a lumberjack's breakfast on the morning of the test in order to avoid the risk of midmorning burnout is more likely to give you indigestion, and drinking twelve cups of coffee to make sure you stay awake will probably make you hyperactive in more ways than one. Stick with the familiar.

The Test Administration

Travel to the test site on a schedule that leaves you feeling unhurried. Make sure you have built in enough flexibility to allow for unexpected holdups. Once you reach the test center, find a place where you can stay relaxed until the time for check-in. Milling about the test center with other test-takers for an hour or two before the exam is not constructive.

After check-in, make certain that there is no problem with your seat assignment—check that you have the light and work space that you require. Then be prepared for a full dose of "hurry up and wait."

After all test-takers are seated, the supervisor will read the test instructions. Listen carefully. You will be told exactly how to mark your answer sheet, the amount of warning you will be given before the end of each section-test (usually 5 minutes), the timing of the break (usually 15 minutes between the second and third sections), and what the "housekeeping" arrangements are.

The test may begin with the 30-minute Writing Sample, or this may appear at the end. Upon its completion, you will work through two of the 35-minute section-tests. The order of the section-tests is scrambled, so not all test-takers are working through the same section-tests at the same time. Next comes a break, and, after that, the last three section-tests are administered. As you begin each section-test, remember to mark at the start of each question set the time at which your plan calls for you to start that set.

Work your way through the question sets, identifying and dumping as many wrong-answer options as you can. Use comparison and contrast to analyze the answer options that remain. If all fails, and you have not been able to identify some of the wrong-answer options, guess. Believe it or not, statistics gathered over the years favor answer options other than (A) and (E) as the best selections, so when guessing, avoid these two options. In fact, it is a good practice to always guess the same answer option—(B), (C), or (D). Do not try to hit the test-maker's choice; let the test-maker hit yours.

Plan on the unexpected when you take the LSAT. Babies have been born, bands have played outside the test-room window, people have walked out and passed out, blizzards have blown, power has failed, plumbing has broken, supervisors have mistimed, fire alarms have sounded, and mysterious smells have wafted across the room. Anticipate the unexpected, and stay relaxed during a crisis. It will pass, and, when order is restored and the test resumes, you do not want to be too distracted to perform at your best.

To be perfectly realistic, you will be distracted from time to time during the many-hour test. You will lose your concentration. When you do, take a short break. Then take three deep breaths, exhaling slowly after each one. Your concentration will be restored, and you will return to maximum performance power.

If you lose all control and panic, freeze, choke, or go blank, stop. Get up and ask permission to leave the test room. Get a drink of water, take a number of deep breaths, and give yourself a chance to regroup outside the test room. Most people quickly regain their composure, return to the test, and complete it without further bother. If you do not regain yours, cancel your score and go. (The cancellation process is described later in this session.) Avoid sitting through the test, waiting for a picture to come onto your screen. If there is no signal from the tower, there can be no picture on the screen. Try again another day.

There is one overarching rule for test-takers: *conform*—just for a few hours. Do not fight the process, your plan, your techniques, the questions, or the answer options. Forget tricks, quibbles, creativity, or proving the test-maker wrong.

Avoid leaving stray marks and incomplete erasures on your answer sheet. Always mark every correct answer in the test book, and write your name on it. If your answer sheet were to be lost, having every answer marked in a test book with your name on it could save you from having to retake the test. Are answer sheets lost?—yes. Often?—rarely.

Assorted Alerts

As your work in previous sessions has shown you, the techniques designed to neutralize the test-maker's obfuscation patterns and strategies simultaneously facilitate wrong-answer identification and superior test performance. There are also a number of patterns and strategies that the test-maker uses episodically with all LSAT question types. Being alert to these further patterns and strategies while applying the other test-taking techniques you have learned will

enhance your identification of wrong answers and your test performance.

The first alert relates to the test-maker's use of absolutes and qualifiers—*always, never, some, few, all, none, every, many,* and similar terms usually flag a pivotal or decisive condition. When you encounter an absolute or a qualifier in a statement or answer option, focus your full attention on its implications within the question context. It is not coincidental—the use of an absolute or qualifier is intentional and significant.

The test-maker's use of negatives and exceptions is frequently an obfuscation strategy. Be alert to NOT, EXCEPT, and their progeny and relatives (they are usually capitalized, as shown here). The rate of best-answer selection falls substantially for many test-takers when negatives and exceptions are involved. Because the large majority of LSAT statements, questions, and answer options involve positives, you anticipate a positive and often overlook a negative. So, when you first see a negative or an exception in a statement, question, or answer option, note it boldly to keep yourself alert to the point as you work through the question.

When a double negative appears—a NOT in the statement and a CANNOT in the question, or a CANNOT in the question and a NOT in an answer option—a double alert is called for. A similar double alert applies to the combination of a negative and an exception. For example, such questions as "All of the following are not true EXCEPT. . . ." require redoubled concentration for you.

The mismatched answer-option structure also deserves an alert. When you encounter an answer-option set in which four of the options present a similar word pattern and the fifth is totally different, your eye is drawn to the different one as a possible answer. It usually is not.

Be alert to questions and answer options that appear later in a series based on a single statement. You may often be attracted to an answer because your thinking has been influenced by the preceding questions and answer options. If you find yourself falling prey to this phenomenon, try considering questions and answer options out of the sequence in which they appear. Work through the last first or the middle last.

Be especially alert to the multiple-option format. Recall that it appears to be more difficult because more than one of the Roman numeral options can satisfy the required conditions. For most test-takers, performance suffers on questions employing this format.

HOW DO YOU MAKE POSTTEST DECISIONS?

Debriefing

Immediately upon completion of the test and before you leave the test center, take a few minutes to note particulars of the test and the administration that you are able to remember. For future reference, record the order of the section-tests, the number of question sets you completed, special difficulties encountered, surprises, uncertainties, and the like. At some point during the next 24 hours, review these notes. It is desirable to conduct this debriefing with someone else—preferably someone familiar with the LSAT.

The objectives of this debriefing are to ascertain any significant discrepancies between your test plan and your actual performance and to identify any factors that had a negative impact on your performance. If you deviated significantly from your test plan or encountered a problem that you are convinced means you did not perform well on the test, the possibility of canceling your test score arises.

Cancellation

Once the test administration has begun, your options with respect to the test score are to do nothing or to cancel your score. If you do nothing, your answer sheet is scored and the score reported. If you cancel your score, it is not reported, but the fact that the score was canceled is reported. Thus, you cancel your score only when the debriefing produces solid information that an informed person other than yourself interprets as a significant deviation from your test plan or a serious problem. A mere sense of unease about your performance or a feeling that you did not perform as well as you might have does not constitute a clear and convincing reason to cancel your score.

You have five working days to cancel your test score. There is no reason to rush to cancel with less than full information and an informed perspective to guide your decision. If you do decide to cancel, you must do so in writing to LSAS, Box 2000-T, Newtown, PA 18940. A mailgram, telegram, or letter requesting that your score be canceled is sufficient. (At the time of this writing, a request by fax does not meet the stated requirements of LSAS.) You do not need to explain your decision, so don't.

In addition to your name and your Social Security (USA), Social Insurance (Canada), or LSAS identification number, your request to cancel must also include the test date, test center, and test center code of the administration involved. The score you would have received is not reported to you or to the law schools.

Postmortems

Reviewing test questions, answer selections, and the like with fellow test-takers seldom provides any reliable information about your performance. In fact, the typical LSAT postmortem tends to confound posttest decision making. The prospect of getting any benefit from a postmortem is so slight that you should make every effort to avoid such after-test comparisons. Stick with the debriefing as the most effective way of making informed posttest decisions.

Retakes

There is no restriction on the number of times you may take the LSAT. Of course, totally different questions are used at each administration of the test. And the average of an applicant's test scores is reported to law schools in addition to the scores themselves.

Studies done over a period of many years show that most—but certainly not all—people who retake the LSAT do score higher on the retake. The same studies show that the increase is small for the majority, and the score increase appears to be even smaller when averaged. For example, a score improvement of four points on a retake results in an averaged score increase of only two points.

Only when your pretest data indicate that a large score improvement could be realized is a retake recommended. From the perspective of most admission committees, the reflection of a very small or nonexistent score increase seems to cast a shadow rather than a glow on an applicant.

WHAT ABOUT TEST RESULTS?

The Wait

The wait for test results is relatively long. It generally takes between four and six weeks for results to be reported. The test-maker waits for nearly all answer sheets to be received, processed, and checked before issuing scores. There is no way to hurry the process along.

The Check

Your test score is issued on an LSAT Candidate Report form. The report is accompanied by a photocopy of your answer sheet and a copy of all scored test questions.

Your LSAT answer sheet is scored by a machine that "reads" the blackened bubbles and produces a score report reflecting what was "seen." The score report also includes your answer selection and the best selection for each question on the test. When the two failed to match, your perfect score was reduced by one. Check every answer on your score report against your answer sheet.

What the scoring machine "sees" is what you get. The machine can mistakenly interpret a stray mark, incomplete erasure, or similar phenomenon and not give you proper credit. If you have misplaced a series of answers, the machine does not know. By checking your answer sheet for any discrepancies, you can identify problems.

The most direct way to resolve a problem of this nature is the hand-scoring process. Upon your request and the payment of a fee, your answer sheet will be scored by hand, but this will take place only after machine scoring and score reporting are completed. Write to LSAS at Box 2000, Newtown, PA 18940, and describe the problem fully. Include exhibits with your description. If, for example, you misplaced a series of responses on your answer sheet, specify where the misplacement started and stopped, and indicate the misplacement on a photocopy of the photocopy of your answer sheet. Any verifiable problem will be resolved and a revised score report issued.

It is very important that you complete this checking process immediately upon receipt of your score report.

The Response

Your test results ought to reflect your test plan. If there is a substantial difference between the expected and actual results, carefully review your performance, and determine the nature and extent of the differences. Based upon your review, decide whether a retake of the test is warranted.

Your test results will provide you with options and choices. Law school admission is not quite as predictable as the LSAT, but with some well-guided research and counseling, realistic options and choices can be defined clearly and quickly acted upon. Just as you balanced your speed and accuracy to achieve optimal performance on the LSAT section-tests, you should balance your prospects and objectives for admission to develop an optimal list of law schools to which you should apply. Based upon this list, complete your plan by applying to the law schools that suit you.

ARE THERE ANY LAST WORDS OF ADVICE?

Now that you have reached this point, you know that there is a better way to prepare for the LSAT. If you consistently apply the techniques acquired through the fifteen success sessions and three Red Alerts in this book and assiduously avoid the reflexes developed through your many years of academic conditioning, you will put the LSAT in its place—working for you.

May you take advantage of the LSAT in every way on your test day!

LSAT Practice Tests

LAW SCHOOL ADMISSION TEST SIMULATIONS

On the following pages are two examples of what a real LSAT is like. According to the test-taking strategies you have developed during the course of your training, you may use these tests in one of two ways.

First, you could work only on those sections of the tests that you feel require additional practice. Use the individual section-tests of this simulation as if each is a pretest, employing the 9-12-18 system to sharpen your test-taking techniques (Sections 1 and 3 contain Relationships problems, Sections 2 and 5 contain Arguments problems, and Section 4 contains Passages problems). Review the sessions on the particular question type before beginning, and be sure to follow the instructions for each section-test carefully.

The second way to approach these simulated tests is to treat them as if you were taking an actual LSAT. In this case, you would spend 35 minutes on each of the five section-tests (remember the experimental section?), in effect putting the 9-12-18 system through a dry run in preparation for this 3-hour-and-25-minute test. Work only on one section during the 35 minutes allowed, and do not work on or review other sections. Take a 15-minute break between Sections 3 and 4 of the test. After Section 5, spend 30 minutes on the Writing Sample.

Whichever method of working through the questions you choose, mark the best answers in the book, and, when you have finished a question set, transfer your choices to the answer sheet (page 162 for Practice Test 1; page 200 for Practice Test 2). For ease of use, you might want to photocopy the answer sheet before working on the questions.

Quick-Score Answers to Practice Test 1 are on page 191, the Explanatory Answers for Practice Test 1 begin on page 192.

Quick-Score Answers to Practice Test 2 are on page 229, the Explanatory Answers for Practice Test 2 begin on page 230.

Law School Admission Test Simulation Answer Sheet

SECTION 1	SECTION 2	SECTION 3	SECTION 4	SECTION 5
1. Ⓐ Ⓑ Ⓒ Ⓓ Ⓔ	1. Ⓐ Ⓑ Ⓒ Ⓓ Ⓔ	1. Ⓐ Ⓑ Ⓒ Ⓓ Ⓔ	1. Ⓐ Ⓑ Ⓒ Ⓓ Ⓔ	1. Ⓐ Ⓑ Ⓒ Ⓓ Ⓔ
2. Ⓐ Ⓑ Ⓒ Ⓓ Ⓔ	2. Ⓐ Ⓑ Ⓒ Ⓓ Ⓔ	2. Ⓐ Ⓑ Ⓒ Ⓓ Ⓔ	2. Ⓐ Ⓑ Ⓒ Ⓓ Ⓔ	2. Ⓐ Ⓑ Ⓒ Ⓓ Ⓔ
3. Ⓐ Ⓑ Ⓒ Ⓓ Ⓔ	3. Ⓐ Ⓑ Ⓒ Ⓓ Ⓔ	3. Ⓐ Ⓑ Ⓒ Ⓓ Ⓔ	3. Ⓐ Ⓑ Ⓒ Ⓓ Ⓔ	3. Ⓐ Ⓑ Ⓒ Ⓓ Ⓔ
4. Ⓐ Ⓑ Ⓒ Ⓓ Ⓔ	4. Ⓐ Ⓑ Ⓒ Ⓓ Ⓔ	4. Ⓐ Ⓑ Ⓒ Ⓓ Ⓔ	4. Ⓐ Ⓑ Ⓒ Ⓓ Ⓔ	4. Ⓐ Ⓑ Ⓒ Ⓓ Ⓔ
5. Ⓐ Ⓑ Ⓒ Ⓓ Ⓔ	5. Ⓐ Ⓑ Ⓒ Ⓓ Ⓔ	5. Ⓐ Ⓑ Ⓒ Ⓓ Ⓔ	5. Ⓐ Ⓑ Ⓒ Ⓓ Ⓔ	5. Ⓐ Ⓑ Ⓒ Ⓓ Ⓔ
6. Ⓐ Ⓑ Ⓒ Ⓓ Ⓔ	6. Ⓐ Ⓑ Ⓒ Ⓓ Ⓔ	6. Ⓐ Ⓑ Ⓒ Ⓓ Ⓔ	6. Ⓐ Ⓑ Ⓒ Ⓓ Ⓔ	6. Ⓐ Ⓑ Ⓒ Ⓓ Ⓔ
7. Ⓐ Ⓑ Ⓒ Ⓓ Ⓔ	7. Ⓐ Ⓑ Ⓒ Ⓓ Ⓔ	7. Ⓐ Ⓑ Ⓒ Ⓓ Ⓔ	7. Ⓐ Ⓑ Ⓒ Ⓓ Ⓔ	7. Ⓐ Ⓑ Ⓒ Ⓓ Ⓔ
8. Ⓐ Ⓑ Ⓒ Ⓓ Ⓔ	8. Ⓐ Ⓑ Ⓒ Ⓓ Ⓔ	8. Ⓐ Ⓑ Ⓒ Ⓓ Ⓔ	8. Ⓐ Ⓑ Ⓒ Ⓓ Ⓔ	8. Ⓐ Ⓑ Ⓒ Ⓓ Ⓔ
9. Ⓐ Ⓑ Ⓒ Ⓓ Ⓔ	9. Ⓐ Ⓑ Ⓒ Ⓓ Ⓔ	9. Ⓐ Ⓑ Ⓒ Ⓓ Ⓔ	9. Ⓐ Ⓑ Ⓒ Ⓓ Ⓔ	9. Ⓐ Ⓑ Ⓒ Ⓓ Ⓔ
10. Ⓐ Ⓑ Ⓒ Ⓓ Ⓔ	10. Ⓐ Ⓑ Ⓒ Ⓓ Ⓔ	10. Ⓐ Ⓑ Ⓒ Ⓓ Ⓔ	10. Ⓐ Ⓑ Ⓒ Ⓓ Ⓔ	10. Ⓐ Ⓑ Ⓒ Ⓓ Ⓔ
11. Ⓐ Ⓑ Ⓒ Ⓓ Ⓔ	11. Ⓐ Ⓑ Ⓒ Ⓓ Ⓔ	11. Ⓐ Ⓑ Ⓒ Ⓓ Ⓔ	11. Ⓐ Ⓑ Ⓒ Ⓓ Ⓔ	11. Ⓐ Ⓑ Ⓒ Ⓓ Ⓔ
12. Ⓐ Ⓑ Ⓒ Ⓓ Ⓔ	12. Ⓐ Ⓑ Ⓒ Ⓓ Ⓔ	12. Ⓐ Ⓑ Ⓒ Ⓓ Ⓔ	12. Ⓐ Ⓑ Ⓒ Ⓓ Ⓔ	12. Ⓐ Ⓑ Ⓒ Ⓓ Ⓔ
13. Ⓐ Ⓑ Ⓒ Ⓓ Ⓔ	13. Ⓐ Ⓑ Ⓒ Ⓓ Ⓔ	13. Ⓐ Ⓑ Ⓒ Ⓓ Ⓔ	13. Ⓐ Ⓑ Ⓒ Ⓓ Ⓔ	13. Ⓐ Ⓑ Ⓒ Ⓓ Ⓔ
14. Ⓐ Ⓑ Ⓒ Ⓓ Ⓔ	14. Ⓐ Ⓑ Ⓒ Ⓓ Ⓔ	14. Ⓐ Ⓑ Ⓒ Ⓓ Ⓔ	14. Ⓐ Ⓑ Ⓒ Ⓓ Ⓔ	14. Ⓐ Ⓑ Ⓒ Ⓓ Ⓔ
15. Ⓐ Ⓑ Ⓒ Ⓓ Ⓔ	15. Ⓐ Ⓑ Ⓒ Ⓓ Ⓔ	15. Ⓐ Ⓑ Ⓒ Ⓓ Ⓔ	15. Ⓐ Ⓑ Ⓒ Ⓓ Ⓔ	15. Ⓐ Ⓑ Ⓒ Ⓓ Ⓔ
16. Ⓐ Ⓑ Ⓒ Ⓓ Ⓔ	16. Ⓐ Ⓑ Ⓒ Ⓓ Ⓔ	16. Ⓐ Ⓑ Ⓒ Ⓓ Ⓔ	16. Ⓐ Ⓑ Ⓒ Ⓓ Ⓔ	16. Ⓐ Ⓑ Ⓒ Ⓓ Ⓔ
17. Ⓐ Ⓑ Ⓒ Ⓓ Ⓔ	17. Ⓐ Ⓑ Ⓒ Ⓓ Ⓔ	17. Ⓐ Ⓑ Ⓒ Ⓓ Ⓔ	17. Ⓐ Ⓑ Ⓒ Ⓓ Ⓔ	17. Ⓐ Ⓑ Ⓒ Ⓓ Ⓔ
18. Ⓐ Ⓑ Ⓒ Ⓓ Ⓔ	18. Ⓐ Ⓑ Ⓒ Ⓓ Ⓔ	18. Ⓐ Ⓑ Ⓒ Ⓓ Ⓔ	18. Ⓐ Ⓑ Ⓒ Ⓓ Ⓔ	18. Ⓐ Ⓑ Ⓒ Ⓓ Ⓔ
19. Ⓐ Ⓑ Ⓒ Ⓓ Ⓔ	19. Ⓐ Ⓑ Ⓒ Ⓓ Ⓔ	19. Ⓐ Ⓑ Ⓒ Ⓓ Ⓔ	19. Ⓐ Ⓑ Ⓒ Ⓓ Ⓔ	19. Ⓐ Ⓑ Ⓒ Ⓓ Ⓔ
20. Ⓐ Ⓑ Ⓒ Ⓓ Ⓔ	20. Ⓐ Ⓑ Ⓒ Ⓓ Ⓔ	20. Ⓐ Ⓑ Ⓒ Ⓓ Ⓔ	20. Ⓐ Ⓑ Ⓒ Ⓓ Ⓔ	20. Ⓐ Ⓑ Ⓒ Ⓓ Ⓔ
21. Ⓐ Ⓑ Ⓒ Ⓓ Ⓔ	21. Ⓐ Ⓑ Ⓒ Ⓓ Ⓔ	21. Ⓐ Ⓑ Ⓒ Ⓓ Ⓔ	21. Ⓐ Ⓑ Ⓒ Ⓓ Ⓔ	21. Ⓐ Ⓑ Ⓒ Ⓓ Ⓔ
22. Ⓐ Ⓑ Ⓒ Ⓓ Ⓔ	22. Ⓐ Ⓑ Ⓒ Ⓓ Ⓔ	22. Ⓐ Ⓑ Ⓒ Ⓓ Ⓔ	22. Ⓐ Ⓑ Ⓒ Ⓓ Ⓔ	22. Ⓐ Ⓑ Ⓒ Ⓓ Ⓔ
23. Ⓐ Ⓑ Ⓒ Ⓓ Ⓔ	23. Ⓐ Ⓑ Ⓒ Ⓓ Ⓔ	23. Ⓐ Ⓑ Ⓒ Ⓓ Ⓔ	23. Ⓐ Ⓑ Ⓒ Ⓓ Ⓔ	23. Ⓐ Ⓑ Ⓒ Ⓓ Ⓔ
24. Ⓐ Ⓑ Ⓒ Ⓓ Ⓔ	24. Ⓐ Ⓑ Ⓒ Ⓓ Ⓔ	24. Ⓐ Ⓑ Ⓒ Ⓓ Ⓔ	24. Ⓐ Ⓑ Ⓒ Ⓓ Ⓔ	24. Ⓐ Ⓑ Ⓒ Ⓓ Ⓔ
25. Ⓐ Ⓑ Ⓒ Ⓓ Ⓔ	25. Ⓐ Ⓑ Ⓒ Ⓓ Ⓔ	25. Ⓐ Ⓑ Ⓒ Ⓓ Ⓔ	25. Ⓐ Ⓑ Ⓒ Ⓓ Ⓔ	25. Ⓐ Ⓑ Ⓒ Ⓓ Ⓔ
26. Ⓐ Ⓑ Ⓒ Ⓓ Ⓔ	26. Ⓐ Ⓑ Ⓒ Ⓓ Ⓔ	26. Ⓐ Ⓑ Ⓒ Ⓓ Ⓔ	26. Ⓐ Ⓑ Ⓒ Ⓓ Ⓔ	26. Ⓐ Ⓑ Ⓒ Ⓓ Ⓔ
27. Ⓐ Ⓑ Ⓒ Ⓓ Ⓔ	27. Ⓐ Ⓑ Ⓒ Ⓓ Ⓔ	27. Ⓐ Ⓑ Ⓒ Ⓓ Ⓔ	27. Ⓐ Ⓑ Ⓒ Ⓓ Ⓔ	27. Ⓐ Ⓑ Ⓒ Ⓓ Ⓔ
28. Ⓐ Ⓑ Ⓒ Ⓓ Ⓔ	28. Ⓐ Ⓑ Ⓒ Ⓓ Ⓔ	28. Ⓐ Ⓑ Ⓒ Ⓓ Ⓔ	28. Ⓐ Ⓑ Ⓒ Ⓓ Ⓔ	28. Ⓐ Ⓑ Ⓒ Ⓓ Ⓔ
29. Ⓐ Ⓑ Ⓒ Ⓓ Ⓔ	29. Ⓐ Ⓑ Ⓒ Ⓓ Ⓔ	29. Ⓐ Ⓑ Ⓒ Ⓓ Ⓔ	29. Ⓐ Ⓑ Ⓒ Ⓓ Ⓔ	29. Ⓐ Ⓑ Ⓒ Ⓓ Ⓔ
30. Ⓐ Ⓑ Ⓒ Ⓓ Ⓔ	30. Ⓐ Ⓑ Ⓒ Ⓓ Ⓔ	30. Ⓐ Ⓑ Ⓒ Ⓓ Ⓔ	30. Ⓐ Ⓑ Ⓒ Ⓓ Ⓔ	30. Ⓐ Ⓑ Ⓒ Ⓓ Ⓔ

Practice Test 1

The questions in this section are based on a set of conditions. A diagram may be helpful in the answer selection process. Select the best answer to each question, and mark the corresponding space on the answer sheet.

Questions 1–6

A student is preparing a report on statehood. The source material is incomplete, but the following is known.

Wyoming became a state before Ohio.
Kansas became a state before Wyoming.
Ohio became a state after Maine.

1. Which of the following CANNOT be true?

    (A) Kansas was a state before Maine.
    (B) Maine was a state before Wyoming.
    (C) Ohio was a state before Kansas.
    (D) Wyoming was a state before Maine.
    (E) Kansas was a state before Ohio.

2. Which of the following must be true?

    (A) Kansas was a state before Maine.
    (B) Wyoming was a state before Kansas.
    (C) Maine was a state before Kansas.
    (D) Ohio was a state before Maine.
    (E) Kansas was a state before Ohio.

3. If Texas was a state before Maine, which of the following must be true?

    (A) Texas was a state first.
    (B) Texas was a state before Kansas.
    (C) Wyoming was a state before Texas.
    (D) Texas was a state before Ohio.
    (E) Maine was a state before Texas.

4. If Kansas became a state before Maine, Wyoming became a state after Maine, and Vermont was last to become a state, which of the following must be the order of statehood, first to last?

    (A) Vermont, Wyoming, Maine, Ohio, Kansas
    (B) Wyoming, Ohio, Kansas, Vermont, Maine
    (C) Maine, Kansas, Ohio, Vermont, Wyoming
    (D) Kansas, Maine, Wyoming, Ohio, Vermont
    (E) Ohio, Wyoming, Vermont, Kansas, Maine

5. If Utah became a state before Ohio, and Florida became a state after Wyoming, which of the following CANNOT be true if Maine became a state after Utah and before Florida?

    (A) Utah was a state before Wyoming.
    (B) Florida was a state before Ohio.
    (C) Florida was a state before Kansas.
    (D) Maine was a state before Ohio.
    (E) Wyoming was a state before Florida.

6. If Alaska became a state after Iowa and Wyoming, which of the following must be true?

    (A) Alaska was a state before Maine.
    (B) Iowa was a state before Wyoming.
    (C) Iowa was a state before Ohio.
    (D) Alaska was a state before Ohio.
    (E) Kansas was a state before Alaska.

Questions 7–12

T lives in a smaller house than her brother.
T lives in a larger house than her parents.
T's children live with T.
T has no other relatives.

7. If four females and two males live in smaller houses than T's brother, how many of T's children are boys and girls, respectively?

    (A) 1, 0
    (B) 0, 1
    (C) 2, 1
    (D) 1, 2
    (E) 2, 0

8. If T's relative U lives in a larger house than her relative S, and both U and S are the same sex, what relationship could U be to S?

    (A) father to son
    (B) mother to daughter
    (C) daughter to mother
    (D) grandfather to grandson
    (E) son to father

9. If T's relative U lives in a larger house than T's relative S, all of the following may be true EXCEPT

    (A) S is U's son
    (B) S is U's mother
    (C) U is younger than S
    (D) S is younger than U
    (E) U and S are both female

10. If T's relative U is not as old as T, who is not as old as her relative V, what relationship can U NOT be to V?

    (A) grandson
    (B) uncle
    (C) nephew
    (D) son
    (E) granddaughter

11. If, of all T's relatives who could possibly be either older or younger than T, none are the same age or older, how many of T's relatives must be younger than T?

    (A) less than 2
    (B) 2
    (C) 2 or 3
    (D) 3
    (E) more than 3

12. If the number of males related to T equals the number of females related to T, which of the following can be true?

    (A) T has exactly 4 children.
    (B) T has exactly 3 children.
    (C) T has exactly 1 child.
    (D) T has exactly 6 children.
    (E) T has exactly 2 children.

Questions 13–18

Busses 1, 2, and 3 make one trip each day, and they are the only ones that riders A, B, C, D, E, F, and G take to work.

    Neither E nor G takes bus 1 on a day when B does.
    G does not take bus 2 on a day when D does.
    When A and F take the same bus, it is always bus 3.
    C always takes bus 3.

13. Which of the following groups consists of riders who CANNOT take bus 1 to work on the same day?

    (A) A, D, G
    (B) D, E, F
    (C) D, E, G
    (D) E, F, G
    (E) B, D, G

14. Traveling together to work, B, C, and G could take which of the same busses on a given day?

    (A) 1 only
    (B) 2 only
    (C) 3 only
    (D) 2 and 3 only
    (E) 1, 2, and 3

15. The maximum number of riders who could take bus 2 to work on a given day must be

    (A) 3
    (B) 4
    (C) 5
    (D) 6
    (E) 7

16. Traveling together to work, B, D, E, F, and G could take which of the same busses on a given day?

    (A) 1 only
    (B) 2 only
    (C) 3 only
    (D) 1 and 3 only
    (E) 2 and 3 only

17. On a day when each of the riders takes one of the three busses to work, exactly how many riders CANNOT take any bus other than bus 2?

    (A) 0
    (B) 1
    (C) 2
    (D) 3
    (E) 4

18. Which of the following could be a group of riders that takes bus 1 to work on a given day?

    (A) A, C, E, G
    (B) A, D, E, G
    (C) A, E, F, G
    (D) B, D, E, F
    (E) B, D, E, G

Questions 19–24

Angela, Bruce, Cora, Dora, and Elmer live at different points along a straight east-west highway.

> Angela lives 5 miles away from Bruce.
> Cora lives 7 miles away from Dora.
> Elmer lives 2 miles away from Cora.
> Bruce lives 3 miles away from Cora.
> The distance between houses is measured by straight line only.

19. Which of the following could be true?

    (A) Dora lives 9 miles from Elmer.
    (B) Dora lives 2 miles from Bruce.
    (C) Angela lives 5 miles from Cora.
    (D) Elmer lives 2 miles from Bruce.
    (E) Angela lives 18 miles from Dora.

20. Which of the following must be true?

    (A) The distance between Elmer's and Bruce's houses is greater than the distance between Cora's and Angela's houses.
    (B) The distance between Bruce's and Elmer's houses is shorter than the distance between Cora's and Dora's houses.
    (C) Of the group, Dora lives farthest from Cora.
    (D) Cora lives closer to Dora than she does to Angela.
    (E) Elmer lives closer to Cora than Angela does.

21. Which of the following statements must be FALSE?

    (A) Angela and Cora live 12 miles apart.
    (B) Angela and Dora live 5 miles apart.
    (C) Bruce and Dora live 10 miles apart.
    (D) Elmer and Dora live 9 miles apart.
    (E) Elmer and Bruce live 5 miles apart.

22. If Bruce and Dora live east of Cora, which of the following must be the distance between Bruce's and Dora's houses?

    (A) 10 miles
    (B) 8 miles
    (C) 5 miles
    (D) 4 miles
    (E) 2 miles

23. If Bruce and Elmer live east of Cora, and Dora lives west of Cora, which of the following must be true?

    (A) Dora lives closer to Elmer than Cora does to Bruce.
    (B) Cora lives closer to Dora than Elmer does to Bruce.
    (C) Elmer lives closer to Cora than Bruce does to Elmer.
    (D) Bruce lives closer to Elmer than Cora does to Dora.
    (E) Angela lives closer to Bruce than Cora does to Elmer.

24. If Cora, starting from her house, visits Dora, Bruce, and Elmer in that order and then returns home, what is the smallest number of miles she walks?

    (A) 14
    (B) 15
    (C) 16
    (D) 17
    (E) 18

SECTION 2   **TIME—35 MINUTES**   **24 QUESTIONS**

Evaluate the reasoning contained in the brief statements, and select the best answer. Do not make implausible, superfluous, or incompatible assumptions. Select the best answer to each question, and mark the corresponding space on the answer sheet.

1. Well-designed clothing was once described as the hallmark of a stylish person. We agree, and our clothing is designed for stylish people. Their lifestyles are well-defined. They do everything in good taste. And they search out well-designed clothing as the guarantee of good workmanship.

This advertisement is intended to suggest which of the following conclusions?

(A) Well-designed clothing defines a lifestyle.
(B) Good taste is important in clothing design.
(C) Workmanship guarantees good design.
(D) Purchasers of this brand of clothing will be stylish.
(E) Appearance is the hallmark of purchasers of this brand of clothing.

2. Native American tribes seeking monetary reparations from the government are often told, "There is neither wealth nor wisdom enough in the world to compensate in money for all the wrongs in history."

Which of the following most weakens the argument above?

(A) Prior wrongs should not be permitted as a justification for present wrongs.
(B) Even though all wrongs cannot be compensated for, some wrongs can be.
(C) Since most people committed wrongs, the government should compensate for wrongs with money.
(D) Monetary reparations upset social order less than other forms of reparation.
(E) Since money is the basic cause of the wrongs, should it not be the cure?

3. A mother told her daughter, "You lie too much. You cannot be believed. When you start telling me the truth, I will start believing you."

Which of the following is assumed by the mother's statement?

(A) The mother has explained what is wrong about lying.
(B) The mother has determined that her daughter knows what a lie is.
(C) The mother knows when the daughter has been truthful.
(D) The mother is routinely truthful with her daughter.
(E) The mother believes her daughter ultimately will tell the truth.

4. Manufacturing products using glass made from sand rather than materials made from other natural resources can save energy, despite the fact that the initial cost is high.

Which of the following, if true, does NOT support the above argument?

(A) Manufacturing wood and metal products requires energy that could have been more efficiently used to make glass.
(B) Unlike metal and wood products, those made from glass must be discarded rather than repaired when they break.
(C) Aluminum products require much more energy to produce than do those made of glass.
(D) Fiberglass insulation is much more energy efficient than insulation made with other materials.
(E) Glass cookware transfers heat more efficiently than that made from metal.

5. The United States gets 5 percent of its oil from Mexico. If Mexico raises the price of its oil by 20 percent, that will result in an increase of 1 percent (5 percent times 20 percent) in the price of oil products in the United States.

Which of the following is an assumption upon which the above argument depends?

(A) Oil prices in the United States are not affected by inflation in Mexico.

(B) Other countries will not increase oil exports to the United States.

(C) The price increase will not result in a decrease in the sales of Mexican oil products.

(D) People will not substitute other products for those made from Mexican oil.

(E) A 1 percent price increase in oil products will not be recognized by the buying public.

6. Historians, by trade, describe events that are confused as to motive and significance. Therefore, historians, however well-intentioned, primarily traffic in half-truths and lies. But novelists are free from such burdens. Even though they relate many things that are untrue, their characterizations are not offered as true and, therefore, are not half-truths or lies.

Which of the following, if true, would be an extension of the argument above?

(A) Historians and novelists, by trade, characterize events and, therefore, are required to deal in half-truths and lies.

(B) Poets offer their writing as truth in perception and, thus, do not deal in half-truths and lies.

(C) Journalists report on motives and the significance of events and, like historians, traffic primarily in half-truths and lies.

(D) Nonfiction writers select information to support their point and, thus, deal in half-truths.

(E) Economists characterize statistics and, therefore, do not deal in half-truths and lies.

7. The policy of equal pay for women continues to erode the importance of the mother's role in society.

The above argument can be criticized for which of the following reasons?

(A) The importance of a role is not related to the pay for that role.

(B) Equal pay for women is unrelated to motherhood.

(C) All women are not mothers.

(D) Society continues to devalue motherhood.

(E) When someone gains in a society, someone else loses.

8. The Earth receives energy in the form of heat from the sun and discharges heat energy into space by its own emissions. The heat energy received undergoes many transformations. But in the long run, no significant amount of heat energy is stored on the Earth, and there is no continuing trend toward higher or lower temperatures.

Which of the following sentences provides the most logical continuation of this paragraph?

(A) It is obvious, therefore, that much of the heat energy that reaches the Earth is transformed by some means not yet understood.

(B) Thus, it is imperative that we develop a way to use solar energy before it is dissipated into outer space.

(C) As a result, the amount of heat energy lost by the Earth must closely approximate the amount gained from the sun.

(D) The Earth would become as hot as the sun without the many transformations of heat energy.

(E) The Earth's slow but persistent receding from the sun prevents it from overheating.

Questions 9–10

Lecturer: On average, the majority of Americans enjoy the highest standard of living of any people in the world.

Critic: There are thousands of Americans who have annual incomes of less than $3,000 per year.

9. Which of the following best describes the critic's response?

(A) It is not inconsistent with the lecturer's statement.
(B) It cites data confirming the lecturer's statement.
(C) It fails to distinguish between cause and effect.
(D) It generalizes from too small a number of cases.
(E) It resorts to emotional language.

10. A logical criticism of the lecturer's statement would focus on the existence of

(A) a country in which the majority of people enjoy a higher standard of living than that of the American people
(B) a country with a higher level of employment than America
(C) poor Americans who receive federal aid
(D) a higher level of inflation in America than in other countries
(E) many poor American families that are so isolated that they are not included in statistical surveys

Questions 11–12

The position that the prohibition of morally offensive works is wrong in principle is hardly tenable. There certainly are circumstances in which censorship could be desirable. If it were shown that all or most people of a certain type who saw a film thereafter committed a burglary or murder that they would not otherwise have committed, no one would deny that public exhibition of the film should be prohibited. To admit this is to admit that censorship is not wrong in principle. But to approve the principle of censorship on these grounds does not, of course, commit one to approve censorship in every form.

11. Which of the following can be inferred from the paragraph above?

(A) No film affects any 2 individuals in the same way.
(B) The causal connection between specific acts and exposure to specific films is not established.
(C) We cannot anticipate the abuses to which censorship may lead.
(D) People not exposed to morally offensive works will commit socially offensive acts.
(E) There can be no relationship between a general principle and specific practices.

12. The paragraph questions the position that censorship is wrong in principle by

(A) pointing out the ambiguity of a key term
(B) rehearsing facts that are not generally known
(C) questioning the truth of a factual generalization
(D) exposing a logical inconsistency
(E) presenting a hypothetical case

13. No Vikings carried watches. Some Vikings were explorers. Therefore, some explorers did not carry watches.

Which of the following is logically most similar to the argument above?

(A) Everyone who eats too much candy will be sick. I do not eat too much candy and will, therefore, probably avoid sickness.
(B) All dogs are excluded from this motel, but many dogs are friendly. Therefore, some friendly animals are kept out of this motel.
(C) People who want to avoid the pain of dental work will see the dentist twice a year. My children refuse to have their cavities filled. Therefore, my children like pain.
(D) Some who are athletic are young people, and all young people can run. Therefore, everyone who can run is young.
(E) Hawaii is a beautiful place. Some Hawaiians emigrate to California. Therefore, California is a beautiful place.

14. Many people confuse reasons and causes. Any justification for performing an action is a reason. Anything that makes performing an action necessary is a cause—for example, a strong urge, hunger, an intense desire, social pressure, or some brain disorder. Those people who believe that the same thing may be both a reason for performing an action and its cause are clearly mistaken.

Which of the above examples of a cause that makes an action necessary best fits the description of a cause of an action rather than a justification for it?

(A) "hunger"
(B) "some brain disorder"
(C) "social pressure"
(D) "a strong urge"
(E) "an intense desire"

15. One form of reasoning holds that by eliminating all possible explanations until only one remains, that one should be accepted. Critics argue that the flaw in this form of reasoning is that one cannot know about all possible explanations.

Which of the following examples best supports this criticism?

(A) the possible causes of heart disease
(B) the possible results of rolling dice
(C) the possible family members who left the house unlocked
(D) the possible candidates running for mayor of Atlanta, Georgia
(E) the possible countries with nuclear weapons

16. Doctor: The law of genetics holds that if both parents have brown eyes, then they can have only brown-eyed children.

Patient: That is not true; my mother has blue eyes, and I have brown eyes.

The patient has misinterpreted the doctor's statement to mean that

(A) only brown-eyed people can have blue-eyed children
(B) brown-eyed people cannot have blue-eyed children
(C) people with blue eyes invariably have blue-eyed children
(D) parents with the same eye color have children with a different eye color
(E) parents with different eye colors have children with the same eye color

17. Certain similarities between prehistoric art and the art of children has led some people to the mistaken conclusion that either early humans had the mentality of children or that they were as unskilled as children. These conclusions assume which of the following?

(A) Art that is considered sophisticated today must always have been considered sophisticated.
(B) What is easy for humans today must always have been easy.
(C) The significance of art is consistent over time.
(D) Prehistoric humans painted in the same way that children now paint.
(E) Modern humans have learned from prehistoric man.

18. During the cultural revolution in China under Chairman Mao, thousands of "enemies of the republic" were killed. When Mao's critics accused him of confusing his personal enemies with enemies of the republic, he responded, "I deny the accusation, and the proof is that you are still alive."

Which of the following assumptions was Mao making?

(A) All the enemies of the republic are dead.

(B) His critics are his personal enemies.

(C) Some personal enemies are also enemies of the republic.

(D) Enemies of the republic are not personal critics.

(E) Those killed were personal enemies.

19. Today, neither scientists nor the pharmaceutical companies for which they work are willing to run the risk of being wrong. In the past, these scientists were encouraged to experiment with imaginative hypotheses that had a high probability of failure. If this situation continues, the country's drug-development work will come to a standstill.

The point of the argument above is that

(A) scientists are too concerned about failure

(B) scientists are not concerned about the outcome of experimentation

(C) risk should be an issue in experimental research

(D) scientific advances repay extensive experimentation

(E) support for drug research is vanishing

20. In his latest book, John does some clever writing, but even he might have been encouraged to use more everyday language.

Which of the following has a logical structure most like that of the above statement?

(A) The fertilizer serves some valuable purposes, but the smell of it when it is used is offensive.

(B) The latest sermon was effective as inspirational writing, but it did not offer the path to realizing the objectives it outlined.

(C) The star's last movie contained the usual bit of impressive acting, but her director should have advised her to act more like an average person.

(D) The chef at the resort makes wonderful desserts, but the manager should explain how to portion them more reasonably.

(E) Cage was a brilliant composer, but only a few people are able to understand his music.

21. The end of overcrowding at colleges and universities provides them with the opportunity to improve the quality of the educational services they offer. As enrollment declines, services and campus facilities should better serve student needs.

If true, which of the following statements most weakens the above conclusion?

(A) The quality of educational services does not depend on the variety of services offered.

(B) Fees paid by students are the major source of funding for educational services.

(C) Educational services are a critical factor in a student's choice of school.

(D) As campus facilities grow older, their maintenance becomes more expensive.

(E) Student needs are different than they were when colleges and universities were overcrowded.

22. When pregnant laboratory rats are given caffeine equivalent to the amount a human would consume by drinking six cups of coffee per day, an increase in the incidence of birth defects results. When asked if the government would require warning labels on products containing caffeine, a spokesperson stated that it would not, because if the finding of these studies were to be refuted in the future, the government would lose credibility.

Which of the following is most strongly suggested by the government's statement above?

(A) A warning that applies to a small population is inappropriate.

(B) Very few people drink as many as six cups of coffee a day.

(C) There are doubts about the conclusive nature of studies on animals.

(D) Studies on rats provide little data about human birth defects.

(E) The seriousness of birth defects involving caffeine is not clear.

23. The Mercers are avid sailors. They have a child who will never be able to accompany them sailing because he is afraid of water.

Upon which of the following assumptions does the conclusion above depend?

(A) The Mercers will not take their child sailing.

(B) Avid sailors are not afraid of water.

(C) The Mercer's child will never want to sail.

(D) Sailors cannot be afraid of water.

(E) The Mercer's child may overcome his fear of water.

24. Sam: Olive oil can help prevent heart attacks, according to physicians.

Betty: It cannot. My mother cooked with olive oil her entire life, and she died of a heart attack last year.

Betty's statement can best be countered by pointing out that

(A) Betty's mother was an exception

(B) other factors could have nullified the influence of the olive oil

(C) Betty does not know that her mother always cooked with olive oil

(D) It has never been scientifically proven that olive oil causes heart attacks

(E) Betty's mother might have used olive oil irregularly

SECTION 3   **TIME—35 MINUTES**   **24 QUESTIONS**

The questions in this section are based on a set of conditions. A diagram may be helpful in the answer selection process. Select the best answer to each question, and mark the corresponding space on the answer sheet.

Questions 1–6

A restaurant franchise has several locations in Ames County that are designated by the letters A, B, C, D, etc. The restaurants have the following relationships to the Central Office and one another:

A is northwest of the Central Office.

B is northeast of the Central Office.

C is northeast of the Central Office, but C is located farther east than B.

D is south (but not necessarily due south) of the Central Office.

E is southwest of the Central Office.

A is farther north than C and farther west than D.

E is farther west than A.

G is southeast of the Central Office and farther east than B.

1. If a delivery truck travels in a straight line from E to the Central Office and continues in exactly the same direction, it could pass directly by which of the following?

    (A) the northwest corner of D
    (B) the southeast corner of G
    (C) the northwest corner of A
    (D) the west side of A
    (E) the east side of G

2. If F is located due north of the Central Office, which of the following could be true?

    (A) F is located due north of G.
    (B) F is located west of E.
    (C) F is located east of B.
    (D) F is located due west of C.
    (E) F is located due north of E.

3. A restaurant located precisely midway between C and G must be

    (A) farther east than B
    (B) north of the Central Office
    (C) farther south than B
    (D) farther south than A
    (E) south of the Central Office

4. Which of the following CANNOT be the location of D?

    (A) southwest of A
    (B) northeast of C
    (C) southeast of E
    (D) southeast of G
    (E) northwest of G

5. Which of the following CANNOT be true?

    (A) B is precisely midway between E and G.
    (B) B is precisely midway between C and D.
    (C) B is precisely midway between C and E.
    (D) G is precisely midway between C and E.
    (E) D is precisely midway between C and E.

6. If G is southeast of D, and D is farther east than B, which of the following must be true?

    (A) The Central Office is closer to D than to G.
    (B) E is closer to D than to G.
    (C) E is closer to G than to D.
    (D) E is closer to the Central Office than to G.
    (E) C is closer to D than to G.

Questions 7–12

Six college officers—H, I, J, K, L, and M—are seated at equal distances around a circular table according to a list of personal preferences submitted by each officer.

The secretary and the treasurer have no preference as to where they sit.

The president must be seated directly opposite the vice president.

The 2 trustees cannot sit together.

H must sit next to either J or K.

While it is unclear who occupies which office, M is neither the president nor a trustee.

The vice president is either L or J.

Either H or I or both are trustees.

7. If, in satisfying all of the above conditions, the officers are seated around the table in the order K, I, J, H, L, and M, all of the following may be true EXCEPT

    (A) J is the vice president
    (B) H is a trustee
    (C) I is the president
    (D) K is the treasurer
    (E) M is the secretary

8. If H is seated between K and L, and M is seated opposite H, what is a complete and accurate listing of every officer who could be sitting next to M?

    (A) president, vice president
    (B) president, vice president, secretary
    (C) president, vice president, trustee, secretary, treasurer
    (D) trustee, secretary, treasurer
    (E) vice president, trustee, secretary, treasurer

9. If J, the secretary, must sit across from one of the trustees, how might the officers be arranged clockwise in order to satisfy all conditions?

    (A) L, M, I, K, J, H
    (B) K, M, J, L, H, I
    (C) J, K, L, H, M, I
    (D) K, I, H, J, M, L
    (E) I, J, K, M, H, L

10. If the president has M to her right and H to her left, which is NOT an acceptable arrangement for the other three officers, assuming that their order starts with H and goes around the table clockwise?

    (A) J, K, L
    (B) I, J, L
    (C) K, J, I
    (D) K, L, I
    (E) L, J, K

11. If the officers are seated around the table clockwise in the order J, H, I, K, M, and L, and I is the treasurer, who are the 2 trustees?

    (A) I and K
    (B) H and J
    (C) H and K
    (D) I and J
    (E) H and L

12. If the officers are seated around the table clockwise in the order H, J, K, L, M, and I, all of the following must be true EXCEPT

    (A) M is the secretary
    (B) H is not the treasurer
    (C) J is not the vice president
    (D) I is a trustee
    (E) either J or K is a trustee

Questions 13–18

Holly Hauling has six vehicles. The Kenworth, Mack, and White are trucks; the Chevrolet, Dodge, and Ford are vans.

Holly always fuels and washes the trucks before the vans.

Within the respective groups, Holly fuels the vehicles that hold comparatively more fuel before she fuels those that hold comparatively less.

Holly washes the vehicles in their respective groups in the opposite order of their fueling.

The White holds more fuel than the Chevrolet, and no vehicle holds both more than the Chevrolet and less than the White.

The Dodge holds more than the Mack, and no vehicle holds both less than the Dodge and more than the Mack.

Only the Ford and the Kenworth hold the same amount of fuel.

13. If the Kenworth is fueled first and the White third, which of the following must be true?

    (A) The Ford is fueled fifth.
    (B) The Ford is fueled last.
    (C) The Chevrolet is fueled fifth.
    (D) The Chevrolet is fueled last.
    (E) The Dodge is fueled fourth.

14. If the White is washed first, which of the following could NOT be possible?

    (A) The Kenworth is fueled before the White.
    (B) The Mack is fueled before the Kenworth.
    (C) The Chevrolet is fueled before the Ford.
    (D) The Dodge is fueled after the Ford.
    (E) The Ford is fueled before the Chevrolet.

15. If the Mack is fueled first and the White third, which of the following must be true?

    (A) The Ford is washed first.
    (B) The Dodge is washed second.
    (C) The Kenworth is washed second.
    (D) The White is washed third.
    (E) The Chevrolet is washed third.

16. Which of the following is NOT a possible order in which the vehicles are washed?

    (A) Kenworth, White, Mack, Ford, Chevrolet, Dodge
    (B) Mack, Kenworth, White, Dodge, Ford, Chevrolet
    (C) Mack, White, Kenworth, Dodge, Chevrolet, Ford
    (D) White, Kenworth, Mack, Chevrolet, Ford, Dodge
    (E) White, Mack, Kenworth, Ford, Dodge, Chevrolet

17. Suppose Holly does not wash the trucks first but alternates by washing a van and then a truck. If the Mack is fueled first, it would NOT be possible for which pair of vehicles to be washed sequentially?

    (A) the Kenworth immediately before the Chevrolet
    (B) the Chevrolet immediately before the White
    (C) the White immediately before the Ford
    (D) the Dodge immediately before the Mack
    (E) the Ford immediately before the Dodge

18. If Holly fuels the trucks after the vans on a day the White is washed second and the Dodge is washed fourth, the order of fueling must be

    (A) Chevrolet, Dodge, Ford, White, Mack, Kenworth
    (B) Chevrolet, Ford, Dodge, White, Kenworth, Mack
    (C) Ford, Chevrolet, Dodge, Kenworth, White, Mack
    (D) Ford, Dodge, Chevrolet, Kenworth, Mack, White
    (E) Dodge, Chevrolet, Ford, Mack, White, Kenworth

Questions 19–24

There are six distinct building groups in a large office complex. From smallest to largest, respectively, the groups are constructed of aluminum, brick, concrete, glass, stone, and wood. The building groups are designated Groups 1 through 6.

Group 1, which is not stone, is larger than Group 3.

Group 2 is larger than Group 5 and Group 6.

Group 2 is smaller than Group 4.

Group 3 is larger than Group 6.

19. What material must Group 6 be made of if Group 3 is smaller than Group 5?

   (A) aluminum
   (B) brick
   (C) concrete
   (D) glass
   (E) stone

20. From smallest to largest, which of the following is a possible arrangement of the groups?

   (A) 5, 3, 6, 1, 2, 4
   (B) 6, 3, 1, 5, 2, 4
   (C) 6, 3, 1, 2, 5, 4
   (D) 6, 3, 5, 2, 1, 4
   (E) 6, 5, 3, 2, 1, 4

21. If Group 1 is concrete, Group 3 must be which of the following?

   (A) aluminum
   (B) brick
   (C) glass
   (D) stone
   (E) wood

22. Which of the following CANNOT be a possible arrangement of the groups from smallest to largest?

   (A) 5, 6, 3, 1, 2, 4
   (B) 5, 6, 3, 2, 4, 1
   (C) 6, 5, 2, 4, 3, 1
   (D) 6, 5, 3, 1, 2, 4
   (E) 6, 5, 4, 3, 2, 1

23. If Group 5 is glass, Group 2 could be made of which of the following materials?

   (A) concrete
   (B) stone
   (C) wood
   (D) brick
   (E) aluminum

24. If Group 4 is stone, Group 1 could be made of which of the following materials?

   (A) concrete
   (B) glass
   (C) brick
   (D) aluminum
   (E) wood

SECTION 4 — TIME—35 MINUTES — 28 QUESTIONS

The questions in this section are based on what is stated or implied in the passage. Select the best answer to each question, and mark the corresponding space on the answer sheet.

Line A. L. Macfie makes the distinction between what he calls the Scottish method, characteristic of Adam Smith's approach to problems of social policy, and the scientific
(5) or analytical method, which is more familiar to modern social scientists. In the former, the center of attention lay in the society as observed rather than in the idealized version of the society considered as an
(10) abstraction. Smith did have an underlying model or paradigm for social interaction; he could scarcely have discussed reforms without one. But his interest was in making the existing social structure "work better,"
(15) in terms of the norms that he laid down, rather than in evaluating the possible limitations of the structure as it might work ideally if organized on specific principles.

Frank Knight suggested that critics of
(20) the free-enterprise system are seldom clear as to whether they object to the system because it does not work in accordance with its idealized principles or because it does, in fact, work in some approximation
(25) to these principles. There is no such uncertainty with respect to Adam Smith. He was critical of the economic order of his time because it did not work in accordance with the principles of natural liberty. He
(30) was not, and need not have been, overly concerned with some ultimate evaluation of an idealized structure.

Smith's methodology has been turned on its head by many modern scientists. The
(35) post-Pigovian theory of welfare economics has largely, if not entirely, consisted of a search for conceptual flaws in the working of an idealized competitive economic order, conceived independently of the flawed and
(40) imperfect order that may be observed to exist. Partial correctives are offered in both the theory of the second-best and in the

still-emerging theory of public choice, but the perfect-competition paradigm continues
(45) to dominate applied economic policy discussions.

This methodological distinction is important in our examination of Smith's conception of justice. In one sense, John
(50) Rawls's efforts in defining and delineating "a theory of justice" are akin to those of the neoclassical economists who first described the idealized competitive economy. By contrast, Adam Smith saw no need for
(55) defining in great detail the idealized operation of a market system and for evaluating this system in terms of strict efficiency criteria. Similarly, he would have seen no need for elaborating in detail a
(60) complete "theory of justice" for defining those principles that must be operative in a society that would be adjudged to be "just." In comparing Smith with Rawls, therefore, we must somehow bridge the contrasting
(65) methodologies. We can make an attempt to infer from Smith's applied discussion of real problems what his idealized principles of justice might have embodied. Or we can infer from John Rawls's treatment of
(70) idealized principles what his particular application of these might be in an institutional context.

1. Which of the following best describes the passage's objective?

   (A) distinguishing between the Scottish and Pigovian theories of justice
   (B) supporting Adam Smith's concept of justice
   (C) comparing Smith's and Rawls's views of a just society
   (D) supporting John Rawls's theory of justice
   (E) analyzing the contrasting methodologies of Smith and Rawls

2. According to the passage, all of the following are methods used to explain social policy EXCEPT

    (A) the Scottish method
    (B) the theory of welfare economics
    (C) the perfect-competition paradigm
    (D) the scientific method
    (E) the principles of natural liberty

3. According to the passage, John Rawls's "theory of justice" is similar to which of the following?

    (A) the description of the free-enterprise system
    (B) the description of the efficiency of the market system
    (C) the description of the idealized structure of natural liberty
    (D) the description of the idealized competitive economy
    (E) the description of the society considered as an abstraction

4. It can be inferred from the passage that Adam Smith was

    (A) not interested in achieving a just society
    (B) concerned with improving the operation of society
    (C) not worried about efficiency in the operation of society
    (D) indifferent to the economic operation of society
    (E) anxious to achieve an idealized operation of society

5. The author of the passage is presenting which of the following?

    (A) a recitation of methods of approaching social problems
    (B) an analysis of various economic systems
    (C) a comparison of the theories of Knight, Rawls, and Smith
    (D) an exposition of various theories of justice
    (E) an argument supporting idealized versions of social order

6. Which of the following is most likely to be the next sentence of the passage?

    (A) Since Smith planned a book on jurisprudence, there is a reason to develop his theory of justice.
    (B) The practical application of theories of what is "just" is guided by principles of natural justice.
    (C) In what follows, both of these routes will be explored.
    (D) Neither Rawls nor Smith was successful in dealing with real problems.
    (E) Rawls's "theory of justice" is difficult to apply to questions of natural liberty.

7. The author's purpose in finding a bridge between the Rawls and Smith methodologies (lines 63–65) is to

    (A) facilitate understanding of their philosophies
    (B) identify principles that each feels are just
    (C) explore their views toward an idealized market system
    (D) permit comparison of their concepts of justice
    (E) support their attempts to reform society

Line   Many, perhaps most, well-disposed,
practical people would, if they had to
designate a philosophy that comes closest
to expressing their unstated principles, pick
5   utilitarianism. The philosophy that pro-
claims as its sovereign criterion the
procuring of the greatest good for the
greatest number has indeed served as a
powerful engine of legal reform and
10 rationalization. And it is a crucial feature of
utilitarianism that it is consequences that
count. Now it is interesting that some
judgments that are actually made in the law
and elsewhere do not appear to accord
15 with this thoroughgoing consequentialism.
For instance, both in law and morals there
are many instances of a distinction being
made between direct and indirect intention—i.e., the distinction between, on the
20 one hand, the doing of evil as an end in
itself or, on the other hand, bringing about
the same evil result as a consequence of
one's direct ends or means. So also the
distinction is drawn between the conse-
25 quences that we bring about by our actions

and consequences that come about through
our failures to act. Also, when bad consequences ensue from our actions and what
was done was in the exercise of a right or
30 privilege, the law is less likely to lay those
bad consequences at our doorstep. And,
finally, if the only way to prevent some
great harm would be by inflicting a lesser
harm on ourselves or on others, then too
35 the law is inclined to absolve us of responsibility for that avoidable greater harm. It is
as if the net value of the consequences
were not crucial, at least where net benefit
is procured by the intentional infliction of
40 harm.

   Not only are these distinctions drawn
in some moral systems, but there are
numerous places in the law where they are
made regularly. Since in utilitarianism and
45 consequentialism in general the ultimate
questions must always be whether and to
what extent the valued end-state (be it
happiness or possession of true knowledge)
is obtained at a particular moment, it is
50 inevitable that the judgments on the human
agencies that may affect this end-state must
be wholly instrumental: Human actions can
be judged only by their tendency to
produce the relevant end-states.

55   Indeed, it may well be that even the
point and contents of normative judgments—whether legal or moral—are
concerned not just with particular end-
states of the world but also with how
60 end-states are brought about. These kinds
of substantive judgments take the form:
There are some things one should just
never do—kill an innocent person, falsely
accuse a defendant in a criminal proceed-
65 ing, engage in sex for pay. These are to be
contrasted to judgments that this or that is
an unfortunate, perhaps terrible, result that
(other things being equal) one would want
to avoid. The former are—very generally—
70 judgments of right and wrong. It is wrong
to do this or that, even if the balance of
advantages favors it; a person is right to do
some particular thing (help a friend, protect
his client's interests) even though more
75 good will come if he does not.

8. The author's point in the passage is
   primarily that

   (A) law and utilitarianism are not always
   compatible
   (B) utilitarianism is the operating philosophy of most people
   (C) consequentialism is the basis for legal
   reform
   (D) direct and indirect intentions lead to
   different end-states
   (E) judgments about human actions can
   be made only by the resulting end-
   states

9. Which of the following is NOT a feature of
   utilitarianism?

   (A) Results are considered important.
   (B) Consequences are considered important.
   (C) The valued end-state is considered
   important.
   (D) The means of achieving results are
   considered important.
   (E) The net value of consequences is
   considered important.

10. Which of the following is an example of
    judgments that may conflict with the
    utilitarian philosophy?

    (A) It is legally acceptable to base judge-
    ments on the net consequences of
    acts.
    (B) It is legally acceptable to act for the
    greatest good to the greatest number.
    (C) It is legally acceptable for human
    actions that produce more harm than
    good to be punished.
    (D) It is legally acceptable for bad conse-
    quences to flow from the exercise of
    an individual's right or privilege.
    (E) It is not legally acceptable to avoid a
    small harm to oneself, even if the
    result is a great harm to another.

11. The point of the last paragraph is to

   (A) explain the differences between utilitarianism and consequentialism

   (B) contrast judgments of right and wrong with other types of judgments

   (C) discuss the role of intention in both law and words

   (D) distinguish between the results of actions and inaction

   (E) develop a rationale upon which to judge human actions

12. It can be inferred from the passage that the author is concerned with which of the following?

   (A) legal reform

   (B) false accusations

   (C) results of human inaction

   (D) means used to produce results

   (E) aspirations producing human action

13. The passage suggests that utilitarianism

   (A) explains all legal and moral judgments

   (B) explains only judgments of right and wrong

   (C) explains some judgments in law and morals

   (D) explains judgments of direct and indirect intentions

   (E) explains judgments of right and privilege

14. The author's attitude about utilitarianism as a philosophy is best described as

   (A) somewhat critical

   (B) generally supportive

   (C) mostly accepting

   (D) totally convinced

   (E) nearly convinced

Line Although lawyers frequently reason in terms of models, they tend to reason, in Henry Steiner's terms, in *prose* models. I think there are some real advantages of the
5 symbolic-logic type of reasoning in the law. Although lawyers pride themselves on their method of argumentation and on being logicians, actually a lot of their arguments are very flabby. One way of teasing them is
10 to say, "Well, let's write this problem down in formal terms and abstract systems; let's agree on a rigorous abstract definition of this concept or behavioral principle and derive its logical implications." And then
15 you allege that two situations they consider as absolutely distinct are really formally identical. That is what the model says. And if they are not formally identical, what really is the distinction? How has the model
20 been misspecified? You ask them whether they may be making a distinction without a difference.

     I think that the benefit of formal logic is that it sets out very nakedly, with all of
25 its warts and pimples exposed, whatever difficulties there are in the argumentation. By using prose, a lot of that is swept under the carpet. Lawyers invoke the forces of "equity" and "fairness" on both sides of
30 precisely the same set of facts. Two arguments produce equity and fairness "clearly or obviously," as they put it, while pointing in different directions.

     Formal models can be built assuming
35 that all people act in accord with the Kantian categorical imperative—or pick any principle you want. The desirable thing is to write it down, to define your terms as well as you can, say what you mean, and
40 then argue about it.

     Those of us who have been making models for a long time realize that all models are bad, but some models are worse than others. Part of the seduction of
45 mathematical models is that they look much more rigorous than they are. They are always abstractions; there is always something wrong with them, something left out of consideration. But I think that this is
50 no less true in the physical sciences, where the models are supposed to be very good. My chemist friends tell me that the fundamental laws of chemistry are contradicted every day in the laboratory. In the
55 last analysis, I think the way one ought to look at this is as a method of argumentation. I feel that for a lot of uses in the law, it will demonstrate to you problems you did not think existed, inconsistencies, and
60 incidences of illogic. Although we are never going to get all of the answers from formal models, we would be foolish not to take them for what they are worth.

     And if the Landes and Posner thesis
65 stimulated this argument, that is precisely what "writing it down" is supposed to accomplish.

15. The passage can best be summarized as

(A) an analysis of law as a social science
(B) a comparison of formal and flabby models
(C) an argument for the use of formal models by lawyers
(D) a criticism of the method of argumentation of lawyers
(E) a challenge to the value of models in the sciences

16. According to the passage, which of the following applies to both prose models and formal models?

(A) expose all imperfections
(B) require precise definition of terms
(C) appear to be more rigorous than they are
(D) not demonstrably useful in the law
(E) a method of argumentation

17. The author contends that all of the following are benefits of using formal models EXCEPT

(A) determining that an argument is making a distinction without a difference
(B) locating something left out of consideration
(C) demonstrating inconsistencies in an argument
(D) setting out difficulties with the form of argumentation
(E) assisting in the derivation of the logical implications of an argument

18. The author defines a "flabby" argument (line 9) as one that

(A) is not internally contradicted
(B) is presented in prose
(C) is too abstract
(D) is not logically rigorous
(E) is formally identical to another

19. According to the passage, the primary purpose of "writing it down" is to

(A) avoid contradictions in arguments
(B) pick the principle for the model
(C) provide the basis for argumentation
(D) determine the worth of an argument
(E) identify distinctions without differences

20. The passage indicates that models are used as all of the following EXCEPT

(A) as a method of argumentation
(B) as a source of answers to problems
(C) as a form of reasoning used by lawyers
(D) as a method to identify problems with logic
(E) as a technique to ensure equity

21. Which of the following, if true, most weakens the author's argument about formal models?

(A) Abstract symbols are the same as words.
(B) Behavioral principles are hard to reduce to abstract symbols.
(C) Models are regularly contradicted by facts.
(D) Formal models are as illogical as prose models.
(E) Prose models are routinely used by scientists.

22. Which of the following is implied by the author of the passage?

(A) Symbols are inefficient expressions of behavioral principles.
(B) A lawyer should not use an argument on both sides of a set of facts.
(C) Prose is not a useful form of argumentation.
(D) Omissions are a problem with formal models.
(E) Mathematical inconsistencies are a problem with formal models.

Line   Applying communications theory to legal discourse has foundered on a lack of clear conception of what the theory means in the context of law and can tell attorneys

5   about the legal process. Communications theory is not a unified body of thought. It has three quite distinct branches. The first, "syntactics," is concerned with the logical arrangement, transmission, and receipt of

10   signals or signs. The second is "semantics," which is concerned with the meaning of signals to people. The third is "pragmatics," which is the study of the impact of signal transmission on human behavior.

15   The key concepts of syntactics are "information," "redundancy," and "feedback," of which the first two are best discussed together. For the telegraphic engineer, information is the content of the

20   signal that could not have been predicted

by the receiver; it is a probability concept. The more probable the transmission of a given sign, the less information its actual transmission conveys. "Redundancy" is the
25 opposite of information. It is the introduction of repetition or pattern into the message. If the telegrapher sends each message twice, his second sending is redundant and contains less information
30 than his first.

The ideal transmission, then, in terms of pure "information," would contain no repetition and no pattern. The engineer finds it wise, however, to introduce
35 redundancy at the cost of reducing the information content of the message, because otherwise, any loss of information due to malfunctions in the transmission system would be undetectable and irreme-
40 diable. It is only when we can predict, at least partially, what message we are going to receive that we can spot an erroneous transmission or substitution in the message and call for its correction. The ideal
45 message, then, will contain the highest proportion of information and the lowest proportion of redundancy necessary to identify and correct errors in transmission.

Thus it will be seen that redundancy
50 and information, in syntactic terms, are reciprocals of each other. But the situation is more complicated when we consider the semantic dimension of communication, for both information and redundancy convey
55 meaning. And the line is even more blurred when we consider the pragmatics of communication. Weakland has said, "There is no redundancy," his point being, of course, that repetitions and patterns in
60 messages do have significance to partici- pants in the communication process. Such redundancies carry a freight of meaning, knowledge, and stimuli to the receiver and in this important sense are not redundant.
65 In the law, the strongest argument that an attorney can make is that the current case is "on all fours" with many previous cases, all of which were decided by repeatedly applying the same legal
70 principle. So it is that, in terms of commu- nications theory, the rules of legal discourse seem to require attorneys to suppress as much information and transmit as much redundancy as possible.

23. The passage can best be characterized as

(A) an explanation of the principles of communications theory
(B) a description of conflict between information and redundancy
(C) an interpretation of syntactics applied to aspects of legal discourse
(D) an exposition of redundancy
(E) a review of the branches of thought in communications theory

24. According to the passage, which of the following describes an ideal transmission in terms of pure information?

(A) A, 2, #, +, s, ?, c, p, %, $
(B) A, C, A, E, A, G, A, I, A, K
(C) 1, 2, 3, 4, 5, 6, 5, 4, 3, 2, 1
(D) @, %, &, @, %, &, @, %, &
(E) 8, 1, 9, 1, 7, 1, 6, 1, 5, 1, 4, 1

25. According to the passage, which of the following is an unambiguous example of syntactic redundancy?

(A) the transmission of the dash in dot-dot-dash
(B) the transmission of the dash in dot-dot-dash when two dots are always followed by a dash
(C) the transmission of a dot in dot-dot- dash
(D) the transmission of a dot when two dashes are never followed by a dot
(E) the transmission of the dash in dot-dot-dash when two dots are never followed by a dash

26. In the context of the passage, "on all fours" (line 67) most likely refers to

(A) a type of information in terms of communications theory
(B) a legal principle that is applied to many different cases
(C) the most recent example in a series of cases
(D) a type of argument lawyers use to distinguish one case from another
(E) a case that is exactly the same as previous cases

27. According to the passage, which of the following is NOT true?

    (A) Patterns in messages are significant to communicating.

    (B) Legal discourse requires maximum redundancy.

    (C) Information in a message can be predicted by a telegraphic engineer.

    (D) Redundancy in a message reduces the information transmitted.

    (E) Information is the opposite of redundancy.

28. Which of the following best reflects the author's view about the application of communications theory to legal discourse?

    (A) Syntactics tell lawyers very little about the legal process.

    (B) Redundancy accounts for the difference between strong and weak legal arguments.

    (C) Engineering, not law, has been the profession making use of communications theory.

    (D) Communications theory is too difficult for lawyers to understand clearly.

    (E) Legal discourse is dominated by the attempt to present pure information.

Evaluate the reasoning contained in the brief statements, and select the best answer. Do not make implausible, superfluous, or incompatible assumptions. Select the best answer to each question, and mark the corresponding space on the answer sheet.

1. There are no great writers in Largo because freedom of expression does not exist there.

   The conclusion above depends upon which of the following assumptions?

   (A) In the absence of freedom of expression, great writers do not develop.
   (B) If there is freedom of expression, there will be many great writers.
   (C) Where there is no freedom of expression, great writers turn to politics.
   (D) Great writers leave places that do not have freedom of expression.
   (E) Great writers must express themselves freely.

2. Archaeologists have determined that the bison was the primary source of meat for the cave dwellers, but their caves also contained the bones of birds, snakes, and fish, which indicates that they also liked to eat these animals.

   Which of the following, if true, would weaken the conclusion reached in the statement above?

   (A) Drawings of snakes and fish were made by cave dwellers.
   (B) Cave dwellers were not always able to eat what they liked.
   (C) Birds, rather than cave dwellers, may have brought snakes and fish to the caves to eat.
   (D) Cave dwellers ate grains and berries.
   (E) The bones of birds, snakes, and fish found in the caves were from small animals.

3. Some psychologists believe that humans, like porpoises, are benevolent creatures by nature. These psychologists assume that human nature is essentially disposed to benevolent conduct. To account for social evils, psychologists have to blame institutions that corrupt the native disposition of humans.

   The psychologists' argument described above would be most strengthened if it were to explain how

   (A) a way of life consistent with benevolent ideals is possible in the modern world
   (B) people can be persuaded to abandon technology, urbanization, and mass production
   (C) benevolent conduct can result from humans living in accordance with their own natural dispositions
   (D) benevolent dispositions give rise to evil institutions
   (E) corrupt institutions can be eliminated or reformed

4. Whenever the sky is cloudy and rain is falling, Bob wears his slicker. Whenever the sky is cloudy and rain is not falling, Bob ties his slicker around his waist. Sometimes rain falls when the sky is not cloudy.

   If the statements above are true, and it is true that Bob is not wearing his slicker, which of the following must also be true?

   (A) Bob has tied his slicker around his waist.
   (B) The sky is not overcast.
   (C) The sky is not cloudy, and rain is not falling.
   (D) The sky is cloudy, and/or rain is not falling.
   (E) The sky is not cloudy, and/or rain is not falling.

5. Only excellent musicians can be professors at Juilliard. No insensitive people are great lovers of poetry. No one who is not sensitive can be a lover. There are no excellent musicians who are not great lovers of poetry. Therefore, all Juilliard professors are lovers.

Which of the following inferences leading to the conclusion above is NOT valid?

(A) All Juilliard professors are excellent musicians.
(B) Juilliard professors are sensitive people.
(C) Sensitive people are lovers.
(D) Great lovers of poetry are sensitive people.
(E) Excellent musicians are great lovers of poetry.

6. Since plaznium evaporates in air, and this cube did not evaporate when it was exposed to air, it is not plaznium.

Which of the following is most like the argument above?

(A) Since no cats have hooves, and Fifi is a cat, Fifi does not have hooves.
(B) Since owls feed only at night, the bird feeding in daylight is not an owl.
(C) Since this box is made of brass, and boxes not made of brass are better than brass boxes, this brass box is not as good as a box not made of brass.
(D) Since chicks are never furry, and this animal is not furry, it is not a chick.
(E) Since every Canarbik dog is black or white, and Fido is a Canarbik, Fido cannot be gray.

7. Some ocean-liner captains are alcoholics. Ocean-liner captains who are alcoholics are dangerous. Every captain of an ocean liner is responsible for the care of the passengers.

The above leads to which of the following conclusions?

(A) All ocean-liner passengers are in the care of an alcoholic.
(B) Some ocean-liner passengers are dangerous when they drink.
(C) Some ocean-liner passengers are in the care of a dangerous person.
(D) All ocean-liner captains are dangerous when they drink.
(E) Some ocean-liner captains are dangerous when they drink.

8. Because coal is a nonrenewable resource, states that produce coal will experience problems that will never be faced by the lumber-processing industry.

Which of the following, if true, most weakens this argument?

(A) The resources required to log forests cannot be replenished.
(B) States with economies dominated by coal are trying to develop forest products.
(C) Lumber-producing states must secure much of the food they require from other states.
(D) Renewable resources are a significant part of the economies of coal-producing states.
(E) Coal-producing states depend on money from coal sales to buy lumber.

9. A criminal justice study has found that 82 percent of people presented with eyewitness testimony regarding a crime were willing to convict the accused. However, only 58 percent of the same people were willing to convict the accused when presented with lie-detector, fingerprint, and handwriting evidence from experts.

Which of the following conclusions is most reasonably supported by the above study results?

(A) Most crimes do not involve eyewitness and expert testimony.
(B) An accused can only be convicted by evidence that eliminates all reasonable doubt.
(C) Most people do not understand expert evidence.
(D) Prosecutors can ensure conviction by presenting both eyewitness and expert testimony.
(E) Jurors think eyewitness testimony leaves less room for doubt than does expert testimony.

10. By 1997, the number of 18-year-olds will be dramatically lower than it was in 1961, when population growth in the United States reached its highest point. This decline in the number of potential college students will result in large enrollment decreases at colleges in the United States.

    If true, which of the following would most weaken the conclusion of the above argument?

    (A) Colleges prospered in the 1950s with lower enrollments than there are today.
    (B) By 1997, there will be more colleges than there are today.
    (C) Colleges will compete more aggressively for students when the number of 18-year-olds declines sharply.
    (D) In the future, more older students will enter college than ever before.
    (E) College enrollments in the 1960s were inflated by students avoiding the draft.

11. The contemporary film is a form of mass entertainment rather than an important art form. It fascinates, amuses, and distracts but fails to elevate the human spirit and deepen awareness. Film can be ignored if one is looking for art rather than escape.

    Which of the following is NOT implied by the argument above?

    (A) When looking for art, film can be ignored.
    (B) Contemporary film is not an important art form.
    (C) Film is an amusement.
    (D) In the past, film was an important art form.
    (E) Film is a form of escape.

Questions 12–13

Critics who claim that the sale of U.S. military equipment to other countries is destabilizing and leads to war take a narrow view of history. War occurs when one country gains a military advantage over another. By selling arms, the United States can ensure that the military balance among countries is maintained and war avoided.

12. The above argument depends on which of the following assumptions?

    (A) Arms sales by the United States do not lead to wars between countries.
    (B) Critics do not understand military history.
    (C) Countries can accurately determine one another's military strength.
    (D) Arms imbalances stimulate conflict between countries.
    (E) Critics misunderstand the principle of military balance between countries.

13. Which of the following, if true, most weakens the above argument?

    (A) Military equipment is usually used to intimidate rather than to actually conduct war.
    (B) A country's military strength depends on military equipment rather than on the expertise of military commanders.
    (C) The sale and delivery of military equipment is usually known only by the two countries involved.
    (D) The military advantages of all countries are well known by the United States.
    (E) Military equipment sold by the United States to other countries is less sophisticated than the equipment it produces for itself.

14. A study by the motor-vehicle bureau shows that only 3 percent of all cars fail the annual safety inspection because of defective lights. Consequently, the bureau has decided to discontinue inspecting lights, because the benefit is not worth the expense involved.

Which of the following, if true, is the greatest weakness in the decision of the bureau?

(A) Studies in other states show that a larger percentage of cars have defective lights.

(B) Cars with defective lights often have safety problems that are not part of the inspection.

(C) Lights are maintained in good working order because of the inspection requirement.

(D) Most cars fail inspection for more than one defect.

(E) Inspecting for defective lights costs less than 2 percent of the annual budget of the motor-vehicle bureau.

Questions 15–16

The public's right to know is an inadequate justification for exposing people's private lives to public scrutiny. Only when the public welfare is involved does the public have a right to know information about a person's private life.

15. Which of the following, if true, most weakens the position taken in the above argument?

(A) The public seldom knows which activities promote its welfare.

(B) The public seldom wants much of the information exposed to it.

(C) It is seldom possible to discover the most intimate details of someone's personal life.

(D) The public seldom understands the implications of the information exposed to it.

(E) It is seldom possible to determine which information involves the public welfare.

16. Which of the following best expresses the underlying point of the above argument?

(A) Public welfare is the greatest good.

(B) A justification is not a reason.

(C) Personal privacy is an important right.

(D) The common good is an insufficient justification.

(E) Public rights supersede individual privacy.

17. A study shows that there is a strong positive relationship between voting and political involvement.

Which of the following CANNOT be inferred from this finding?

(A) Political involvement and voting appear to be interrelated.

(B) People who are not involved in politics are less likely to vote than those who are involved.

(C) After people become involved in politics, they vote more frequently than before.

(D) People who vote are more likely to be involved in politics.

(E) Voting is a form of political involvement.

Questions 18–19

A survey of students concludes that some students prefer physics to history; all students prefer history to geometry; no students prefer history to economics; and all students prefer biology to history.

18. Based on the survey results, which of the following must represent students' preferences?

(A) Some students prefer geometry to physics.

(B) Some students prefer physics to geometry.

(C) Some students prefer biology to economics.

(D) Some students prefer geometry to economics.

(E) Some students prefer physics to economics.

19. Based on the survey results, which of the following CANNOT represent students' preferences?

    (A) Some students prefer geometry to physics.
    (B) Some students prefer physics to geometry.
    (C) Some students prefer biology to economics.
    (D) Some students prefer economics to biology.
    (E) Some students prefer physics to economics.

20. Voters who complain about a trusted politician's betrayal remind me of the tale of the man who nursed a starving snake back to health. Afterward, the snake bit the man, who then complained about the snake's ingratitude. The snake responded to the complaint by saying, "You knew I was a snake when you saved me."

    Which of the following can be derived from the argument above?

    (A) Don't cut off your nose to spite your face.
    (B) Things are not always what they seem.
    (C) Chickens always come home to roost.
    (D) Nature cannot be changed.
    (E) Take the bitter with the sweet.

21. Representatives of dairy producers say that government subsidies are needed to ensure that milk processors produce sufficient amounts for children. If there are no milk-price subsidies, processors will attempt to meet the demand for cheese and butter before producing milk.

    Which of the following can be inferred from the above argument?

    (A) The demand for milk is volatile, often leading to underproduction and shortages.
    (B) Processors have produced sufficient milk in the past because they understood the needs of hungry children.
    (C) Cheese and butter produce greater profits for processors than does milk.
    (D) Representatives of dairies have a lobby that is powerful enough to ensure the passage of favorable subsidies.
    (E) Dairy representatives are trying to avoid a surplus of cheese and butter.

22. The sculpture of the woman was carved during the early Greek period. The shape of the fingers, the style of hair, and the design of her sandals indicate the early period. The tilt of the chin and the closed eyes are frequently found in early Greek sculpture.

    Which of the following is an assumption upon which this argument is based?

    (A) The period of a work of art can be established with certainty.
    (B) Certain attributes of works of art are typical of specific periods.
    (C) Tilted chins and closed eyes always appear together in Greek sculpture.
    (D) Sculptures of women first appeared in the early Greek period.
    (E) Closed eyes are characteristic of early art.

23. The village is overrun by poisonous snakes. The mayor argues that paying a $10 bounty for each dead snake turned in by a villager will result in ridding the village of snakes.

    Which of the following does NOT weaken the mayor's argument?

    (A) The bounty ensures that breeding the snakes is in the economic interest of the villagers.
    (B) Village taxes will triple if the mayor's proposal is implemented.
    (C) The villagers do not trust the mayor.
    (D) The snakes control the rat population, so the villagers will not kill the snakes.
    (E) A drug company pays villagers $15 for each live snake delivered to it.

24. Spring Lake does not appear to be good for sailing. I have gone to the lake many times this year, and each time the water was too rough for sailing.

Which of the following most closely parallels the above argument?

(A) It appears that we will move to Spring Lake this year. The city is simply too rough for safe living.

(B) Economy-grade gasoline apparently does not prevent my car from running rough. It appears that a good grade of fuel is required.

(C) It appears that the cost of housing at Spring Lake is prohibitive. I looked at a number of houses last month, and they cost much more than I could afford.

(D) I am withdrawing from Spring Lake College. Two months at school was sufficient to prove that college was too rough for me.

(E) It appears that I will never play the clarinet. I began lessons many times, but each time, I quit.

LSAT WRITING SAMPLE TOPIC

Complete the short writing exercise on the topic that follows. You have only 30 minutes to plan, organize, and write your sample. WRITE ONLY ON THE TOPIC SPECIFIED.

Alice Anderson is a senior at John Paul Jones University. She has been offered two positions as a result of her outstanding record in her major, television and radio broadcasting. As her counselor, you are to write an argument favoring one of the two offers. Two considerations guide your decision:

- Alice has a large student-loan debt that she has to begin to repay immediately upon graduation.
- Alice has as her career goal a position as a network-news anchorperson.

WAND is the only television station serving a large area located some 250 miles north of the capital of the state. The station has offered Alice a job as a reporter whose principal assignments would be to cover the activities of local governments, politics, and business. In addition to her assigned stories, Alice would have the opportunity to independently prepare stories for possible broadcast. Because the station is small, has a very stable staff, and has limited growth prospects, Alice's chances for advancement are not good. WAND's owner is a former network executive who purchased the station in order to get away from the pressures of broadcasting in major markets. Alice would get only a modest salary at WAND, and she would have to supplement her income with outside work.

KBSC is one of three television stations located in the state capital. The station has offered Alice a job as a production assistant in the news department. She would primarily do background research and check facts and sources for the producers and reporters. Production assistants who work hard are promoted to positions as special-assignment reporters in about two years. There are many special-assignment reporters competing for assignments, most of which involve covering minor events such as political dinners, award ceremonies, and concerts and writing human-interest stories. Most special-assignment reporters spend at least five years covering minor events before moving into a position as a general report-anchorperson. KBSC would pay Alice a salary in excess of the amount she would need to live comfortably in the city.

190

QUICK-SCORE ANSWERS

Section 1	Section 2	Section 3	Section 4	Section 5
1. **C**	1. **D**	1. **A**	1. **C**	1. **A**
2. **E**	2. **B**	2. **D**	2. **B**	2. **C**
3. **D**	3. **C**	3. **A**	3. **D**	3. **B**
4. **D**	4. **B**	4. **B**	4. **B**	4. **C**
5. **C**	5. **C**	5. **A**	5. **A**	5. **C**
6. **E**	6. **C**	6. **A**	6. **C**	6. **B**
7. **D**	7. **C**	7. **A**	7. **D**	7. **C**
8. **E**	8. **C**	8. **C**	8. **E**	8. **A**
9. **A**	9. **A**	9. **D**	9. **E**	9. **E**
10. **B**	10. **A**	10. **A**	10. **D**	10. **D**
11. **D**	11. **E**	11. **E**	11. **B**	11. **D**
12. **B**	12. **E**	12. **A**	12. **D**	12. **C**
13. **E**	13. **B**	13. **C**	13. **C**	13. **C**
14. **C**	14. **C**	14. **C**	14. **A**	14. **C**
15. **B**	15. **A**	15. **C**	15. **C**	15. **E**
16. **C**	16. **C**	16. **E**	16. **E**	16. **C**
17. **A**	17. **C**	17. **E**	17. **B**	17. **E**
18. **B**	18. **A**	18. **C**	18. **D**	18. **A**
19. **A**	19. **A**	19. **A**	19. **C**	19. **A**
20. **B**	20. **C**	20. **B**	20. **E**	20. **D**
21. **A**	21. **B**	21. **B**	21. **D**	21. **C**
22. **D**	22. **C**	22. **E**	22. **D**	22. **B**
23. **D**	23. **D**	23. **B**	23. **C**	23. **C**
24. **A**	24. **B**	24. **E**	24. **A**	24. **C**
			25. **B**	
			26. **E**	
			27. **D**	
			28. **B**	

EXPLANATORY ANSWERS

In the following answer guide, the credited responses appear in bold type and the visualizations that make the credited response clear appear before the answers to each question set. Use the visualization to guide you in determining the credited answer.

Section 1

Questions 1–6

Statehood   A, F, K, O, T, V, W

Earlier   Later

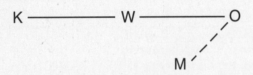

1. **The correct answer is (C).** Ohio was a state before Kansas.

2. **The correct answer is (E).** Kansas was a state before Ohio.

3. **The correct answer is (D).** Texas was a state before Ohio.

4. **The correct answer is (D).** Kansas, Maine, Wyoming, Ohio, Vermont

5. **The correct answer is (C).** Florida was a state before Kansas.

6. **The correct answer is (E).** Kansas was a state before Alaska.

Questions 7–12

Houses   T
              T's Children
              Brother
              Parents

Smaller   Larger

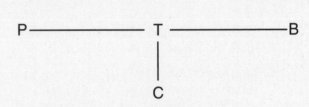

7. **The correct answer is (D).** 1, 2

8. **The correct answer is (E).** son to father

9. **The correct answer is (A).** S is U's son.

10. **The correct answer is (B).** uncle

11. **The correct answer is (D).** 3

12. **The correct answer is (B).** T has exactly 3 children.

Questions 13–18

Riders—A, B, C, D, E, F, G

Busses—1, 2, 3

  Bus

    1 if B then no E or G

    2 if D then no G

    3 C always

    4 when A and F take the same bus

13. **The correct answer is (E).** B, D, G

14. **The correct answer is (C).** 3 only

15. **The correct answer is (B).** 4

16. **The correct answer is (C).** 3 only

17. **The correct answer is (A).** 0

18. **The correct answer is (B).** A, D, E, G

Questions 19–24

19. **The correct answer is (A).** Dora lives 9 miles from Elmer.

20. **The correct answer is (B).** The distance between Bruce's and Elmer's houses is shorter than the distance between Cora's and Dora's houses.

21. **The correct answer is (A).** Angela and Cora live 12 miles apart.

22. **The correct answer is (D).** 4 miles

23. **The correct answer is (D).** Bruce lives closer to Elmer than Cora does to Dora.

24. **The correct answer is (A).** 14

SECTION 2

In the following answer guide, the credited responses appear in bold type and the guide that directs you toward the credited response appears within the answer-choice context. The first reference is to the point of the argument and the second is to the nature of the issue involved.

1. **The correct answer is (D).** Purchasers of this brand of clothing will be stylish.

   Point—Stylish people wear well-designed clothing.

   Issue—Extension question/conclusion

2. **The correct answer is (B).** Even though all wrongs cannot be compensated for, some wrongs can be.

   Point—Money cannot compensate for historic wrongs.

   Issue—Extension question/assumption

3. **The correct answer is (C).** The mother knows when the daughter has been truthful.

   Point—Tell the truth and I will believe you.

   Issue—Extension question/assumption

4. **The correct answer is (B).** Unlike metal and wood products, those made from glass must be discarded rather than repaired when they break.

   Point—Products made from glass can save energy.

   Issue—Extension question/weakening evidence

5. **The correct answer is (C).** The price increase will not result in a decrease in the sales of Mexican oil products.

   Point—Raising oil prices 20 percent will cause a 1 percent increase in the U.S.

   Issue—Extension question/assumption

6. **The correct answer is (C).** Journalists report on motives and the significance of events and, like historians, traffic primarily in half-truths and lies.

   Point—Those who try to describe events engage in half-truths and lies.

   Issue—Extension question/conclusion

7. **The correct answer is (C).** All women are not mothers.

   Point—Equal pay for women detracts from motherhood.

   Issue—Extension question/weakening evidence

8. **The correct answer is (C).** As a result, the amount of heat energy lost by the Earth must closely approximate the amount gained from the sun.

   Point—The Earth does not store energy.

   Issue—Extension question/conclusion

9. **The correct answer is (A).** It is not inconsistent with the lecturer's statement.

   Point—All Americans do not enjoy a high standard of living.

   Issue—Description question/nature of response

10. **The correct answer is (A).** a country in which the majority of people enjoy a higher standard of living than that of the American people

    Point—All Americans do not enjoy a high standard of living.

    Issue—Extension question/weakening evidence

11. **The correct answer is (E).** There can be no relationship between a general principle and specific practices.

    Point—Censorship is appropriate in some circumstances.

    Issue—Extension question/conclusion

12. **The correct answer is (E).** presenting a hypothetical case

    Point—Censorship is appropriate in some circumstances.

    Issue—Description question/tactic

13. **The correct answer is (B).** All dogs are excluded from this motel, but many dogs are friendly. Therefore, some friendly animals are kept out of this motel.

    Point—All have one attribute, some have another attribute; therefore, some have both attributes.

    Issue—Extension question/same point, new context

14. **The correct answer is (C).** "social pressure"

    Point—Causes require actions; reasons justify actions.

    Issue—Extension question/conclusion

15. **The correct answer is (A).** the possible causes of heart disease

    Point—Accepting the only explanation does not take all possible explanations into account.

    Issue—Description question/example

16. **The correct answer is (C).** people with blue eyes invariably have blue-eyed children

    Point—Children have the same color eyes as their parent(s)

    Issue—Extension question/conclusion

17. **The correct answer is (C).** The significance of art is consistent over time.

    Point—Similar results connote similar causes, regardless of context.

    Issue—Extension question/assumption

18. **The correct answer is (A).** All the enemies of the republic are dead.

    Point—Any living critic proves that Mao did not have personal enemies killed.

    Issue—Extension question/assumption

19. **The correct answer is (A).** scientists are too concerned about failure

    Point—Risking failure is no longer tolerated in drug development.

    Issue—Extension question/conclusion

20. **The correct answer is (C).** The star's last movie contained the usual bit of impressive acting, but her director should have advised her to act more like an average person.

    Point—Those producing exceptional work should use more common devices.

    Issue—Extension question/same point, new context

21. **The correct answer is (B).** Fees paid by students are the major source of funding for educational services.

    Point—As demands on resources decrease, services and facilities should improve.

    Issue—Extension question/weakening evidence

22. **The correct answer is (C).** There are doubts about the conclusive nature of studies on animals.

    Point—If the government acts prematurely, it loses credibility.

    Issue—Extension question/conclusion

23. **The correct answer is (D).** Sailors cannot be afraid of water.

    Point—The Mercer child will not sail because of his fear of water.

    Issue—Extension question/conclusion

24. The correct answer is (B). other factors could have nullified the influence of the olive oil

Point—Olive oil did not prevent heart attack in Betty's mother.

Issue—Extension question/weakening evidence

SECTION 3

In the following answer guide, the credited responses appear in bold type and the visualizations that make the credited response clear appear before the answers to each question set. Use the visualization to guide you in determining the credited answer.

Questions 1–6

Location   A, B, C, D, E, G

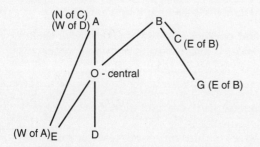

1. **The correct answer is (A)**. the northwest corner of D

2. **The correct answer is (D)**. F is located due west of C.

3. **The correct answer is (A)**. farther east than B

4. **The correct answer is (B)**. northeast of C

5. **The correct answer is (A)**. B is precisely midway between E and G.

6. **The correct answer is (A)**. The Central Office is closer to D than to G.

Questions 7–12

Seating   H, I, J, K, L, M

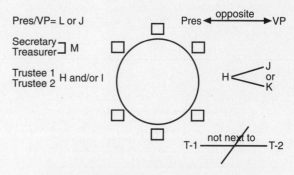

Pres/VP= L or J

Secretary / Treasurer—] M

Trustee 1 / Trustee 2   H and/or I

7. **The correct answer is (A)**. J is the vice president

8. **The correct answer is (C)**. president, vice president, trustee, secretary, treasurer

9. **The correct answer is (D)**. K, I, H, J, M, L

10. **The correct answer is (A)**. J, K, L

11. **The correct answer is (E)**. H and L

12. **The correct answer is (A)**. M is the secretary

Questions 13–18

Trucks - K, M, W   Fuel and wash - trucks before vans
Fuel larger tanks before smaller
Vans - C, D, F   Wash smaller before larger

Tank Size

Larger ————————————————— Small

K

equals ——— D ——— M ——————W more than C

F

13. **The correct answer is (C)**. The Chevrolet is fueled fifth.

14. **The correct answer is (C)**. The Chevrolet is fueled before the Ford.

15. **The correct answer is (C)**. The Kenworth is washed second.

16. **The correct answer is (E)**. White, Mack, Kenworth, Ford, Dodge, Chevrolet

17. **The correct answer is (E)**. the Ford immediately before the Dodge

18. **The correct answer is (C)**. Ford, Chevrolet, Dodge, Kenworth, White, Mack

Questions 19–24

Smallest ─────────────────────── Largest

Alum, Brick, Concrete, Glass, Stone, Wood

Groups 1- 6

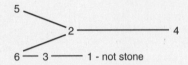

19. **The correct answer is (A).** aluminum

20. **The correct answer is (B).** 6, 3, 1, 5, 2, 4

21. **The correct answer is (B).** brick

22. **The correct answer is (E).** 6, 5, 4, 3, 2, 1

23. **The correct answer is (B).** stone

24. **The correct answer is (E).** wood

SECTION 4

In the following answer guide, the credited responses appear in bold type and the guide that directs you to the place in the passage that accounts for the credited response appears within the answer-choice context. The first reference is to the paragraph number in the passage that accounts for the credited response and the second number refers to the relevant sentence in the paragraph. The reference will appear as 2/4 for example. This means paragraph 2 and sentence 4 within paragraph 2.

1. **The correct answer is (C).** comparing Smith's and Rawls's views of a just society—Paragraph 4/Sentence 5

2. **The correct answer is (B).** the theory of welfare economics. For (A) *the Scottish method* and (D) *the scientific method*, see 1/1; for (C) *the perfect-competition paradigm*, see 3/3; and for (E) *the principles of natural liberty*, see 2/3.

3. **The correct answer is (D).** the description of the idealized competitive economy—Paragraph 4/Sentence 2

4. **The correct answer is (B).** concerned with improving the operation of society—Paragraph 1/Sentence 4

5. **The correct answer is (A).** a recitation of methods of approaching social problems—Most inclusive of the five answer choices

6. **The correct answer is (C).** In what follows, both of these routes will be explored.—Paragraph 4/Sentence 7

7. **The correct answer is (D).** permit comparison of their concepts of justice—Paragraph 4/Sentences 6 and 7

8. **The correct answer is (E).** judgments about human actions can be made only by the resulting end-states—Paragraph 2/Sentence 2

9. **The correct answer is (E).** The net value of consequences is considered important. Only (A), (B), (C), and (D) are mentioned as features of utilitarianism. See the importance of (A) *results*, 3/3; (B) *consequences*, 1/3; (C) *valued end-state*, 2/2; and (D) *means of achieving results*, 3/1.

10. **The correct answer is (D).** It is legally acceptable for bad consequences to flow from the exercise of an individual's right or privilege.—Paragraph 1/Sentence 8

11. **The correct answer is (B).** contrast judgments of right and wrong with other types of judgments—Paragraph 4/Sentence 5

12. **The correct answer is (D).** means used to produce results—Paragraph 3/Sentence 1 and Paragraph 2/Sentence 2

13. **The correct answer is (C).** explains some judgments in law and morals—Paragraph 1/Sentence 2

14. **The correct answer is (A).** somewhat critical—Paragraph 1/Sentence 4

15. **The correct answer is (C).** an argument for the use of formal models by lawyers—Paragraph 1/Sentence 8

16. **The correct answer is (E).** a method of argumentation—Paragraph 1/Sentence 6

17. **The correct answer is (B).** locating something left out of consideration. Only (A), (C), (D), and (E) are benefits of using formal models. For (A) *determining that an argument is making a distinction without a difference*, see 1/8; for (C) *demonstrating inconsistencies in an argument*, see 4/7; for (D) *setting out difficulties with the form of argumentation*, see 2/1; and for (E) *assisting in the derivation of the logical implications of an argument*, see 1/4.

18. **The correct answer is (D).** is not logically rigorous—Paragraph 1/Sentence 4

19. **The correct answer is (C).** provide the basis for argumentation—Paragraph 3/Sentence 2

20. **The correct answer is (E).** as a technique to ensure equity. Only (A), (B), (C), and (D) describe uses for models as argued in the passage. For models used (A) *as a method of argumentation*, see 4/7; (B) *as a source of answers to problems,* see 4/8; (C) *as a form of reasoning used by lawyers*, see 1/1; and (D) *as a method to identify problems with logic*, see 4/7.

21. **The correct answer is (D).** Formal models are as illogical as prose models.—Paragraph 2/Sentences 1 and 2

22. **The correct answer is (D).** Omissions are a problem with formal models.—Paragraph 4/Sentence 3

23. **The correct answer is (C).** an interpretation of syntactics applied to aspects of legal discourse—Paragraph 1/Sentence 1

24. **The correct answer is (A).** A, 2, #, +, s, ?, c, p, %, $ — Paragraph 3/Sentence 1

25. **The correct answer is (B).** the transmission of the dash in dot-dot-dash when two dots are always followed by a dash—Paragraph 2/Sentence 6

26. **The correct answer is (E).** a case that is exactly the same as previous cases—Paragraph 5/Sentence 1

27. **The correct answer is (D).** Redundancy in a message reduces the information transmitted.—Paragraph 4/Sentence 4

28. **The correct answer is (B).** Redundancy accounts for the difference between strong and weak legal arguments.—Paragraph 5/Sentence 2

SECTION 5

In the following answer guide, the credited responses appear in bold type and the guide that directs you toward the credited response appears within the answer-choice context. The first reference is to the point of the argument and the second is to the nature of the issue involved.

1. **The correct answer is (A).** In the absence of freedom of expression, great writers do not develop.

    Point—Neither great writers nor freedom of expression exist in Largo.

    Issue—Extension question/assumption

2. **The correct answer is (C).** Birds, rather than cave dwellers, may have brought snakes and fish to the caves to eat.

    Point—Cavemen ate bison, birds, snakes, and fish.

    Issue—Extension question/weakening evidence

3. **The correct answer is (B).** people can be persuaded to abandon technology, urbanization, and mass production

    Point—The natural benevolence of people is corrupted by institutions.

    Issue—Extension question/strengthening evidence

4. **The correct answer is (C).** The sky is not cloudy, and rain is not falling.

    Point—Bob is not in the slicker he wears when it is cloudy and rainy.

    Issue—Extension question/conclusion

5. **The correct answer is (C).** Sensitive people are lovers.

    Point—Excellent musicians love poetry.

    Issue—Description question/Sensitivity not involved in argument

6. **The correct answer is (B).** Since owls feed only at night, the bird feeding in daylight is not an owl.

    Point—Reasoning from properties of plaznium to a conclusion.

    Issue—Description question/structure of argument

7. **The correct answer is (C).** Some ocean-liner passengers are in the care of a dangerous person.

   Point—Captains who care for passengers may be dangerous alcoholics.

   Issue—Extension question/conclusion

8. **The correct answer is (A).** The resources required to log forests cannot be replenished.

   Point—Coal is a nonrenewable resource—trees are a renewable resource.

   Issue—Extension question/weakening evidence

9. **The correct answer is (E).** Jurors think eyewitness testimony leaves less room for doubt than does expert testimony.

   Point—Jurors find expert testimony less persuasive than eyewitness testimony.

   Issue—Extension question/conclusion

10. **The correct answer is (D).** In the future, more older students will enter college than ever before.

    Point—College enrollment will decline when the number of 18-year-olds declines.

    Issue—Extension question/weakening evidence

11. **The correct answer is (D).** In the past, film was an important art form.

    Point—Contemporary film is not an art form.

    Issue—Extension question/unsupported conclusion

12. **The correct answer is (C).** Countries can accurately determine one another's military strength.

    Point—U.S. can assure military balance of power by selling arms to other countries.

    Issue—Extension question/assumption

13. **The correct answer is (C).** The sale and delivery of military equipment is usually known only by the two countries involved.

    Point—U.S. can assure military balance of power by selling arms to other countries.

    Issue—Extension question/weakening evidence

14. **The correct answer is (C).** Lights are maintained in good working order because of the inspection requirement.

    Point—Turn-signal inspection identifies few defective lights.

    Issue—Extension question/weakening evidence

15. **The correct answer is (E).** It is seldom possible to determine which information involves the public welfare.

    Point—Public welfare is the only justification for exposing people's private lives.

    Issue—Extension question/weakening evidence

16. **The correct answer is (C).** Personal privacy is an important right.

    Point—Public welfare is the only justification for exposing people's private lives.

    Issue—Extension question/conclusion

17. **The correct answer is (E).** Voting is a form of political involvement.

    Point—Voting and political involvement have a strong relationship.

    Issue—Extension question/conclusion

18. **The correct answer is (A).** Some students prefer geometry to physics.

    Point—All prefer history to geometry—some prefer physics to history.

    Issue—Extension question/conclusion

19. **The correct answer is (A).** Some students prefer geometry to physics.

    Point—All prefer history to geometry—some prefer physics to history.

    Issue—Extension question/conclusion

20. **The correct answer is (D)**. Nature cannot be changed.

    Point—A snake will bite a hand that fed it.

    Issue—Extension question/conclusion

21. **The correct answer is (C)**. Cheese and butter produce greater profits for processors than does milk.

    Point—Without government subsidies, more milk would be used for cheese and butter.

    Issue—Extension question/conclusion

22. **The correct answer is (B)**. Certain attributes of works of art are typical of specific periods.

    Point—Many characteristics differentiate early Greek period sculpture.

    Issue—Extension question/assumption

23. **The correct answer is (C)**. The villagers do not trust the mayor.

    Point—By paying a bounty for snakes, the mayor will rid the town of them.

    Issue—Extension question/NOT weakening evidence

24. **The correct answer is (C)**. It appears that the cost of housing at Spring Lake is prohibitive. I looked at a number of houses last month, and they cost much more than I could afford.

    Point—Spring Lake is too rough for sailing.

    Issue—Description question/structure of argument

Law School Admission Test Simulation Answer Sheet

SECTION 1	SECTION 2	SECTION 3	SECTION 4	SECTION 5
1. Ⓐ Ⓑ Ⓒ Ⓓ Ⓔ	1. Ⓐ Ⓑ Ⓒ Ⓓ Ⓔ	1. Ⓐ Ⓑ Ⓒ Ⓓ Ⓔ	1. Ⓐ Ⓑ Ⓒ Ⓓ Ⓔ	1. Ⓐ Ⓑ Ⓒ Ⓓ Ⓔ
2. Ⓐ Ⓑ Ⓒ Ⓓ Ⓔ	2. Ⓐ Ⓑ Ⓒ Ⓓ Ⓔ	2. Ⓐ Ⓑ Ⓒ Ⓓ Ⓔ	2. Ⓐ Ⓑ Ⓒ Ⓓ Ⓔ	2. Ⓐ Ⓑ Ⓒ Ⓓ Ⓔ
3. Ⓐ Ⓑ Ⓒ Ⓓ Ⓔ	3. Ⓐ Ⓑ Ⓒ Ⓓ Ⓔ	3. Ⓐ Ⓑ Ⓒ Ⓓ Ⓔ	3. Ⓐ Ⓑ Ⓒ Ⓓ Ⓔ	3. Ⓐ Ⓑ Ⓒ Ⓓ Ⓔ
4. Ⓐ Ⓑ Ⓒ Ⓓ Ⓔ	4. Ⓐ Ⓑ Ⓒ Ⓓ Ⓔ	4. Ⓐ Ⓑ Ⓒ Ⓓ Ⓔ	4. Ⓐ Ⓑ Ⓒ Ⓓ Ⓔ	4. Ⓐ Ⓑ Ⓒ Ⓓ Ⓔ
5. Ⓐ Ⓑ Ⓒ Ⓓ Ⓔ	5. Ⓐ Ⓑ Ⓒ Ⓓ Ⓔ	5. Ⓐ Ⓑ Ⓒ Ⓓ Ⓔ	5. Ⓐ Ⓑ Ⓒ Ⓓ Ⓔ	5. Ⓐ Ⓑ Ⓒ Ⓓ Ⓔ
6. Ⓐ Ⓑ Ⓒ Ⓓ Ⓔ	6. Ⓐ Ⓑ Ⓒ Ⓓ Ⓔ	6. Ⓐ Ⓑ Ⓒ Ⓓ Ⓔ	6. Ⓐ Ⓑ Ⓒ Ⓓ Ⓔ	6. Ⓐ Ⓑ Ⓒ Ⓓ Ⓔ
7. Ⓐ Ⓑ Ⓒ Ⓓ Ⓔ	7. Ⓐ Ⓑ Ⓒ Ⓓ Ⓔ	7. Ⓐ Ⓑ Ⓒ Ⓓ Ⓔ	7. Ⓐ Ⓑ Ⓒ Ⓓ Ⓔ	7. Ⓐ Ⓑ Ⓒ Ⓓ Ⓔ
8. Ⓐ Ⓑ Ⓒ Ⓓ Ⓔ	8. Ⓐ Ⓑ Ⓒ Ⓓ Ⓔ	8. Ⓐ Ⓑ Ⓒ Ⓓ Ⓔ	8. Ⓐ Ⓑ Ⓒ Ⓓ Ⓔ	8. Ⓐ Ⓑ Ⓒ Ⓓ Ⓔ
9. Ⓐ Ⓑ Ⓒ Ⓓ Ⓔ	9. Ⓐ Ⓑ Ⓒ Ⓓ Ⓔ	9. Ⓐ Ⓑ Ⓒ Ⓓ Ⓔ	9. Ⓐ Ⓑ Ⓒ Ⓓ Ⓔ	9. Ⓐ Ⓑ Ⓒ Ⓓ Ⓔ
10. Ⓐ Ⓑ Ⓒ Ⓓ Ⓔ	10. Ⓐ Ⓑ Ⓒ Ⓓ Ⓔ	10. Ⓐ Ⓑ Ⓒ Ⓓ Ⓔ	10. Ⓐ Ⓑ Ⓒ Ⓓ Ⓔ	10. Ⓐ Ⓑ Ⓒ Ⓓ Ⓔ
11. Ⓐ Ⓑ Ⓒ Ⓓ Ⓔ	11. Ⓐ Ⓑ Ⓒ Ⓓ Ⓔ	11. Ⓐ Ⓑ Ⓒ Ⓓ Ⓔ	11. Ⓐ Ⓑ Ⓒ Ⓓ Ⓔ	11. Ⓐ Ⓑ Ⓒ Ⓓ Ⓔ
12. Ⓐ Ⓑ Ⓒ Ⓓ Ⓔ	12. Ⓐ Ⓑ Ⓒ Ⓓ Ⓔ	12. Ⓐ Ⓑ Ⓒ Ⓓ Ⓔ	12. Ⓐ Ⓑ Ⓒ Ⓓ Ⓔ	12. Ⓐ Ⓑ Ⓒ Ⓓ Ⓔ
13. Ⓐ Ⓑ Ⓒ Ⓓ Ⓔ	13. Ⓐ Ⓑ Ⓒ Ⓓ Ⓔ	13. Ⓐ Ⓑ Ⓒ Ⓓ Ⓔ	13. Ⓐ Ⓑ Ⓒ Ⓓ Ⓔ	13. Ⓐ Ⓑ Ⓒ Ⓓ Ⓔ
14. Ⓐ Ⓑ Ⓒ Ⓓ Ⓔ	14. Ⓐ Ⓑ Ⓒ Ⓓ Ⓔ	14. Ⓐ Ⓑ Ⓒ Ⓓ Ⓔ	14. Ⓐ Ⓑ Ⓒ Ⓓ Ⓔ	14. Ⓐ Ⓑ Ⓒ Ⓓ Ⓔ
15. Ⓐ Ⓑ Ⓒ Ⓓ Ⓔ	15. Ⓐ Ⓑ Ⓒ Ⓓ Ⓔ	15. Ⓐ Ⓑ Ⓒ Ⓓ Ⓔ	15. Ⓐ Ⓑ Ⓒ Ⓓ Ⓔ	15. Ⓐ Ⓑ Ⓒ Ⓓ Ⓔ
16. Ⓐ Ⓑ Ⓒ Ⓓ Ⓔ	16. Ⓐ Ⓑ Ⓒ Ⓓ Ⓔ	16. Ⓐ Ⓑ Ⓒ Ⓓ Ⓔ	16. Ⓐ Ⓑ Ⓒ Ⓓ Ⓔ	16. Ⓐ Ⓑ Ⓒ Ⓓ Ⓔ
17. Ⓐ Ⓑ Ⓒ Ⓓ Ⓔ	17. Ⓐ Ⓑ Ⓒ Ⓓ Ⓔ	17. Ⓐ Ⓑ Ⓒ Ⓓ Ⓔ	17. Ⓐ Ⓑ Ⓒ Ⓓ Ⓔ	17. Ⓐ Ⓑ Ⓒ Ⓓ Ⓔ
18. Ⓐ Ⓑ Ⓒ Ⓓ Ⓔ	18. Ⓐ Ⓑ Ⓒ Ⓓ Ⓔ	18. Ⓐ Ⓑ Ⓒ Ⓓ Ⓔ	18. Ⓐ Ⓑ Ⓒ Ⓓ Ⓔ	18. Ⓐ Ⓑ Ⓒ Ⓓ Ⓔ
19. Ⓐ Ⓑ Ⓒ Ⓓ Ⓔ	19. Ⓐ Ⓑ Ⓒ Ⓓ Ⓔ	19. Ⓐ Ⓑ Ⓒ Ⓓ Ⓔ	19. Ⓐ Ⓑ Ⓒ Ⓓ Ⓔ	19. Ⓐ Ⓑ Ⓒ Ⓓ Ⓔ
20. Ⓐ Ⓑ Ⓒ Ⓓ Ⓔ	20. Ⓐ Ⓑ Ⓒ Ⓓ Ⓔ	20. Ⓐ Ⓑ Ⓒ Ⓓ Ⓔ	20. Ⓐ Ⓑ Ⓒ Ⓓ Ⓔ	20. Ⓐ Ⓑ Ⓒ Ⓓ Ⓔ
21. Ⓐ Ⓑ Ⓒ Ⓓ Ⓔ	21. Ⓐ Ⓑ Ⓒ Ⓓ Ⓔ	21. Ⓐ Ⓑ Ⓒ Ⓓ Ⓔ	21. Ⓐ Ⓑ Ⓒ Ⓓ Ⓔ	21. Ⓐ Ⓑ Ⓒ Ⓓ Ⓔ
22. Ⓐ Ⓑ Ⓒ Ⓓ Ⓔ	22. Ⓐ Ⓑ Ⓒ Ⓓ Ⓔ	22. Ⓐ Ⓑ Ⓒ Ⓓ Ⓔ	22. Ⓐ Ⓑ Ⓒ Ⓓ Ⓔ	22. Ⓐ Ⓑ Ⓒ Ⓓ Ⓔ
23. Ⓐ Ⓑ Ⓒ Ⓓ Ⓔ	23. Ⓐ Ⓑ Ⓒ Ⓓ Ⓔ	23. Ⓐ Ⓑ Ⓒ Ⓓ Ⓔ	23. Ⓐ Ⓑ Ⓒ Ⓓ Ⓔ	23. Ⓐ Ⓑ Ⓒ Ⓓ Ⓔ
24. Ⓐ Ⓑ Ⓒ Ⓓ Ⓔ	24. Ⓐ Ⓑ Ⓒ Ⓓ Ⓔ	24. Ⓐ Ⓑ Ⓒ Ⓓ Ⓔ	24. Ⓐ Ⓑ Ⓒ Ⓓ Ⓔ	24. Ⓐ Ⓑ Ⓒ Ⓓ Ⓔ
25. Ⓐ Ⓑ Ⓒ Ⓓ Ⓔ	25. Ⓐ Ⓑ Ⓒ Ⓓ Ⓔ	25. Ⓐ Ⓑ Ⓒ Ⓓ Ⓔ	25. Ⓐ Ⓑ Ⓒ Ⓓ Ⓔ	25. Ⓐ Ⓑ Ⓒ Ⓓ Ⓔ
26. Ⓐ Ⓑ Ⓒ Ⓓ Ⓔ	26. Ⓐ Ⓑ Ⓒ Ⓓ Ⓔ	26. Ⓐ Ⓑ Ⓒ Ⓓ Ⓔ	26. Ⓐ Ⓑ Ⓒ Ⓓ Ⓔ	26. Ⓐ Ⓑ Ⓒ Ⓓ Ⓔ
27. Ⓐ Ⓑ Ⓒ Ⓓ Ⓔ	27. Ⓐ Ⓑ Ⓒ Ⓓ Ⓔ	27. Ⓐ Ⓑ Ⓒ Ⓓ Ⓔ	27. Ⓐ Ⓑ Ⓒ Ⓓ Ⓔ	27. Ⓐ Ⓑ Ⓒ Ⓓ Ⓔ
28. Ⓐ Ⓑ Ⓒ Ⓓ Ⓔ	28. Ⓐ Ⓑ Ⓒ Ⓓ Ⓔ	28. Ⓐ Ⓑ Ⓒ Ⓓ Ⓔ	28. Ⓐ Ⓑ Ⓒ Ⓓ Ⓔ	28. Ⓐ Ⓑ Ⓒ Ⓓ Ⓔ
29. Ⓐ Ⓑ Ⓒ Ⓓ Ⓔ	29. Ⓐ Ⓑ Ⓒ Ⓓ Ⓔ	29. Ⓐ Ⓑ Ⓒ Ⓓ Ⓔ	29. Ⓐ Ⓑ Ⓒ Ⓓ Ⓔ	29. Ⓐ Ⓑ Ⓒ Ⓓ Ⓔ
30. Ⓐ Ⓑ Ⓒ Ⓓ Ⓔ	30. Ⓐ Ⓑ Ⓒ Ⓓ Ⓔ	30. Ⓐ Ⓑ Ⓒ Ⓓ Ⓔ	30. Ⓐ Ⓑ Ⓒ Ⓓ Ⓔ	30. Ⓐ Ⓑ Ⓒ Ⓓ Ⓔ

Practice Test 2

The questions in this section are based on a set of conditions. A diagram may be helpful in the answer selection process. Select the best answer to each question, and mark the corresponding space on the answer sheet.

Questions 1–6

Five golfers, C, D, E, F, and G, play a series of matches in which the following are always true of the results.

Either C is last and G is first or C is first and G is last.

D finishes ahead of E.

Every golfer plays in and finishes every match.

There are no ties in any match; that is, no 2 players ever finish in the same position in a match.

1. If exactly 1 golfer finishes between C and D, which of the following must be true?

   (A) C finishes first.
   (B) G finishes first.
   (C) F finishes third.
   (D) D finishes fourth.
   (E) E finishes fourth.

2. Which of the following CANNOT be true?

   (A) E finishes second.
   (B) F finishes second.
   (C) F finishes third.
   (D) E finishes ahead of F.
   (E) F finishes ahead of D.

3. If D finishes third, which of the following must be true?

   (A) G finishes first.
   (B) C finishes first.
   (C) E finishes ahead of F.
   (D) F finishes ahead of E.
   (E) F finishes behind D.

4. If C finishes first, in how many different orders is it possible for the other golfers to finish?

   (A) 1
   (B) 2
   (C) 3
   (D) 4
   (E) 5

5. Which of the following additional conditions makes it certain that F finishes second?

   (A) C finishes ahead of D.
   (B) D finishes ahead of F.
   (C) F finishes ahead of D.
   (D) D finishes behind G.
   (E) G finishes behind F.

6. If a sixth golfer, H, enters a match and finishes ahead of F and behind D, which of the following CANNOT be true?

   (A) D finishes ahead of G.
   (B) H finishes ahead of E.
   (C) E finishes third.
   (D) F finishes fourth.
   (E) H finishes fifth.

Questions 7–12

The state presidents of the Half Century Club are comparing ages at the Club's annual meeting.

The Kansas president is older than the Wyoming president.

The Ohio president is younger than the Maine president.

7. If the president from Ohio is younger than the president from Wyoming, which of the following CANNOT be true?

(A) The Kansas president is younger than the Maine president.
(B) The Maine president is younger than the Wyoming president.
(C) The Ohio president is younger than the Kansas president.
(D) The Wyoming president is younger than the Maine president.
(E) The Kansas president is younger than the Ohio president.

8. If the president from Wyoming is older than the president from Ohio, which of the following must be true?

(A) The Kansas president is older than the Maine president.
(B) The Wyoming president is older than the Kansas president.
(C) The Maine president is older than the Kansas president.
(D) The Wyoming president is older than the Maine president.
(E) The Kansas president is older than the Ohio president.

9. If the Texas president is older than the Maine president, which of the following must be true?

(A) The Texas president is the oldest president.
(B) The Texas president is older than the Kansas president.
(C) The Wyoming president is older than the Texas president.
(D) The Texas president is older than the Ohio president.
(E) The Kansas president is older than the Texas president.

10. If the Vermont president is younger than the Maine president, the Wyoming president is older than the Maine president, and the Ohio president is the youngest, which of the following is the second-oldest president?

(A) Vermont
(B) Wyoming
(C) Maine
(D) Kansas
(E) Ohio

11. If the Utah president is older than the Ohio president and the Florida president is younger than the Wyoming president, which of the following CANNOT be true if the age of the Maine president is between the ages of the Utah and Florida presidents?

(A) The Utah president is older than the Wyoming president.
(B) The Florida president is older than the Ohio president.
(C) The Florida president is older than the Kansas president.
(D) The Maine president is older than the Ohio president.
(E) The Wyoming president is older than the Florida president.

12. If the Alaska president is older than the Iowa, Maine, and Wyoming presidents, which of the following must be true?

(A) The Iowa president is older than the Maine president.
(B) The Iowa president is older than the Wyoming president.
(C) The Iowa president is older than the Ohio president.
(D) The Alaska president is older than the Ohio president.
(E) The Kansas president is older than the Alaska president.

Questions 13–18

There are four parallel train tracks at a railroad station, numbered 1 through 4 from left to right. Tracks 1 and 2 are northbound, tracks 3 and 4 are southbound. A train coming from the north will arrive on a southbound track. A train coming from the south will arrive on a northbound track.

A round-trip train must arrive on a track adjacent to a track going the other direction.

A local train can only arrive immediately after either an express or a metroliner.

Two consecutive trains cannot use the same track.

13. If three trains, P, Q, and R, arrive at the station on tracks 2, 4, and 1, respectively, and in that order, what could be true about the trains?

   I. P is an express.

   II. P and R are metroliners.

   III. Q and R are locals.

   (A) I only
   (B) II only
   (C) III only
   (D) I and II only
   (E) I, II, and III

14. If two northbound locals, a southbound express, and a round-trip metroliner coming from the north are all approaching the station, what is the order in which the tracks can be used, from first to last?

   (A) 2,3,4,1
   (B) 1,2,3,4
   (C) 3,2,1,4
   (D) 1,3,2,4
   (E) 4,1,3,2

15. If five trains arrive on tracks 1,3,1,4, and 2, in that order, and the second train to arrive is not a local, what is the maximum number of trains that could be locals?

   (A) 1
   (B) 2
   (C) 3
   (D) 4
   (E) 5

16. Train Q, a northbound express; train R, a round-trip express coming from the south; train S, a northbound metroliner; and trains T and U, both southbound locals, are arriving at the station, though not necessarily in that order.

   In what order and on what track can each train arrive?

   (A) S on track 1, U on track 4, Q on track 2, T on track 4, R on track 3
   (B) R on track 2, T on track 3, S on track 1, Q on track 1, U on track 4
   (C) R on track 2, U on track 3, S on track 1, T on track 3, Q on track 2
   (D) Q on track 2, T on track 4, R on track 3, U on track 4, S on track 1
   (E) T on track 3, Q on track 2, S on track 1, U on track 4, R on track 2

17. If six trains arrive on tracks 1,2,1,3,4,3, in that order, and there are two locals, what are the maximum and minimum numbers, respectively, of trains that could be expresses?

   (A) 3,0
   (B) 3,2
   (C) 4,2
   (D) 2,1
   (E) 4,0

18. If four trains arrive at the station, and none of them arrives on track 3, what must be true about the trains?

   (A) None are round-trip trains.
   (B) Two of the trains are not northbound locals.
   (C) The number of locals equals the number of southbound trains.
   (D) There are more northbound trains than there are southbound trains.
   (E) The greatest number of locals cannot exceed the greatest number of express trains.

Questions 19–24

Five friends, Carol, Ed, Jenny, Rick, and Walt, go to the beach. Each person either brings something (food, blankets, or umbrella) or does something for the trip (drives or pays the tolls along the route).

Two people are brother and sister. They are the only two of the group of friends who are related to each other.

One person meets the others on the beach when they arrive. This person brings the umbrella. The driver of the group that meets the person on the beach is male.

When Ed brings the food, Walt does not drive.

The brother pays the tolls.

When Carol or Jenny brings the blankets, Rick drives.

19. If Ed brings the food, which of the following must be true?

   (A) Carol brings the blankets.
   (B) Rick drives.
   (C) Jenny does not bring the blankets.
   (D) Carol does not bring the umbrella.
   (E) Jenny meets the others at the beach.

20. If Rick drives, what CANNOT be true?

   (A) Jenny brings the umbrella.
   (B) Ed pays the tolls.
   (C) Ed brings the food.
   (D) Walt is Jenny's brother.
   (E) Carol is Rick's sister.

21. If Walt brings the food, Rick CANNOT

   (A) drive
   (B) be Jenny's brother
   (C) bring the umbrella
   (D) be Carol's brother
   (E) pay the tolls

22. If Carol brings the umbrella, which of the following CANNOT be true?

   (A) Carol is Rick's sister.
   (B) Ed pays no tolls.
   (C) Jenny brings neither blankets nor food.
   (D) Ed brings the food.
   (E) Jenny does not bring the blankets.

23. If Ed brings the food, Rick must

   (A) drive
   (B) pay tolls
   (C) bring the blankets
   (D) bring the umbrella
   (E) be someone's brother

24. If Jenny brings the blankets, which two people CANNOT be related?

   (A) Carol and Ed
   (B) Carol and Rick
   (C) Jenny and Walt
   (D) Carol and Walt
   (E) Jenny and Ed

SECTION 2   TIME—35 MINUTES   24 QUESTIONS

Evaluate the reasoning contained in the brief statements, and select the best answer. Do not make implausible, superfluous, or incompatible assumptions. Select the best answer to each question, and mark the corresponding space on the answer sheet.

1. All quiet people are harmless.

   No harmless people are easily identified.

   The premises above lead to which of the following conclusions?

   (A) Quiet people are not easily identified.
   (B) Most people who are easily identified are harmless.
   (C) No harmless people are quiet.
   (D) Some easily identified people are quiet.
   (E) All quiet people are easily identified.

2. I don't believe that ambitious people are good parents. Of course, there are some parents who have successful careers and well-raised children. But these parents are not really ambitious. Were they ambitious, they could not devote the necessary time and energy to raising their children well.

   Which of the following best explains the flawed reasoning in the author's argument?

   (A) It relies on a word with two different meanings.
   (B) It bases an absolute conclusion upon relative evidence.
   (C) It assumes the conclusion.
   (D) It generalizes from inappropriate specifics.
   (E) It depends on a false analogy.

3. Arthritis specialists understand that effective treatment must do more than relieve pain. So, the medicine arthritis specialists prescribe most has both an anti-pain and anti-inflammation ingredient. These same ingredients are found in Arthrelief. Use Arthrelief to combat arthritic pain.

   The advertisement above does NOT assume which of the following?

   (A) Arthritis specialists provide authoritative information on effective medication for arthritis.
   (B) Arthritis specialists use Arthrelief because it contains anti-inflammation medicine.
   (C) A medicine containing ingredients prescribed for arthritis will be effective.
   (D) Arthrelief only combats arthritic pain.
   (E) Arthritis specialists prescribe Arthrelief most.

4. Testing the reasoning abilities of illiterate people has proven to be particularly challenging to psychologists. When illiterate people are given tasks that are designed to require them to reason to a conclusion, they are relatively successful when the mechanical devices used in the test are familiar ones. But if the devices used in the test are unfamiliar to the illiterate person, they are relatively unsuccessful at performing analogous tasks.

   Which of the following conclusions can be reasonably drawn from the information above?

   (A) Reasoning abilities of illiterate people should not be tested using tasks that do not involve familiar devices.
   (B) Literacy is required in order to test the reasoning abilities of people through the use of mechanical devices.
   (C) Testing illiterate people for reasoning abilities is relatively unsuccessful.
   (D) Mechanical devices are a poor substitute for words in reasoning to a conclusion.
   (E) Unfamiliar tasks provide a better measure of reasoning ability than do familiar tasks.

5. Japanese workers exercise each day in their workplaces. American employers do not require daily exercise, and, as a result, American workers are more overweight and much less fit and suffer more sickness and injuries than their Japanese counterparts. American workers will only become as productive as the Japanese if they are required to exercise on a daily basis.

Which of the following, if true, most weakens the above argument?

(A) Daily exercise does not reduce or prevent incidents of sickness.
(B) Daily exercise does not reduce the severity of on-the-job injuries.
(C) Daily exercise does not contribute greatly to Japanese worker fitness.
(D) Daily exercise does not contribute greatly to Japanese worker productivity.
(E) Daily exercise does not result in significant weight loss.

6. Dictatorships or centralized governments result from the political indifference of a country's people. If people were not politically indifferent, all governments would be democratic or decentralized.

Which of the following could NOT be inferred from the above argument?

(A) Democratic governments result from politically active people.
(B) Dictatorships only exist in countries whose people are politically indifferent.
(C) Politically active people are responsible for decentralized governments.
(D) A country with a democratic government must have politically active people.
(E) Centralized governments are the responsibility of the politically indifferent.

7. Which is the most logical arrangement of the sentences?

I.   By reducing its standard of living the United States can conserve energy.

II. Yet, the United States aspires to energy independence.

III. Studies confirm that the only certain path to energy independence is through conservation.

IV. More than 20 percent of the energy consumed by the United States is imported.

(A) I, II, III, IV
(B) I, III, IV, II
(C) II, III, IV, I
(D) III, IV, I, II
(E) IV, II, III, I

8. Dr. Bartels concludes that governments waste the money they spend in support of higher education. His argument is based on longitudinal research that shows that fewer than 20 percent of persons with college degrees are working in the field of their training five years after receiving their degrees.

Dr. Bartels makes the assumption that

(A) higher education in a field is valuable training only for that field
(B) what is desirable at one time will continue into another
(C) higher education can be valued only in degrees awarded
(D) work areas are directly related to college-degree areas
(E) higher education should not be a governmental concern

9. Ninety percent of the students taking as few as two Alert tablets daily got better grades in school. Improve your grades, get Alert today!

Which of the following could be offered as a valid criticism of the advertisement above?

(A) It does not state that Alert tablets cause grade improvement.
(B) Using medication to get good grades is cheating.
(C) Taking more Alert will result in greater grade improvement.
(D) It suggests that only 10 percent of students do not use Alert daily.
(E) Being alert in school does not always result in improved grades.

10. According to dog lovers, the principal virtue of the dog is its general friendliness toward all people. According to cat lovers, the principal virtue of the cat is its exclusive friendliness toward its provider.

Which of the following is true of the claims of both dog and cat lovers?

(A) Pet friendliness toward a provider is unworthy.
(B) They come from sources that apply the same standard.
(C) Animals cannot be judged by standards for human behavior.
(D) Animal lovers are friendly.
(E) Friendliness is a virtue.

11. In Canada, a family can stay overnight in a litter-free public campground on a clear lake for less than it costs to spend a day at a filthy public beach in the United States. Why must public beaches in the United States be so expensive and dirty?

Which of the following, if true, most weakens the above argument?

(A) Campgrounds in Canada are little used.
(B) Beaches in the United States are intensely used.
(C) There are more public campgrounds in Canada than there are public beaches in the United States.
(D) There are more public beaches in the United States than there are public campgrounds in Canada.
(E) Public beaches in Canada are no cleaner or cheaper than those in the United States.

12. Computers have been programmed to play poker. Because of the way they are programmed, computers reproduce human strategies, such as bluffing. Apparently, they make decisions for the same reasons as human players.

The author of this note

(A) uses scientific evidence to support the conclusion
(B) proposes a common cause for similar effects
(C) grounds the argument on the double meaning of the word "reason"
(D) states a conclusion and then explains how it was reached
(E) argues from an analogy to reconcile an apparent contradiction

13. The Department of Agriculture will stop inspecting milk processing plants because no citations have been issued in the past two years.

If true, which of the following most strengthens the decision?

(A) Processors will cut corners if the threat of inspection is removed.
(B) Milk processing is very automated.
(C) The source of milk is known, so compensation can be had for any problem that occurs.
(D) The Department budget has been cut by 30 percent.
(E) The industry association has standards that exceed the legal requirements.

14. Rites of adulthood are more frequently found in societies where the differences between adults and children are not clear. The purpose of such rites is to formally impose adult responsibilities on participants.

The above argument would be most strengthened if it were found that

(A) children do not generally behave as adults prior to the rites
(B) children generally accept the rites without question
(C) adults generally approve of the rites
(D) formal rites are prevalent in such societies
(E) children do not generally accept adult responsibilities prior to the rites

15. Attempts to make public-transportation facilities accessible to physically challenged people are misguided. Only the most athletic of the physically challenged are able to get to the stops and stations where it is possible for them to take advantage of special devices installed on buses and trains.

Which of the following most strengthens the argument above?

(A) It is extremely expensive to install special devices on buses and trains to accommodate the physically challenged.

(B) More physically challenged people have access to motorized wheelchairs than ever before.

(C) Very few physically challenged people use facilities in the places where they have been installed.

(D) Special-access facilities to public buildings have increased their use by physically challenged people.

(E) Physically challenged people on buses and trains are at greater safety risk than others.

Questions 16–17

Every time a business grants financial credit to an individual, the business assumes the risk of the individual not being able to make all the agreed-upon payments. Credit bureaus assist businesses in their efforts to evaluate the risks involved with the extension of credit to individual purchasers. The financial history of individuals is maintained and reported on by credit bureaus. Credit bureaus assist debtors as well as creditors by preventing them from assuming greater debt resulting from the work of credit bureaus, which holds losses and prices down and, thus, benefits consumers generally. The few concerns for individual privacy that have been raised about credit bureaus hardly offset their financial value to business and consumer alike.

16. Which of the following is assumed by the above argument?

(A) Business would have no way to make credit decisions without credit bureaus.

(B) Risk of nonpayment is difficult for most businesses to assess.

(C) Purchasers attempt to secure more credit than they can afford.

(D) Credit bureaus seldom make errors in their reports about individuals' financial histories.

(E) Financial histories are complex and difficult to develop and maintain.

17. According to the above argument, harm that results from the use of credit bureaus by businesses is

(A) offset by the need for individual financial histories

(B) minimal, because so few errors are made in their reports

(C) acceptable, because business requires financial histories

(D) justified by the economic value to business and society

(E) essential to the effective extension of credit to individuals

18. Harold is a better writer of short stories than Stan and a better novelist, too. Thus, Harold is indubitably a better playwright as well.

Given the information in the passage, which of the following is a belief about Harold that can be most justifiably attributed to the speaker?

(A) Harold is more versatile than Stan.

(B) Harold is a better writer than Stan.

(C) Harold is altogether more effective than Stan.

(D) Harold is more cultivated than Stan.

(E) Harold is more artistically talented than Stan.

19. The average salary of a college graduate is only 22 percent greater than that of a high school graduate. In 1969, the difference was 55 percent. In addition, college graduates' salaries have not kept up with inflation. For most, the rewards of a college education will not justify the cost of tuition and lost income while getting a degree.

Which of the following, if true, most weakens the above argument?

(A) Since 1969, the incomes of few groups have kept pace with inflation.
(B) Since 1969, college education costs have outpaced inflation by nearly 100 percent.
(C) Since 1969, more high school graduates have decided to seek a college degree.
(D) Since 1969, the unemployment rate for college graduates is lower than that for high school graduates.
(E) Since 1969, there has been a steady decline in the number of high school graduates in the job market.

20. Genetic engineering places the nature-versus-nurture argument in stark relief. Not only will physical qualities (nature) of individuals be altered by manufacturing processes, but intellectual, emotional, and spiritual qualities will be modified as well. Those who argue that the altering of human qualities violates the laws of nature ignore the reality that people are already the result of engineering in the form of their manufactured education, socialization, and environment (nurture).

Which of the following, if true, supports the above argument?

(A) Manufacturing techniques do not alter spiritual qualities of individuals.
(B) By definition, the laws of nature cannot be altered.
(C) Manufacturing of education and intellect are markedly different.
(D) Engineering of genes and environment are virtually the same.
(E) Qualities of individuals and societies are virtually the same.

Questions 21–22

There is an inherent fallacy in the reasoning of Shea, who suggests that all of his readers ought to attend the retrospective of Beatles music offered by the Springfield Pops because "the Beatles have had as great an influence on the musical development of our day as Beethoven had on his." Stalin had great influence on the political development of his time, but no one suggests that people should rush to Moscow to pay homage at his tomb.

21. The point of the above argument is that

(A) Shea confuses influence with merit
(B) Shea confuses politics with music
(C) Shea confuses the Beatles with Beethoven
(D) Shea confuses honor with attendance
(E) Shea confuses popularity with importance

22. Which of the following is analogous to Stalin's tomb in the argument above?

(A) the Springfield Pops
(B) musical influence
(C) Beethoven
(D) attendance at the Beatles retrospective
(E) Shea's readers

23. Ann has vacationed at three different Florida resorts and has enjoyed each of them very much. Thus, Ann is confident that she will enjoy vacationing at the newly opened resort in the Florida keys.

Which of the following statements does NOT alter the probability that vacationing at the new Florida resort will be enjoyable?

(A) All three resorts Ann previously visited are in north Miami Beach, and the new resort is in south Miami Beach.
(B) The new resort was unfavorably reviewed in a national travel magazine.
(C) The manager of the new resort was trained at the same hotel-management school as 2 of the 3 managers of the other three resorts.
(D) The owner of the new resort has been in the resort business for thirty years.
(E) The architect of the other three resorts did not design the new resort.

24. A recent survey has found that the number of high school students that attend a house of worship regularly has increased 60 percent in the past decade. This increase in religious exposure appears to have significantly reduced cheating on tests and improved class participation.

Which of the following, if true, most weakens the inference made above?

(A) Religious leaders frequently speak out for academic honesty.

(B) Not all students responded to the survey.

(C) Recently the high school changed from proctored exams to an honor system.

(D) Social reasons account for the attendance of most students at services.

(E) Cheating is not considered to be a major problem by most teachers.

The questions in this section are based on a set of conditions. A diagram may be helpful in the answer selection process. Select the best answer to each question, and mark the corresponding space on the answer sheet.

Questions 1–6

Six building contractors—L, M, N, O, P, and Q—bid on the construction of a new school. Each submits one bid stating the total price for constructing the building. The school board must award the job to the lowest bidder.

P bids less than N but more than Q.

O bids less than P but more than M.

Q bids less than N but more than L.

No two bids are equal to each other.

1. Which of the following could be the ranking of the contractors' bids?

(A) M, Q, O, P, L, N
(B) M, L, O, Q, P, N
(C) L, Q, M, P, O, N
(D) Q, M, O, L, P, N
(E) L, M, Q, N, P, O

2. If O submits the third-highest bid, which of the following contractors could get the job?

(A) M only
(B) L only
(C) Q or M
(D) M or L
(E) Q or L

3. If O submits one of the lowest two bids, which of the following must be true?

(A) N submits the second-highest bid.
(B) L submits the third-lowest bid.
(C) P submits the third-highest bid.
(D) Q submits the fourth-highest bid.
(E) L submits the fourth-lowest bid.

4. If L submits the lowest bid, all of the following must be true EXCEPT

(A) M submits a lower bid than O
(B) Q submits a higher bid than M
(C) Q submits a lower bid than P
(D) P submits a higher bid than O
(E) M submits a lower bid than P

5. If M submits the second-lowest bid, which of the following can be a ranking of the contractors' bids?

(A) L, M, Q, O, P, N
(B) Q, M, L, O, P, N
(C) O, M, L, Q, P, N
(D) L, M, Q, P, O, N
(E) L, M, P, O, Q, N

6. Which of the following contractors could submit the lowest bid and the second-lowest bid, respectively?

(A) Q and N
(B) M and Q
(C) Q and L
(D) L and P
(E) Q and M

Questions 7–12

Ten students—L, M, N, O, P, Q, R, S, T, and U—graduated from Naquapaug High School in the years 1971-1975, two students per year.

M graduated the year before Q.

P and R graduated together before 1975.

Q and N did not graduate in the same year.

S and T graduated together.

7. All of the following are possible orders of graduation, starting with the 1971 pair of graduates EXCEPT

(A) S, T; P, R; M, O; Q, N; L, U
(B) S, T; P, R; M, N; Q, O; L, U
(C) O, U; M, N; Q, L; P, R; S, T
(D) P, R; M, U; Q, L; N, O; S, T
(E) L, U; M, N; Q, O; P, R; S, T

8. Which of the following could be in the pairs that graduated in 1971, 1973, and 1975, respectively?

   (A) O, U, N
   (B) O, L, U
   (C) L, N, S
   (D) S, N, P
   (E) L, O, U

9. If Q, T, and U graduated in 1972, 1973, and 1975, respectively, and O and M graduated together, which of the following must be true?

   (A) L graduated in 1972.
   (B) N graduated in 1974.
   (C) P graduated two years before N.
   (D) R graduated before 1974.
   (E) S graduated the year before O.

10. If O and U graduated together, and Q graduated in 1974, which of the following must be true?

    (A) N graduated in 1974.
    (B) N graduated in 1972.
    (C) L graduated in 1974.
    (D) R graduated in 1972.
    (E) T graduated in 1971.

11. If P graduated in 1973, and L and O graduated together, which of the following are the only years in which N could be one of the pair of graduates?

    (A) 1971 and 1972
    (B) 1971 and 1974
    (C) 1971 and 1975
    (D) 1972 and 1974
    (E) 1972 and 1975

12. If L, O, and U each graduated in an even-numbered year, which of the following must be true?

    (A) P graduated in 1971.
    (B) O graduated in 1972.
    (C) Q graduated in 1972.
    (D) N graduated in 1973.
    (E) S graduated in 1975.

Questions 13–18

On any day their schedules permit, Adam, Beth, Cary, Dana, and Edith each set up a sales table at a flea market.

Edith will set up only when Cary does not.

Dana will set up only when Adam does not.

Cary will set up only when Dana does.

Beth will set up only when Edith does.

Adam will always set up.

13. Who will set up on a day when the schedules of only Adam, Beth, and Cary permit them to sell?

    (A) Adam only
    (B) Beth only
    (C) Cary only
    (D) Adam and Beth only
    (E) Beth and Cary only

14. How many will set up on a day when the schedules of only Adam, Beth, and Cary permit them to sell?

    (A) one
    (B) two
    (C) three
    (D) four
    (E) five

15. Which of the following groups of people could set up on the same day?

    (A) Adam, Beth, and Cary
    (B) Adam, Cary, and Dana
    (C) Cary, Dana, and Edith
    (D) Beth, Dana, and Edith
    (E) Beth, Cary, and Edith

16. If a buyer wanted to be certain that both Beth and Cary were set up on the same day, which of the following must be set up also?

    (A) Dana and Edith
    (B) Adam
    (C) Edith
    (D) Adam and Dana
    (E) Adam and Edith

17. Which of the following could set up on a day when the schedules of only Beth, Cary, and Edith permit them to sell?

- **(A)** Beth only
- **(B)** Cary only
- **(C)** Edith only
- **(D)** Cary and Edith only
- **(E)** Beth and Edith only

18. How many will set up on a day when the schedules of only Beth, Cary, and Dana permit them to sell?

- **(A)** Zero
- **(B)** One
- **(C)** Two
- **(D)** Three
- **(E)** Four

Questions 19–24

A, B, and C are dentists and S, T, U, and V are hygienists assigned to work for them.

A and B each have exactly two hygienists assigned to them.

C sometimes is assigned one hygienist and sometimes two.

T is assigned to A and one other dentist.

Each hygienist is assigned to at least one dentist.

19. If S and T are assigned to the same two dentists, V must work for

- **(A)** both A and B
- **(B)** both A and C
- **(C)** either A or B
- **(D)** either A or C
- **(E)** either B or C

20. If V is assigned to both B and C, which of the following must be true?

- **(A)** U is assigned to B.
- **(B)** S is assigned to A.
- **(C)** T and U are assigned to the same dentist.
- **(D)** S and T are assigned to the same dentist.
- **(E)** U is assigned to only one dentist.

21. If T and V both are assigned to the same two dentists, S must work for

- **(A)** both A and B
- **(B)** both A and C
- **(C)** either A or B
- **(D)** either A or C
- **(E)** either B or C

22. If U is assigned to B and C, and V is assigned to B, S must work for

- **(A)** A only
- **(B)** B only
- **(C)** C only
- **(D)** both A and B
- **(E)** both A and C

23. Whenever S is assigned to only one dentist and C is assigned only one hygienist, which of the following must be true?

- **(A)** S is assigned to C.
- **(B)** V is assigned to two dentists.
- **(C)** U is assigned to only one dentist.
- **(D)** T is assigned to C.
- **(E)** U is assigned to A.

24. If S is assigned to both B and C, which of the following must be true?

- **(A)** T and V are assigned to the same dentist.
- **(B)** V is assigned to A.
- **(C)** U and V are assigned to the same dentist.
- **(D)** U is assigned to B.
- **(E)** U is assigned to only one dentist.

SECTION 4   TIME—35 MINUTES   28 QUESTIONS

The questions in this section are based on what is stated or implied in the passage. Select the best answer to each question, and mark the corresponding space on the answer sheet.

Line Without a doubt, the role of firearms in American violence is much greater today than a decade ago. Rates of gun violence and the proportion of violent acts that are
(5) committed by guns have increased substantially, even after the Gun Control Act went into effect. Behind these increases lies the probability that handgun ownership has become at least a subcultural institution in
(10) the big cities that are the main arena of American violence. During this period, regional differences in gun ownership and use have been moderated as the large Northeastern cities that were traditionally
(15) areas of low ownership and use have experienced large increases in handgun use.

The special role of the handgun in urban violence is one of the more obvious
(20) lessons of the data that are reported. Over the past ten years, rates of handgun homicide have increased more than three times as much as homicides by all other means. The data reported suggest, but do
(25) not compel, other conclusions about patterns of handgun ownership and violence in the United States. First, the sharp rise in the proportion of violence attributable to handguns in Northeastern
(30) cities may lead to modification of the hypothesis that general patterns of handgun ownership determine the extent to which handguns are used in violent episodes. While it is still true that those regions with
(35) the highest general levels of gun ownership have the highest proportion of gun use in violence, the past decade has produced an increase in handgun use in the Northeast that leaves cities in that region closer to but
(40) still below the average handgun share of violence. This could be due to a substantial rise in handgun ownership in the general

population in these cities, but that would mean that a vast Northeastern urban
(45) handgun arsenal has been accumulating during the past ten years. It is more likely that handgun ownership increased substantially among subcultural groups disproportionately associated with violence without
(50) necessarily affecting other parts of the population.

If one adopts a "subcultural" explanation of the relationship between gun ownership and violence, hypotheses about
(55) the effect of increases or decreases in handgun ownership on handgun violence should take a slightly more complicated form. One would predict that high levels of handgun ownership produce high levels of
(60) handgun violence for two reasons: More handguns are available at a moment of perceived need, and high ownership rates necessarily suggest high levels of handgun availability to all potential consumers. Low
(65) general levels of handgun ownership, on the other hand, become the necessary but not sufficient condition of low levels of handgun violence. If the lower-than-average general ownership levels are still high
(70) enough to create relatively easy handgun availability and if both handgun ownership and propensity for violence are concentrated in discrete subpopulations, lower-than-average general ownership is an
(75) inadequate insurance policy against increases in handgun violence. It is only when ownership levels are low enough to have an impact on handgun availability that low aggregate ownership will depress
(80) handgun involvement in rates of subcultural violence. Efforts to limit handgun supply on a national basis by limiting legitimate production, or imports, or both will not require a large federal street police force.
(85) At the point when market controls make illicit gun production profitable, some police work will obviously be needed, along the lines of controls on illicit liquor production.

1. The primary purpose of the passage is to

   (A) criticize the Gun Control Act
   (B) describe the role of the handgun in urban violence
   (C) advocate limiting handgun availability
   (D) explain the growth of handgun violence
   (E) point out the increase in the urban handgun arsenal

2. If true, the "subcultural" explanation of gun ownership and violence means that

   (A) all parts of the population own more guns
   (B) general patterns of gun ownership determine their use in violent episodes
   (C) higher levels of gun ownership produce higher levels of violence
   (D) gun ownership by people associated with violence has greatly increased
   (E) guns are now primarily owned by the violent elements of urban society

3. The author refers to the Gun Control Act to

   (A) dramatize the increase in gun-related violence
   (B) criticize the government for gun-related violence
   (C) point out the statute's total ineffectiveness
   (D) minimize the importance of gun-control legislation
   (E) argue for more enforcement of the statute

4. Which of the following, if true, would most weaken the author's argument concerning handgun ownership in Northeastern cities?

   (A) Handgun ownership among Boston drug dealers has increased 300 percent in the last ten years.
   (B) Handgun ownership among organized crime figures in New Jersey has increased dramatically in the last ten years.
   (C) Handgun ownership among convicted criminals has increased in the last ten years.
   (D) Handgun ownership among middle-class New Yorkers has increased fourfold in the last ten years.
   (E) Handgun ownership among middle-class Philadelphians has increased slightly in the last ten years.

5. Which of the following may be inferred from the passage?

   (A) The rate of growth in gun ownership in the Northeast is greater than that of other regions.
   (B) Gun ownership in the Northeast is greater than that of other regions.
   (C) There is little data available concerning the growth of gun ownership in urban areas.
   (D) High levels of handgun ownership do not necessarily result in increased violence.
   (E) High levels of handgun ownership in urban areas do not necessarily result in increased violence.

6. The passage suggests which of the following?

   (A) High levels of handgun ownership are not related to perceived needs among consumers.
   (B) More violent acts are committed by means other than handguns.
   (C) Urban violence is due to subcultural differences among residents.
   (D) The number of homicides not involving handguns has increased in the past ten years.
   (E) Lower-than-average handgun ownership will result in lower violence.

7. The author would likely disagree that which of the following would reduce handgun violence?

   (A) regulation of handgun imports
   (B) reduction of handgun ownership in certain subcultural groups
   (C) regulation of handgun possession
   (D) reduction of handgun ownership levels
   (E) regulation of handgun production

Line   Software is like hardware in that it causes
       machines to perform tasks. Software is
       merely a replacement for hardware
       components that could otherwise perform
5   the same function. Software is often
       embedded in hardware and part of an
       overall hardware system. Like hardware,
       software can often serve as a tool for
       creating other items. Like hardware,
10   software needs maintenance work from
       time to time to operate properly.

Software is unlike hardware, however, in a great many ways. Software is, for example, easy and cheap to replicate as compared with hardware. Once the first copy has been produced, software can be almost endlessly replicated at almost no cost, regardless of how complex it is. One of the consequences of this characteristic is that the government tends to think that additional copies of software ought to be deliverable at a very low cost, whereas industry, which is concerned about recouping its research and development costs and which tends to regard the sale of software as the sale of a production facility (as if one bought a General Motors factory when one bought a truck produced by GM), thinks that sales at higher price levels are necessary to make the software business viable. A second consequence of low-cost replicability is that the software industry, for the most part, tends to make its products available only on a highly restrictive licensing basis, rather than selling copies outright.

Another important difference between software and hardware is that software may be wholly subject to a very lengthy lawful monopoly (i.e., a copyright) as well as being held as a trade secret, whereas hardware may be subject to a much shorter monopoly (i.e., a patent) and most often cannot be held as a trade secret. Moreover, quite often hardware is either not patented at all or only subject to partial patent protection. A high standard of inventiveness is required for patent, while copyright requires only the most minimal originality. Hardware, unlike software, cannot be copyrighted at all. As a result, it tends to be much harder to get competition for software procurements and maintenance than for hardware, which means that it is even easier for the government to find itself in a sole-source position as to software than as to hardware. Moreover, because software engineering is still in the early stages of development, it is generally more difficult to specify how software, as opposed to hardware, should be developed for particular functions and to estimate the cost and development schedule for it.

Software, which consists of a stream of electrical impulses, is also virtually "invisible" as compared with hardware, which means that it is more difficult to detect if someone delivers very similar or nearly identical software on a second development contract. Again, because software engineering is a developing art, software is likely to contain many undetected defects that will need to be corrected while in the user's possession.

Unlike hardware, software is readily changeable; that is, new capabilities can be added to software without additional plant or material costs. Often, all that is required is some intellectual labor. All of these factors tend to make software maintenance and enhancement a much bigger part of computer system life-cycle planning than is the case with hardware.

8. The passage is primarily concerned with

   (A) correcting misimpressions about hardware and software
   (B) explaining the nature of software
   (C) minimizing apparent difficulties with software
   (D) comparing hardware and software
   (E) describing computer system life-cycle planning

9. According to the passage, which of the following is true?

   (A) Hardware and software cannot perform the same functions.
   (B) Software can make hardware cheaper.
   (C) Software can be located within hardware.
   (D) Software cannot be copyrighted.
   (E) Hardware is readily changeable.

10. According to the passage, all of the following is true EXCEPT

   (A) the cost of duplicating software is low
   (B) very little software is sold outright
   (C) hardware is often not patented
   (D) software requires minimal originality
   (E) hardware is readily changeable

11. According to the passage, which of the following characteristics does NOT apply to both hardware and software?

   (A) It can be held as a trade secret.
   (B)· It can be copyrighted.
   (C) It can create other items.
   (D) It can be subject to a monopoly.
   (E) It can be maintained.

12. Which of the following can be inferred from the passage?

   (A) Hardware is more expensive than software.
   (B) It is more profitable to sell copies of software than hardware.
   (C) Software maintenance is a relatively competitive business.
   (D) Procurement of hardware is not a competitive business.
   (E) Software is licensed because it is too expensive to buy.

13. Which of the following can be inferred from the passage?

   (A) Ownership rights in software can be better protected than those in hardware.
   (B) Copyrighted software requires greater inventiveness than does hardware.
   (C) Ownership rights in hardware can be better protected than those in software.
   (D) Patented hardware requires greater inventiveness than does software.
   (E) Patented hardware is difficult to specify for particular functions.

14. The argument that one purchased the factory when one purchased a truck made at the factory (lines 27–29) is most like which of the following?

   (A) One purchased the typewriter when one purchased the book that prepared the manuscript.
   (B) One purchased the cruise when one purchased the cruise ship.
   (C) One purchased the restaurant when one purchased the dinner prepared there.
   (D) One purchased the office building when one leased an office located in the building.
   (E) One purchased the health club when one purchased a membership to use the club facilities.

Line We customarily identify the concept of status with its conventional indices, such as wealth, title, and occupation. But there is nothing sacred about these indices; they are
5 merely the most convenient and concrete manifestations in everyday life of different social positions. If every member of society routinely tested his strength in court several times each year instead of once or twice a
10 lifetime, we would immediately recognize court performance as a direct measure of social position, perhaps even more revealing of the pecking order than conventional indices, such as power.
15 Of course, in no society, not even a litigious one like premodern New Haven, does the court play so vital a role as this in the life of the community. Nevertheless, if other societies show the same positive
20 correlation between status and court performance found in New Haven, we will be compelled to admit that individual court appearances—infrequent though they are—are revelatory of group status when
25 treated collectively. Of course, one cannot assume on the basis of this one study of a single society that court performance is always and everywhere a reliable index of status. Only a considerable accumulation of
30 confirmatory studies of other communities and courts could justify the use of the voluntary appearance ratio as an independent measure of status. But if, as in the case of New Haven, it can be shown for a given
35 community that court performance is strongly correlated with the more conventional indices of status over a long period of time, then it seems reasonable to treat court performance itself as an index of
40 status in that community. Doing so may be extremely advantageous because, unlike most indices of status, court performance can be reconstructed on a year-to-year basis.
45 If court performance can be shown to reflect the static distribution of power and advantage in the community—as has been done for New Haven—then by tracing court performance through time, on a
50 year-to-year basis, it should be possible to reveal shifts of power and advantage as they take place. Court records exploited in this manner might serve as a weather vane of social change. The gentry controversy in

55 English history stands as the classic
illustration of the difficulty of reconstruct-
ing an account through time of the relative
position of two classes, using only economic and demographic data. Of all the
60 kinds of data relating to group status, none
is more likely to be recorded and be
preserved in as complete a form as court
records. A continuous year-by-year account
of group status would be virtually impos-
65 sible to reconstruct from surviving economic data, but such an account may be
feasible for societies with complete court
records. Such a methodological tool should
be useful to any historian who wants to test
70 hypotheses postulating the rise or fall of a
class or other large group.

15. The author views court records primarily as

(A) surviving other available records about
society
(B) a source of more reliable data about
society
(C) reflecting distribution of power in
society
(D) a means of tracing changes in group
status in society
(E) reporting on tests of strength within a
society

16. The term "positive correlation" in lines
19–20 refers to which of the following?

(A) the relationship between individual
and group status
(B) the relationship between group status
and frequency of court appearance
(C) the relationship between individual
court appearance and social position
(D) the relationship between the pecking
order and group status in the community
(E) the relationship between power shifts
and frequency of court appearance

17. The passage suggests that which of the
following is an indication of individual
social status?

(A) wealth
(B) occupation
(C) title
(D) court performance
(E) power

18. Which of the following, if true, would most
weaken the author's thesis?

(A) There is an inverse relationship
between wealth and court appearances.
(B) There is a negative relationship
between age and court appearances.
(C) There is a random relationship
between occupation and court
appearances.
(D) There is a positive relationship
between title and court appearances.
(E) There is a direct relationship between
land ownership and court appearances.

19. If true, which of the following would best
support the author's thesis?

(A) There is little correlation between the
New Haven findings and those of
other towns.
(B) There is a positive correlation between
the New Haven findings and those of
other towns.
(C) There is a positive correlation between
wealth and court appearances in New
Haven and those of other towns.
(D) There is little correlation between
occupations and court appearances in
New Haven and those of other towns.
(E) There is a direct relationship between
land ownership in New Haven and ten
surrounding towns.

20. Which of the following is most likely the
author of the passage?

(A) a sociologist
(B) a genealogist
(C) a heraldrist
(D) an anthropologist
(E) a legal historian

21. The passage suggests that all of the follow-ing would be advantages of using court records and performance as a means of social status determination EXCEPT

 (A) court records can be reconstructed over long periods of time
 (B) court appearances change with status within the society
 (C) court records are generally preserved in most jurisdictions
 (D) court appearances can be treated collectively to reflect status
 (E) court procedures remain the same over long periods of time

Line Much advertising is patently uninformative: Rational consumers should not care what sort of breakfast cereal is eaten by famous baseball players. Nonetheless, advertisers
5 spend large sums of money on these sorts of messages as well as many others of equal value as information. Rational consumers should not be influenced by such messages, and rational advertisers should not spend
10 money on messages without influence.

  There are two types of goods: search goods and experience goods. A search good is one whose salient characteristics can be ascertained by presale inspection (e.g., the
15 comfort of a pair of shoes); experience goods are those that must be consumed to be evaluated (e.g., the taste of a candy bar). The role of advertising differs depending on which type of good is involved. In the case
20 of search goods, where the consumer can and will easily determine for himself whether the goods are what he wants, advertisers have little incentive to misrepre-sent the quality of their goods. Thus,
25 advertisers simply urge the consumer to make the inspection, and their message should be largely informative and truthful. In the case of the experience good, the consumer can determine quality only by
30 purchasing and using the good. The function of advertising, therefore, is to get the consumer to try the product. Here, advertisers might have an incentive to mislead and make false claims.
35 With respect to advertising, then, the characteristics of goods and services form a continuum, from those in which it is very easy to detect the truth or falsity of advertising claims (search goods: The truth

40 of the claim can be ascertained before purchase) through experience goods (where the truth of the claim can be detected only after purchase and use) through credence goods (where the validity
45 of advertisements may never be deter-mined).

  As we move along this continuum from search to credence characteristics, misrepresentation becomes relatively more
50 profitable, since detection by consumers becomes more expensive. Nonetheless, it is in the case of credence characteristics that self-protection becomes most difficult and in which some legal remedy would seem
55 most important.

  For any one purchase where credence qualities are involved, the consumer cannot be sure that he is getting a desirable good; i.e., there is a low probability of his finding
60 out whether claims about any one good are true or false. However, if the consumer buys many goods from the same source, the probability of ascertaining that claims about one of those goods are false would
65 be increased. In this situation, claims about individual goods have credence characteris-tics; but the reputation of the seller of all of the goods is an experience characteristic. It may be that consumer trust in the reputa-
70 tion of the intermediary is misplaced in the situation of mail-order advertisements carried by magazines. Although the consumer may rely on the publisher of the magazine to police their advertisers,
75 Consumers Union claims that in fact such policing is minimal or nonexistent.

22. Which of the following best states the primary objective of the passage?

 (A) to point out that advertising reliability varies by type of good
 (B) to contrast advertising purposes for three types of goods
 (C) to differentiate between advertising for two types of goods
 (D) to discuss the role of advertising as information
 (E) to question the trustworthiness of magazine mail-order advertising

23. According to the passage, the consumer can determine the quality of experience goods by which of the following?

    (A) advertising
    (B) inspection
    (C) consumption
    (D) policing
    (E) reputation

24. According to the passage, each of the following is true EXCEPT which statement?

    (A) Search-goods advertising is likely to be informative and truthful.
    (B) Mail-order advertising in magazines is not likely to be truthful.
    (C) Experience-goods advertisers have incentive to mislead.
    (D) Credence-goods advertisements may never be determined to be valid.
    (E) Advertisers spend large sums of money on informative messages.

25. Which of the following articles is the most likely source of the passage?

    (A) "The Economics of Advertising"
    (B) "The Law of False Advertising"
    (C) "Advertising by Type of Good"
    (D) "Analysis of the Function of Advertising"
    (E) "Advertising and the Quality of Goods"

26. It can be inferred from the passage that which of the following are credence goods?

    (A) auto transmission oil
    (B) vitamin pills
    (C) plant fertilizer
    (D) eyeglasses
    (E) air conditioner

27. Which of the following best describes the author's attitude toward advertising?

    (A) Many advertisers and consumers do not act rationally.
    (B) Many advertisers spend too much money on ads.
    (C) Many consumers are influenced by advertising.
    (D) Many advertisers are not interested in informing consumers.
    (E) Many consumers use advertising to determine the quality of goods.

28. The author implies which of the following in the passage?

    (A) Search-goods consumers are easily misled by advertising.
    (B) Experience-goods consumers purchase by mail order.
    (C) Credence-goods consumers require statutory protection.
    (D) Experience-goods consumers ascertain value by inspection.
    (E) Credence-goods consumers depend on seller credibility.

SECTION 5   TIME—35 MINUTES   24 QUESTIONS

Evaluate the reasoning contained in the brief statements, and select the best answer. Do not make implausible, superfluous, or incompatible assumptions. Select the best answer to each question, and mark the corresponding space on the answer sheet.

1. Hitler was born in <u>1889</u> and became chancellor of Germany in <u>1933</u>. On December 7, 1941, he was <u>52</u> years old and had been in power for <u>8</u> years. Hirohito was born in <u>1901</u> and became emperor of Japan in <u>1926</u>. On December 7, 1941, he was <u>40</u> years old and had been in power for <u>15</u> years.

   The four underlined figures for each man total 3,882.

   Which of the following most accurately describes the total 3,882?

   (A) It is significant, but its meaning is not clear.
   (B) It is insignificant and coincidental.
   (C) Important leaders share significant events and figures.
   (D) It is politically significant only.
   (E) There is more significance in figures than is usually acknowledged.

2. It is acceptable to support one corrupt faction in a war against another in Nicaragua. And it is acceptable to send troops to Grenada to oust a Communist leader. But it is unacceptable to use force to get food to thousands of isolated and starving people in Sudan because it would interfere with that nation's internal affairs.

   The author makes a point by

   (A) identifying incongruities in the use of force
   (B) analyzing evidence of the use of force
   (C) attacking proprieties in the use of force
   (D) complaining about irrationality in the use of force
   (E) arguing for a more pervasive use of force

3. "Return my pocket watch!"

   "How did you get it?"

   "My father gave it to me."

   "How did your father get it?"

   "His father gave it to him."

   "How did your grandfather get it?"

   "He won it in a poker game."

   "Good, we will play poker for it."

   Which of the following is best inferred from the statement, "Good, we will play poker for it"?

   (A) Gambling achieves objectives effectively.
   (B) Past practice validates future action.
   (C) Meaningful customs transcend generations.
   (D) Possession is a privilege not a right.
   (E) Wanting another's possessions is instinctive.

4. Kaminski's disparaging reviews of the book call her abilities as a critic into question since the book became an immediate best-seller.

   Which of the following, if true, would most weaken the author's questioning of Kaminski's critical ability?

   (A) Immediate success of books is quickly forgotten.
   (B) Book critics often disagree with each other.
   (C) Sales of a book are not always indicative of its value.
   (D) The significance of a book is not known for years.
   (E) Critics often change their views about books.

Questions 5–6

If a writer is truly emotional, his writing will comprise his deepest feelings about the world; and one would expect such feelings to appear in his work, if not dominate it. Many societies and people are very emotional, and their writing has as its principal function the expression and integration of deep feeling. This suggests that writing must be either emotional or trivial, that only emotional people can be great writers, and that writing cannot flourish in a technical society.

5. The writing of emotional people demonstrates

   (A) feelings are not integrated in other ways
   (B) only emotional writing can be great
   (C) the expression of deep feeling
   (D) writing cannot flourish in a technical society
   (E) one type of writing is better than another

6. On which of the following assumptions is the author's position based?

   (A) Great writers must be emotional.
   (B) Societies must be emotional or technical.
   (C) Feelings dominate an emotional writer's work.
   (D) Writing is emotional or trivial.
   (E) A writer's purpose is to express emotion.

Questions 7–8

It is almost as safe to assume that an artist of any dignity is against his country, i.e., against the environment in which God hath placed him, as it is to assume that his country is against the artist. He differs from the rest of us mainly because he reacts sharply and in an uncommon manner to phenomena that leave the rest of us unmoved, or, at most, merely annoy us vaguely. Therefore, he takes to artistic endeavor, which is at once a criticism of life and an attempt to escape from life.

The more the facts are studied, the more they bear out these generalizations. In those fields of art, at all events, which concern themselves with ideas as well as with sensations, it is almost impossible to find any trace of an artist who was not actively hostile to his environment and, thus, an indifferent patriot. From Dante to Tolstoy and from Shakespeare to Mark Twain, the story is ever the same. Names suggest themselves instantly: Goethe, Shelley, Byron, Balzac, Cervantes, Swift, Dostoevsky, Carlyle, Moliere, and Pope were each a bitter critic of his time and nation.

7. Which of the following, if true, would most strongly refute the author's argument?

   (A) Artists are generally honored by their countries.
   (B) Artists best recognize life's difficulties.
   (C) Artists usually escape from their countries.
   (D) Artists generally venerate their countries.
   (E) Artists are best known in their own countries.

8. The author's argument most depends upon which of the following assumptions?

   (A) Most people are annoyed by phenomena that make an artist hostile.
   (B) Art defines in the abstract events and sensations that are uncommon.
   (C) The purpose of art is to both find fault with and escape from life.
   (D) In order to be an artist of dignity, a person must be an indifferent patriot.
   (E) Life is actively hostile to the artistic endeavors of most artists.

9. In a recent survey, the majority of respondents answered "no" to the question, "Should free hypodermic needles be provided by the government to drug addicts on welfare?"

   The survey results can be best criticized because the question structure

   (A) presented more than one issue to respondents
   (B) presented a choice that suggested a negative reply
   (C) presented respondents an impossible value judgment
   (D) presented an issue to largely unaffected respondents
   (E) presented a controversial issue out of context

222

10. When it rains, the crops grow; but it hasn't rained recently, so the crops must not be growing.

Which of the following arguments is logically most similar to the one above?

(A) When people are old, they complain about their health; but our town has no health problems, so it must have no old people.

(B) When a town has health problems, so it must also have many old people.

(C) When people are old, they complain about their health; but one can complain about one's health and yet not be old.

(D) When people complain about their health, they get old; but no one is complaining about their health, so we must have no people getting old.

(E) When a town has people complaining about their health, it must also have old people; our town has many people complaining about their health, so it must have many old people.

Questions 11–12

The proposal to divert one third of the flow of the Delaware River to supply New York City with water ought to be a matter of great concern to the people who live in the Delaware Valley. The interests of the people of the Delaware Valley are being put aside so that growth can continue in an already overdeveloped area. Fresh water is a natural resource in the same sense that oil and coal are natural resources. Do Texas and Alaska give away their oil? Does West Virginia give away its coal? Why should Pennsylvania and New Jersey supply New York or any other place with fresh water? If the growth of New York is capped by limited fresh water, so much the better.

11. The author assumes which of the following to be fact rather than opinion?

(A) Diverting the Delaware River is a matter of great concern to people in the Delaware Valley.

(B) Oil, coal, and fresh water are natural resources.

(C) The purpose of diverting the Delaware River is to allow New York City to continue to grow.

(D) The interests of New York and the Delaware Valley conflict.

(E) The Delaware River supplies New York with water.

12. Which of the following, if true, would most weaken the author's argument?

(A) New York City is permanently committed to zero growth.

(B) The diversion will not reduce water availability to people in the Delaware Valley.

(C) New York City will pay Pennsylvania and New Jersey for each gallon of water diverted.

(D) The diversion will reduce the risk of flooding in the Delaware Valley.

(E) New York City will get water from Vermont if the Delaware River is not diverted.

13. If the present moment contains no living and creative choice and is totally and mechanically the product of the matter and moment of the moment before, so, then, was that moment the mechanical effect of the moment that preceded it and so on until we arrive at a single cause of every later event, of every act and suffering of man.

Which of the following would NOT be supported by the above argument?

(A) a theory postulating a mechanistic origin of the universe

(B) a theory postulating suffering as a requisite for creativity

(C) a theory postulating a deterministic explanation of history

(D) a theory postulating that there are no choices in the present moment

(E) a theory postulating a single cause of all events

14. Baxter defends paternal authority and the preservation of the family in her most recent work. But other aspects of her thinking more convincingly demonstrate that she cannot be considered a feminist. For example, she fails to appreciate that the full realization of a woman's capacities depends on her securing the same political, economic, and civil rights as those afforded me.

Which of the following inferences is NOT supported by the above argument?

- **(A)** Paternal authority is not generally supported by feminists.
- **(B)** The family is not generally supported by feminists.
- **(C)** Baxter feels that women do not need rights equal to men's.
- **(D)** Women's capacities have not been fully realized.
- **(E)** Baxter feels that women and men have unequal capacities.

15. Many children in urban schools are forced to learn in dilapidated classrooms with few modern teaching aids. Compared to children in suburban schools with their computers, labs, and the latest advances in educational resources, the urban student is truly deprived.

The point of the author's argument is best stated by which of the following?

- **(A)** Modern educational aids should be provided for urban children.
- **(B)** Urban and suburban children should be educated in the same schools.
- **(C)** Urban schoolchildren should not be required to compete with suburban schoolchildren.
- **(D)** Unequal resources for urban and suburban children should be investigated.
- **(E)** Suburban school resources should be combined with those of urban schools if an ideal education is to be achieved.

16. A philosopher makes arguments that frequently are not logical in order to demonstrate that rationality is not as valuable as irrationality to us humans. Consequently, the philosopher should not be expected to use the same arguments as those whose positions are rationally based.

The argument above is most similar to which of the following?

- **(A)** A philosopher's arguments focus on the flaws in logical reasoning of those who oppose her.
- **(B)** A writer often uses great restraint when describing mayhem.
- **(C)** A female author was not taken seriously, so she used a male pseudonym when establishing her reputation.
- **(D)** A novel is judged to be boring because it describes a boring situation.
- **(E)** A philosopher's reasoning is complicated because he was trained in a tradition that often uses complicated reasoning.

Question 17–18

United States treaty negotiations with Japan about trade involve the basic question, "Can the Japanese be trusted?" But treaties are based on self-interest rather than on trust. There would be no need to have treaties if countries trusted one another. A treaty is an alternative to trust; one that formally recognizes that each country finds an advantage in the agreement.

17. Which of the following is an argument made above?

- **(A)** If the Japanese can be trusted, the United States should negotiate treaties with Japan.
- **(B)** If the Japanese cannot be trusted, the United States should not negotiate treaties with Japan.
- **(C)** If Japan and the United States have common trade interests, a treaty between the countries should be negotiated.
- **(D)** If Japan and the United States sign a treaty, interests of each will be served by the agreement.
- **(E)** If Japanese and United States interests are different, a treaty dealing with those interests will not be signed.

18. Which of the following is NOT supported by the author's argument above?

   (A) Treaties are made only between countries that trust one another.
   (B) Treaties further the self-interest of countries.
   (C) Treaties formally recognize an advantage one country has over another.
   (D) Treaties do not serve mutual interests of countries.
   (E) Treaties serve as reasonable alternatives to trust.

19. Tests done on the employees of a chemical plant showed that 28 percent had abnormal chromosome patterns. Chemical fumes, radiation, and airborne particulates are among the causes of abnormal chromosome patterns.

Which of the following would most support the conclusion that chemical fumes were responsible for employees' abnormal chromosome patterns?

   (A) Abnormal chromosome patterns can be altered.
   (B) Nonemployees in the area also develop abnormal chromosome patterns.
   (C) Employees of other chemical plants do not develop abnormal chromosome patterns.
   (D) Abnormal chromosome patterns are not necessarily harmful.
   (E) Employees of most chemical plants develop abnormal chromosome patterns.

20. "None of the legislators we polled are in favor of this bill?"

"That cannot be true. There are six legislators who introduced the bill and support it."

Which of the following can be inferred from the above exchange?

   (A) Legislators who do not favor the bill may support it.
   (B) The only legislators who favor the bill are those who introduced it.
   (C) Only legislators who do not favor the bill were polled.
   (D) Some legislators refused to participate in the poll.
   (E) Legislators might indicate that they favor a bill when they do not.

21. The Audubon Society Falcon Watch reports that there were 2,487 more falcon sightings in 1988 than there were in 1987. This proves that an increase in the falcon population has finally been realized.

Which of the following, if true, most weakens the above argument?

   (A) Falcons regularly move from area to area in search of food.
   (B) Falcons have been introduced into urban environments.
   (C) Development in falcon nesting areas is being restricted.
   (D) The Society intensified its falcon sighting program in 1988.
   (E) The Society database about falcons improved in 1988.

22. The following notice was received by Mary Castle, a scientist.

"We regret that your article cannot be accepted. Page limitations in the *Journal* force the editor to return many worthy and well-written articles."

All of the following may be inferred from the above, EXCEPT

   (A) only well-written articles were accepted for publication
   (B) Castle's article was considered to be well-written
   (C) Castle's article was found to be too long for the *Journal*
   (D) Castle's article was considered to be worthy of publication
   (E) writing was not the only factor in deciding which articles to publish

Questions 23–24

The drug Thalidomide caused unforeseen birth defects in thousands of babies; therefore, thorough testing of the effects of all new drugs should be required before release to the public.

23. Which of the following is an assumption made in the argument above?

   (A) Birth defects caused by Thalidomide could have been prevented by testing.
   (B) Thalidomide produced more harmful birth defects than any drug before it.
   (C) The benefits of Thalidomide are not outweighed by its harmful side effects.
   (D) Thalidomide producers acted irresponsibly in putting such a dangerous drug on the market.
   (E) Less harmful drugs were available to treat the problems treated by Thalidomide.

24. The argument above is most similar to which of the following?

   (A) Exposure to loud music has been shown to be harmful to teenage hearing; therefore, teens should not be permitted to listen to loud music.
   (B) The value of research is hard to determine; therefore, amounts spent for research should be reduced.
   (C) The Ford Pinto has been found to have a design defect; therefore, it should be replaced by the manufacturer.
   (D) Teenage drivers have caused some of the worst auto accidents; therefore, driving tests for teenagers should be more rigorous than for others.
   (E) Generic drugs are less expensive than brand-name drugs; therefore, doctors should prescribe only generic drugs.

LSAT WRITING SAMPLE TOPIC

Complete the short writing exercise on the topic that follows. You have only 30 minutes to plan, organize, and write your sample. WRITE ONLY ON THE TOPIC SPECIFIED.

As the director of the Carthage University Press, you must recommend to the board of managers a long-range plan to counteract the Press's financial decline. You must choose between merging with a high-quality publisher or changing your publishing policy in a way that would greatly increase income. Two considerations guide your decision:

- The plan must provide a relatively permanent solution to the financial problems of the Press.
- The Press must maintain its tradition of only publishing work of the highest quality, using the very best paper, printing, and binding.

By merging with Lisle & Fish, Ltd., savings would result from combined sales, advertising, management, and printing, and a strong financial future would be ensured. Lisle & Fish has an impeccable reputation in the industry, and its taste is fastidious. If the companies merged, however, Carthage would lose its autonomy, and Lisle & Fish policies would control, including the use of somewhat lower-quality paper, printing, and binding.

On the other hand, by changing the Carthage publishing policy and introducing a series of annotated works of Shakespeare for use in high school and college courses, a permanently enlarged market would result. Professor Barth, the series' editor, produces popular and effective material but is not a highly respected scholar. And the Shakespeare series would require Carthage to publish in paperback form, which Carthage has refused to do for decades because it felt its reputation would suffer.

QUICK-SCORE ANSWERS

Section 1	*Section 2*	*Section 3*	*Section 4*	*Section 5*
1. **E**	1. **A**	1. **B**	1. **C**	1. **B**
2. **A**	2. **C**	2. **D**	2. **D**	2. **A**
3. **D**	3. **A**	3. **B**	3. **A**	3. **B**
4. **C**	4. **A**	4. **B**	4. **D**	4. **C**
5. **C**	5. **D**	5. **A**	5. **A**	5. **C**
6. **D**	6. **D**	6. **C**	6. **C**	6. **B**
7. **E**	7. **E**	7. **A**	7. **C**	7. **D**
8. **E**	8. **D**	8. **C**	8. **D**	8. **C**
9. **D**	9. **A**	9. **A**	9. **C**	9. **A**
10. **B**	10. **E**	10. **D**	10. **E**	10. **D**
11. **C**	11. **E**	11. **B**	11. **B**	11. **B**
12. **D**	12. **B**	12. **E**	12. **B**	12. **C**
13. **D**	13. **E**	13. **A**	13. **D**	13. **B**
14. **E**	14. **E**	14. **A**	14. **C**	14. **E**
15. **B**	15. **C**	15. **D**	15. **D**	15. **A**
16. **C**	16. **C**	16. **A**	16. **B**	16. **E**
17. **E**	17. **D**	17. **E**	17. **D**	17. **D**
18. **E**	18. **B**	18. **C**	18. **A**	18. **D**
19. **B**	19. **C**	19. **E**	19. **B**	19. **E**
20. **E**	20. **D**	20. **E**	20. **E**	20. **C**
21. **C**	21. **A**	21. **E**	21. **E**	21. **D**
22. **C**	22. **A**	22. **A**	22. **A**	22. **E**
23. **A**	23. **A**	23. **C**	23. **C**	23. **A**
24. **B**	24. **D**	24. **E**	24. **E**	24. **D**
			25. **D**	
			26. **A**	
			27. **A**	
			28. **C**	

EXPLANATORY ANSWERS

In the following answer guide, the credited responses appear in bold type and the visualization that makes the credited response clear appears before the answers to each question set. Use the visualization to guide you in determining the credited answer.

SECTION 1

Questions 1–6

Golf   C, D, E, F, G

Last   First

←——————————————————→

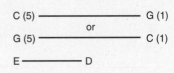

C (5) ———————— G (1)
             or
G (5) ———————— C (1)

E ———— D

No ties - all play

1. **The correct answer is (E).** E finishes fourth.

2. **The correct answer is (A).** E finishes second.

3. **The correct answer is (D).** F finishes ahead of E.

4. **The correct answer is (C).** 3

5. **The correct answer is (C).** F finishes ahead of D.

6. **The correct answer is (D).** F finishes fourth.

Questions 7–12

Ages   A, F, I, K, M, O, T, U, V, W

Younger   Older

W ——————— K

O ——————— M

7. **The correct answer is (E).** The Kansas president is younger than the Ohio president.

8. **The correct answer is (E).** The Kansas president is older than the Ohio president.

9. **The correct answer is (D).** The Texas president is older than the Ohio president.

10. **The correct answer is (B).** Wyoming

11. **The correct answer is (C).** The Florida president is older than the Kansas president.

12. **The correct answer is (D).** The Alaska president is older than the Ohio president.

Questions 13–18

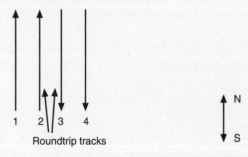

1   2   3   4

Roundtrip tracks

2 consecutive trains cannot use same track

Local after express or metro

13. **The correct answer is (D).** I and II only

14. **The correct answer is (E).** 4, 1, 3, 2

15. **The correct answer is (B).** 2

16. **The correct answer is (C).** R on track 2, U on track 3, S on track 1, T on track 3, Q on track 2

17. **The correct answer is (E).** 4, 0

18. **The correct answer is (E).** The greatest number of locals cannot exceed the greatest number of express trains.

Questions 19–24

| Beach | C, E, J, R, W |
| | Food, Blankets, Umbrella, Drives, Pays |

Brother - Sister
First brings umbrella
Driver = male
Brother pays
When E brings food - W not drive
When C or J brings blankets - R drives

19. **The correct answer is (B).** Rick drives.

20. **The correct answer is (E).** Carol is Rick's sister.

21. **The correct answer is (C).** bring the umbrella

22. **The correct answer is (C).** Jenny brings neither blankets nor food.

23. **The correct answer is (A).** drive

24. **The correct answer is (B).** Carol and Rick

SECTION 2

In the following answer guide, the credited responses appear in bold type and the guide that directs you toward the credited response appears within the answer choice context. The first reference is to the point of the argument and the second is to the nature of the issue involved.

1. **The correct answer is (A).** Quiet people are not easily identified.

   Point—All people have one attribute. All with the one attribute have a second attribute.

   Issue—Extension question/conclusion

2. **The correct answer is (C).** It assumes the conclusion.

   Point—Ambitious people are not good parents. Good parents are not ambitious people.

   Issue—Description question/tactic

3. **The correct answer is (A).** Arthritis specialists provide authoritative information on effective medication for arthritis.

   Point—Connect Arthrelief to the most prescribed medicine.

   Issue—Extension question/NOT assumption

4. **The correct answer is (A).** Reasoning abilities of illiterate people should not be tested using tasks that do not involve familiar devices.

   Point—Testing results for illiterates vary by the devices used to test.

   Issue—Extension question/conclusion

5. **The correct answer is (D).** Daily exercise does not contribute greatly to Japanese worker productivity.

   Point—Americans and Japanese vary in terms of daily exercise and productivity.

   Issue—Extension question/weakening evidence

6. **The correct answer is (D).** A country with a democratic government must have a politically active people.

   Point—Political indifference is required by dictators and central governments.

   Issue—Extension question/conclusion

7. **The correct answer is (E).** IV, II, III, I

   Point—The path to follow to U. S. energy independence

   Issue—Extension question/order of evidence to conclusion

8. **The correct answer is (D).** work areas are directly related to college degree areas

   Point—It is wasteful to spend for training that is little used.

   Issue—Extension question/assumption

9. **The correct answer is (A).** It does not state that Alert tablets cause grade improvement.

   Point—Students who use Alert get good grades.

   Issue—Extension question/strengthening conclusion

10. **The correct answer is (E).** Friendliness is a virtue.

    Point—Dogs and cats express friendliness differently.

    Issue—Extension question/conclusion

11. **The correct answer is (E).** Public beaches in Canada are no cleaner or cheaper than those in the United States.

    Point—Canadian public campgrounds compare favorably with U. S. public beaches.

    Issue—Extension question/weakening evidence

12. **The correct answer is (B).** proposes a common cause for similar effects

    Point—Computers and people play poker in the same way.

    Issue—Description question/tactic

13. **The correct answer is (E).** The industry association has standards that exceed the legal requirements.

    Point—Inspections identify no violations.

    Issue—Extension question/conclusion

14. **The correct answer is (E).** children do not generally accept adult responsibilities prior to the rites

    Point—Rites that formally impose adult responsibilities are found in societies with unclear differences between adults and children.

    Issue—Extension question/strengthening evidence

15. **The correct answer is (C).** Very few physically challenged people use facilities in the places where they have been installed.

    Point—Devices to help the physically impaired use public transportation help only very athletic people.

    Issue—Extension question/strengthening evidence

Questions 16–17

16. **The correct answer is (C).** Purchasers attempt to secure more credit than they can afford.

    Point—Credit bureaus provide valuable services with little personal intrusion by reducing business losses and preventing consumers from overextending their financial obligations.

    Issue—Extension question/assumption of behavior

17. **The correct answer is (D).** justified by the economic value to business and society

    Point—Credit bureaus provide valuable services with little personal intrusion by reducing business losses and preventing consumers from overextending their financial obligations.

    Issue—Extension question/conclusion

18. **The correct answer is (B).** Harold is a better writer than Stan.

    Point—Harold writes better short stories and novels than does Stan.

    Issue—Extension question/conclusion

19. **The correct answer is (C).** Since 1969, more high school graduates have decided to seek a college degree.

    Point—The value of a college education has dropped significantly over time.

    Issue—Extension question/weakening evidence

20. **The correct answer is (D).** Engineering of genes and environment are virtually the same.

    Point—Engineering produces change in many characteristics of people.

    Issue—Extension question/strengthening evidence

Questions 21–22

21. **The correct answer is (A).** Shea confuses influence with merit

    Point—Similar influence requires similar recognition.

    Issue—Extension question/conclusion

22. **The correct answer is (A).** the Springfield Pops

    Point—Similar influence requires similar recognition.

    Issue—Extension question/same structure/new context

23. **The correct answer is (A).** All three resorts Ann previously visited are in north Miami Beach, and the new resort is in south Miami Beach.

    Point—Florida resorts are enjoyable to Ann.

    Issue—Extension question/insignificant evidence

24. The correct answer is (D). Social reasons account for the attendance of most students at services.

> Point—There is an inverse relationship between cheating and religious exposure.

> Issue—Extension question/weakening evidence

SECTION 3

In the following answer guide, the credited responses appear in bold type and the visualizations that make the credited response clear appear before each question set. Use the visualization to guide you in determining the credited answer.

Questions 1–6

Bids   L, M, N, O, P, Q

Lowest   Highest

K —— Q —— P —— N

M —— O —— P

1. The correct answer is (B). M, L, O, Q, P, N

2. The correct answer is (D). M or L

3. The correct answer is (B). L submits the third-lowest bid.

4. The correct answer is (B). Q submits a higher bid than M

5. The correct answer is (A). L, M, Q, O, P, N

6. The correct answer is (C). Q and L

Questions 7–12

Graduation   L, M, N, O, P, Q, R, S, T, U

                1971 - 1975 - Two per year

1971   1975

M ——1—— Q

P and Q in '71 to '74

S and T together

Q not with N

7. The correct answer is (A). S, T; P, R; M, O; Q, N; L, U

8. The correct answer is (C). L, N, S

9. The correct answer is (A). L graduated in 1972.

10. The correct answer is (D). R graduated in 1972.

11. The correct answer is (B). 1971 and 1974

12. The correct answer is (E). S graduated in 1975.

Questions 13–18

Table set-ups   A, B, C, D, E

B must E
C must D
E not with C
D not with A
A always sets up

13. The correct answer is (A). Adam only

14. The correct answer is (A). one

15. The correct answer is (D). Beth, Dana, and Edith

16. The correct answer is (A). Dana and Edith

17. The correct answer is (E). Beth and Edith only

18. The correct answer is (C). two

Questions 19–24

Dentists - A, B, C   Hygienists all assigned
Hygienists - S, T, U, V

A and B - 2 hygienists each
C - 1 or 2 hygienists
T assign A and B or C

19. The correct answer is (E). either B or C

20. The correct answer is (E). U is assigned to only one dentist.

21. The correct answer is (E). either B or C

22. The correct answer is (A). A only

23. The correct answer is (C). U is assigned to only one dentist.

24. The correct answer is (E). U is assigned to only one dentist.

SECTION 4

In the following answer guide, the credited responses appear in bold type and the guide that directs you to the place in the passage that accounts for the credited response appears within the answer-choice context. The first reference is to the paragraph number in the passage that accounts for the credited response and the second number refers to the relevant sentence in the paragraph. The reference will appear as 2/4 for example. This means paragraph 2 and sentence 4 within paragraph 2.

1. **The correct answer is (C).** advocate limiting handgun availability—Paragraph 3/Sentence 6

2. **The correct answer is (D).** gun ownership by people associated with violence has greatly increased—Paragraph 2/Sentence 7

3. **The correct answer is (A).** dramatize the increase in gun-related violence—Paragraph 1/Sentence 2

4. **The correct answer is (D).** Handgun ownership among middle-class New Yorkers has increased fourfold in the last ten years.—Paragraph 2/Sentences 6 and 7

5. **The correct answer is (A).** The rate of growth in gun ownership in the Northeast is greater than that of other regions.—Paragraph 2/Sentence 5

6. **The correct answer is (C).** Urban violence is due to subcultural differences among residents. —Paragraph 1/Sentences 3 and 4

7. **The correct answer is (C).** regulation of handgun possession—Paragraph 3/Sentence 4

8. **The correct answer is (D).** comparing hardware and software—Paragraph 1/Sentence 1; Paragraph 2/Sentence 1

9. **The correct answer is (C).** Software can be located within hardware.—Paragraph 1/Sentence 3

10. **The correct answer is (E).** hardware is readily changeable. According to the passage, choices (A), (B), (C), and (D) are all true. For (A), the cost of duplicating software is low, see 2/1; for (B), very little software is sold outright, see 2/5; for (C), hardware is often not patented, see 3/2; and for (D), software requires minimal originality, see 3/3.

11. **The correct answer is (B).** It can be copyrighted.—Paragraph 3/Sentence 1

12. **The correct answer is (B).** It is more profitable to sell copies of software than hardware.—Paragraph 2/Sentences 2 and 4

13. **The correct answer is (D).** Patented hardware requires greater inventiveness than does software.—Paragraph 3/Sentence 3

14. **The correct answer is (C).** One purchased the restaurant when one purchased the dinner prepared there.—Production Capacity/Production Result

15. **The correct answer is (D).** a means of tracing changes in group status in society—Paragraph 1/Sentence 3

16. **The correct answer is (B).** the relationship between group status and frequency of court appearance—Paragraph 2/Sentence 2

17. **The correct answer is (D).** court performance—Paragraph 2/Sentence 5

18. **The correct answer is (A).** There is an inverse relationship between wealth and court appearances.—Paragraph 2/Sentence 5

19. **The correct answer is (B).** There is a positive correlation between the New Haven findings and those of other towns.—Paragraph 2/Sentence 4

20. **The correct answer is (E).** a legal historian—Paragraph 5/Sentence 6

21. **The correct answer is (E).** court procedures remain the same over long periods of time. According to the passage, choices (A), (B), (C), and (D) are all true. For (A), court records can be constructed over long periods of time, see 3/5; for (B), court appearances change with status within the society, see 3/1; for (C), court records are generally preserved in most jurisdictions, see 3/4; and for (D), court appearances can be treated collectively to reflect status, see 3/5.

22. **The correct answer is (A).** to point out that advertising reliability varies by type of good—Paragraph 2/Sentence 3

23. **The correct answer is (C).** consumption—Paragraph 2/Sentence 2

24. The correct answer is (E). Advertisers spend large sums of money on informative messages. According to the passage, choices (A), (B), (C), and (D) are all true. For (A), search goods advertising is likely to be informative and truthful, see 2/5; for (B), mail order advertising in magazines is not likely to be truthful, see 5/4; for (C), experienced goods advertisers have incentive to mislead, see 3/1; and for (D), credence goods advertisements may never be determined to be valid, see 3/1.

25. The correct answer is (D). "Analysis of the Function of Advertising"—Paragraph 1/Sentence 1

26. The correct answer is (A). auto transmission oil—Paragraph 3/Sentence 1

27. The correct answer is (A). Many advertisers and consumers do not act rationally.—Paragraph 1/Sentence 3

28. The correct answer is (C). Credence-goods consumers require statutory protection.—Paragraph 4/Sentence 2

SECTION 5

In the following answer guide, the credited responses appear in bold type and the guide that directs you toward the credited response appears within the answer-choice context. The first reference is to the point of the argument and the second is to the nature of the issue involved.

1. The correct answer is (B). It is insignificant and coincidental.

Point—Significant figures in two peoples lives total the same number.

Issue—Description question/characterize the number

2. The correct answer is (A). identifying incongruities in the use of force

Point—The acceptable use of force varies by context.

Issue—Description question/tactic

3. The correct answer is (B). Past practice validates future action.

Point—Past is prologue

Issue—Extension question/conclusion

4. The correct answer is (C). Sales of a book are not always indicative of its value.

Point—Able criticism anticipates the market reaction.

Issue—Extension question/weakening evidence

Questions 5–6

5. The correct answer is (C). the expression of deep feeling

Point—Emotional societies produce better writing than technical societies.

Issue—Description question/rephrasing

6. The correct answer is (B). Societies must be emotional or technical.

Point—Emotional societies produce better writing than technical societies.

Issue—Extension question/assumption

Questions 7–8

7. The correct answer is (D). Artists generally venerate their countries.

Point—Artists oppose their environments.

Issue—Extension question/weakening evidence

8. The correct answer is (C). The purpose of art is to both find fault with and escape from life.

Point—Artists oppose their environments.

Issue—Extension question/assumption

9. The correct answer is (A). presented more than one issue to respondents

Point—Drug addicts on welfare should not get free needles.

Issue—Description question/tactic

10. The correct answer is (D). When people complain about their health, they get old; but no one is complaining about their health, so we must have no people getting old.

Point—If : then—Not if : not then

Issue—Extension question/same structure/ new context

Questions 11–12

11. **The correct answer is (B).** Oil, coal, and fresh water are natural resources.

    Point—Natural resources should not be given away by a state.

    Issue—Extension question/assumption

12. **The correct answer is (C).** New York City will pay Pennsylvania and New Jersey for each gallon of water diverted.

    Point—Natural resources should not be given away by a state.

    Issue—Extension question/weakening evidence

13. **The correct answer is (B).** a theory postulating suffering as a requisite for creativity

    Point—Excluding matters of choice, the present is the product of past actions.

    Issue—Extension question/NOT conclusion

14. **The correct answer is (E).** Baxter feels that women and men have unequal capacities.

    Point—For various reasons Baxter is not a feminist.

    Issue—Extension question/NOT conclusion

15. **The correct answer is (A).** Modern educational aids should be provided for urban children.

    Point—Suburban students have more educational resources than urban students.

    Issue—Extension question/conclusion

16. **The correct answer is (E).** A philosopher's reasoning is complicated because he was trained in a tradition that often uses complicated reasoning.

    Point—Because they do not, they should not be expected to.

    Issue—Extension question/same structure/ new context

Questions 17–18

17. **The correct answer is (D).** If Japan and the United States sign a treaty, interests of each will be served by the agreement.

    Point—Treaties serve self-interest, not trust.

    Issue—Extension question/conclusion

18. **The correct answer is (D).** Treaties do not serve mutual interests of countries.

    Point—Treaties serve self-interest, not trust.

    Issue—Extension question/NOT conclusion

19. **The correct answer is (E).** Employees of most chemical plants develop abnormal chromosome patterns.

    Point—Plant environment may produce abnormal chromosome patterns in workers.

    Issue—Extension question/strengthening evidence

20. **The correct answer is (C).** Only legislators who do not favor the bill were polled.

    Point—Some legislators support the bills and some do not.

    Issue—Extension question/conclusion

21. **The correct answer is (D).** The Society intensified its falcon sighting program in 1988.

    Point—More sightings result from more falcons.

    Issue—Extension question/weakening evidence

22. **The correct answer is (E).** writing was not the only factor in deciding which articles to publish

    Point—Worthy and well-written articles are not always published.

    Issue—Extension question/conclusion

Questions 23–24

23. **The correct answer is (A).** Birth defects caused by Thalidomide could have been prevented by testing.

   Point—Testing will detect unforeseen
   effects in new drugs.

   Issue—Extension question/assumption

24. **The correct answer is (D).** Teenage drivers have caused some of the worst auto accidents; therefore, driving tests for teenagers should be more rigorous than for others.

   Point—Testing will detect unforeseen
   effects in new drugs.

   Issue—Extension question/same structure/
   new context

Appendix

PAYING FOR LAW SCHOOL

If you're considering attending law school but fear you don't have enough money, don't despair. Financial support for graduate and professional study does exist, although, admittedly, the information about support sources can be difficult to find.

For those of you who have applied for financial aid as undergraduates, there are some differences for law students you'll notice right away. For one, most aid to undergraduates is based primarily on need (although the number of colleges that now offer undergraduate merit-based aid is increasing). But law school aid is more often based on academic merit. Second, as a law student, you are automatically declared "independent" for federal financial aid purposes, meaning your parents' income and assets information is not required in assessing your need for federal aid. And third, at some law schools, the awarding of aid may be administered by the law school itself, not the financial aid office.

FINANCIAL AID MYTHS
- Financial aid is just for poor people.
- Financial aid is just for smart people.
- Financial aid is mainly for minority students.
- I have a job, so I must not be eligible for aid.
- If I apply for aid, it will affect whether or not I'm admitted.
- Loans are not financial aid.

BE PREPARED
Being prepared for law school means you have to put together a financial plan. Before you enter law school, you should have answers to these questions:

- What should I be doing now to prepare for the cost of my law education?
- What can I do to minimize my costs once I arrive on campus?

- What financial aid programs are available at each of the schools to which I am applying?
- What financial aid programs are available outside the university, at the federal, state, or private level?
- What financing options do I have if I cannot pay the full cost from my own resources and those of my family?
- What should I know about the loans I am being offered?
- What impact will these loans have on me when I complete my program?

You'll find your answers in three guiding principles: think ahead, live within your means, and keep your head above water.

THINK AHEAD
The first step in putting together your financial plan comes from thinking about the future: the loss of your income while you're attending school, your projected income after you graduate, the annual rate of inflation, additional expenses you will incur as a student and after you graduate, and any loss of income you may experience later from unintentional periods of unemployment, pregnancy, or disability. The cornerstone of thinking ahead is following a step-by-step process.

1. *Set your goals.* Decide what and where you want to study, and determine an appropriate level of debt.
2. *Take inventory.* Collect your financial information and add up your assets—bank accounts, stocks, bonds, real estate, business and personal property. Then subtract your liabilities—money owed on your assets, including credit card debt and car loans—to yield your net worth.

Estimated Loan Repayment Schedule Monthly Payments for Every $1,000 Borrowed

Rate	5 years	10 years	15 years	20 years	25 years
5%	$18.87	$10.61	$ 7.91	$ 6.60	$ 5.85
8%	20.28	12.13	9.56	8.36	7.72
9%	20.76	12.67	10.14	9.00	8.39
10%	21.74	13.77	10.75	9.65	9.09
12%	22.24	14.35	12.00	11.01	10.53
14%	23.27	15.53	13.32	12.44	12.04

3. *Calculate your need.* Compare your net worth with the costs at the schools you are considering to get a rough estimate of how much of your assets you can use for your schooling.

4. *Create an action plan.* Determine how much you'll earn while in school, how much you think you will receive in grants and scholarships, and how much you plan to borrow. Don't forget to consider inflation and possible life changes that could affect your overall financial plan.

5. *Review your plan regularly.* Measure the progress of your plan every year and make adjustments for such things as increases in salary or other changes in your goals or circumstances.

LIVE WITHIN YOUR MEANS

The second step in being prepared is knowing how much you spend now so you can determine how much you'll spend when you're in school. Use the standard cost of attendance budget published by your school as a guide. But don't be surprised if your estimated budget is higher than the one the school provides, especially if you've been out of school for a while. Once you've figured out your budget, see if you can pare down your current costs and financial obligations so the lean years of law school don't come as too large a shock.

KEEP YOUR HEAD ABOVE WATER

Finally, the third step is managing the debt you'll accrue as a law student. Debt is manageable only when considered in terms of five things:

1. Your future income

2. The amount of time it takes to repay the loan

3. The interest rate you are being charged

4. Your personal lifestyle and expenses after graduation

5. Unexpected circumstances that change your income or your ability to repay what you owe

To make sure your educational debt is manageable, you should borrow an amount that requires payments of between 8 and 15 percent of your starting salary.

The approximate monthly installments for repaying borrowed principal at 5, 8-10, 12, and 14 percent are indicated in the chart above.

Use this table to estimate your monthly payments on a loan for any of the five repayment periods (5, 10, 15, 20, and 25 years). The amounts listed are the monthly payments for a $1000 loan for each of the interest rates. To estimate your monthly payment, choose the closest interest rate and multiply the amount of the payment listed by the total amount of your loan and then divide by 1,000. For example, for a total loan of $15,000 at 9 percent to be paid back over ten years, multiply $12.67 times 15,000 (190,050) divided by 1,000. This yields $190.05 per month.

If you're wondering just how much of a loan payment you can afford monthly without running into payment problems, consult the chart on page 241.

Of course, the best way to manage your debt is to borrow less. While cutting your personal budget may be one option, you also may wish to investigate asking your family for help. Although the federal government considers you "independent," your parents and family may still be willing and able to help pay for your graduate education. If your family is not open to just giving you money, they may be open to making a low-interest (or deferred-interest) loan. Family loans usually have more attractive interest

HOW MUCH CAN YOU AFFORD TO REPAY?

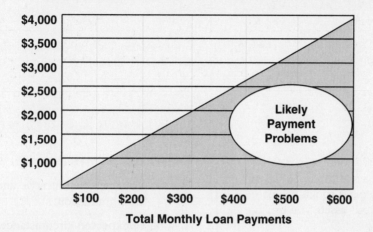

Monthly Income (after taxes) / $4,000 / $3,500 / $3,000 / $2,500 / $2,000 / $1,500 / $1,000

Likely Payment Problems

$100 $200 $300 $400 $500 $600

Total Monthly Loan Payments

This graph shows the monthly cash-flow outlook based on your total monthly loan payments in comparison with your monthly income earned after taxes. Ideally, to eliminate likely payment problems, your monthly loan payment should be less than 15% of your monthly income.

rates and repayment terms than commercial loans. They may also have tax consequences, so you may want to check with a tax adviser.

ROLL YOUR LOANS INTO ONE

There's a good chance that as a law student you will have two or more loans included in your aid package, plus any money you borrowed as an undergraduate. That means when you start repaying, you could be making loan payments to several different lenders. Not only can the record keeping be a nightmare, but with each loan having a minimum payment, your total monthly payments may be more than you can handle. If you owe more than $7500 in federal loans, you can combine your loans into one consolidated loan at either a flat 9 percent interest rate or a weighted average of the rates on the loans consolidated. Your repayment can also be extended to up to thirty years, depending on the total amount you borrow, which will make your monthly payments lower (of course, you'll also be paying more total interest). With a consolidated loan, some lenders offer graduated or income-sensitive repayment options. Consult with your lender or the U.S. Department of Education about the types of consolidation provisions offered.

PLASTIC MANIA

Any section on managing debt would be incomplete if it didn't mention the responsible use of credit cards. Most law students hold one or more credit cards, and many students find themselves in financial difficulties because of them. Here are two suggestions: use credit cards only for convenience, never for extended credit; and, if you have more than one credit card, keep only the one that has the lowest finance charge and the lowest limit.

CREDIT: DON'T LET YOUR PAST HAUNT YOU

Many schools will check your credit history before they process any private educational loans for you. To make sure your credit rating is accurate, you may want to request a copy of your credit report before you start law school. You can get a copy of your report by sending a signed, written request to one of the three national credit reporting agencies at the addresses listed below. Include your full name, social security number, current address, any previous addresses for the past five years, date of birth, and daytime phone number. Call the agency before you request your report so you know whether there is a fee for this report. Note that you are entitled to a free copy of your credit report if you have been denied credit within the last sixty days. In addition, Experian currently

CREDIT REPORTING AGENCIES

Equifax
P.O. Box 105873
Atlanta, Georgia 30348
800-685-1111

Experian
P.O. Box 2002
Allen, Texas 75013
888-397-3742
800-972-0322 (TTY/TDD)
Web site: www.experian.com/product/
consumer/index.html

Trans Union Data Corporation
P.O. Box 390
760 Sproul Road
Springfield, Pennsylvania 19064-0390
610-690-4909

provides complimentary credit reports once every twelve months.

Credit criteria used to review and approve student loans can include the following:

- Absence of negative credit

- No bankruptcies, foreclosures, repossessions, charge-offs, or open judgments

- No prior educational loan defaults, unless paid in full or making satisfactory repayments

- Absence of excessive past due accounts; that is, no 30-, 60-, or 90-day delinquencies on consumer loans or revolving charge accounts within the past two years

TYPES OF AID AVAILABLE

There are three types of aid: money given to you (grants, scholarships, and fellowships), money you earn through work, and loans.

Grants, Scholarships, and Fellowships

Most grants, scholarships, and fellowships are outright awards that require no service in return. The one major exception for law students is ROTC aid, which can be very generous, but entails a commitment to serve as an officer in the military branch providing the aid. Often these gift aid programs provide the cost of tuition and fees plus a stipend to cover living expenses. Some are based exclusively on financial need, some exclusively on academic merit, and some on a combination of need and merit. As a rule, grants are awarded to those with financial need, although they may require the recipient to have expertise in a certain field. Fellowships and scholarships often connote selectivity based on ability—financial need is usually not a factor.

Federal Support

The provision of free federal money in the form of grants and scholarships for the training of future lawyers has never ranked very high as a national priority. This is especially noticeable compared with what is available to prospective doctors, teachers, or scientific researchers. The only notable federal grant program for lawyers is the newly enacted Thurgood Marshall Legal Educational Opportunity Program to aid low-income, minority, or disadvantaged students seeking a law school education. The Marshall program, to be administered by the Department of Education, provides information, preparation, and financial assistance to students so they may gain access to and complete a law school education. The U.S. Department of Education or one of the law schools that you are interested in should have more details about this new program.

State Support

Many states offer grants for graduate study. States grant approximately $64 million per year to graduate students. To qualify for a particular state's aid you must be a resident of that state. Residency is established in most states after you have lived there for at least twelve consecutive months prior to enrolling in school. Many states provide funds for in-state students only; that is, funds are not transferable out of state. Contact your state scholarship office to determine what aid it offers.

Institutional Aid

Educational institutions using their own funds provide between $2 and $3 billion in graduate assistance in the form of fellowships, tuition waivers, and assistantships. In the field of law, most scholarship aid comes from the institutions themselves. Consult each school's catalog for information about their aid programs.

Aid from Foundations

Certain foundation grants available to other graduate students, such as the Harry S. Truman Scholarships, are also open to law school students. Most foundations provide support in areas of interest to them. The Association of Trial Lawyers of America and the Harry A. Blackmun Scholarly Foundation are a couple of the national foundations that make awards specifically to law school students. Addresses for these are: Harry S. Truman Scholarship Foundation, 712 Jackson Place, NW, Washington DC 20006; Association of Trial Lawyers of America, 1050 31st Street, NW, Washington DC 20007; Harry A. Blackmun Scholarship Foundation, 118 West Mulberry Street, Baltimore, MD 21201-3600. The Foundation Center of New York publishes several reference books on foundation support for graduate study. For more information, call 212-620-4230 or access their Web site at http://fdncenter.org.

Financial Aid for Minorities and Women

Bureau of Indian Affairs. The Bureau of Indian Affairs (BIA) offers aid to students who are at least one-quarter American Indian or native Alaskan and from a federally recognized tribe. Contact your tribal education officer, BIA area office, or call the Bureau of Indian Affairs at 202-208-3710.

In addition, below are some books available that describe financial aid opportunities for women and minorities.

The Directory of Financial Aids for Women by Gail Ann Schlachter (Reference Service Press, 1999) lists sources of support and identifies foundations and other organizations interested in helping women secure funding for graduate study.

Books such as *Financial Aid for Minorities* (Garrett Park Press, 1998) describe financial aid opportunities for minority students.

Disabled students are eligible to receive aid from a number of organizations. *Financial Aid for the Disabled and Their Families* by Gail Ann Schlachter and R. David Weber (Reference Service Press, 2000) lists aid opportunities for disabled students. The Vocational Rehabilitation Services in your home state can also provide information.

Researching Grants and Fellowships

The books listed below are good sources of information on grant and fellowship support for graduate education and should be consulted before you resort to borrowing. Keep in mind that grant support varies dramatically from field to field.

Annual Register of Grant Support: A Directory of Funding Sources 2000 (R.R. Bowker, 1999). This is a comprehensive guide to grants and awards from government agencies, foundations, and business and professional organizations.

Corporate Foundation Profiles, (Foundation Center, 1998). This is an in-depth, analytical profile of 195 of the largest company-sponsored foundations in the United States. Brief descriptions of an additional 1,000 company-sponsored foundations are also included. There is an index of subjects, types of support, and geographical locations.

The Foundation Directory (Foundation Center, 2000). This directory, with a supplement, gives detailed information on U.S. foundations with brief descriptions of the purpose and activities of each.

The Grants Register 2000, 18th ed. Edited by Ruth Austen (St. Martin's, 1999). This lists grant agencies alphabetically and gives information on awards available to law students, young professionals, and scholars for study and research.

Peterson's Grants for Graduate and Postdoctoral Study, 5th ed. (Peterson's, 1998). This book includes information on 1,400 grants, scholarships, awards, fellowships, and prizes. Originally compiled by the Office of Research Affairs at the Graduate School of the University of Massachusetts at Amherst, this guide is updated periodically by Peterson's.

Graduate schools sometimes publish listings of support sources in their catalogs, and some provide separate publications, such as the *Graduate Guide to Grants,* compiled by the Harvard Graduate School of Arts and Sciences. For more information, call 617-495-1814.

THE INTERNET: A NEW SOURCE OF FUNDING INFORMATION

If you have not explored the financial resources on the World Wide Web, your research is not complete. A wealth of information is now available on the Web, ranging from loan and entrance applications to minority grants and scholarships.

Web Mailing Lists

There is a mailing list, or newsgroup, called GRANTS-L, for announcements of grants and fellowships of interest to law students. To subscribe, send mail to listproc@listproc.gsu.edu with "subscribe GRANTS-L YOUR NAME" in the body of the message.

University-Specific Information on the Web

Universities are now in the process of creating Web financial aid directories. Applications of admission can be downloaded from the Web to start the graduate process. After that, detailed information can be obtained on financial aid processes, forms, and deadlines. University-specific grant and scholarship information can also be found, and more may be learned about financing information by using the Web than by an actual visit to the school. Questions can be answered on line.

Scholarships on the Web

When searching for scholarship opportunities, be sure to search the Web. Many benefactors and other scholarship donors are creating pages on the Web listing pertinent information with regard to their specific scholarship. You can reach this information through a variety of methods. For example, you can find a directory listing minority scholarships, quickly look at the information on line, decide if it applies to you, and then move on. New scholarship pages are being added to the Web daily.

The Web also lists many services that will look for scholarships for you. Some of these services cost money and advertise more scholarships per dollar than any other service. While some of these might be helpful, surfing the Web and using the traditional library resources on available scholarships is often just as productive and free.

Bank and Loan Information on the Web

Banks and loan servicing centers are creating pages on the Web, making it easier to access loan information. Having the information on screen in front of you instantaneously is more convenient than being put on hold on the phone. Any loan information, such as interest rate variations, descriptions of loans, loan consolidation programs, and repayment charts, can be found on the Web.

LOANS

Most needy law students borrow to finance their law programs. There are basically two sources of student loans—the federal government and private loan programs. You should read and understand the terms of these loan programs before submitting your loan application.

Federal Loans

Federal Stafford Loans. The Federal Stafford Loan Program offers government-sponsored, low-interest loans to students either through the Department of Education or a private lender, such as a bank, credit union, or savings and loan association.

There are two components of the Federal Stafford Loan program. Under the *subsidized* component of the program, the federal government pays the interest accruing on the loan while you are enrolled in law school on at least a half-time basis. Under the *unsubsidized* component of the program, you pay the interest on the loan from the day proceeds are issued. Eligibility for the federal subsidy is based on demonstrated financial need as determined by the financial aid office from the information you provide on the Free Application for Federal Student Aid (FAFSA). A cosigner is not required, since the loan is not based on creditworthiness.

Although Unsubsidized Federal Stafford Loans may not be as desirable as Subsidized Federal Stafford Loans from the consumer's perspective, they are a useful source of support for those who may not qualify for the subsidized loans or who need additional financial assistance.

Eligible borrowers may borrow up to $8500 per year through the Subsidized Stafford Loan Program, up to a maximum of $65,500, including undergraduate borrowing. In addition to loans through the Subsidized Stafford Loan Program, law students may borrow up to an additional

$10,000 per year through the unsubsidized component of the Federal Stafford Loan Program. You may borrow up to the cost of the school in which you are enrolled or will attend, minus estimated financial assistance from other federal, state, and private sources, with a maximum of $138,500, including undergraduate borrowing. Graduate students who borrow the maximum allowable amounts each year can receive a total of $18,500; $8500 through the *subsidized* program and an additional $10,000 through the *unsubsidized* program.

The interest rate for the Federal Stafford Loans varies annually and is set every July. The rate during in-school, grace, and deferment periods is based on the 91-Day U.S. Treasury Bill rate plus 1.7 percent, capped at 8.25 percent. The rate in repayment is based on the 91-Day U.S. Treasury Bill rate plus 2.3 percent, capped at 8.25 percent.

Two fees are deducted from the loan proceeds upon disbursement: a guarantee fee of up to 1 percent, which is deposited in an insurance pool to ensure repayment to the lender if the borrower defaults, and a federally mandated 3 percent origination fee, which is used to offset the administrative cost of the Federal Stafford Loan Program.

Under the *subsidized* Federal Loan Program, repayment begins six months after your last enrollment on at least a half-time basis. Under the *unsubsidized* program, repayment of interest begins within thirty days from disbursement of the loan proceeds, and repayment of the principal begins six months after your last enrollment on at least a half-time basis. Some lenders may require that some payments may be made even while you are in school, although most lenders will allow you to defer payments and will add the accrued interest to the loan balance. Under both components of the program, repayment may extend over a maximum of ten years with no prepayment penalty.

Federal Perkins Loans. The Federal Perkins Loan is a long-term loan available to students demonstrating financial need and is administered directly by the school. Not all schools have these funds, and some may award them to undergraduates only. Eligibility is determined from the information you provide on the FAFSA. The school will notify you of your eligibility.

Eligible law students may borrow up to $6,000 per year, up to a maximum of $40,000, including undergraduate borrowing (even if your previous Perkins Loans have been repaid). The interest rate for Federal Perkins Loans is 5 percent, and no interest accrues while you remain in school at least half-time. There are no guarantee, loan, or disbursement fees. Repayment begins nine months after your last enrollment on at least a half-time basis and may extend over a maximum of ten years with no prepayment penalty.

Deferring Your Federal Loan Repayments. If you borrowed under the Federal Stafford Loan Program or the Federal Perkins Loan Program for previous undergraduate or graduate study, some of your repayments may be deferred (i.e., suspended) when you return to law school, depending on when you borrowed and under which program.

There are other deferment options available if you are temporarily unable to repay your loan. Information about these deferments is provided at your entrance and exit interviews. If you believe you are eligible for a deferment of your loan repayments, you must contact your lender to complete a deferment form. The deferment must be filed prior to the time your repayment is due, and it must be refiled when it expires if you remain eligible for deferment at that time.

Law Access Loan Program

In an effort to ensure that new and continuing law students have an adequate opportunity to finance their legal education at the law school of their choice, the Law School Admission Council (LSAC), in cooperation with other higher education and financial institutions, sponsors student loans. The Law Access program offers a wide range of services to law students attending LSAC member schools approved by the American Bar Association. Through Law Access, students can obtain five types of loans: Federal Stafford Loans; Federal Supplemental Loans for Students; Law Access Loans (LAL); Private Bar Examination Loans (BEL); and private Federal Consolidation Loans. For further information, contact the Law Access Loan Program, Box 2500, Newtown, PA 18940; 800-282-1550.

Supplemental Loans

Many lending institutions offer supplemental loan programs and other financing plans, such as the ones described below, to students seeking assistance in meeting their expected contribution toward educational expenses.

If you are considering borrowing through a supplemental loan program, you should carefully consider the terms of the program and be sure to "read the fine print." Check with the program sponsor for the most current terms that will be applicable to the amounts you intend to borrow for graduate study. Most supplemental loan programs for graduate study offer unsubsidized, credit-based loans. In general, a credit-ready borrower is one who has a satisfactory credit history or no credit history at all. A creditworthy borrower generally must pass a credit test to be eligible to borrow or act as a cosigner for the loan funds.

Many supplemental loan programs have a minimum annual loan limit and a maximum annual loan limit. Some offer amounts equal to the cost of attendance minus any other aid you will receive for graduate study. If you are planning to borrow for several years of graduate study, consider whether there is a cumulative or aggregate limit on the amount you may borrow. Often this cumulative or aggregate limit will include any amounts you borrowed and have not repaid for undergraduate or previous graduate study.

The combination of the annual interest rate, loan fees, and the repayment terms you choose will determine how much the amount is that you will repay over time. Compare these features in combination before you decide which loan program to use. Some loans offer interest rates that are adjusted monthly, some quarterly, some annually. Some offer interest rates that are lower during the in-school, grace, and deferment periods, and then increase when you begin repayment. Most programs include a loan "origination" fee, which is usually deducted from the principal amount you receive when the loan is disbursed and must be repaid along with the interest and other principal when you graduate, withdraw from school, or drop below half-time study. Sometimes the loan fees are reduced if you borrow from a qualified cosigner. Some programs allow you to defer interest and/or principal payments while you are enrolled in law school. Many programs allow you to capitalize your interest payments; the interest due on your loan is added to the outstanding balance of your loan, so you don't have to repay immediately, but this increases the amount you owe. Other programs allow you to pay the interest as you go, which will reduce the amount you later have to repay.

For more information about supplemental loan programs or to obtain applications, call the customer service phone numbers of the organizations listed below, access the sponsor's site on the World Wide Web, or visit your school's financial aid office.

CitiAssist Loans. An unsubsidized, credit-based loan for graduate students, sponsored by Citibank. Telephone: 888-812-5030; Web site: http://www.studentloan.com.

GradExcel Loan. An unsubsidized, credit-based loan for credit-ready graduate and professional students enrolled at least half-time, sponsored by Nellie Mae. Telephone: 800-367-8848; Web site: http://www.nelliemae.com.

LawAchiever Loan. An unsubsidized, credit-based loan for law students enrolled at least half-time, sponsored by Key Education Resources. Telephone: 800-KEY-LEND; Web site: http://www.keybank.com/educate.

PEP Loan. An unsubsidized, credit-based loan for credit-ready law students enrolled at least half-time, sponsored by the Education Resources Institute. Telephone: 800-255-8374; Web site: http://www.teri.org.

Law Access Loan. An unsubsidized, credit-based loan for creditworthy law students enrolled at least half-time, sponsored by the Access Group. Telephone: 800-282-1550; Web site: http://www.accessgroup.org.

LawLoan. An unsubsidized, credit-based loan for law students enrolled at least half-time, sponsored by Sallie Mae. Telephone: 888-239-4269; Web site: http://www.salliemae.com.

How to Apply

All applicants for federal aid must complete the Free Application for Federal Student Aid (FAFSA). This application must be completed *after* January 1 preceding enrollment in the fall. On this form you report your income and asset information for the preceding calendar year and specify which schools will receive the data. Two to four weeks later you'll receive an acknowledgment on which you can make any corrections. The schools you've designated will also receive the information and may begin asking you to send them documents (usually your U.S. income tax return) that verify what you reported.

In addition to the FAFSA, some law schools want additional information and will ask you to complete the CSS Financial Aid PROFILE. If your school requires this form, it will be listed in the PROFILE registration form available in college financial aid offices. Other schools use their own supplemental application. Check with your financial aid office to confirm which forms they require.

If you have already filed your federal income tax for the year, it will be much easier for you to complete these forms. If not, use estimates, but be certain to notify the financial aid office if your estimated figures differ from the actual ones once you have calculated them.

Application Deadlines

Application deadlines vary. Some schools require you to apply for aid when applying for admission; others require that you be admitted before applying for aid. Aid application instructions and deadlines should be clearly stated in each school's application material. The FAFSA must be filed after January 1 of the year you are applying for aid, but the Financial Aid PROFILE can be completed earlier, in October or November.

Determining Financial Need

Eligibility for need-based financial aid is based on your income during the calendar year prior to the academic year in which you apply for aid. Prior-year income is used because it is a good predictor of current-year income and is verifiable. If you have a significant reduction in income or assets after your aid application is completed, consult a financial aid counselor. If, for example, you are returning to school after working, you should let the financial aid counselor know your projected income for the year you will be in school. Aid counselors may use their "professional judgment" to revise your financial need, based on the actual income you will earn while you are in law school.

Need is determined by examining the difference between the cost of attendance at a given institution and the financial resources you bring to the table. Eligibility for aid is calculated by subtracting your resources from the total cost of attendance budget. These standard student budgets are generally on the low side of the norm. So if your expenses are higher because of graduate bills, higher research travel, or more costly books, for example, a financial aid counselor can make an adjustment. Of course, you'll have to document any unusual expenses. Also, keep in mind that with limited grant and scholarship aid, a higher budget will probably mean either more loan or more working hours for you.

Tax Issues

Since the passage of the Tax Reform Act of 1986, grants, scholarships, and fellowships may be considered taxable income. That portion of the grant used for payment of tuition and course-required fees, books, supplies, and equipment is excludable from taxable income. Grant support for living expenses is taxable. A good rule of thumb for determining the tax liability for grants and scholarships is to view anything that exceeds the actual cost of tuition, required fees, books, supplies related to courses, and required equipment as taxable.

- If you are employed by an educational institution or other organization that gives tuition reimbursement, you must pay tax on the value that exceeds $5250.

- If your tuition is waived in exchange for working at the institution, the tuition waiver is taxable. This includes waivers that come with teaching or research assistantships.

- Other student support, such as stipends and wages paid to research assistants and teaching assistants, is also taxable income. Student loans, however, are not taxable.

- If you are an international student you may or may not owe taxes depending upon the agreement the United States has negotiated with your home country. The United States has tax treaties with more than forty countries. You are responsible for making sure that the school you attend follows the terms of the tax treaty. If your country does not have a tax treaty with the United States, you may have as much as 30 percent withheld from your paycheck.

A FINAL NOTE

While amounts and eligibility criteria vary from field to field as well as from year to year, with thorough research you can uncover many opportunities for graduate financial assistance. If you are interested in graduate study, discuss your plans with faculty members and advisers. Explore all options. Plan ahead, complete forms on time, and be tenacious in your search for support. No matter what your financial situation, if you are academically qualified and knowledgeable about the different sources of aid, you should be able to attend the law school of your choice.

Patricia McWade
Dean of Student Financial Services
Georgetown University

NOTES

NOTES